W9-CMQ-104

WOODROW WILSON CENTER SERIES

Unsilent revolution

Other books in the series

Michael J. Lacey, editor, *Religion and Twentieth-Century American Intellectual Life*

Michael J. Lacey, editor, *The Truman Presidency*

Joseph Kruzel and Michael H. Haltzel, editors, *Between the Blocs: Problems and Prospects for Europe's Neutral and Nonaligned States*

William C. Brumfield, editor, *Reshaping Russian Architecture: Western Technology, Utopian Dreams*

Mark N. Katz, editor, *The USSR and Marxist Revolutions in the Third World*

Walter Reich, editor, *Origins of Terrorism: Psychologies, Ideologies, Theologies, States of Mind*

Mary O. Furner and Barry Supple, editors, *The State and Economic Knowledge: The American and British Experiences*

Michael J. Lacey and Knud Haakonssen, editors, *A Culture of Rights: The Bill of Rights in Philosophy, Politics, and Law—1791 and 1991*

Unsilent revolution

Television news and American public life, 1948–1991

ROBERT J. DONOVAN and RAY SCHERER

WOODROW WILSON INTERNATIONAL
CENTER FOR SCHOLARS

AND

CAMBRIDGE
UNIVERSITY PRESS

Published by the Press Syndicate of the University of Cambridge
The Pitt Building, Trumpington Street, Cambridge CB2 1RP
40 West 20th Street, New York, NY 10011-4211, USA
10 Stamford Road, Oakleigh, Victoria 3166, Australia

© Robert J. Donovan and Raymond L. Scherer 1992

First published 1992
Reprinted 1992

Printed in the United States of America

Library of Congress Cataloging-in-Publication Data
Donovan, Robert J.
Unsilent revolution: television news and American public life,
1948–1991 / Robert J. Donovan and Ray Scherer.
p.   cm. — (Woodrow Wilson Center series)
Includes bibliographical references and index.
ISBN 0–521–41829–1 (hard). — ISBN 0–521–42862–9 (pbk.)
1. Television broadcasting of news—United States—History—20th
century.   2. United States—Politics and government—1945–1989.
3. United States—Politics and government—1989–   I. Scherer, Ray.
II. Title.   III. Series.
PN4888.T4D66   1992
070.1′95—dc20   91–41189
                                          CIP

A catalog record for this book is available from the British Library

ISBN 0-521-41829-1 hardback
ISBN 0-521-42862-9 paperback

To
Barbara and Gerry

WOODROW WILSON INTERNATIONAL CENTER FOR SCHOLARS

BOARD OF TRUSTEES

The Center is the "living memorial" of the United States of America to the nation's twenty-eighth president, Woodrow Wilson. The U.S. Congress established the Woodrow Wilson Center in 1968 as an international institute for advanced study, "symbolizing and strengthening the fruitful relationship between the world of learning and the world of public affairs." The Center opened in 1970 under its own presidentially appointed board of trustees.

In all its activities the Woodrow Wilson Center is a nonprofit, nonpartisan organization, supported financially by annual appropriations from the U.S. Congress, and by the contributions of foundations, corporations, and individuals. Conclusions or opinions expressed in Center publications and programs are those of the authors and speakers and do not necessarily reflect the views of the Center staff, fellows, trustees, advisory groups, or any individuals or organizations that provide financial support to the Center.

Woodrow Wilson International Center for Scholars
Smithsonian Institution Building
1000 Jefferson Drive, S.W.
Washington, D.C. 20560
(202) 357–2429

Contents

Preface

On live television over the past four decades:

*Men walking on the moon. Scud missiles exploding in Israel. Pres-
ident Kennedy's coffin being loaded onto a hearse at Andrews Air
Force Base. The Berlin Wall crumbling. Police dogs and firehoses
terrorizing African Americans in Birmingham. The House Judiciary
Committee voting on articles of impeachment against President
Nixon. Chinese troops shooting students in Tiananmen Square in
Beijing. Mobs burning the American flag in front of the U.S. Embassy in Tehran. Iraqi soldiers surrendering in the desert. Kurdish
exiles starving on the northern borders of Iraq. Russia's Boris Yeltsin, atop a tank in Moscow, exhorting defiance.*

These scenes affected untold millions of television viewers. They even
influenced public policy and political decisions. This book is not a history
of television news, however. Its purpose is to tell an intimate story of
how television news since 1948 has affected American moods, American
society and institutions, American politics and politicians.

When television news moved to the center of the political process in
the 1950s, it changed that process from top to bottom. Sometimes the
change was for the worse. Politicians are now obsessed with sound bites
and image making. Sometimes it was for the better. Televised debates
between presidential nominees are a valuable public service. For good or
ill, television has drastically changed U.S. politics. To be sure, no exact
way has been devised to measure the power of television news. But, then,
who can measure precisely the influence of the *New York Times* or other
major newspapers? In his celebrated attack on television news in Des
Moines in 1969, Vice-President Spiro T. Agnew begrudgingly acknowledged the networks' important contributions:

The networks have made "hunger" and "black lung disease" national issues
overnight. The TV networks have done what no other medium could have done

ix

in terms of dramatizing the horrors of war. The networks have tackled our most
difficult social problems with a directness and immediacy that is the gift of their
medium. They have focused the nation's attention on its environmental abuses
... on pollution in the Great Lakes and the threatened ecology of the Ever-
glades.[1]

Television news has been a potent and steady force for change in many
fields. Speaking of its influence on newspapers, James K. Batten, president and chief executive officer of Knight-Ridder Newspapers, said,
"Television set in motion a tide and keeps us going in that direction."[2]
Reuven Frank, former president of NBC News, observed, "Television
news has the power to transmit the experience itself rather than information about the experience."[3] Specifically, he was alluding to the shooting of President Ronald Reagan in 1981. Dr. Leo Bogart, former executive vice-president of the Newspaper Advertising Bureau, noted "live TV's
unique ability to provide entree into history as it is made."[4] An extraordinary case was the coverage of the Persian Gulf War in 1991.

This book is divided into two parts. The twelve chapters of Part I
describe particular episodes when television news changed the course of
events and built or destroyed the careers of public figures. Here are the
stories of the civil rights struggles in the South; the manned space program; the assassination and funeral of President Kennedy; the riots of
1965, the "long hot summer" of 1967, and the aftermath of the 1968
assassination of Dr. Martin Luther King, Jr.; the Vietnam War; the Iranian hostage crisis of 1979–81; and the Ethiopian famine of the mid-
1980s. Also described in Part I are the Army-McCarthy hearings and the
fall, rise, and fall of Richard M. Nixon. Each of the twelve episodes highlights how television news has changed the social and political fabric of
America.

Part II describes how television news has affected and will continue to
affect four areas of politics: the presidency, diplomacy and terrorism,
Congress, and presidential campaigning. It also explains and analyzes the
competition between print journalism and broadcast journalism. By the
1950s, newspaper editors were aware that their electronic competitors
would win contests of timeliness and emotional impact. It became obvious that newspapers had to rely on their special strengths by providing
background, investigation, and analysis. A special case was sports journalism. When television cameras began covering games and matches,
viewers could watch all the action and follow the scoring. This outdated
the standard way of writing a sports story. Besides writing differently,

sports reporters met the new competition by delving into social problems in sports, such as drugs, betting, and abuses in college recruiting.

In the postwar years many newspapers disappeared through mergers and loss of revenue. Many factors were responsible, although television competition was a root cause. Most of the failures were of afternoon papers. Dense traffic and suburban sprawl made early delivery impossible. The newspapers that have survived are very different from what they were in 1950 in appearance, content, and style.

This book concludes with television's impact on four dramatic stories of 1989–91: Tiananmen Square, the Berlin Wall, the Persian Gulf War, and the failed Russian coup. Television's coverage of the shooting of prodemocracy demonstrators in the heart of Beijing disillusioned the world about the once promising regime of Deng Xiaoping. On the threshold of their own revolution, East Germans watched the television coverage of Tiananmen Square and drew strength from it. Television also was a window through which they could view revolutionary changes in Poland, Czechoslovakia, and other countries once dominated by Communist rulers. With utter clarity television showed the world the welcome end of an era.

The Persian Gulf War was the first war waged live, at least in part, on television. The effect at home was gripping. Patriotism soared. The burden of the Vietnam War was lifted. President George Bush won acclaim. Gen. H. Norman Schwarzkopf became a folk hero. His role misunderstood, Peter Arnett of CNN became in some eyes a villain.

During the second Russian revolution, of August 1991, the whole world experienced three days of extraordinary events as the coup plotters were unable to seal off the Soviet Union electronically.

The coverage of Tiananmen Square, the Berlin Wall, the Gulf War, and the sudden collapse of communism in the Soviet Union extended the role and influence of television news as a prime medium of international communications.

Cosmic events aside, even in its early days, television news made a critical impact on social conditions in the United States. This book begins with that story.

Acknowledgments

Most of this book was written while we were guest scholars in the Media Studies Project of the Woodrow Wilson International Center for Scholars in Washington, D.C., in 1988–90. Peter Braestrup, organizer of the project, and Philip S. Cook, its first director, helped us immensely. We received a research grant from the Florence and John Schumann Foundation and remember with fondness its late president William B. Mullins. We also are indebted to his associate Evelyn Rooney. For the decision to publish this book, our thanks go to Joseph F. Brinley, Jr., an editor at the Woodrow Wilson Center, to Charles Blitzer, its director, and to Samuel F. Wells, Jr., the deputy director. Our thanks too to the perspicacious copy editor, Barbara de Boinville.

Advice and help in research, which are hallmarks of the Center, were invaluable. Among the many, in and out of the Center, who helped us were Lawrence W. Lichty, the new director of the Media Studies Project; Douglas Gomery, its senior researcher; Marjorie White; Byron A. Parham; Martha Ann Overland; Ariadne Allen; James Devitt; Kathleen Hall Jamieson; Barbara Matusow; Jack Nelson; Edward Fouhy; Peter Backlund; John M. Logsdon; and Yvonne Egertson. Finally, we thank the many people who granted us interviews and whose names appear in this book.

I

Twelve episodes

1

Police dogs, firehoses, and television cameras: shockwaves from the south

It was a tense morning when fall term at Central High School in Little Rock opened on September 4, 1957. By eight o'clock, troops of the Arkansas National Guard lined the block. A menacing-looking crowd had gathered. Opposite the main entrance stood a cluster of photographers and reporters, including John Chancellor of NBC and Robert Schakne of CBS. The night before, Gov. Orval E. Faubus had ordered the National Guard to bar entrance to Central High School to nine newly enrolled African-American students. His order defied the U.S. Supreme Court, which had ruled more than three years earlier, on May 17, 1954, that racial segregation of public schools was unconstitutional. The next year the Court had ordered desegregation to proceed "with all deliberate speed."

On the morning of September 4 the school buses were rolling, and their riders included the African-American children. Shortly before 8:30 a school bus arrived. Out stepped a nervous but outwardly composed fifteen-year-old African-American girl named Elizabeth Eckford. Crisply dressed and carrying books under her left arm, she started toward the school, but a guardsman told her to cross the street. A mob followed her. Someone shouted, "Lynch her!" Elizabeth looked for a friendly face but saw none. Instead she heard someone snarl, "No nigger bitch is going to get in our school. Get out of here!"[1] To his later regret, Schakne went up to the girl and held his microphone in her face for a comment. She was too frightened to say a word. Years later he recalled the incident:

We had no idea that our form of journalism would essentially change the way the country thought. I think it did in Little Rock in a very substantial way. I think people saw things [on television] they didn't quite comprehend if they had just read [about] them. But we didn't know that. When I [saw] Elizabeth Eckford walking down the street . . . and went up to her with a microphone I did what a reporter does. You see a person there, a central part of the story, and you go in and talk to [her], but I did not realize then [that] television changed the rules somewhat. I wouldn't today walk up to a fifteen-year-old girl at the center of a mob and thrust a microphone in her face when she was petrified. . . . But we didn't know that this was essentially a different medium in some very fundamental ways and that the impact of what we did was going to be very different. At the time we were very primitive.[2]

Schakne had come to television news from the International News Service, which was absorbed by the United Press in 1958. He acknowledged that when he was assigned to Little Rock by CBS, largely uninstructed, he did not yet understand this new medium. "We knew how to cover stories as newspapers covered stories, but we were inventing television. . . . The whole process of changing television into a serious news medium happened to coincide with the civil rights movement."[3]

Peter J. Boyer, a former *New York Times* writer on television, described the movement as "the first running story of national importance that television fully covered." The effect on the the story and on the developing medium was lasting. "Television brought home to the nation the civil rights struggle in vivid images that were difficult to ignore, and for television it was a story that finally proved the value of TV news gathering as opposed to mere news dissemination."[4]

Television in 1957 was very different from what it is today. Television news had been in existence for only nine years at the time of Little Rock. News programs were still in black and white and lasted fifteen minutes. Television had covered the Korean War, crudely by modern standards, and national political conventions. But the passion and panorama of years of upheaval in the Old Confederacy posed greater challenge.

Chancellor was challenged that morning in Little Rock. "Sometimes as I walked down the streets," he recalled, "a car with four men in it would just idle along beside me, block after block. It worked: I was scared. Sometimes at the glass telephone booth across from the high school the mob would wait until I had New York on the line and then start rocking the booth back and forth, trying to knock it over."[5]

Chancellor heard the standard jeer "Nigger lover" as well as the usual litanies about miscegenation. It took courage to point a camera at a crowd looking for blood.[6] In the 1950s, none of the networks had bureaus in the South. The television reporters who were rushed there after the crisis erupted in Little Rock were, for the most part, unfamiliar with the region and its ways. They also were relatively young and inexperienced. In 1957 Chancellor was thirty and Schakne thirty-one. For years, they remained grateful for the tutelage they received from *New York Times* reporters already on the scene, notably John N. Popham and Claude F. Sitton.

The safety of the cameramen was jeopardized by the bulkiness of the film cameras. "They were totally helpless walking around under these giant cameras and cables," recalled Karl Fleming of *Newsweek,* who was long in the thick of the coverage of the South. "I saw these guys get beaten up so many times, helpless—totally helpless. They had no defenses. It was always the cops who would beat them up, practically always. For if it wasn't them, they would stand aside and smirk while the local rednecks pounded the hell out of them."[7]

NBC had equipped its reporters with boxlike tape recorders that hung suspended from the shoulder. Fortunately, Chancellor happened to be wearing one when he was in Mississippi in 1955 covering the Emmett Till murder case. Till, a fourteen-year-old African-American youth from Chicago, had gone to Money, Mississippi, to see relatives. Flippantly, it appears, he called, "Bye, baby," to a young white woman clerk in a country candy store as he was departing. A group of white men tracked him down and killed him. The alleged murderers were put on trial in Mississippi before an all-white male jury and were promptly acquitted.

The local atmosphere was venomous while Chancellor was interviewing African Americans and whites on their reactions to the trial. He suddenly noticed white men in bib overalls closing in on him from behind. Instinctively, he knew there was no easy way out of trouble because his pursuers were already between him and his car. As a last resort he swung around and pointed the recorder at them.

"All right," he said, "come on. The whole world is going to know what you're doing to me."

"It worked," he related afterward. They backed off. Evidently, the men mistook the tape recorder for a camera, which could have caught their faces and their actions on film.[8]

The largest events of the civil rights movement followed Little Rock. Faubus's resistance collapsed on September 24, 1957, when Eisenhower deployed the 101st Airborne Division to open Central High School. The nine minority students were admitted, but the physical resistance to desegregation continued. The elemental bitterness raised by civil rights issues and the depth of regional division were of a kind that had not been seen on American soil since the Civil War. All too often causing injury and death, the struggle was to continue until Jim Crow rule had finally been broken by the Civil Rights Act of 1964 and the Voting Rights Act of 1965.

Eugene J. Roberts, Jr., who for more than three years covered the South as a reporter for the *New York Times,* said that it was the civil rights story that made him realize the force of television news. Police dogs looked like police dogs in newspaper and magazine photos, but on television the dogs snarled. Wallace Westfeldt, a reporter for the *Nashville Tennessean* in the 1950s and later executive producer of the "Huntley-Brinkley Report," observed that television coverage of the civil rights struggle "gave that story a color and attraction and emphasis that newspapers couldn't do. Even without any commentary, a shot of a big white man spitting and cursing at black children did more to open up the national intellect than my stories ever could."[9]

Hostile southerners believed that the presence of television cameras generated violence. Certainly, television reporters saw themselves as part of the story. Indubitably, the camera, especially at night when the lighting drew a crowd, was often a catalyst for disturbance. This was the case in varying degrees in the riots in Watts in 1965, in northern cities in 1967, and in Chicago during the Democratic National Convention of 1968. To lessen the problem the networks devised guidelines for coverage of tumultuous scenes. For example, cameras were to be turned off if a gathering mob tried to play to television in a way that might lead to rioting. Television cameras also could be a safeguard for demonstrators. Jack Nelson, who covered the South for the *Los Angeles Times,* observed this time and again.

The law enforcement people supposedly were there always to protect. Sometimes ... they had confrontations with the civil rights demonstrators. What they used to do, particularly for the print media, was put tape over their badges so you wouldn't get their badge number when they clubbed somebody. But if the camera got their face, it didn't make any difference whether they had the tape on the badge or not. There's no question about it, that having [television] there was a protection ... for the demonstrators ... [and] for the reporters.[10]

Especially in southern rural areas, communications created exasperating problems for newspaper and television journalists. Driving from Memphis to Greenville, Mississippi, on a story and needing to make a telephone call, Eugene Roberts once found every pay phone along more than thirty miles of highway had been sabotaged. Rumor had it that the

Ku Klux Klan had cut the wires to frustrate the press. Roberts and his colleagues complained to AT&T, and the company lent them a mobile unit that followed them for a while. At some point the reporters rented a flatbed truck to cover one of the intercity civil rights marches. Climbing back on one day they noticed a grocery counter box for cheese crackers tied with a ribbon. For the moment no one was in a mood for cheese crackers. "The driver," Roberts related, "kept asking whose box this was, and no one seemed to know. After about three days he opened the box, and there was a copperhead in it. The driver literally went straight up."[11]

Despite all the hostility the civil rights movement created, many southern newspapers and the local news departments of many southern television and radio stations largely ignored what was happening. No satisfactory coverage of the regional crisis was provided even by the otherwise most enlightened southern papers. The renowned *Atlanta Constitution* did not send a reporter 170 miles to cover the confrontation at Selma between civil rights marchers and police forces. Instead the paper used wire service stories.

The ire of the southern press was exemplified by a dateline in the *Nashville Banner* after President Eisenhower dispatched the 101st Airborne to Central High School. With echoes of Confederate times, the dateline read, "With U.S. Forces in Little Rock." On September 26, 1957, an accompanying front-page editorial entitled "Storm Troopers Must Go" referred to the division's vehicles as "Brownell's panzer units" (a reference to Herbert Brownell, Jr., then attorney general of the United States).

The University of Mississippi held a conference in 1987 on journalism and the civil rights movement. All but a few southern newspapers of the 1950s and 1960s were sternly criticized by the participants—editors and reporters who had been involved in the coverage of the South during those two decades. Their complaint was not simply that the southern press reneged on its duty to report the news but that they did so because of the owners' opposition to racial desegregation.

Hodding Carter III, a journalist, the son of the distinguished editor of the *Delta Democrat–Times* of Greenville, told the conference, "The overwhelming majority of all southern decision-makers in journalism were people who played a very strong and active game in opposing change."[12]

In southern city after southern city, regardless of size, "the pressures of local government, the pressures of local business, the pressures of the local police made themselves felt," noted John Seigenthaler, the editor of the *Nashville Tennessean*. He added that "in too many cities cowardice ruled. Retrenchment ruled. It was a profanation of what journalism was supposed to be about."[13]

This "peer review" at the University of Mississippi praised a few papers for their handling of the civil rights upheaval. They included the *Norfolk Virginian–Pilot*, the *Charlotte News and Observer*, and the *McComb* (Miss.) *Enterprise–Journal*. McComb was a hotbed of segregationist sentiment. The newspaper was boycotted. John O. Emmerich, Jr., the managing editor, was knocked down in a drugstore in an argument over coverage and editorial comments on the Freedom Riders. The night his mother died a cross was burned in front of his house. For this atrocity he received a note of apology from a member of the Ku Klux Klan, regretting not the cross-burning but its grim timing.[14]

From the start the *New York Times* took the lead in covering the story in the South. The Associated Press and United Press International played their usual indispensable role of providing daily spot news. Relman Morin of the AP won a Pulitzer Prize for his reporting from Little Rock. As time went on, the news magazines, the *Los Angeles Times*, the *New York Herald Tribune*, the *Washington Star*, the *Washington Post*, the *Baltimore Sun*, and the *Chicago Tribune* did good work. Newspapers from other parts of the country, however, were hard to find in the South. A few southerners subscribed to the *New York Times* and the *Wall Street Journal*, but that was about all.

Only television, radio, the AP, and UPI regularly carried the daily news story from the South to all other parts of the United States. Of these, television was by far the most compelling because of its visual impact. Doubtless, television news influenced northern newspaper and magazine editors to keep playing the story year after year when they might have preferred to give readers something different for a change. Noting that his editors followed the story on television nightly, Arlie W. Schardt, who covered the South for *Time*, observed:

I think in terms of just basic interest by editors, certainly television coverage helped. If television was giving that kind of priority to it, it can't help but at least subconsciously be influencing the editors to feel, "My God, this is one of the main stories again this week." There's a tendency to want to drop something after a while, but I think that everybody's sense of history was caught as this went along. It really was a tremendously dramatic day-by-day and then week-by-week and even month–by-month development.[15]

It was not only southern newspapers that shunned the civil rights story. Local broadcasts, as distinct from network shows, on southern television and radio stations also to a large extent turned away. Seigenthaler said that one Nashville television station in particular and probably all three of them "absolutely refused to report on civil rights news as it broke in that town. And had it not been for the networks coming on the screen after the local news, the story of the civil rights movement in that city would not have been told on television." At the time of the Emmett Till murder and the subsequent trial, John Herbers, who later covered the South for the *New York Times,* was head of a small UPI bureau in Mississippi. He found that in much of the state "a sort of blanket opposition" against reporting the case developed among radio, television, and most newspapers. "I kept getting pressures from broadcasters and publishers [indicating] that they didn't want this kind of news reporting," he related. "UPI at that time was very heavily dependent on broadcast stations for their revenues in this state. So I had to find a way to report news and without enraging these people to the extent they would cancel the service. I think we were able to do it by just a lot of hard work."[16]

The detestation of out-of-town television crews by many southerners was mirrored in segregationists' names for the networks: NBC was the Nigger Broadcasting Company, ABC was the Afro Broadcasting Company, and CBS was the Coon (or Communist) Broadcasting System. Some of the managers of southern stations affiliated with the networks were none too enthusiastic about transmitting to New York certain of the day's news reports by network crews. Occasionally, Fred L. Beard, general manager of WLBT in Jackson, which was affiliated with ABC and NBC, tried to talk network reporters out of the stories they had prepared to file. "Fred would sometimes bring them into his office and sit down and try to convert them to the segregationist point of view," Richard R. Sanders, then the station's news director, recalled.[17]

WLBT subscribed to UPI service. Another UPI reporter in Mississippi was Cliff Sessions, a native of the state. One of his stories on civil rights, which WLBT received on its news ticker, threw Beard into a rage. Beard was prominent in a white Citizens' Council. His objection to the story was that it quoted Medgar Evers, an organizer in Mississippi for the National Association for the Advancement of Colored People. Beard denounced Sessions to his face.

"He thought that Medgar didn't deserve to be quoted like this, and he thought I had given him too much space on the wire," Sessions related.

I tried to explain to him my thinking and the news business. And the more we talked the more upset he got. He turned red and you could see the veins sticking out. He finally started screaming at me. He said, "Well, you're an integrationist, aren't you?" And I just turned away from him and started walking down the hall. There were several people standing in the corridor, and he said, screaming louder, "Crawl back under your rock." And as I walked away, I can remember him standing at the foot of some stairs. "Crawl back under your rock," he said, "You've been exposed."[18]

Beard assigned a man to rummage through the waste paper to retrieve carbon copies to keep him abreast of what the network reporters were writing. The station's egregious unfairness to the cause of African Americans was branded by the *Nation* as "electronic racism."[19]

Beard's broadcasting policies eventually led to his ouster. In 1963 a slide reading "Sorry, Cable Trouble" cut an NBC documentary off WLBT just as the documentary was about to report on a sit-in at the Woolworth store in Jackson, according to Fred W. Friendly. In his book *The Good Guys, the Bad Guys, and the First Amendment,* he added:

The Huntley-Brinkley nightly news program was reportedly occasionally interrupted when it was covering civil rights, and sometimes, prior to news reports on the Today show, a WLBT announcer would warn, "What you are about to see is an example of biased, managed, Northern news. Be sure to stay tuned at seven twenty-five to hear your local newscast."[20]

The WLBT license was held by the Lamar Life Broadcasting Company, a subsidiary of the Lamar Life Insurance Company owned by the Murchison family of Texas. In 1964 the United Church of Christ petitioned the Federal Communications Commission on grounds of unfairness to African Americans to deny the renewal of the WLBT license. The station promised reforms. Beard was replaced. The FCC then voted a one-year renewal. But the U.S. Court of Appeals in the District of Columbia ordered a hearing. Ultimately, Lamar Life lost its license to broadcast over WLBT.

Many places in the South were dangerous for journalists to cover. Montgomery, Alabama, was such a place. Police tended to believe that reporters were allied with civil rights workers. And civil rights workers were often viewed as either pawns of the communists or outright communists themselves. Sometimes reporters and cameramen had to flee to African-American neighborhoods to take refuge in houses, churches, and, in at least one case, a funeral parlor. At the bus station in Montgomery on Saturday morning, May 20, 1961, a crowd of white men armed with lead pipes, bottles, and baseball bats waited for the arrival of a Grey-hound bus filled with Freedom Riders. The riders were students and other civil rights activists who had been crisscrossing the South that spring, testing enforcement of a Supreme Court decision prohibiting racial discrimination on interstate buses. The waiting crowd was resolved to keep the riders out of Montgomery. As the bus rolled into the terminal, the passengers noted that the streets were empty. When the bus door opened the passengers heard nothing and could see on the arrival platform only a group of reporters and photographers. The armed men were momentarily screened from their view. Then when the reporters began to question the travelers, the waiting men attacked. Storming past Norman Ritter, Atlanta bureau chief for *Time–Life,* they slapped Maurice (Moe) Levy, an NBC cameraman. During the brawl that erupted, Ritter was clubbed to the ground. A Birmingham television reporter was beaten, and one of the attackers grabbed the camera of Don Urbrock of *Life* and kept smashing his face with it. Reporters who tried to flee were chased.

The next year a French reporter, Paul Guihard, was shot in the back and killed on a fierce night at the University of Mississippi, in Oxford. Another man died, and others in the crowd suffered ghastly injury. Open warfare had erupted over the admission of James Meredith, an African American, by order of a federal district court. President John F. Kennedy had first dispatched a large number of civilian law-enforcement officials to keep order. Before the night was over, however, word of Meredith's presence in the university caused such rioting and shooting that Kennedy had to send federal troops to the campus for the first time since the Civil War. Two hundred persons were arrested. Safety was purely a matter of chance. Because most of the battling was at night, the story was particularly difficult for television news to cover. Dan Rather, in the South on one of his first big assignments for CBS, later described the horror of that night:

Whenever anyone turned on a light—which meant every time we needed to film—one or more bullets would attempt to knock it out. We had to film and move, film and move. After a while we worked out a pattern: turn on our battery-powered, portable light, film for fifteen seconds by actual count, turn off the light—if we didn't get hit—and then run, because we were bound to catch gunfire or bricks, or both. We had no way of protecting ourselves, except to avoid the crowds, keep moving and stay low.[21]

Reporters and cameramen developed other stratagems for averting bodily harm. To conceal their identity from hostile crowds, reporters often didn't take any notes or else furtively jotted them in narrow note-books they could hide in their pockets. Some northern reporters removed their coats and ties to shed their citified look. Claude Sitton one day in McComb did more: "I took off my shirt, rolled it up, stomped on it, got it dirty, put it on, unbuttoned it down to here"—pointing to his navel—"messed up my hair, put some dirt on my shoes, went down and sat on the courthouse lawn with a piece of grass in my mouth, chewing the grass, and just watched what was going on."[22]

No rolling his shirt in the dust for Rather. He and his crew made a rule of dressing well. "That decision may sound frivolous," he wrote later.

But the rule proved important as a symbol, because this was the first indication to these people that we meant business. I could walk in wearing blue jeans and a plaid shirt—and some did—and fade into the crowd and work around the edges. But that way was not as effective as showing up with my shoes shined, pants pressed, coat on and tie straight. That said, "I'm a professional. Here to do a job. I want to get along. But don't try to con or intimidate me."[23]

In covering the civil rights movement, Sitton and Karl Fleming of *Newsweek* often traveled together. "We would check into a motel," Fleming explained,

and the instant we got in the room the police chief would be on the phone and say, "Hey, you guys, what's going on?" They had a network of informers which consisted of Citizens' Council people riding around in these pick-up trucks with the whiplash antennas and the rifles plainly showing in the windows. They, to-gether with the Klan people and the police chiefs, kept the white rednecks, so-called, informed at all times where we were. . . . We were quite careful not to get in motels that had a cul-de-sac where there was no escape.[24]

Sitton and Fleming drove together in June 1964 from Meridian to Philadelphia, Mississippi, to investigate a report that three civil rights volunteers were missing. Andrew Goodman, a student at Queens College in New York City, and Michael Schwerner, of Brooklyn, were white. The third missing man was James Chaney of Mississippi, an African American who worked for the Congress on Racial Equality. When Sitton and Fleming arrived at the Delphian Motel in Philadelphia, three men threatened that if they did not leave town quickly, the two journalists might be reported missing, too.

"You fellows are wasting your time," Sitton replied. "If you shoot, the *New York Times* will have fifteen reporters in here tomorrow."

Later he and Fleming, joined by Nicholas von Hoffman, then of the *Chicago Sun-Times*, went to the sheriff's office to inquire about the missing men (whose bodies, pierced by bullets, were later found in an earthen dam). When the journalists left, a hostile crowd followed them. As Sitton listened to the ever louder cries of the gang at their heels, he saw a sign ahead: Turner Hardware Store. It was owned by the uncle of Turner Catledge, the executive editor of the *New York Times*. Catledge had assured Sitton that his uncle was ready to help a *Times* man if he needed it. The three reporters bolted for the store and, safely inside, Sitton recalled his executive editor's assurances. The proprietor's reply utterly astounded the three reporters.

"If you were black," the hardware dealer said, as Sitton later recalled his words, "I might do something to help you. But you got no business here, and I'm not going to lift a hand to help you."

Fleming remembers saying when the three reporters were back on the sidewalk, "Claude, it's a good thing you've got a lot of pull in this town or we'd be in big trouble here."

They managed to make it back, unharmed, to the motel.

"A few minutes later," Fleming recalled, "an automobile pulled up at the door, and four guys were sitting in it. They opened the car door so we could see two shotguns. They were passing around a quart fruit jar of corn liquor. We got in our car and beat a hasty retreat back to Meridian."

Peter Jennings of ABC had an even worse time of it in Mississippi. "My cameraman and I were chased out of Natchez by the Klan," he related. "I phoned my boss in New York. I was very shaken. He called the governor of Mississippi and said, 'If my boys don't get protection, I'm coming down there with forty cameras to do the Mississippi story.' Before long there was a patrol car outside the motel, keeping an eye on my boss's boys."[25]

Some journalists, especially some members of television crews, carried handguns in self-defense. Rather, however, "laid down the rule that no CBS crewman could carry a weapon of any kind, including a pocket-knife." This prohibition, he later explained, "had less to do with any aversion I might have felt toward handguns than with my professional judgment that it would be best for us not to be armed." His rule was disobeyed, and Rather had good reason to be grateful that it was. While he was filming a demonstration in Birmingham one evening, a roughneck jammed a shotgun into his ribs and threatened to blow him to pieces. "I knew the man wasn't kidding when I felt the pressure of the sawed-off shotgun," Rather said. He described what followed.

In the next instant, suddenly reaching around from the other side of the camera, there appeared a .38 on a .44 base revolver. One of our crew, the sound man, had jammed the [revolver] against the redneck's temple. [The sound man] was an Alabaman ... who worked for the local station and hired out to us on his days off. He was country and had the habit of calling other people "Sonny." He said to the man with the shotgun, "Sonny, I think you want to stroll." Quickly the shotgun dropped to "Sonny's" side. This tough was wide-eyed and scared. He had good reason to be. . . . I remember the sound man holding the gun steady and saying, as we backed away toward our car, "If you think I'm bluffing, gents, just try me."[26]

"That scene," Rather concluded, "could have turned into a bloody mess. I have to admit I lectured our gun-wielding hero and told him I'd rather not see him carry a gun again. But he knew I was thinking how thankful I was that he had violated the rule."[27]

On yet another occasion a local photographer hired by Rather was chased by some men with sawed-off cue sticks. The photographer fled into a clothing store and hid in a back room by hanging with his hands from a rack of men's suits. As he was being hunted, he suffered a heart attack. After a long convalescence he recovered.

Occasionally networks took steps to protect their crews. "At times when we'd go into scary areas," Richard Valeriani, then of NBC, said, "the network would send retired or off-duty Chicago cops with guns down to protect us. Sometimes you felt you needed these bodyguards."[28]

But guns did not always frighten journalists. Sometimes a joke was all that was needed to ease tension. During his coverage of racial trouble in St. Augustine, Charles Quinn of NBC arranged to interview some members of the Ku Klux Klan. At their insistence the interview took place in a woods. When he arrived, Quinn saw that the Klan members had guns sticking conspicuously from their pockets.

"All right," one of them snapped at him, "tell me which one is the Communist, Huntley or Brinkley?"

"I don't know," Quinn replied.

Plainly, the answer did not satisfy the armed questioner.

"I think it is Brinkley," Quinn said. "I think he's the one."

That cleared the air. The interview proceeded, and NBC ran it.[29]

The civil rights revolution in the South began when a man and the eye of the television film camera came together, giving the camera a focal point for events breaking from state to state, and the man, Martin Luther King, Jr., high exposure on television sets from coast to coast. The beginning was the arrest of Mrs. Rosa Parks in Montgomery on December 1, 1955, for her refusal to yield her seat on a municipal bus to a white passenger. King was the young pastor of the Dexter Avenue Baptist Church in Montgomery. He became the leader not only of the local protest against Mrs. Parks's arrest but also of a wider movement to outlaw racial segregation on the buses. His prominence began to spread well beyond Montgomery when his house was bombed and when he was indicted along with hundreds of other members of the Montgomery Improvement Association, which had launched a boycott of the city buses.

The boycott made the front pages of major newspapers such as the *New York Times* and the *New York Herald Tribune*. "Even network television began covering events there," wrote King's biographer David J. Garrow, "with one ABC commentator comparing the protesters to Gandhi and the bankruptcy of white Montgomery's position to that of the British in India."[30]

From the earliest days of the civil rights movement, reporters were aware of King's determination to rely on television, newspapers, and magazines to attract attention to his cause. His plan, Garrow wrote, was to "arouse the conscience of the nation through radio, TV, and newspapers."[31] Herbert Kaplow, then an NBC reporter, recalled that King "understood from the first time I met him the importance of television. But he didn't hoke it up. He didn't have to. He had all the tools for good television to start with." King's dignity, his courage, his philosophy of nonviolence, his eloquence and rolling cadences made him an appealing performer on television. "He was not a leader," Kaplow explained, "who would make the grand entrance. He would just come in and right away . . . sort of subconsciously you would say, 'Hey, that fellow's not trying to promote himself so much . . . as his cause.' But he understood and . . . would try to tell you what was going on."[32]

King and reporters often dealt with each other with the greatest informality. After a rough night in the streets of St. Augustine, Florida, Charles Quinn looked for King and found him in someone's kitchen, munching on a chicken leg and sipping a glass of milk.

"Chuck, man, are you still in town?" King asked in surprise. He had just seen Quinn's interview with the Klan on television. King warned him that Quinn's life was in danger. One Klansman was after him. "No,"

Quinn calmly replied. From experience he knew better: The fellow would love him for putting him on television.[33]

Through the extraordinary communication of television, scenes of civil conflict were conveyed to tens of millions of Americans, from the president on down. One episode after another built pressure in the country for action to terminate the rule of Jim Crow. By late 1956 King and his followers had triumphed in Montgomery without resort to violence: The U.S. Supreme Court affirmed a lower court decision outlawing segregation on the city's buses. From there King turned to the historic task of ending all legalized segregation in the South. His primary goal was to end discriminatory election practices, particularly literacy tests that effectively barred African Americans from voting. In Birmingham King's further aims included desegregation of large stores, more opportunities for jobs for African Americans in those stores, and establishment of biracial committees to negotiate desegregation of schools.

Birmingham was where King and his followers encountered a character who was to help them immeasurably, if painfully. With police dogs and firehoses, spectacular props on television especially, Birmingham Police Commissioner Eugene T. (Bull) Connor brutalized peaceable marchers. King and his assistants knew that firehoses were in reality *their* best weapon, not Connor's. They understood it was how the hoses and the dogs looked on television screens and in newspaper and magazine photographs that counted. King nudged his helpers "to find some way to make Bull Connor tip his hand."[34] According to Hodding Carter III, the late New York civil rights advocate Allard Lowenstein said that it took police dogs in Birmingham to sell civil rights to Des Moines.[35] Indeed King's organization in Birmingham was apt to call off a planned demonstration if no mob turned up to attack marchers or if no television cameras were in evidence.

In the spring of 1963, Americans for Democratic Action held its annual convention in Washington. For a month beforehand Joseph L. Rauh, Jr., and other leaders of the liberal organization had tried unsuccessfully to get the White House to agree to a meeting with President Kennedy. Then just as the convention was about to end, Rauh received an urgent telephone call asking him to see Kenneth P. O'Donnell, the president's appointments secretary. The night before, television news had shown the riots in Birmingham, and the next morning—the day of O'Donnell's call—the *New York Times* had run on its front page a photograph of Connor's police dogs and firehoses on the attack. When Rauh got to the White House, he found O'Donnell "consumed," as Rauh put it, with the photograph. "Kenny now wanted to set up a meeting for us with the president," Rauh said, "but it was too late. The convention was all but over."[36]

The scenes in Birmingham were having an effect—across the nation and at 1600 Pennsylvania Avenue. On May 4, 1963, Kennedy said that the brutal televised attacks on women and children made him "sick." "I can understand," he added, "why the Negroes in Birmingham are tired of being asked to be patient." Public reaction against the southern militant segregationists was so great that Kennedy privately referred to his civil rights legislation of 1963 as "Bull Connor's bill." The designation, Attorney General Robert F. Kennedy said later, "summarizes the idea that what Bull Connor did down there—the dogs and the hoses and the pictures with the Negroes—is what created a feeling in the United States that more was needed to be done. Until that time, people were not worked up about it or concerned about it."[37] The same could fairly well be said of the Kennedy administration. In their notable study *Racial Attitudes in America,* Howard Schuman, Charlotte Steeh, and Lawrence Bobo wrote, "The changes in Kennedy's thoughts and attitudes were probably indicative of the thoughts of many Northern whites who witnessed, through television and other media, the brutality of Bull Connor and other white supremacists."[38]

The shift in John Kennedy's attitude was easy to plot. Despite a strong civil rights plank in the 1960 Democratic platform, he temporized on legislation in his first year in office. For one thing, he did not wish to alienate influential southerners in Congress, whose support he wanted on other issues. For another, he felt the nation was not yet ready for sweeping civil rights reforms. In 1962 Kennedy endorsed perennial civil rights proposals such as outlawing the poll tax and easing standards for passing literacy tests. But it was not until 1963 and the nationally televised brutalities in Birmingham that he faced up to the "moral crisis" in the country.[39] He submitted to Congress on June 19 a bill that prohibited segregation in all interstate public accommodations, cut off funds for federal programs countenancing discrimination, and eased educational standards for voting in federal elections. It also included measures to facilitate public school integration.

Although the civil rights march on Washington on August 28, 1963, was commonly called the "black march," thousands of whites participated.

Like Marian Anderson's historic concert in 1939, Dr. King's "I have a dream" speech was delivered against the backdrop of the Lincoln Memorial. Though he spoke in the afternoon, the CBS and ABC networks covered it live. NBC did special reports from 4:30 to 6:00 P.M. and from 11:15 to midnight. The other two networks also did specials in the evening. Frequent reruns of this famous speech have done much to immortalize Martin Luther King.

On the Labor Day following the march, NBC devoted its entire nighttime schedule to a three-hour documentary entitled "The American Revolution of '63." Twice as long as any scheduled public affairs program on television in the past, it examined both sides of the civil rights issue. Writing about it afterward, Robert Kintner, then president of NBC, said:

Waiting outside the American home, in the days before television, was a human face that seldom had entered there: the Negro citizen, who was not welcomed as a guest, a colleague, an acquaintance. Television put Negro Americans into the living rooms of tens of millions of white Americans for the first time.[40]

While Kennedy's civil rights legislation was still bumping along a rutty road in Congress, he was assassinated. The next year, in an atmosphere more conducive to action because of the tragedy in Dallas on November 22, 1963, President Lyndon B. Johnson coaxed a considerably strengthened civil rights bill through Congress. The act outlawed discrimination in restaurants, cafeterias, lunch rooms, soda fountains, theaters, concert halls, sports arenas, and all but very small hotels, motels, and lodging houses. King was pleased with its enactment but wanted a stronger law to assure African Americans the ballot.

The seeds of the Civil Rights Act of 1964 were sewn in Birmingham. The seeds of the Voting Rights Act of 1965 were sewn in Selma, in Dallas County, Alabama. Half the voting population in Dallas County was African American, yet only 1 percent of voting-age African Americans were registered to vote, compared with 65 percent of whites. In Selma itself a mere 156 of 15,000 African Americans of voting age were registered.[41] Beginning early in 1965, King used Selma not only as a classic example of the denial of the ballot to African Americans but also as a boiler to put pressure on Johnson to introduce a new bill. In Selma, King's foil was the hot-headed Sheriff James G. Clark, Jr., of Dallas County. Not satisfied with police dogs and firehoses, Clark also resorted to cattle prods, bullwhips, and a club-wielding mounted posse. His viciousness worked in King's favor. Of Clark, one of King's assistants said, "We should put him on the staff."[42] "If anyone got manipulated [by King]," said Jack Bass, who wrote on the South in newspapers, books, and television, "it wasn't the media—it was Bull Connor and Sheriff Clark."[43]

King staged a registration drive in Selma, and television filmed the scene: marchers of all ages roughed up and poked with cattle prods. Demonstrations after dark could be especially dangerous. In nearby Marion, Alabama, Richard Valeriani and Charles Quinn, both of NBC, decided to cover a night march even though they were aware of the danger. No sooner had they arrived on the scene than segregationists sprayed their camera lens with black paint. Without warning, the street lights were turned off. Lawmen with billyclubs and handguns fell upon the demonstrators. A young black, Jimmie Lee Jackson, who, according to Garrow, was trying to shield his mother from blows, was fatally shot. Valeriani was standing beside his useless camera when a roundhouse blow from an ax handle sent him staggering into the arms of a cameraman. Dazed but aware of what was happening, Valeriani saw a state trooper take the ax handle from the assailant but make no effort to arrest him. "I guess you've done enough damage with that tonight," the trooper remarked to the man, blandly.

"Some guy came up to me," Valeriani later recalled, "and said, 'You need a doctor?' I reached back and touched my head. When I pulled my hand away it was all bloody. And I said, 'Yeah, I think I do. I'm bleeding. I think I do need a doctor.' And then he thrust his face right up next to mine, and he said, 'We don't have doctors for people like you.' And he walked away."[44]

The police did call an ambulance that took Valeriani to a hospital. The next day NBC put him on the air from his hospital bed. His head was bandaged, and his speech was still slurred.

Some nights later the Reverend James J. Reeb, a white Unitarian minister from Boston, was clubbed to death in Selma. Two days before, he and two other white Unitarian ministers had been attacked outside a restaurant while visiting Selma in support of the civil rights movement. Demonstrations of sympathy in several northern cities underscored the rising conviction that racial conflict had to stop.

Meanwhile King made plans for a fifty-four mile–walk from Selma to Montgomery, the state capital, there to lay the case for voting rights before a reluctant governor, George Wallace. On March 7, 1965, a column of six hundred set out on a route that ran across the Edmund Pettus Bridge in East Selma. The marchers never reached the other side. Sheriff

Clark ordered them to disperse. The marchers asked for a parley. None
was granted. When the ultimatum expired, the combined police forces
stormed the marchers. The most startling sight was the stampede of Clark's
horses through the heart of the screaming crowd, the riders clubbing left
and right. The mayhem took place before a gallery of press and television
reporters and photographers. By evening the whole country was the witness. ABC interrupted a movie to flash pictures of the punishment in
Selma. In a stark juxtaposition of symbols, the movie was *Judgment at
Nuremberg,* a tale about racial hatred in Nazi Germany. "As I watched
the reruns of the Selma confrontation on television," Lyndon Johnson
wrote in his memoirs, "I believed that my feelings were shared by millions of Americans throughout the country, North and South."[45]

One of Johnson's most dramatic moments as president was his appearance before a joint session of Congress to appeal for enactment of
the Civil Rights Act of 1965.

"At times," he said, "history and fate meet at a single place to shape
a turning point in man's unending search for freedom. So it was at Lexington and Concord. So it was at Appomattox. So it was last week in
Selma, Alabama."[46]

The joint session, of course, was televised, and viewers across the country
could share with those in the House chamber the surprise at Johnson's
sudden boldness of gesture. It was not just African Americans, he said,
as he neared his climax, "but really it is all of us who must overcome the
crippling legacy of bigotry and injustice." Then, pausing, he raised his
arms, and, quoting the anthem of the civil rights movement—words from
an old Baptist hymn—said, "And we shall overcome."[47] Members of
both parties rose to their feet, and in the galleries some of the audience,
black and white, wept.

Johnson's bill passed. Television played an important part. Burke
Marshall, assistant attorney general in charge of the civil rights division
of the Department of Justice under Kennedy and, until 1965, under Johnson, later said: "Television made it possible. Everybody in the business
thought that to be true. Congressional mail, White House mail, Justice
Department mail—it was an outpouring of public opinion. An enormous
outpouring."[48] Steven F. Lawson, in his book on southern African Americans and electoral politics, described the powerful effect on Congress.
"To be sure southern politicos attacked the . . . measure, but their customary combativeness was missing. No match for the bipartisan interracial coalition in defense of the right to vote, southern congressmen

watched helplessly as their colleagues overwhelmingly voted to extend first-class citizenship rights to blacks."[49]

The essence of the national mood that resulted in the victories of the civil rights movement were captured on the Senate floor by Everett McKinley Dirksen, a Republican from Illinois. He said: "The time has come for equality of opportunity in sharing in government, in education, and in employment. It will not be stayed or denied. It is here."[50]

The price of this victory was high. Perhaps the worst tragedy of the civil rights movement occurred on September 15, 1963, when a blast of dynamite ripped through the Sixteenth Street Baptist Church in Birmingham. Four African-American girls attending Sunday school were killed. The next morning the *Atlanta Constitution* carried an angry yet eloquent column by Eugene Patterson, the editor of the editorial page. It began: "A Negro mother wept in the street Sunday morning in front of a Baptist Church in Birmingham. In her hand she held a shoe, one shoe, from the foot of her dead child. We hold that shoe with her. Every one of us in the white South holds that small shoe in his hand."

Patterson excoriated the "sick criminals" and "politicians who heat the kettles of hate" and "little men who have their nigger jokes." But, he concluded:

Let us not lay the blame on some brutal fool who didn't know any better.

We know better. We created the day. We bear the judgment. May God have mercy on the poor South that has been so led. . . . If our South is ever to be what we wish it to be, we will plant a flower of nobler resolve for the South now upon these four small graves that we dug.[51]

In New York, Cronkite learned of the editorial and ordered a crew to film Patterson reading it. Afterward Patterson supposed an excerpt of a few seconds of reading might run on the CBS network. What happened he related later:

I tuned it in and, sure enough, Cronkite had given up this huge chunk of his time for me, just sitting at my desk [reading] the column from beginning to end. That was the beginning of my education as to the impact of television. Within a week or two I received close to two thousand letters, telegrams, or phone calls from all over the nation. When a newspaper editor gets 20 letters he usually feels he has scored big with a column. The magnified reach that television brought to this piece bewildered me. For every one who felt moved to communicate there must have been a hundred or a thousand who responded [in spirit] but stayed silent.[52]

For decades African Americans in the South had been oppressed and beaten. Enlightened leaders had long appealed for a new order but without success. Then, in the 1960s, millions of African Americans began to see on television the world beyond the slums and glimpse all that had been denied them. Television, as Frank Mankiewicz and Joel Swerdlow wrote,

nurtured a cadre of young shock troops for . . . the civil rights movement. These were the members of the Television Generation who believed in what they saw and were prepared to demand that the promises of America be kept. It was television which gave them the notion that they, and their demands, were legitimate.

And it was television that showed white America that segregation was not. In short, television was "a perfect tool for organizing a revolution."[53]

2

Exit Joe McCarthy

In 1954 the U.S. Senate condemned Joe McCarthy, effectively ending his witch-hunt for Communists in America. The Wisconsin Republican had become an "embarrassment to his own party." [1] The causes of embarrassment were many: the senator's persecution of people he investigated, his sensationalism, his crudeness, and, a matter of no small consequence, his reckless antagonizing of the popular new Republican president, Dwight D. Eisenhower. The condemnation probably would not have occurred if McCarthy had not embarrassed his party and if television had not exposed him to the nation. The story of McCarthy's downfall is also the story of two leading television figures. One was Edward R. Murrow, the most respected radio and television reporter of his time. His eyewitness reports of the Battle of Britain, which began with his dramatic signature, "This— is London," made him famous. The other man was Robert E. Kintner, the president of ABC. Each separately took actions that exposed McCarthy on national television in some of his most flagrant moments.

As early in the history of television as 1954, Murrow was worried about the power of television news—worried, in fact, about the power of this instrument in his own hands. From his years of covering Europe's drift to war, he understood the evils of broadcast propaganda. His anxiety early in March 1954, when he was stationed in New York, arose out of the preparations for one of the weekly editions of his CBS television program "See It Now." In this particular broadcast he planned to step outside the role of newscaster and into that of prosecutor of Senator McCarthy. For four years McCarthy had been using television, radio, the press, the Senate floor, and Senate committee hearings to smear and frighten individual Americans, including government officials, by badgering them

23

as alleged Communists. He had never exposed a single Communist spy, but this did nothing to slow his depredations. His red-baiting had caused turmoil in two administrations—Truman's and Eisenhower's—and embarrassed the United States abroad. Chairman of the Permanent Subcommittee on Investigations of the Senate Committee on Government Operations, McCarthy had created an uproar in the fall of 1953 over the possibility of Communist infiltration of the U.S. Army. Nowhere was the reaction angrier than in the White House. If anyone then personified the army, it was five-star Dwight Eisenhower, commander-in-chief, formerly supreme Allied commander in Europe, and later army chief of staff. Yet while the president fumed, McCarthy besieged the Department of Defense, the army in particular.

One phase of the controversy sprang from the efforts of McCarthy's staff to obtain preferential treatment for a recently drafted private, G. David Schine. Heir to a hotel fortune, Schine had been a "consultant" to the subcommittee and was a favorite friend of Roy M. Cohn, the chief counsel to the subcommittee. Cohn upbraided army officials, civilian and military, for not having done more to lighten Schine's duties.

Overshadowing this unsavory affair was a bitter fight between McCarthy and an obscure New York dentist, Irving Peress. In October 1952 the army had commissioned Dr. Peress, and a year later he was routinely promoted to the rank of major under the provisions of the federal law drafting doctors. Within a month, however, military authorities had discovered that the dentist had declined to answer questions about his political beliefs. He had been a member of the left-wing American Labor party.

The adjutant general ordered the First Army to discharge Peress within ninety days. Before that deadline expired, McCarthy stepped in and summoned Peress before the subcommittee. In his usual terrier fashion, the senator clamped his teeth into Peress and wouldn't let him go. When the dentist declined to answer questions about his politics, McCarthy branded him a "Fifth Amendment Communist" and demanded that he be court-martialed. To jettison the problem the army gave the dentist an honorable discharge instead. Not missing a trick, McCarthy called to the stand Brig. Gen. Ralph W. Zwicker, commandant at old Camp Kilmer, New Jersey, where Peress was stationed. McCarthy demanded the names of all officers involved in the decision to give the major an honorable discharge. On advice of counsel, Zwicker refused to say. McCarthy retorted that Zwicker, who had been decorated for heroism in World War II, was "not fit to wear" his uniform.

Robert T. Stevens, a South Carolina textile manufacturer, who had become secretary of the army and was out of his milieu in a political brawl, then ordered Zwicker not to testify further. Stevens said he would testify in Zwicker's place. An intraparty free-for-all ensued. Republican leaders of the Senate finally tried to calm things by having Stevens join McCarthy at a supposedly private luncheon on February 24. For the administration the outcome was deplorable. Duped and naive, Stevens allowed McCarthy to get word out that the Eisenhower administration had surrendered. A headline in the *New York Times* the next day read, "Stevens Bows to McCarthy at Administration Behest. Will Yield Data on Peress." In "near hysteria," according to Eisenhower, Stevens offered to resign, but Eisenhower rejected the suggestion.[2]

In private the president stormed about the affair and blamed the press for making McCarthy a celebrity. In public Eisenhower could not summon the political spunk to voice his own loathing of McCarthy and McCarthyism. Below all the quarreling on the surface, a deeper issue was at stake. McCarthy had challenged the president's constitutional rights by demanding access to the army's confidential files on loyalty and security. McCarthy threatened to subpoena the files of the Loyalty and Security Appeals Board that had passed on some of the cases the subcommittee was investigating. Robert Griffith, a leading historian of the McCarthy bane, later wrote about the constitutional conflict. It was "between the right of the president to withhold information and the right of Congress to know."[3] In the end Eisenhower told Republican congressional leaders that he would permit no testimony on private discussions within the executive branch and directed the Department of Defense to withhold any confidences that might breach the integrity of the presidency.

On his evening radio program on February 23, Murrow questioned how long McCarthy was to be allowed to "delve into departmental matters, goad subordinates into criticism of their superiors, taint them with insinuations of Communist sympathies, and impugn the judgment and integrity to the demoralization of their department."[4] In this criticism Murrow had not stepped far ahead of public opinion. Although McCarthy was on one of his biggest rampages and had the president himself on the defensive, the senator was in deepening trouble. McCarthy's gullible and hot-headed following may have remained devoted, but the moderate press and moderate Republicans were appalled by his antics. Sen. Ralph E. Flanders, a Republican from Vermont, thus described McCarthy's pursuit of Peress: "He dons his war paint. He goes into his war dance. . . . He goes forth to battle and proudly returns with the scalp of a pink Army dentist."[5] The schism in the Republican party that McCarthy had caused was noted by Gov. Adlai Stevenson of Illinois, the Democratic presidential nominee in 1952 and 1956, only three days before Murrow's documentary was to air. Addressing the Southeastern Democratic Conference in Miami Beach, he called the Republicans "a party divided against itself, half McCarthy and half Eisenhower." It was a measure of how telling Stevenson's words were that the Republican National Committee demanded free air time to reply—and received it. And it was a measure of how McCarthy's standing had declined when he also demanded free time and was denied it.

Murrow scheduled the "See It Now" program on McCarthy for March 9, 1954. At CBS no one seems to have been in doubt about the controversy the show would ignite. The corporate side more or less averted its gaze and would pay for no promotion or advertising of the program. Murrow and Fred Friendly, the producer, put up fifteen hundred dollars of their own money to buy an advertisement in the *New York Times*.[6] Given the turmoil in the Republican party over McCarthy, Murrow's thirty-minute program could scarcely have come at a more pertinent time. He began by explaining to the audience that the story would be told mainly in the senator's own recorded words and pictures. If McCarthy were to feel "that we have done violence to his words or pictures . . . an opportunity will be afforded him on this program." Murrow employed a point-counterpoint technique: a quote by McCarthy and then a refutation.

Here was McCarthy captured on video in his favorite trick of declaring "I hold in my hand" and then never revealing what supposedly secret proof of villainy he held in his hand. There was Murrow disclosing that the supposedly incriminating document was a committee hearing transcript that anyone could have bought for two dollars.

Here was McCarthy asserting that the American Civil Liberties Union had "been listed as a front for . . . the Communist party." There was Murrow reporting, "The Attorney General's list does not and never has listed the ACLU as subversive. Nor does the FBI or any other federal government agency."

One strip of film caught McCarthy associating Adlai Stevenson with treason through mock confusion of his name with that of Alger Hiss. This notorious ruse occurred in a speech by McCarthy during the 1952 campaign. He had used the line, "Alger—I mean Adlai." By that time Hiss, a former government official, had been convicted and jailed for perjury in denying under oath that he had passed classified documents to a Communist espionage ring.[7]

A showman first and foremost, McCarthy carried his bag of expressions to hearings, and Murrow's film caught him closely in his malevolent look. McCarthy also had a panting, humorless laugh, and viewers were treated to this grace also. Summarizing what he perceived to be the dangers of McCarthyism, Murrow appealed to Americans not to let fear of communism drive them into an age of unreason:

This is no time for men who oppose Senator McCarthy's methods to keep silent—or for those who approve. We *can* deny our heritage and our history but we cannot escape responsibility for the result. There is no way for a citizen of a republic to abdicate his responsibility. . . .

The actions of the junior senator from Wisconsin have caused alarm and dismay amongst our allies abroad and given considerable comfort to our enemies. And whose fault is that? Not really his. He didn't create this situation of fear, he merely exploited it; and rather successfully.

Cassius was right. "The fault, dear Brutus, is not in our stars, but in ourselves."[8]

The response was an indication of the force of television news in only its sixth year. The next afternoon the pro-McCarthy New York *Journal–American,* a Hearst newspaper, carried the headline "Telecast Rip at McCarthy Stirs Storm." CBS was inundated with more than one hundred thousand letters, telegrams, and telephone calls, heavily supporting Murrow. The senders of messages ranged from Chief Justice Earl Warren to Albert Einstein. A new Gallup Poll showed a drop in McCarthy's approval rating. *Variety* called Murrow "practically . . . a national hero." In its "Week in Review" section the following Sunday, March 14, the *New York Times* raised the question whether the tide had turned against McCarthy.[9]

The beleaguered senator, two days after the Murrow broadcast, began a prolonged, well-publicized counterattack. He accepted Murrow's offer of a chance to reply, and on April 6 appeared on "See It Now." Among other things, he characterized Murrow as "a symbol, the leader and the cleverest of the jackal pack, which is always found at the throat of anyone who dares to expose individual Communists and traitors." Although the pummeling of Murrow by McCarthy and his supporters went on, it was the original Murrow program that had scored.

By chance, Murrow scored a few more points the day after Mc-Carthy's appearance on "See It Now." Eisenhower happened to have scheduled a White House press conference on April 7. Joseph C. Harsch of the *Christian Science Monitor* and NBC asked the president whether he would "care to say anything to us about the loyalty and patriotism of Edward R. Murrow?" Eisenhower's reply was wonderfully typical of the general in such a circumstance. "I am going to say nothing at all about that," he began.

First of all, I don't comment about people. . . . I will say this: I have known this man for many years; he has been one of the men I consider my friend among your profession. . . . So far as indulging in philosophical discussion, I can't remember any instance; but I do say that he has been one of those that over the years, in the war, when he was working in London, and so on, I always thought of him as a friend.[10]

A *New York Post* headline had no problem groping through the verbiage: "Ike Backs Murrow. Calls Joe's Target 'His Friend.' "

For all the turmoil generated by "See It Now" and by McCarthy's charges voiced in and out of his subcommittee, the stormy Army-McCarthy hearings did not begin until more than a month after the Murrow broadcast. The Permanent Subcommittee on Investigations held the hearings to investigate the charges raised by and against McCarthy and by and against Roy Cohn as chief counsel. Because McCarthy as chairman of the subcommittee was in reality the prosecutor at the hearings and a witness as well, he had to sit at the table as a nonmember but under a friendly acting chairman, Sen. Karl E. Mundt, a Republican from South Dakota. The arrangement was a sham; McCarthy continually intervened by invoking points of order.

The hearings opened before a full house on April 22, 1954, and went on for thirty-five days. On the first and second days they were televised by ABC, NBC, and a small network of the time, Dumont. CBS passed up live coverage because, of all the networks then, it had the most daytime billings and stood to lose the most money by preempting regular programs. After the second day, NBC looked at the early ratings and abandoned live coverage in favor of later filmed summaries. Along with DuMont, ABC was still on the job on the third day.

The president of ABC was Robert Kintner, a stout, gruff, vodka-drinking executive, who could terrify anyone who did not know that he had a softer side. Kintner stubbornly believed that the hearings could pay off for television. He saw the big play newspapers were giving them, and newspaper work was where he had learned his trade, beginning as a Wall Street reporter for the *New York Herald Tribune.* In his dilemma over whether to follow NBC in dropping live coverage of the hearings, he asked John Daly, head of ABC News, how much it would cost to cover the hearings to the end. The network was then in a perilous financial condition.

"How do I know?" Daly answered. "Half a million dollars—maybe more."

Holding the decision in abeyance, Kintner said he would call Daly before the day was out.

"He called me about 5:42," Daly recalled. "I picked up the phone, and he said, 'Kintner,' and I said, 'Yup,' and he said, 'Go.' That probably was the most courageous decision ever taken in such a context."

According to Daly, "ABC was looking at a million-three of red ink," because of a misguided contract with the National Collegiate Athletic Association for coverage of college sports.

"All of us vice-presidents were called in one evening," he related, "and Mr. Kintner said to us, 'I want every budget in every department cut 20 percent by the close of business tomorrow night. No excuses will be accepted.' That's how dire a condition he had come into."[11]

"Remember," Kintner said later, "in those days the other two networks were just beginning to program their daytime soap operas. We didn't have any on ABC, so it didn't matter what shows we preempted. . . . [W]e took over an unbelievably large audience. People all over the country stopped listening to their radios and watching their soaps and stayed glued to what we were showing on ABC."[12]

The hearings made a better drama than the soaps did. "Major affiliates of CBS and NBC," according to Daly, "dumped their soap operas and their general programming and started asking for permission to pick up the ABC feed."[13]

When NBC terminated coverage after the second day, Chicago, like any other city, would have been blacked out unless ABC stayed with the hearings. *Newsweek* reported that Marshall Field, Jr., owner of the liberal *Chicago Sun–Times,* offered to give the ABC affiliate in Chicago "several thousand dollars a day" if that was what it took to keep the hearings on the air.[14] In the end, his generosity was not put to the test.

For its coverage of the Army-McCarthy hearings, ABC won a Peabody Award. "It was ABC that really held the mirror up to Joe McCarthy," recalled Fred Friendly, producer of the Murrow program. "It was a historic decision. Let it be recorded that Kintner emerges as the hero of that period."[15]

The televised hearings were a widely viewed spectacle. After they had ended in June 1954, a Gallup Poll reported that 89 percent of their respondents on the subject said they had followed the hearings. For McCarthy, carrying on through 187 hours of television before audiences estimated to be as large as 20 million at a time, the display was a calamity.[16]

To many television viewers, McCarthy's underling, Roy Cohn, was repulsive in manner and looks. Although Private Schine was not called as a witness, testimony about his and Cohn's efforts to get preferential treatment for him in the army struck many people as an outrage. Gen. Cornelius E. Ryan, commandant at Fort Dix, New Jersey, testified that Schine had been granted (usually at the request of McCarthy's subcommittee) sixteen passes compared with three or four that other enlisted men normally would have received during the same period. Ryan declared that his aide had been called by Cohn, who complained that two of Schine's officers did "everything they could to make it difficult for Private Schine and that he [Cohn] was not going to forget their names."

The subcommittee also had heard testimony from Schine's company commander at Fort Dix, Cap. Joseph J. M. Miller. On Private Schine's first day at the base, Miller said, Schine began to tell him that if Miller "ever wanted to take a little trip to Florida," Schine's family ran a resort hotel there. Thinking he was being proffered a favor, the captain terminated the conversation. Miller testified that he once came upon Schine seeking a favor from his sergeant. When the captain upbraided Schine, the private asked the captain to lower his voice. According to the captain, the private "put his hand on my shoulder," "attempted to draw me aside," and said that "it was his purpose to remake the American military establishment along modern lines."[17]

McCarthy denounced Eisenhower's "iron curtain" around confidential Department of Defense records that he wanted to see. In fact, the senator practically advocated insubordination. All federal employees, he said, should understand that "it is their duty to give us any information which they have about graft, corruption, communism, treason, and that there is no loyalty to a superior officer which can tower above and beyond their loyalty to their country." In a statement approved by the president, Attorney General Herbert Brownell, Jr., replied that execution of the laws was the sole and fundamental duty of the executive and that "responsibility can't be usurped by an individual who may seek to set himself above the laws of our land."[18]

McCarthy's unruly conduct at the hearings, typified by his intrusion with points of order, began to be ridiculed by comedians on television. Soon Jackie Gleason, Steve Allen, Bob Hope, and Milton Berle were mimicking him on the air with cries of "Mr. Chairman, Mr. Chairman" and shouts of "point of order."

Five days before the end of the televised hearings a stunning confrontation occurred that proved anything but a joke for McCarthy. The senator met his match in an unlikely adversary, the urbane and mild-mannered Joseph L. Welch of the Boston law firm of Hale & Dorr. Welch had been retained by the army as special counsel. When he came to address the committee, he was strikingly precise and even a touch theatrical. The drama hinged on a young member of Welch's firm, Frederick G. Fisher, Jr., who was brought to Washington to help in the preparation of the army's case. He didn't stay long. Welch reluctantly told Fisher that he had better not work on the case after Fisher confided that he had belonged to the National Lawyers Guild while he had been enrolled as a student at Harvard Law School. During the period of anti-Communist fervor, the organization had been accused of having left-wing tendencies. Although Fisher had been a member for only a short time and although Fisher's current politics were not suspect (he was secretary of the conservative Young Republicans League in Newton, Massachusetts), Welch smelled trouble. If his affiliation with the guild were to come up and be aired on national television, it might hurt Fisher professionally, Welch told his young colleague.

Cohn and McCarthy's counsel, Edward Bennett Williams, urged the senator not to mention Fisher during the hearings. After all, Welch had never recommended Fisher for counsel to the subcommittee. But McCarthy could not resist. On June 9 he became annoyed at Welch's interrogation of Cohn at the hearings. Concerning Cohn's probe for subversives in the army, Welch archly commented that he hoped Cohn would be quick to report any Communist spy he might find. McCarthy grabbed the floor to say that Welch should be informed "that he has in his law firm a young man named Fisher . . . who has been for a number of years a member of an organization which was named . . . as the legal bulwark of the Communist party." When McCarthy finished, he was grinning at Welch.

The lawyer was not amused. "Until this moment, senator, I think I never really gauged your cruelty or your recklessness." After recalling the circumstance of his sending Fisher back to Boston, Welch continued:

Little did I dream you could be so reckless and so cruel as to do an injury to that lad. . . . I fear he shall always bear a scar needlessly inflicted by you. If it were in my power to forgive you for your reckless cruelty, I [would] do so. I like to think I am a gentleman, but your forgiveness will have to come from someone other than me.[19]

McCarthy again began to speak about Fisher when Welch cut him short.

"Let us not assassinate this lad further, senator. You have done enough. Have you no sense of decency, sir, at long last? Have you left no sense of decency?"

"It seems," McCarthy retorted, "that Mr. Welch is pained so deeply he thinks it is improper for me to give the record, the Communist-front record, of the man whom he wanted to foist upon this committee."

"Mr. McCarthy," Welch responded, "I will not discuss this with you further. You have sat within six feet of me and could have asked me about Fred Fisher. You have brought it out. If there is a God in heaven, it will do neither you nor your cause any good."[20]

Thereupon Welch rose and walked out of the hearing room to the applause of the audience. Viewers across the country saw him go. For once McCarthy was without words. A "*coup de grace* . . . demolishing McCarthy live on camera," Murrow's biographer A. M. Sperber called Welch's riposte.[21] Cohn later described the confrontation with Welch as a terribly damaging blow to McCarthy.[22] Fisher was unfazed. He went on to a distinguished career with Hale & Dorr. He was elected president of the Massachusetts Bar Association and became chairman of the American Bar Association's general practice section.

Two days after McCarthy's exchange with Welch, Senator Flanders entered the hearing room and handed McCarthy a written invitation to be present in the Senate that afternoon when Flanders would make a speech of interest to the senator from Wisconsin. When Flanders took the floor, McCarthy having disdained his invitation, he introduced Senate Resolution 261. It called for the removal of McCarthy from the chairmanship of the Committee on Government Operations and any of its subcommittees unless McCarthy answered charges raised in 1952 by a subcommittee of the Senate Rules Committee. These charges pertained to corruption in McCarthy's finances, but the issue was never resolved. For nearly five months after Flanders's speech, the Senate was torn over the McCarthy question. A select committee was chosen to study it. Almost week by week the case against McCarthy gathered support. A new resolution—Senate Resolution 301—was substituted. Alleging that he had "tended to bring the Senate into dishonor and disrepute, to obstruct the constitutional processes of the Senate, and to impair its dignity," the resolution called for condemnation of McCarthy for having acted "contrary to Senatorial ethics." On December 2, 1954, he was censured by a vote of sixty-seven to twenty-two.

Neither Murrow nor the ABC coverage of the Army-McCarthy hearings had censured McCarthy. The U.S. Senate did. But as Edwin R. Bayley explained in his book on McCarthy, "broadcasting of the hearings made it possible for the Senate to consider censure."[23] Alexander Kendrick, a biographer of Murrow, also acknowledged television's role in McCarthy's downfall. "What [McCarthy] did the Senator may have done to himself, as he would do again in the Army-McCarthy hearings . . . but television showed him doing it. The See It Now broadcast helped persuade people that he was not invincible or immune, and put him on the defensive." Kendrick concluded that the Murrow broadcast apparently "did influence Senators and others who had hitherto tolerated McCarthy, and who possessed the power to do something about him."[24] Professor Griffith's studies convinced him that a slight balance in the Senate, while not exactly supporting McCarthy, nevertheless went along with him and enabled him to survive furious opposition. If the hearings did not destroy the balance, they threatened it, Griffith wrote, adding:

This was why the resolution Senator Ralph E. Flanders introduced on June 11 was so important. The "McCarthy balance" was created by acquiescence, not by support, and its prolongation depended upon the Senate's continued evasion of a direct confrontation with McCarthy. The Flanders resolution, quite simply, threatened to make further evasion impossible.[25]

Speaking at Guildhall in London in 1959, Murrow said McCarthy was censured because he "broke the rules of the club, the United States

Senate. When he began attacking the integrity, the loyalty of fellow Senators, he was censured by that body, and was finished."[26]

The televised hearings made the continuance of McCarthy's power embarrassing and intolerable to an increasing number of Republicans. From New Hampshire to Nebraska, party professionals expressed fear that the spectacle in Washington would hamper fund-raising and hurt Republicans at the polls. "It is now time for the Republican Party to repudiate Joe McCarthy before he drags them all to defeat," Palmer Hoyt, publisher of the *Denver Post,* wrote to President Eisenhower.[27] In their meticulous study of the influence of television news, focusing particularly on Watergate, political scientists Gladys Engel Lang and Kurt Lang offered support for some of these assessments. The hearings, they wrote, "did make an impression on [McCarthy's] fellow legislators; they learned that McCarthy could be challenged. When, after the hearings, powerful political forces on Capitol Hill were finally stirred to action, McCarthy's public performance was among the evidence used to discredit him."[28]

McCarthy was even faced with a revolt in his own subcommittee. Overwhelmingly, the Senate defeated three substitute amendments to dilute the censure resolution.

The final act was a notable event in the history of the Senate. The slow process and McCarthy's steady decline, however, made the 67-to-22 vote somewhat anticlimactic. McCarthy did not lose his Senate seat nor his chairmanship of the permanent investigations subcommittee. Nevertheless his standing was shattered. The press and people in and out of Congress paid ever less attention to him. While fear of communism in America continued, at least its most cynical source evaporated. McCarthy drank heavily. At the age of forty-eight, he died of cirrhosis of the liver on May 2, 1957.

Writing in the *Reporter* magazine on June 8, 1954, Marya Mannes commented: "Week after week on our television screen we have watched a drama of the most compelling sort. Whatever you call them, the Army-McCarthy hearings have been a picture which should obsess the American memory, as it has obsessed all those who have seen it."[29] Not for another twenty years—Watergate—would congressional hearings make such compelling television.

3

Television news and the ups and downs of
Richard Nixon: the 1960 election

Richard Nixon's relationship with most television and print journalists
was as dark and joyless as it was prolonged and complex. For twenty-
two years, six years longer than the period John Kennedy, Lyndon Johnson, and Ronald Reagan spent in the White House, Nixon pursued a
public career that was singularly interwoven with television. No political
figure of the time gained and lost so much from it.

As Franklin Roosevelt had mastered radio, Kennedy was the first president to master television. Johnson, although not a polished performer
before the television camera, made gargantuan lunges at it to turn its
potential to his own advantage. Reagan, a trained actor with a message
and a staff skilled in video techniques, was a conqueror. Through television he won the affection of most of the American people so enduringly
that scandals and blunders could not erase it. But Nixon was obsessed
with television. He repeatedly tried to discredit television and print journalists and menace television networks. His animosities fueled his strategies for communicating with the public. And he was firmly convinced in
1989 that no other institution had controlled his fate as had television
news.[1]

During Nixon's first year in the White House in 1969, he employed
television through appearances on news broadcasts on a scale unequaled
by any president before him.[2] For advice on dealing with the press and
television, he listened to some hard, ruthless men. They advised actions,
wrote Thomas Whiteside in the *New Yorker,* that seemed "to be the
work not of a peacetime government but of some wartime propaganda
bureau operating against an enemy under emergency powers, with coor-

35

dinated policy directives [and] weekly party propaganda lines."[3] Nixon
was explicit with his staff in identifying the press as the enemy. Nixon
papers in the National Archives reveal how certain assistants not only
catered to the president's feelings of hostility but also sought to inflame
it. The idea that the press was viciously against the president must be
hammered home to the public, they argued. Obviously, Nixon did not
need too much goading. On April 30, 1972, in an extraordinary memorandum to H. R. Haldeman, his chief of staff, Nixon said that the press
had "a vested interest in seeing the United States lose" the Vietnam War.[4]

Needless to say, if this memorandum had been disclosed to the public
at the time, it would have caused a storm. Other memorandums also
would have stirred up foul weather if they had been publicized. One
written in 1969 by Jeb Stuart Magruder, the White House deputy director of communications, implied that the Nixon administration should
consider sending agents of the Federal Bureau of Investigation to reporters' homes in the middle of the night to question them about allegedly
unfair stories. On the same subject of dealing with the press and television, but in a different context, Lawrence M. Higby of Haldeman's
office wrote a memorandum. What the White House staff was aiming at,
he said, was "to tear down the institution."[5] Specifically, Higby was referring to NBC's "Huntley-Brinkley Report," which frequently did not
please the White House.

Haldeman understood the power of a television image compared with
the written word. During the planning of Nixon's trip to China in 1972,
he wrote an "action memo" that said, "the picture of the American President being received by a million Chinese is worth 100 times the effect of
the communiqué and other substantive output. In terms of our interest,
television is the overriding factor."[6] In case of a shortage of seats on the
press plane, Haldeman had a solution: "The most important press people
are the TV—even if this means no writing press at all."

At times the line of fire from the White House extended to newspapers
and news magazines. Before the 1972 election Nixon told his staff that
"the discrediting of the press must be our major objective over
the next few months."[7] After he won, the "campaign" continued. No
time was lost. In an action memo dated November 10, 1972, Haldeman
wrote:

Be sure we have established a total embargo on *Time* and *Newsweek* and especially no background material to [*Time* correspondent Hugh] Sidey. . . . [Secre-
tary of State William P.] Rogers is to understand that there is a complete freeze

on The Washington Post and The New York Times and CBS . . . no conversations with them until the Vietnam negotiations are over.[8]

President Nixon's desire to turn the American people against television news programs, their producers, anchors, and reporters was shared by his vice-president, the sharp-tongued Spiro T. Agnew. In a speech in Des Moines on November 13, 1969, he excoriated "a small and unelected elite" of network journalists for allegedly abusing their power over public opinion by the way they reported and interpreted news. A week later in Montgomery, Agnew made a similar attack on newspapers, singling out the *New York Times* and the *Washington Post* for condemnation. Even Haldeman and Ronald L. Ziegler, the White House press secretary, urged Nixon to stop the speech, but Patrick J. Buchanan, a speechwriter, fought for it, and, as William Safire, another speechwriter, recalled, "the President said let 'er rip."[9]

When Nixon referred in 1989 to television news and his fate, he was not only referring to his presidency.[10] As early as August 1948 television was shaping his political career. At that time Nixon was thirty-five years old and in the second year of his first term as a U.S. representative from California. The Committee on Un-American Activities, on which he served, was investigating Alger Hiss, formerly of the State Department. In executive session Whittaker Chambers, a senior editor of *Time,* who had been a member of a Communist underground in the early 1930s, made serious charges against Hiss. He alleged that Hiss had been a member of the underground and had passed classified government documents to a Communist agent. Hiss denied it. The upshot was the most dramatic congressional hearings of the early postwar period, climaxed by confrontation between Hiss and Chambers. Hiss denied that he even recognized Chambers. Eventually, Hiss was convicted and sent to prison for perjury (the statute of limitations on espionage had expired). In committee, Nixon had been a driving force in focusing doubt on Hiss's testimony and was often interviewed on television news in its earliest days. It was his large hand in Hiss's downfall through indictment and conviction for perjury that doubtless intensified many liberals' antipathy toward Nixon, who had a reputation for red-baiting. It helped his standing among conservatives. Nixon ran for the Senate in 1950 and won.

Nixon's role in the Hiss case and in the politics of anticommunism in general was a major consideration in his selection as Eisenhower's running mate in 1952. The Republicans saw anticommunism as a big weapon to turn against the Democrats, and Nixon looked like the right man to fire it. Yet scarcely had he begun to campaign for vice-president after his nomination when he was plunged into a crisis that might have ended his career.

On Sunday, September 14, 1952, Nixon was interviewed on "Meet the Press" by Peter Edson, a columnist for the Scripps-Howard newspapers, and two other journalists. After the broadcast Edson asked Nixon privately about the rumor that Nixon had a fund of about twenty thousand dollars a year in extra income.

Apparently unconcerned, Nixon explained that a fund totaling $18,235 had indeed been established by California supporters. It provided supplementary office and travel expenses, not extra salary for the senator. The fund was public and independently audited. Dana C. Smith, a lawyer and finance chairman of Nixon's senatorial campaign in California in 1950, had originated the fund and directed it. Saying he had nothing to hide, Nixon gave Smith's telephone number in Pasadena to Edson. In the next day or so Edson called Smith and obtained further details that coincided with Nixon's explanation. A straightforward, unsensational column about the fund appeared on September 18. Nixon later characterized Edson's column as objective.[11]

But the same day, the *New York Post,* a partisan Democratic newspaper, appeared with a headline "Secret Nixon Fund." On page 2 was this subhead: "Secret Rich Man's Trust Fund Keeps Nixon in Style Far Beyond His Salary." The story by Leo Katcher began: "Los Angeles— The existence of a 'millionaires' club' devoted exclusively to the financial comfort of Senator Nixon, GOP vice presidential candidate, was revealed today." The scandalous overtones of the *Post* account prompted Democrats to demand Nixon's resignation from the ticket. In shock, Eisenhower and his political advisers concluded that resignation would be in the best interests of the Republican party. Nixon balked, claiming he had done nothing wrong. Finally, a consensus was reached that he should state his case to the public on television and await the reaction.

The Republican party bought a half-hour of television and radio time on NBC on the night of September 23. Since Nixon was campaigning in the West, he would speak from the stage of El Capitan Theater in Hollywood.

Upset and rushed for time though he was, Nixon made a shrewd decision. At the close of his speech he would ask the audience to write or telegraph their reaction not to Eisenhower but to the Republican National Committee, a stronghold of Nixon sentiment. As he phrased it, it was the decision of the committee after the speech that he would abide by. On the twenty-minute ride to the theater from the Ambassador Hotel he and Mrs. Nixon were silent. On the stage Edward A. (Ted) Rogers, Nixon's producer, inquired what movements he might make during the broadcast. "I haven't the slightest idea," Nixon replied. "Just keep the camera on me." At three minutes to air time he tried to read his notes again but felt too tense. Suddenly, he told his wife he did not think he could go through with the speech. Of course, he could, she replied. At the table he bent forward over his notes. Expressionless, Mrs. Nixon sat to one side in an armchair. The light on the camera blinked red. The floorman's finger pointed.

"My fellow Americans," Nixon began, "I come before you tonight as a candidate for the vice-presidency and as a man whose honesty and integrity has [*sic*] been questioned." On the black-and-white television screens he came across as emotional but controlled, earnest but not intense or troubled. At times he was maudlin, and even folksy. But the earnest appeal of the young candidate worked. What the audience saw was a devoted family man who spent his money prudently. Nixon explained the workaday nature of the fund—an issue that had already lost force after the *Chicago Tribune* reported that Adlai Stevenson, as governor of Illinois, had a similar one. Nixon artfully contrasted his wife Pat with a former stenographer in the Truman White House named Lauretta Young. A year or so before, Mrs. Young had turned out in an $8,450 royal pastel mink coat given to her husband, a businessman and former government employee. He had accepted it from the attorney for a client who had sought government loans and may have felt obligated to the husband.

"I should say this," Nixon told his large national audience, "that Pat doesn't have a mink coat. But she does have a respectable Republican cloth coat, and I always tell her that she would look good in anything."[12]

Nixon did archly confess that he and Pat had accepted a gift:

A man down in Texas [he said] heard Pat on the radio mention the fact that our two youngsters would like to have a dog and, believe it or not, the day before we left on this campaign trip we got a message from Union Station in Baltimore, saying they had a package for us. We went down to get it. You know what it was?

It was a little cocker spaniel dog, in a crate that he had sent all the way from

Texas—black and white, spotted, and our little girl Tricia, the six-year-old, named it Checkers. And, you know, the kids, like all. kids, loved that dog, and I just want to say this, right now that regardless of what they say about it, we are going to keep it.[13]

This principle established, he went on to criticize Stevenson, quote Lincoln ("God must have loved the common people, he made so many of them"), and exalt Eisenhower. "And remember, folks, Eisenhower is a great man. Folks, he is a great man, and a vote for Eisenhower is a vote for what is good for America."[14]

After watching the speech on television in Cleveland, Eisenhower turned to Republican National Chairman Arthur E. Summerfield and said, "Well, Arthur, you certainly got your seventy-five thousand dollars' worth tonight."[15]

Nixon's performance on television and radio unleashed a deluge of support. To handle the wave of favorable telegrams to the Republican National Committee headquarters in Washington, Western Union had to rush in extra operators. Mailed checks and telegraphed money orders totaled sixty thousand dollars, almost enough to pay for the broadcast. The committee headquarters in Washington received three hundred thousand letters and telegrams signed by more than a million people. Republican committees in the states also were swamped with telegrams, running 350-to-1 in support of Nixon. The television audience was estimated at 58 million, one of the largest up to that point. Newspaper stories about the Checkers speech produced a frenzied response. Theodore H. White wrote:

One must mark 1952 as the date that Richard Nixon discovered how spectacular the influence of television could be when, with his masterful . . . "Checkers speech," he reached for the first time, nationally, to stir the emotions of Middle America and override the decisions of the party masters for his dismissal. . . . Its success scored [in] the mind of every realistic politician. Television would change the mechanics of all future American campaigning.[16]

Instead of being dumped from the ticket, Nixon was inaugurated vice-president on January 20, 1953. "That broadcast," Garry Wills wrote, "saved Nixon's career, and made history."[17]

On July 24, 1959, at the invitation of Premier Nikita S. Khrushchev, Nixon went to Moscow to open the first U.S. exhibition ever held in the Soviet Union. Much was at stake on this trip. With the next Republican convention a year away, the vice-president was the leading, though not yet assured, candidate for the 1960 presidential nomination. Many were watching to see how he would deal with America's primary adversary in the cold war.

Nixon's briefings had convinced him that he would face a bullying man intent on dominating conversation. Indeed, when the two met privately in the Kremlin, Khrushchev assailed him about the recent passage in Congress of the Captive Nations Resolution decrying Soviet domination of Eastern Europe. Khrushchev's argumentativeness continued until it was time for Nixon to open the U.S. exhibit. Afterwards, the two men stopped at an RCA display of a model television studio. Nixon later recalled what happened next:

A young engineer asked if we would like to try out a new color television taping system by recording greetings that could be played back during the exhibition. Khrushchev seemed suspicious, but when he saw a group of Soviet workmen near the display, the actor in him took over. Before I knew what he was doing he had scrambled onto the platform and was talking for the cameras and playing to the gallery.[18]

The first report from the exhibition to appear on American television was confined to the scene at the RCA exhibit. And it caught Nixon lecturing Khrushchev about his threats of Soviet competition against the United States. "If this competition in which you plan to outstrip us is to do the best for both of our peoples and for peoples everywhere," Nixon said, "there must be a free exchange of ideas. You must not be afraid of ideas. After all, you don't know everything."[19] Back home the networks repeatedly showed this scene of Nixon "standing up to the Russians." As Nixon often told his staff, "What's on the tube is what counts."[20] Later, during a visit to a model American kitchen, Khrushchev again seized the initiative. He goaded Nixon on American accomplishments, called the United States inept in trading, predicted that Soviet technology would soon surpass America's, and continually took advantage of Nixon's resolve to keep his visit decorous. Before the tour of the U.S. exhibit was over Nixon had taken a good deal of bullying. Fortunately for Nixon, the bulky television cameras could not be moved at the pace of Nixon's and Khrushchev's stroll. Although the "kitchen debate," as it became known, was not televised, the episode was fully covered by American newspapers, and one photo caught Nixon pointing his finger at Khrushchev. This good fortune led William Safire to challenge the notion prevailing among Nixon and his staff that only television was important.[21]

NBC decided to assemble all the film it had on Nixon in Moscow and

Poland, where he visited briefly, for a one-hour documentary. After his return to Washington, Nixon went to the studio and, with the help of a correspondent who had covered the trip, flawlessly narrated his experiences to a national audience. The nomination of Nixon at the Republican convention in 1960 reflected to some extent the delegates' confidence that in him they had a man who could hold his own with Khrushchev.

Thus, when Nixon began to campaign against the Democratic presidential nominee, Sen. John F. Kennedy, he had two major television triumphs to his credit: the Checkers speech and the Khrushchev debates. They augured well for his bid on the presidency. Television, by 1960, had become a powerful force in the political system.

In 1960 the networks were striving to improve their image and reassure viewers of their dedication to the public interest. Television had just sloshed through an embarrassing ordeal resulting from the fixing of weekly quiz programs. Cheating on two immensely popular shows—"Twenty-One" and "The $64,000 Question"—genuinely shocked the public. Network executives, eager to demonstrate their civic-mindedness, conceived of the ideas of televised debates between the Democratic and Republican nominees. In addition to huge audiences, the debates promised another benefit to the networks: a change in the Communications Act of 1934. Section 315 had long rankled broadcasting executives. It required that candidates for the same office be given equal treatment on the air. Longshot presidential contenders from every party, not just the Democratic and Republican nominees, would have to be included, making the debates an impractical multilateral affair.

The networks invited Kennedy and Nixon to debate, subject to congressional action on the Communications Act. Kennedy immediately accepted. The debates would give him a great deal of national exposure, which he then lacked and might not readily get otherwise. Nixon hesitated. He needed the exposure less. Not only had he been in the House and the Senate with Kennedy but also he had been twice elected vice-president. His official trips to Moscow and to Venezuela, where he had encountered dangerous anti-American violence in Caracas, made him better known than Kennedy and seemingly the more experienced in statecraft. Although he had less to gain and more to lose, Nixon agreed to debate, and Congress suspended Section 315.

A number of factors entered into Nixon's decision. The Gallup Poll consistently indicated a close race. Ironically, Nixon's very success in

Moscow argued in favor of a face-to-face confrontation with Kennedy. If Nixon could debate Khrushchev and more than hold his own, why worry about the senator from Massachusetts? Nixon considered himself an excellent debater, his skill dating from his student days at Duke Law School. Certainly, he did not wish, by refusing, to make it appear that he was afraid of Kennedy. Eisenhower admonished him against trying "to be too slick." Nixon assured him that he "was going to be gentlemanly, let Kennedy be the aggressor."[22]

Both candidates were confident that they would "win." According to Theodore White, Nixon was sure he "could take this man on TV."[23] As for Kennedy, he "had no doubt that he could hold his own against Nixon," recalled Lawrence F. O'Brien, one of Kennedy's closest campaign aids.[24]

Four debates were held at staggered intervals during the campaign. They covered different issues. "Since there was no precedent for this kind of televised debate," Nixon wrote of the 1960 encounters, "we could only guess which program would have the larger audience. Foreign affairs was my strong suit, and I wanted the larger audience for that debate. I thought more people would watch the first one, and that interest would diminish as the novelty of the confrontation wore off."[25] He was right. The American Research Bureau estimated the audiences of the four debates, in order, at 75 million, 61 million, 70 million, and 63 million.[26]

Nixon, however, heeded his advisers who were convinced that the last program, nearest election day, would have the biggest audience. Domestic issues were the focus of the first debate, which was held at the CBS studio in Chicago on September 26.

Both candidates arrived in Chicago the day before. Kennedy was much the more rested of the two. Ill luck had befallen Nixon at the start of his campaign. In Greensboro, North Carolina, on August 17, he had bumped his knee getting into a car. An infection set in that forced him to stay in the Walter Reed Army Medical Center in Washington from August 29 to September 9. He lost eight pounds—and looked it. As soon as he was discharged, he began campaigning furiously to make up for time lost and caught a cold.

Nixon did not arrive in Chicago on September 25 until 10:30 P.M., and even at that hour he visited some street rallies that kept him up until well after midnight. On the morning of the 26th he had to address a meeting of the United Brotherhood of Carpenters and Joiners of America. Meanwhile Kennedy arose early and spent four hours with members of his staff preparing for the debate. After lunch he, too, made a brief speech to the same union and then took a nap. Nixon spent practically the entire afternoon reading in preparation for the debate. From all that is known of that day, Kennedy was relaxed, and his opponent was tired and tense. Nixon later wrote: "The tension continued to rise all afternoon. My entire staff obviously felt it just as I did. As we rode to the television studio, conversation was at a minimum as I continued to study my notes up to the last minute."[27] When he got out of the car at the studio he painfully bumped his sore knee again. On greeting Kennedy inside, he was impressed by how fit the senator looked. "We could see that Nixon was nervous," O'Brien recalled. "He tried to be hearty but it didn't come off."[28]

Don Hewitt of CBS was the director of the program. Ted Rogers was present, as Nixon's adviser, as was Kennedy's adviser, Bill Wilson. The vice-president's pallor disturbed Hewitt and Rogers. Aware that Nixon's transparent skin needed make-up under bright studio lights, even though the broadcast was in black and white, Rogers had requested that the vice-president's make-up artist be brought to Chicago, but the campaign staff declined. Hewitt asked Nixon if he would like to be made up. "No," Nixon replied. Kennedy, well sun-tanned, did not need make-up. And, according to Hewitt, Nixon did not want to run the risk of having it reported that he was made up (an unmanly advantage) and Kennedy was not. In the end Nixon did use "Lazy Shave," a powder to cover his five o'clock shadow, but Hewitt did not think it was satisfactory. He recalled:

He looked so bad when he came out that I took one look at him on camera, and went out and I called Frank Stanton, who was then president of CBS, and I said, "Frank, you better come and look at this because I think we're in for some problems here." Frank looked and said to Ted Rogers, "Are you happy with the way your candidate looks?" Ted said, "Sure." Frank said to me, "Then it's not our business. If that's the way they want him to look, that's the way they want him to look."[29]

Nixon used poor judgment in wearing a gray suit against the gray backdrop. He did not stand out on television screens nearly as sharply as Kennedy, who was handsomely dressed in a dark suit, blue shirt, and dark tie. Kennedy's manner in the debate was serious. Nixon smiled often and somewhat nervously. Perhaps because of his sore knee, he sat awkwardly when he was not speaking. His tendency to perspire under studio lights quickly became noticeable, and it caused a quarrel in the control booth while the debate was in progress. Rogers was shocked when, without warning, Hewitt called for a reaction shot that caught Nixon apparently off guard. A reaction shot is one that cuts away from the main action of the moment and focuses on an accompanying scene, which in this case was one of Nixon seated while Kennedy was speaking. The shot showed Nixon wiping his brow and upper lip. Furiously, Rogers maintained that reaction shots had been disallowed by the rules and that Nixon had been brought into the picture unfairly in an undignified pose.

Uncomfortably seated between Rogers and Wilson, Hewitt insisted that no ban on reaction shots had even been discussed. Still, while Rogers was challenging him from one side, Wilson on the other was making demands of his own, as Hewitt recalled. "We need more reaction shots," Wilson said. "You owe me three. We've had three of my man, now we need three of your man." Wilson acknowledged later that the dispute "drove Don Hewitt crazy."[30]

In the first debate as in the remaining three, the two candidates were cautious, even prosaic. Reporters had difficulty deciding what would make the best lead on their stories. No issue had caught fire. Though the debates were historic, the low-keyed exchanges about farm surpluses, education, and care for the aged sometimes bored listeners. No thirty-second sound bites were flung at the camera. Many persons who listened to the first debate on radio rather than watching it on television thought Nixon had the better of it. He was careful about making debating points. But, as Theodore White, the shrewd chronicler of presidential elections in the 1960s and 1970s, observed, Nixon "was debating with Mr. Kennedy as if a board of judges were scoring points; he rebutted and refuted, as he went. . . . Nixon was addressing himself to Kennedy—but Kennedy was addressing himself to the audience that was the nation."[31]

In retrospect, Nixon characterized the first debate as a setback for him. He was in much better health for the last three and at the very least held his own. But those debates did not engage the public to the degree the first one had. Even the first debate failed to cause anything like a decisive swing in either direction in the Gallup Poll. Kennedy retained the slight lead he had held through September. Nixon's sense of a setback contrasted with renewed optimism around Kennedy, whose staff were ecstatic because when Kennedy resumed campaigning after Chicago, he suddenly seemed to attract more excited crowds, as though people were flocking toward a winner. Certainly, the concerns of Eisenhower and other Republicans had been realized; Kennedy, the younger and supposedly less experienced candidate, had looked more presidential on television than Nixon.

Regardless of Nixon's bad knee and haggard look, Kennedy had an élan on television that Nixon could not match. Marshall McLuhan, a Canadian communications scholar, noted the great disparity in their images on television. Describing McLuhan's impressions, journalist Philip Deane wrote that Kennedy was "something like the shy young sheriff—while Mr. Nixon with his very dark eyes that tend to stare, with his slicker circumlocution . . . resembled more the railway lawyer who signs leases that are not in the interests of the folks in the little town."[32]

Because no overriding issues defined the 1960 campaign, the importance of the Kennedy-Nixon debates lay largely in the images projected on television. Whether these images determined the election outcome is hard to say. Kennedy won and returned the Democrats to power after eight years of Eisenhower. The margin of his victory—112,881 votes—was so narrow that it is impossible to single out as decisive any one factor, even one as important as the debates.

4

Television's march on Cape Canaveral

Television helped create national fervor for the venture into space. In doing so, it contributed vastly to the funding for such an undertaking. By 1988 the government had spent about $130 billion on civilian space programs.[1] There were long lulls, however, between the most spectacular space feats. Public attention would wane, and concerns in Congress about costs would rise. Then some new extravaganza would be launched, bringing a nation of television viewers to its feet once again. Renewed public support would renew Congress's willingness to keep spending on space.

This vital role for television in the space program was not at all foreordained. In fact, during the early years when the air force managed the space program, television was locked out of Cape Canaveral. Robert Asman, an NBC producer, remembered what it was like:

Like most military establishments, the Air Force had a feeling that the press was an intrusion, something to be wary of. There was a great deal of concern about security at a time when we were in fierce competition with the Russians. There was a great fear of showing failures, of having our early attempts that might not be successful show up on the air or in the press and that would be bad from a national morale standpoint because we were already behind. Sputnik [1957] was the lead-off, and we were playing catch-up.[2]

In the late 1950s the air force even refused to announce in advance the times of launches, forcing the networks into games of cat-and-mouse, as James Kitchell, who was in charge of NBC's space coverage, recalled. "Since we couldn't get any official word," Herbert Kaplow of NBC said, "we would get a lot of people who worked at Cape Canaveral to come out and meet us behind a tree and say, 'We think something is about to go up.' "[3]

47

Because the space facilities were virtually off limits, Kitchell had to rent a beach house overlooking the cape and set up two telescopes on the porch to scan whatever rockets were on launching pads. "The way we could tell when they were near a launch," said Kaplow,

was by watching the vapor that oozed from the top of the rockets. It could go on for weeks. When the venting stopped, you knew that they were within minutes of a launch. Every little while we said, "Oops, still venting, still venting" and kept on watching. Then all of a sudden the steam would stop, and everybody would jump into action and turn on the cameras.[4]

The television crews were prey to bizarre happenings. Near Kitchell's rented house lived a man who convinced himself that the cameras and telescopes belonged not to a television network but to a foreign espionage ring probing the American space effort. In time he became so overwrought about danger to national security that he hired a bulldozer to dig a ditch as deep as a swimming pool athwart the dirt road connecting Kitchell's house with the highway. Kitchell responded by hiring the same bulldozer operator to fill in the ditch and by obtaining a court order to restrain his neighbor.

After a while it dawned on the air force generals that the launchings were going to be filmed, one way or another. The officers began talking with representatives of the networks and the press on increasingly friendly terms. It was agreed that when a launching was imminent, reporters, photographers, and camera crews would be transported to an observation area on the base, which was equipped with twenty telephones. A major was on hand to distribute press releases one minute after lift-off, a rule to safeguard against announcing a fizzle. For double certainty the telephones remained switched off until the minute had elapsed. Television crews then made a breakneck dash to chartered planes waiting on Merritt Island to fly their film to Orlando or Jacksonville.

The National Aeronautical and Space Act of 1958, passed by Congress one year after the Soviet Union blasted Sputnik into space, elevated the space program to the level of a major governmental enterprise. One provision, little noticed publicly, ensured that manned space flight would not be veiled in secrecy: "The Administration [NASA] shall provide for the widest practicable and appropriate dissemination of information concerning the activities and the results thereof." As far as some experts can recall, no other government body has ever been under such a flat and specific mandate to be open about its activities. A large share of the credit goes to President Dwight D. Eisenhower. John M. Logsdon, a foremost historian of the American space effort, wrote: "Eisenhower was able to prevail in his view that the American space program should be conducted openly, not behind a cloud of secrecy."[5]

Eisenhower opposed the notion of a space race with the Soviets and saw no point to sending men to the moon. In short order his successor turned that policy around. It was just before the flight on May 5, 1961, of the first American astronaut, Comdr. Alan B. Shepard, Jr., that Kennedy telephoned Paul Haney, a NASA information officer, to make sure the event was being covered live by television. When the mission succeeded, Kennedy followed up with an enthusiastic plea for America "to work with the utmost speed and vigor in further development of our space program."[6] There was good reason for haste. A month before the Shepard flight, Yuri A. Gagarin, a Soviet cosmonaut, became the first man to orbit the earth. On May 26, 1961, Kennedy addressed a joint session of Congress to ask for funds to land a man on the moon before the end of that decade, a goal that was met.

In order, the early NASA programs were Mercury for the orbiting of the earth by a one-man capsule, Gemini for the orbiting of a two-man capsule, and Apollo for the moon missions. The idea of taking cameras into space was not just a brainchild of the television networks. NASA intended originally that spacecraft used in all three programs would be equipped for television transmission. In August 1961 Edward R. Murrow, Kennedy's director of the U.S. Information Agency, wrote to NASA Administrator James E. Webb to ask where the matter stood. Webb referred the query to Abraham Silverstein, who was in charge of the Mercury program. Silverstein replied:

There is no doubt that at this time a change in the communication system of this magnitude will compromise the Mercury schedule, the reliability of the entire system and the safety of the pilot. The use of television in our manned flight program must await future flight projects when adequate booster capability will be available to carry the increased payload and when an integrated-communication system can be designed, developed and suitably tested.[7]

While conceding that recent development of relatively lightweight cameras had increased the feasibility of future installation, Silverstein said that their immediate use would complicate communication between capsule and ground controllers.

For a long time the themes of the Silverstein memorandum were repeated to the networks, eager to expand the limits of what was available for televising. It was too late to change designs. Installing cameras would delay flight schedules. Pilots' safety would be compromised. NASA engineers also had many objections: Television aboard spacecraft would have no scientific value. It would drain electric power and impinge on the astronauts' work. It would take up valuable time and add weight on the missions. The astronauts, some of whom were former engineers and test pilots, often went along with these arguments. On some occasions, even when others at NASA agreed on installing cameras, astronauts would use their authority to eliminate them.[8] They felt they had enough to do without being responsible for operating television cameras in space.

The start of the manned space programs was big news, and the promise of spectacular and novel visual displays was seen as an unfailing magnet for large television audiences. Television's own troops moved like a new kind of army into Cape Canaveral and into Houston when the Manned Spacecraft Center (now the Johnson Space Center) was opened there in September 1961. NASA officials quickly felt the weight of this deployment the way harbormasters, mayors, and local suppliers felt the movement of masses of soldiers toward the embarkation points in 1942. The television army rolled in with tons of equipment as well as heavy demands for just one more camera on a pole here or another crew there. Networks took over entire motels. The television army included cameramen, soundmen, reporters, directors, and producers, all scratching for ideas for new shots. The networks also employed auditors, finance directors, and even bankers. During major missions, the NASA pressrooms seethed with people. Including reporters and columnists for newspapers, wire services, and magazines, perhaps more than three thousand journalists were on hand in July 1969 for the story of the first landing of men on the moon.

Even though NASA was a powerful government agency, the phalanxes of network executives and crews were capable of bringing heavy and continuing pressure upon it. The official in the cockpit between the contending forces was Julian W. Scheer, the able NASA director of public affairs. The demands of television news were so broad and the resistance of NASA engineers often so dogged that Scheer dealt less with television reporters than with the network producers, among them Kitchell, Robert Wussler of CBS, and Wallace Pfister of ABC. They found him no pushover.

"Julian Scheer was one of the stumbling blocks we had along the way,"

Kitchell recalled. "There were days that he would be very supportive, very affable. And there were times he fought you tooth and nail. He was not that sympathetic to television. I think he was more concerned with the writing media."[9]

No doubt, Scheer was influenced by his newspaper background. In his youth he was a reporter for the *Charlotte* (N.C.) *News*. Newspaper reporters who covered the space program still like to tell stories about him. On Christmas Eve 1968, after the Apollo 8 astronauts read from the Book of Genesis while orbiting the moon, a Japanese reporter put in a frantic call to Scheer from his Houston hotel. The man was in despair over his failure to take down all the quoted words properly. He asked Scheer to read them to him over the telephone. Instead Scheer gave him roughly these instructions: "In your hotel room open the drawer in the table next to your bed. In it you will find a book. Turn to the first page. There you will see the words you want."[10]

On the night of the first moon landing, the pressroom in Houston was bedlam. Television cameras were everywhere, including the area where the print reporters were writing. The television lights were so glaring that reporters cried to Scheer for relief. He asked the crew in charge to turn them off. The crew told him in so many words to go to the moon. Instead he went to a baseboard and pulled their plug. Sometimes, Scheer said, a network would make what he considered a preposterous request, such as asking to land its own Piper Cub on an aircraft carrier to film a spot in the ocean where a splashdown was about to occur at the end of a mission.

Inevitably, network pressures on NASA brought friction within the NASA staff. An example was a dispute between Scheer and a subordinate, Col. John (Shorty) Powers, who had become something of a celebrity by doing the original countdowns to the launchings. Scheer worried that Powers had become too much the ally of network officials, who courted him assiduously. The colonel loved to go on camera.

"Just before the Gordon Cooper Mercury flight [in 1963]," Scheer said, "Shorty Powers had the feeling that the print media no longer counted and that everything should be geared toward television, that he could control access to the cameras and work well with the correspondents and that he would appear on television." During one of the important missions, Powers caused a row by giving copies of the flight plans to the three networks while refusing to give them to the print reporters. "Everybody," Scheer said, "was up in arms . . . so I confronted Shorty, and he said, 'That's the way it's going; television guys have to know what is going on.' " Scheer relieved Powers of his duties.[11]

Slowly television news became a partner in the government's space program. It was a rare symbiotic relationship: NASA needed commercial television and commercial television needed NASA. In time the Manned Spacecraft Center agreed to assign one astronaut to each network as a technical adviser. According to Brian Duff, then director of public affairs for the center, this led to a tug-of-war: Each network tried to capture the most famous astronauts. "Of course, they did not want a technical expert—they wanted a celebrity," Duff said. "And so they would argue heatedly over who they got. We finally ended up with something like a draft in the major leagues, a complicated lottery to choose an astronaut for each network."[12]

Newspaper reporters often relied on television news to find out what was happening in the distance. John Finney, who was covering the space launches for the *New York Times,* said that in the beginning the paper's trailer at the cape did not have a television set. "But we soon got one," he added. "It was so much easier to watch. Their cameras could get so much closer a view than we could. TV became our monitor."[13] One television set was no longer enough. When Howard Simon, then a science reporter for the *Washington Post,* entered the *Newsweek* trailer at the cape, he saw three sets going, one tuned to each network. The space story, he realized, "had given TV news its big boost. In a subtle way I thought of it as TV's bar mitzvah. Television was becoming a man, developing its own stories. TV had great impact on the public's impression of the space program. At the cape they became dominant."[14] Writer Edwin Diamond described the relationship between television and space as the "perfect match"—a marriage literally made in heaven.[15]

It was no misfortune for NASA that the most celebrated and conspicuous space reporter was Walter Cronkite. During his rise as the anchorman of the "CBS Evening News" in the 1960s, he seized upon the story and lavished enthusiasm on it. "He sometimes seemed more cheerleader than reporter," Barbara Matusow wrote. "The 'eighth astronaut,' they called him. He frowned on stories that reflected poorly on the program."[16]

On February 22, 1962, Col. John H. Glenn, Jr., in five hours orbited the earth three times. Nothing of its kind had so greatly excited the country since Charles A. Lindbergh's New York–to–Paris solo airplane flight in 1927. The estimated television audience for the Glenn mission was a record-breaking 135 million, compared with the previous high mark of 90 million for the final game of the 1959 World Series.[17] Facilities for televising Glenn's splashdown in the Atlantic Ocean were not available. The only action shown on the networks was Glenn's arrival at the launching pad, President Kennedy's preparations in the White House for following the flight, and the fiery lift-off in mid-morning. Once Glenn's capsule was lost from view in the distance, it was never seen again on television screens.

The television pool had requested the right to carry instantaneously Glenn's running reports to ground stations along his journey, but NASA was unwilling to go that far. It insisted on controlling the release of each recording for prior security clearance, after which recordings would be played over the public address system in the pressroom for all to hear. About seven minutes into the flight, Glenn's voice was first heard publicly as he talked with the Bermuda tracking station. Ninety minutes later he was heard reporting the sight of glowing particles outside his capsule. In the end practically all his reports were released. Jack Gould, the television critic, wrote in the *New York Times* the next day that the recordings—"a vivid experience" for listeners—"were incalculably educational in acquainting the layman firsthand with the amount and variety of the data produced."[18]

The coverage on television and in the press paid dividends: public and congressional support at home and praise from abroad for the openness of America's space program compared with the secrecy surrounding the USSR's. "The contrast between our whole system of government and that of the Russians," Glenn later wrote, "has been vividly portrayed to the world by the way in which reporting of our space [program] has been handled."[19]

Recalling that period years later, Brian Duff said: "Some of the network men thought the way to get what they wanted was to attack, attack, attack. And some of them thought you could get it by being polite." Duff went on, however, to mention something more significant than network manners.

"We at NASA," he recalled, "more and more realized that it was in our best interests to make it as easy as possible [for them] to cover the story accurately and completely, that this in the long run was going to serve us. We worked hard at it."[20]

Symbiosis was occurring. At first NASA made it a rule that on the day of a flight live television coverage at Cape Canaveral could not begin earlier than ten minutes before lift-off. The networks protested that this gave them too little time to create an air of anticipation and to build up an audience. They wanted to start broadcasting live pictures forty-eight hours before lift-off. To NASA officials this was a completely unrealistic demand. After weeks of debating, a compromise was reached. Live television could begin a half-hour before a launching (T minus thirty minutes in the lingo of the space program). This worked well for the networks. Live pictures on the morning of a flight could be shown just as the CBS morning news program and NBC's "Today" came on the air on the East Coast.

Having received the go-ahead from NASA for live coverage a half-hour before lift-off, the networks opened a new front, bombarding NASA for live coverage of splashdowns at the end of space missions. Satellite television made this technically possible. An earth station could be mounted on the aircraft carrier assigned to retrieve the downed capsule. In the early sixties the networks could provide live coverage from the scene only by voice. Film from the decks of carriers had to be flown to the nearest television transmitter before it could be released to the networks.

In response to the networks, NASA authorized live coverage of the splashdown of Gemini 10 in July 1966 near the U.S.S. *Wasp,* 340 miles East of Bermuda. But the networks still were not satisfied. They wanted a camera in the rescue helicopter for dramatic shots of the astronauts climbing out of the capsule in heavy seas and into a rubber life raft. The navy recovery experts and Donald K. (Deke) Slayton, then chief of the astronauts, objected. Duff recalled:

"I said, 'Deke, what is it? What's the problem here? It's our NASA camera, our cameraman. It's a great picture, and we ought to have it.'

"And Slayton said, 'I never want anyone to see an American astronaut losing his lunch on that spacecraft.'

"I said, 'Deke, how many guys have done that?' It turns out there was no one. I said, 'Besides, if it happens, it's our cameraman. I mean, we can always point at the ocean or the ship or something.'

"He said, 'We're not going to do it!'

"So I said, 'We've got to see Bob [Dr. Robert R.] Gilruth about this.' Gilruth, the director [of the Manned Spacecraft Center], was a sort of fatherly figure. Gilruth listened to both of us and said, 'Deke, you are going to lose this one.'

"And Slayton, to give him credit, never argued the question again."[21]

In 1968 shortly before the flight of Apollo 7 there was a hitch that threatened televising the subsequent Apollo 11 moon landing. At a conference at Ramey Air Force Base in Puerto Rico, astronaut Walter M. Schirra, Jr., the Apollo 7 commander, objected to having a television camera aboard. George Low, then Apollo program manager at Houston, supported him.

"Low called me," Scheer recalled, "and said, 'That camera weighs too much, and we can't get it on.'

"I said, 'Well, George, then you'll have to take something else off.' "

Scheer won out. The Ramey decision, as he later said, "was a real watershed for the space program."[22] In Apollo 8 viewers on earth reveled in the sight of astronauts in their command module as they sped to encircle the moon but not land. Against the breathtaking backdrop of the moon's surface only sixty nautical miles away the astronauts read from Genesis. Col. Frank Borman on Christmas Eve, 1968, greeted his vast audience: "From the crew of Apollo 8, we pause with good night, good luck, and a Merry Christmas, and God bless all of you, all of you on the good earth."

Apollo 11 was the first event televised live around the world, because Intelsat, an international satellite agency, had just completed its global network. Everyone vied with everyone else for an adequate description of the sight that no one in human history had ever seen before: man on the moon. President Richard Nixon pronounced the eight-day mission "the greatest week in the history of the world since the creation." From his White House telephone he talked with astronauts Neil A. Armstrong and Edwin E. Aldrin, Jr., on the moon. Interestingly, according to an article in *Life* by Albert Rosenfeld, Armstrong would have preferred to keep television out of the command module altogether. "He feels that putting on TV shows is an unnecessary and added chore and nuisance."[23]

For pure drama none of the six remaining Apollo missions could excel Apollo 11, yet for earthbound spectators Apollo 15 in July 1971 offered a most fascinating spectacle. In a camera-equipped electric rover resembling a golf cart, astronauts David R. Scott and Alfred M. Worden took the television audience along as they explored seventeen miles of the moon's surface. Scott demonstrated the correctness of Galileo's reasoning that in a vacuum bodies of different weights fall with equal velocities and with a uniform acceleration. Because the moon travels in a vacuum, when Scott dropped the feather and the hammer from the same height they landed on the surface simultaneously. On their trip the Apollo 15 astronauts collected 173 pounds of moon rock to take back to earth.

The entire performance of all the Apollo missions added up to a big hit with the human race and high audience ratings for the space program. Crosby Noyes, a columnist for the *Washington Star,* commented that the TV show seemed at least as important to the astronauts and the crew in Houston as anything they might have found on the surface of the moon, as though the whole performance was a running commercial for the space program.[24]

Upon the ending of the spectacular Apollo program, network television pulled away from years of regular space coverage because of lack of news. In a 180-degree turn from early doubts about televising space missions, NASA developed in 1974 a television system of its own. The agency took over the complete televising of programs such as Skylab and the space shuttle, and it made its live pictures and film available to the networks.

In the early days of space coverage, the networks debated what to do if an accident occurred while a mission was being televised. They decided the cameras would keep rolling. Chet Hagan, chief producer of NBC's space coverage, explained, "It was felt that it was part of the coverage, however tragic, and that we could not go to black and make believe it didn't happen."[25] NASA adopted a similar policy in the early eighties for its own television system. Robert J. Shafer, NASA's television director, promulgated a rule that coverage was to continue as long as there was anything to see.

On January 28, 1986, NASA turned its cameras on the lift-off of the space shuttle *Challenger.* Seconds later it exploded, killing all of those aboard: six astronauts and Christa McAuliffe, a New Hampshire teacher. In that cruel hour, television news, by hooking into the NASA system, showed the American people the price they must be ready to pay to conquer space. The revelation was written in the fiery devastation in the sky and the mute desolation on the faces of McAuliffe's parents, watching from a nearby grandstand at Cape Canaveral.

"Once again," John Corry wrote in the *New York Times,* "television was the great American hearth. The assumption was that we were all one family."[26] If the *Challenger* had exploded in outer space beyond the eye of the television camera, television could not have done more with the story, essentially, than newspapers could have. But the camera caught the explosion, and the image utterly transcended the power of words. It is the image that sets television apart.

5

Television's supreme hour: the Kennedy funeral

One year before the 1964 presidential election, President John F. Kennedy, accompanied by his wife, went to Texas to try to close rifts within the state's Democratic party. To cover an event of such interest the affiliated local stations had formed a pool, upon which the networks could draw later for the evening news reports. The Kennedys' flight to Dallas from Fort Worth on Friday, November 22, 1963, was a short one. Air Force One touched down at Love Field at 11:25 A.M., central standard time. An early morning rain had stopped, the day was bright and promising.

WFAA-TV, the ABC affiliate in Dallas, had cameras and a mobile cruiser at the airport for a live report on the brief reception for the president before he and Mrs. Kennedy slipped into the back seat of the open presidential limousine. Gov. John B. Connally, Jr., of Texas and Mrs. Connally sat in front of them on jump seats. All were headed downtown where the president was scheduled to address a luncheon at the Dallas Trade Mart. At 1:00 P.M. KRLD-TV, the CBS affiliate in Dallas, had three cameras in the balcony to feed pictures to the pool. The audience was already seated at luncheon tables. Tables for the press were partly filled with reporters not traveling with Kennedy. Suddenly, with a clatter that affronted the guests, these reporters dashed for the exits. Someone had dropped a rumor at the press tables about shots fired at the approaching presidential motorcade. In the scramble all the carefully laid plans for television coverage of the Kennedy visit went up in smoke.

Each of the networks had an experienced reporter traveling with the president: Robert Pierpoint for CBS, Robert MacNeil for NBC, and Robert Clark for ABC. Pierpoint and MacNeil were riding in one of the press

58

buses well back in the motorcade. Clark was in the pool car, six cars behind the presidential limousine. Others in the car were Malcolm Kilduff, acting press secretary for the White House, Robert Baskin of the hometown *Dallas Morning News,* Jack Bell of the Associated Press, and Merriman Smith of United Press International, a genuine star-reporter type of the old school who had been covering the White House since the Roosevelt administration.

Smith, who won a Pulitzer Prize for his work that day, could not have been shouldered out of the way by Paul Bunyan. Smith was so competitively excitable over a big story that on May 8, 1945, he broke his arm dashing out of President Harry S. Truman's office with the flash that Germany had surrendered. As a rule Smith used his seniority to make sure that he was always in the front seat of the pool car. Whenever a radiophone was in a car, he demanded to be seated by it. A phone was in the pool car that day in Dallas—only one—and it was in the dashboard directly in front of him.

As the forward part of the motorcade turned left in Dealey Plaza and passed the Texas School Book Depository, a sudden "bam" sounded somewhere close by. A backfire? A firecracker? Smith counted two more cracks. A gun collector and weekend marksman, he may not have known what type of weapon had been fired but he was certain the sounds were gunshots. Where the bullets came from and where they went he did not know. He simply grabbed the radiophone, called the UPI Dallas bureau, and, at 12:34 P.M. central standard time dictated, "Three shots were fired at President Kennedy's motorcade today in downtown Dallas." Throughout the world the bulletin clacked on UPI printers two minutes before the blood-spattered limousine reached Parkland Memorial Hospital. Despite rage and pummeling by Bell, his competitor from the Associated Press, Smith held the phone almost all the way to the hospital. Clark of ABC, pooling for the networks, had no way to get his hands on it. It would be years before network reporters who covered the White House would be equipped with cellular phones or walkie-talkies.

After the shots the entire motorcade came to a brief stop. Robert MacNeil decided to pull his cameraman and soundman off the bus and rush forward to the president's limousine. Before the NBC team could get there, the first six cars had already broken away from the rest and were racing up Stemmons Freeway to the hospital. In search of a telephone, he dashed for the nearest building—the book depository. As he entered a young man in shirtsleeves was hurrying out—and for good reason. MacNeil asked him where he might find a phone. Just inside, the man replied.[1] The next day Lee Harvey Oswald told the Secret Service that as he left the book depository a man rushed up the steps and asked him where to find a phone.

It was lunchtime in New York when the UPI bulletin bells, signaling a major newsbreak, rang at 1:34 P.M. eastern standard time. Many executives, reporters, and commentators were away from their desks. Not Walter Cronkite of CBS. He was eating cottage cheese and canned pineapple at his desk when an editor bolted in, shouting that shots had been fired at the motorcade in Dallas. Cronkite glanced at the wire copy. "The hell with writing it," he snapped. "Just give me the air." He went to a studio where cameras were always kept "hot," that is, in readiness for just such an emergency. Breaking into a daily serial, "As the World Turns," Cronkite paraphrased the words Merriman Smith had dictated from the speeding pool car. This report on CBS went out at 1:40 P.M., eastern standard time. ABC followed at 1:42 and NBC at 1:45.[2]

Elmer W. Lower, president of ABC News, was swimming at the New York Athletic Club when summoned to take an urgent telephone call. Jesse Zousmer, the new director of television news at ABC, was lunching at a restaurant on Central Park West when a secretary assigned to him only that morning called. Zousmer thrust a twenty-dollar bill at the waiter and cried, "I'll be back for the change." Back in the newsroom, he found himself giving orders to people, some of whom were not sure who he was since he had been on the job only two weeks. On the air, Milton Cross reported the shooting. Meanwhile Zousmer placed a radiophone call to his top commentator, Howard K. Smith, who was aboard a plane on his way back from interviewing President Gamal Abdel Nasser of Egypt. The navigator allowed Smith to stay in the radio compartment for the remainder of the trip to follow the news reports. As soon as he reached his New York office, Smith went on the air, even though he had been up for eighteen hours. Lower asked Smith what he thought he should do next. "If you let me go back to Washington and get a night's sleep, I'll do anything you say," Smith replied. The upshot was that he and Edward P. Morgan took charge of ABC's coverage in the capital the next day.

Julian Goodman, president of NBC News, and Chet Huntley were giving a business lunch in the network's executive dining room when the steward, who had heard the news on his radio, interrupted them. By the time Goodman and Huntley reached the newsroom, the place was humming. Off in a small office, Chet Hagan, a news producer, was working on a summary of the Andrew Johnson administration for a 1964 election handbook the network was preparing. "Calhoun had been dumped—" Hagan had just written when his telephone rang. Frank McGee happened to be passing Hagan's door and picked up the phone for him. The message from the news desk sent the two of them scampering. NBC had an immediate problem. At the moment the network was "down." All affiliated stations were putting on their own programs and thus had control of the air. But at 1:45 NBC took over the network. Grabbing the latest wire service report, Don Pardo, an announcer, read over a news interrupt slide: "President Kennedy and Governor John Connally of Texas were cut down by an assassin's bullet in downtown Dallas and were rushed to an emergency room at Parkland Hospital. The president's limp body was seen cradled in the arms of his wife. There is no information at present on his condition."[3]

The first staff member of NBC News to arrive at the emergency studio, 5HN, next to the control room, was William Ryan. He had in his hand Merriman Smith's bulletin. Goodman told him to stand in front of the camera.

"How can I go on with nothing but this?" Ryan protested.

"Read it slowly from the front to the end," Goodman insisted. "Then start at the back and read it to the front. And then start in the middle and read it toward both sides and by that time we'll have more for you."[4]

Indeed, at 1:53, Ryan was able to report, based on the UPI wire: "Bullet wounds were clearly visible on Governor Connally's chest. Blood was visible on the president's head. He was lying flat on the floor of the presidential car. No answer was given reporters on whether the president is dead. . . . [W]e do not know his condition." At 2:33 McGee reported: "Last rites of the Roman Catholic Church have been administered to President Kennedy. This does not necessarily mean that his condition is fatal." NBC was cautious. A minute earlier UPI had quoted what the priest who administered the rites said: Kennedy was dead.

On that fateful Friday it was payday at CBS. Ernest Leiser, the general manager for news, was on his way back from the bank when an elevator operator told him Kennedy had been shot. Charles Collingwood, a correspondent, and Blair Clark, vice-president of CBS News, were having lunch at the Italian Pavilion on West Fifty-fifth Street. A telephone call from the office sent them flying without paying their bill. A friend of

Kennedy's, Clark held a transistor radio to his ear during the rush to the newsroom in the Graybar Building on Lexington Avenue.

At 2:30 New York time, Malcolm Kilduff at Parkland Hospital officially announced Kennedy's death. CBS had already reported it unofficially—Cronkite stressed this—on the strength of what a doctor at Parkland Hospital had told Dan Rather, one of the reporters there. When Cronkite soon afterward reported the official announcement, his voice broke. He wiped away a tear. Don Hewitt, the producer, could see that Cronkite was worn and bade him take a rest. Collingwood replaced him. Cronkite sat back to telephone his wife only to find a call coming in on his line. The caller was an anonymous woman. She did not know whom she had on the line, but she knew that she wanted to give CBS a good bawling out. "I just want to say," she snapped, "that's the worst bad taste to have that Walter Cronkite on the air when everybody knows he spent all his time trying to get the president."

"This *is* Walter Cronkite," he exploded, "and you're a goddamned idiot!"[5]

Back from the restaurants, the executives had urgent planning to do. For a space shot a network plans for a month. For national political conventions it plans for a year. On November 22, the networks were planning minute by minute. Uncertain of Kennedy's condition and believing Parkland Hospital might be the source of news for some time to come, NBC chartered a Pan American Airlines 707 to go to Dallas. Edwin Newman and thirty-five technicians and cameramen were already in the air when it was disclosed that Air Force One was about to fly Lyndon Johnson and Kennedy's body to Washington. Johnson, who accompanied Kennedy to Texas, was sworn in as president before take-off. In mid-flight the NBC chartered plane turned around. No one yet knew where Kennedy would be buried. Boston was certainly a possible choice. Hence all three networks ordered news teams to Boston to prepare for what obviously would be maximum coverage.

Friday afternoon Julian Goodman telephoned William B. Monroe, chief of the NBC bureau in Washington. "We're going to stay on the air with this as long as it takes," Goodman ordered. "We're going nonstop, and we're knocking off all commercials."[6] The other networks did the same. The loss of advertising revenue for all three networks over four days was more than $32 million—a sum that at today's rates would be several times higher.[7]

At dusk Kennedy's coffin was taken in a hearse from Andrews Air Force Base, where it had arrived from Dallas, to the Bethesda Naval Hospital in suburban Maryland. Right away television technicians began preparing for the funeral, which, it had then been decided, was to be held in Washington. The Chesapeake & Potomac Telephone Company laid six miles of temporary video cables in the streets. A mass of equipment—an electronic army, someone said—moved into Washington. From New York, Philadelphia, Baltimore, Norfolk, and Richmond rolled television trucks as big as moving vans and emblazoned with the networks' symbols and call letters. In the most remarkable on-the-spot technical achievement in the first fifteen years of television news, the cameras were trucked to selective vantage points about the capital. Some would remain under the control of the individual networks. But most of them—forty-one units in twenty-two locations—were assigned to the pool. A toss of the coin determined that the pool operation would be run by two CBS executives, Arthur Kane as producer and Norman Gorin as director. The pool pictures from all remote points were controlled from an electronic bunker (largely banks of monitors) under the east steps of the Capitol.

When Air Force One landed at Andrews at 6:05 P.M. Friday, a huge television audience was already watching. After the plane had come to a stop and the door was opened, the public for the first time saw unmistakable evidence of the unspeakable crime: President Kennedy's coffin draped with an American flag.

Members of his cabinet were two hours west of Honolulu, bound for an economic conference in Japan, when a message arrived for Secretary of State Dean Rusk. It said that the president had been shot, perhaps fatally, in Dallas. Rusk told the pilot to return to Hawaii. A few minutes later Pierre Salinger, the White House press secretary and part of the delegation, told Rusk that a message under the code name "Stranger" had arrived from the White House ordering the plane to return to Washington.

Stranger? Who was *Stranger?*

"It went through Rusk's mind," his biographer Thomas J. Schoenbaum wrote, "that there might be a national or international conspiracy against the government of the United States." For five minutes the secretary and Salinger frantically searched the plane trying to find a code that revealed the identity of "Stranger."

"Finding none," Schoenbaum continued, "Rusk told Salinger to find out who 'Stranger' was: 'We don't know what is happening in Dallas.

Who is the government now?' Salinger broke code to ask the White House. There was relief when the answer came that 'Stranger' was Maj. Harold R. Patterson, a trusted White House communications officer."

Within seconds another message arrived for Rusk. He read it, walked to a microphone in the front of the plane, and said: "Ladies and gentlemen, this is the secretary of state speaking. We have received official confirmation that President Kennedy is dead. I am saddened to tell you this grievous news. We have a new president. God bless our new president and our nation."[8] At first cries of anguish throughout the plane. Then tears. Then silence.

A cold drizzle was falling in Washington on Saturday morning. The networks came on the air at seven o'clock, focusing on the White House. On the North Portico, used by visitors, including that day Harry Truman and Dwight Eisenhower, the door was draped in black. From time to time throughout the day the cameras looked into the hushed East Room, in the center of which the dead president lay in state in a closed coffin covered by the flag. Candles burned at each corner of the coffin, guarded by a soldier, sailor, marine, and airman.

In contrast to the previous day, Washington was somber and calm. It was important for the public to be aware that the government was pulling itself together. Television served this need by showing officials arriving at the Executive Office Building, west of the White House, for President Johnson's first meetings. At noon the networks switched briefly to Dallas for a glimpse of Oswald, an insignificant-looking man whose bleak expression matched the times. The cameras caught him being led to the homicide bureau at police headquarters. Later in the day television showed a scene that was almost unbearable for friends, colleagues, and admirers of John Kennedy. The door to the West Wing of the White House opened, and a mover carried out Kennedy's rocking chair. It had been specially designed to ease his chronic back trouble, aggravated during the Second World War when a Japanese destroyer crashed into his *PT-109* in the Solomon Islands. The rocker was a personal symbol of the Kennedy presidency, its removal an unmistakable sign of transition.

Not always during the four days of nonstop network coverage were extraordinary camera shots available to television. Sometimes, especially at night, there were fairly long intervals between stages of the obsequies. The networks filled in with quickly arranged programs. These might include a short concert by a string quartet or a choir; pictures of Kennedy and Johnson through the years; interviews with prominent persons; and panel discussions on matters ranging from the history of presidential assassination and succession of vice-presidents to the current state of the world and speculation on how Johnson would address it.

At noon on Sunday Mrs. Kennedy and her children, Caroline and John F. Kennedy, Jr., were preparing to join the cortege that would carry the dead president to the Capitol to lie in state overnight. Television cameras covered every angle of view from the North Portico of the White House along Pennsylvania Avenue to the Rotunda under the Capitol dome. At the same hour, in Dallas, police had begun to move Lee Harvey Oswald from the city jail at the police headquarters to the county jail. He was to be taken from one to the other in an armored truck. The networks planned to switch temporarily to Dallas upon word that the prisoner was coming into view. A television pool was not involved; the networks in this case were acting on their own. At 10:30 that morning Goodman, who was in charge of NBC's coverage, received a call from Robert E. Kintner, the president of NBC. Kintner tended to brood over contingencies, and he had not forgotten what had happened on Friday: NBC missed by one city block a chance of catching a picture of the presidential limousine at the moment Oswald pulled the trigger. Anxious not to let any more opportunities escape, Kintner instructed Goodman to "watch Dallas today." He then told him, "I have a feeling about it—get that boy coming out of jail."[9]

This was a critical instruction because Oswald was expected to be in view twice: first emerging from the city jail and then entering the county jail some distance away. Supposedly extraordinary precautions were ordered for his move because, not surprisingly, death threats against Oswald had been made during the night. The basement room in the city jail was thoroughly searched. Policemen with rifles guarded it. Cameras were set up in the hallway through which Oswald would walk. NBC had a live camera (instant sight and sound), with Tom Pettit as the reporter. CBS also had a live camera in the hallway, but it did not catch the signal that Oswald was coming out of the city jail in time to switch immediately from Washington. The worst luck that day was ABC's. Of its two live cameras in the area, one was covering a memorial service for Kennedy in a church in Fort Worth. The other camera was in the county jail in Dallas. "The rationale for that decision," Elmer Lower later wrote, "was that if anyone was going to take a shot at Oswald, he would try at the county jail end where the prisoner would have to walk in the open for fifteen feet."[10]

But Oswald never made it to the county jail. Back at the city jail there suddenly was a stir. Pettit whispered through his microphone circuit, "Let me have it." His producer, Fred Rheinstein, sang out over his line to New York, "Give it to us now!"[11] The NBC network was on live. An elevator door opened. Oswald trudged out, flanked by two detectives. Bound for the armored truck, they led him down a ramp and into an aisle surging with reporters and police. In that throng stood Jack Ruby, a pudgy bum who was connected with a striptease joint in Dallas. He often hung out with cops, so his presence at the jail that afternoon was accepted. As Oswald approached, Pettit looked directly into his face. Then, out of the righthand corner of the NBC screen, appeared the back of a man. The next thing Pettit knew, Ruby, having drawn a .38-caliber revolver from his pocket, thrust it toward Oswald. A shot rang out. Oswald gasped, clutched his stomach, and started to fall.

"He's been shot!" Pettit exclaimed into the microphone.

He's been shot! He's been shot! Lee Oswald has been shot! There's a man with a gun. There's absolute panic, absolute panic here in the basement of the Dallas police headquarters. Detectives have their guns drawn. Oswald has been shot. There's no question about it. Oswald has been shot. Pandemonium has broken loose here in the basement of the Dallas police headquarters.[12]

CBS switched to the scene in time to catch the police grappling with Ruby. Although ABC had its live camera at the wrong jail, its film camera in the city jail caught the shooting from the best angle of all. ABC was able to run the film in stop-motion, which helped to clarify the rapid action of the assassination. Nevertheless, the absence of live coverage was an embarrassment for ABC and led Jesse Zousmer to declare a new rule: "Don't carry a church service from the center of a news story."[13]

If surrealism comes down to fantastic imagery and incongruous juxtaposition of subject matter, Sunday was as surreal a day as Americans alive in 1963 ever endured. Murder and tumult in Dallas. Love and stately grief in Washington. Dressed in black, the thirty-four-year-old widow Jacqueline Kennedy waited with her children on the North Portico of the White House as the military parade to the Capitol formed. A gun carriage drawn by six white horses moved up to receive the coffin. Prancing behind the gun carriage was a spirited black horse, Black Jack, with the traditional empty boot pointed backward, in a stirrup. In the Rotunda of the Capitol the mourners waited. Word of the shooting of Oswald spread among them, but few, if any, knew that by the time the service in the Rotunda began Oswald had died, in Parkland Hospital of all places. Those in the Rotunda heard in the distance, faintly, the U.S. Navy Band and a steady roll of drums. The sound grew louder as the marchers neared. It was a chilling sound. When the cortege reached the Capitol, mourners in the Rotunda could hear, but not see, all that was happening. A twenty-one–gun salute was fired. The band played "Hail to the Chief," not in the usual tempo but as a dirge. And, finally, sadly, for a navy man who had performed bravely in the Pacific, the navy hymn "Eternal Father, Strong to Save." The vast television audience saw the military casket team carry the coffin into the Capitol where Kennedy had served as a member of the House of Representatives and then of the Senate. His coffin was surrounded by old colleagues and friends of both parties. Mike Mansfield of Montana, the Democratic leader of the Senate, awed the audience with a eulogy in which he recalled that in Parkland Hospital Mrs. Kennedy had placed her wedding ring in her dead husband's hand. What followed numbed those who were there and the millions who watched on television. Mrs. Kennedy took the six-year-old Caroline by the hand and led her to the side of the coffin, where both of them knelt. Although no one was near enough to hear Mrs. Kennedy's whisper, what she said was, "We're going to say goodbye to Daddy, and we're going to kiss him goodbye, and tell Daddy how much we love him and how much we'll always miss him."[14] They brushed their lips against the flag.

Outside thousands waited. It had been announced that after the Rotunda had been cleared the public would be admitted to pay homage to President Kennedy. The original plan, to close the doors at 9:00 P.M., was abandoned. By that hour an estimated one hundred thousand already had entered the Rotunda and the line behind them was three miles long. Five abreast, people of all ages passed the coffin, some briefly kneeling, some making the sign of the cross, some leaving flowers. Almost no talk was heard by the television viewers. In time the networks began to broadcast classical music, and the throng seemed to move to the cadences of symphonies and sonatas, hour after hour. By nine o'clock the next morning, when the doors closed, a quarter of a million people had paid their respects.

Monday was the day of the funeral. Producers and directors from the networks and from the television pool had been hard at work for hours planning how to cover it. A last meeting with White House officials took place Sunday night. The unexpected became the norm. The D.C. fire department brought word that the camera platforms in St. Matthew's Cathedral, where Richard Cardinal Cushing would celebrate a pontifical requiem mass, were too wide. Carpenters were dispatched to rebuild them. Camera stands had to be draped in black, microphones concealed. Cameras were to be placed as inconspicuously as possible. One was put in the niche of a pillar on the left aisle, another went next to a confessional, still another in the balcony to the right of the altar. At the request of the White House, no close shots were to be taken of members of the family. Finally came instructions that camera crews inside the cathedral were to wear mourning attire. The pool managers arranged for a clothing rental agency to open at 7:00 A.M. to outfit thirteen technicians.

At 11 o'clock a military parade escorted the coffin from the Capitol to the White House driveway. There gathered heads of state: President Charles de Gaulle of France; Prince Philip, Duke of Edinburgh, husband of Queen Elizabeth II; Chancellor Ludwig Erhard of the Federal Republic of Germany; Anistas I. Mikoyan, first deputy premier of the Soviet Union; President Eamon de Valera of Ireland; King Baudouin of Belgium; Emperor Hailie Selassie of Ethiopia; Prince Norodom Sihanouk of Cambodia. They walked behind the horse-drawn gun carriage to St. Matthew's Cathedral seven blocks away. Altogether ninety-two nations sent delegations. In the procession were twenty-three presidents and three reigning monarchs.

After the mass the coffin was strapped on the gun carriage for the final march to Arlington Cemetery. Standing at the bottom of the cathedral steps watching was the president's three-year-old son.

"John," his mother said, "you can salute Daddy now and say good-bye to him."

John knew what she meant. As William Manchester wrote, John had loved to play soldiers with his father. The boy drew himself up to attention and gave a gallant salute, holding it long enough to move with sorrow millions of watching Americans. In his own last days Cardinal Cushing recalled, "Oh, God, I almost died." Bishop Philip N. Hannan later told Manchester that from the steps as John saluted he looked across the street and saw spectators crumple as though struck.[15] Not all the pageantry of the cortege could have pierced the soul of a people as did John F. Kennedy Jr.'s last salute to his father.

Six white horses drew the gun carriage past the Lincoln Memorial and over Memorial Bridge spanning the Potomac River. To the strains of "Onward, Christian Soldiers," the marchers followed. Those already at the grave site on the Virginia side watched them come. The sky was blue.

The sun sparkled on the Potomac. Flags held high fluttered in the breeze. The beauty of the scene, beheld by television viewers across the nation and around the world, momentarily expunged the ugliness of Dallas. And soon Mrs. Kennedy and the president's brothers, Robert and Edward, lighted the eternal flame.

The coverage of the Kennedy tragedy brought to view history as it was being made. People were not informed of the shooting of Oswald. They *saw* it. They did not have to hear or read about how a new president comported himself publicly in such a difficult time. They *watched* him. No one had to tell them later about the distinguished performance of Jacqueline Kennedy. With admiration and awe, they followed it with their own eyes. From an explosive beginning, the networks quickly fashioned a coherent account of what was happening. They handled the subject with good taste. No irresponsible reports were broadcast that might have rattled the public. The impact of the four-day coverage was so palpable that social scientists were quick to study it. Persons who had first heard reports of the shooting from other persons disbelieved the news until television or radio confirmed it. Television provided "undeniable evidence of the continuing vitality of the American government."[16]

The coverage elevated the stature of the vice-president. As rapidly as possible on Friday, November 22, the networks broadcast material on Johnson's already formidable career, especially in the Senate. "In a matter of hours," according to William A. Mindak and Gerald D. Hursh, Johnson "moved from the relative limbo of the vice-presidency to the status of a 'capable' successor to Kennedy."[17]

Rather than inciting people to action, Mindak and Hursh found, the flow of television pictures "narcotized" them. Seeing events with their own eyes relieved people of immediate anxiety about a possible conspiracy against the government. The few days of television

served as a catalyst to speed up adjustment to the finality of the President's death and to renew faith in the future. . . . People who on Friday exhibited emotional reactions that usually precede collective disorder appeared to have acquired after the funeral a more realistic appraisal of the assassination's implications for the future of the country. . . . The reversal in mood and in perspective was aided considerably by the presence of television.[18]

Perhaps most important, television gave viewers a therapeutic sense of participation in the farewell to Kennedy. Television coverage had the effect of drawing the country together.

A. C. Nielsen reported that the average home in their viewing sample had television tuned to the Kennedy tragedy for 31.6 hours. Some 166 million Americans in more than 51 million homes tuned in. In some homes people watched for more than eleven hours a day.[19] NBC was on the air for seventy-one hours and thirty-six minutes, ABC for sixty hours, and CBS for fifty-five hours. Portions of the broadcasts were seen in twenty-three other countries having a combined population of 600 million people.

After the burial service had ended and family and friends departed, viewers still clung to the scene of the grave. The broadcast continued until the superintendent of the cemetery felt that work must begin on sealing the vault and filling the grave. He did not believe the sight of this work was appropriate for the public, so he ordered the electric plug pulled. Without power, the networks all went dark from Arlington. But viewers had seen tongues of flame—the eternal flame—leap up from the head of the grave.

The president who flew to Texas four days previously to strengthen his political standing was by no means a legendary figure. It was on the scores of millions of television screens in America and around the world that the legend of John Fitzgerald Kennedy was born in the seventy-five hours between Dealey Plaza and Arlington National Cemetery.

6

In the eye of the storm:
television news and the urban riots

After the great milestones of desegregation of the public schools in 1954 and passage of the Civil Rights Act of 1964 and the Voting Rights Act of 1965, the movement for African-American rights took a sharp turn. It was one that had heavy consequences for television news.

The triumphs in the Supreme Court and in Congress during the 1950s and early 1960s sprang, in Juan Williams's words, from "moral imperatives," which were accepted by fair-minded citizens in all regions of the country.[1] To a large extent their support was attracted by the civil rights marches in Alabama and Mississippi that were televised nationwide. In the South the white segregationists hated national television and television journalists, often to the point of physical attacks upon them. Martin Luther King and his nonviolent followers, however, looked upon television news as an ally. But when, after the triumphs of litigation and legislation, African Americans in the late 1960s agitated for more jobs, elimination of poverty, and an end to discrimination in housing in northern cities, they encountered huge and perplexing difficulties. Angered, they lost faith in nonviolence, as King turned his efforts toward ending the Vietnam War. Now there were surges toward black power, "Black is beautiful," black nationalism, sit-ins, and protests in large cities. The aim of these movements was not violence, but in their path lurked risks of violence. And nothing attracts television cameras as violence does—and did. In a reversal of days in the South, African Americans resented the networks for televising their violent actions. Often clashes, sometimes exaggerated, dominated television news. Before long, streets of Newark,

71

Chicago, Detroit, Washington, and Los Angeles became places of conflict between African-American protesters and television crews.

In the changed atmosphere the first grave clash erupted in mid-August of 1965 in Watts, a somewhat isolated Los Angeles neighborhood of small houses and bungalows, occupied predominantly by African Americans. In nearly a week of disorders whole blocks were ignited. One of the consequences of televising this conflict and later riotous incidents in other cities was that it frightened whites and caused political reaction against violence associated with African-American protesters.

Characteristically of the urban riots, the Watts disturbance was triggered by a minor incident—the arrest of a young African-American man for allegedly driving while drunk. After the nearly week-long riot was over, Gov. Edmund G. Brown of California appointed an investigating commission headed by John A. McCone, former director of central intelligence. In one particularly ugly three-day period, according to the final report, "perhaps as many as 10,000 Negroes took to the streets in marauding bands. They looted stores, set fires, beat up white passersby, whom they hauled from stopped cars, many of which were turned upside down and burned, exchanged shots with law enforcement officers, and stoned and shot at firemen. The rioters seem to have been caught up in an insensate rage of destruction."[2]

Serious trouble began the first night. The indignant mother of the alleged drunken driver appeared on the scene, followed by a crowd. Angry shouts were heard, and stones began to fly. At 8:30 P.M. the arresting officers called for reinforcements. Reporters appeared. At 9:25 a rock was hurled through the window of a station wagon belonging to KNXT, a CBS television outlet in Los Angeles. To the crowd the vehicle represented "whitey." It was viewed as no ally, as might have been the case in Selma or Birmingham. Spectators began rocking the car until it turned over on its side and caught fire. The CBS crew—Jack Leppert, the cameraman, and Pierre Adidge, the soundman—were able to crawl out unharmed. Sensing the mood, Police Chief William H. Parker of Los Angeles thought that television crews should stay away to avoid harm. He observed that "cameras attracted exhibitionists and that, once crowds gathered, violence inevitably followed." With seven television stations, Los Angeles was the most competitive news market in the nation. But no words could keep television from going after pictures of violence. "They went ahead," Parker said, "as was their privilege."[3]

At nine o'clock the second night a car clearly marked as the property of ABC News drove into the area of the worst violence of the moment in Watts. The ABC crew was Piers Anderton, the reporter; Ralph Mayer, the cameraman; and Ray Fahrenkopf, the gray-haired, soft-spoken soundman. Fahrenkopf had returned six months earlier from covering the Vietnam War. The first thing he and his colleagues began filming in Watts was policemen putting two African Americans in a patrol car.

"One of the rioters," Fahrenkopf recounted later, "was jumping up and down, angry because he didn't think we were shooting film of the policemen pushing one of the suspects into the car. He was yelling that it was police brutality."

At the request of Mayer, Fahrenkopf walked to the car to pick up another camera, but when he went to rejoin his two colleagues, he discovered that they had been swept farther along by the crowd. The street was dark. Bricks and bottles were flying. Suddenly, an unknown number of men came up behind him. He was struck by a heavy object.

"It broke my shoulder open," he related afterward. "I dropped the camera. Someone shoved me from behind, and I fell. My glasses flew off, together with the hard hat I'd been wearing for protection against the flying stones. They started kicking me in the chin and on the face. Others beat me over the head with their fists. I could hear two colored women who were standing there beside me, pleading for those hoodlums to leave me alone."

Struggling to his feet, he staggered toward a burning car, expecting to find his colleagues there. Instead he ran into another group of menacing demonstrators. He yelled for the police but none heard him. Then the second group beat him savagely. He was knocked face downward. One of the attackers leaped into the air and came down feet first on Fahrenkopf's back. After that he was clubbed on the head, kicked in the face, and left, naked from the waist up, bleeding in the streets. Missing were several teeth, his wristwatch, his wallet, the camera, and the tape recorder. The next day his eyes were so swollen it was feared he had been blinded, but he and his eyesight survived.[4]

Into the Watts battleground, where reporters trying to avoid snipers' bullets crept along behind policemen and national guard convoys, now came the swoop and roar of a helicopter. It belonged to KTLA, Channel 5, an independent Los Angeles station. The two-man helicopter carried a camera with a lens capable of filling a television screen with the picture of a child's wagon from a height of fifteen hundred feet. KTLA had established a reputation for getting to the scene quickly when a story broke in southern California. Portions of its coverage of the clashes between police and African Americans went out to the whole country.

The helicopter over Watts intensified the competition for television coverage of the riots, and directors of other stations were told to hire all the cameramen they could find. From his vantage point as managing editor of the *Los Angeles Times,* Frank Haven later criticized the "breathless journalism, the 'by golly, this is war' attitude of too many TV and radio broadcasts. It kept the city at a fighting pitch long after the riots had waned."[5] Under trying circumstances, he said, breathless journalism was one thing the *Times* tried to avoid. The paper won a Pulitzer Prize for its coverage.

By providing a close-up view, the camera in the helicopter actually affected what happened on the ground. For the police, reporters, and the protesters in action, the pictures from the helicopter were often useful. Never sure where in Watts fresh disorders might erupt, the police and the reporters could monitor KTLA and rush from one location to the other accordingly. From the camera above, police could discover in what area looting might be taking place. They could even see the faces of looters wandering about with items from whiskey to motorized lawn trimmers. One sequence from the helicopter showed a man and a woman stealing a huge couch. Conversely, rioters could single out areas where they could safely go because the police had hurried somewhere else.

Hal Humphrey, a columnist for the *Los Angeles Times,* recalled how exciting the helicopter coverage was—excitement "frequently heightened . . . with inflammatory commentary and unconfirmed reports." At times, he said, the reporter in the air "got carried away with what he saw and repetitiously harangued his audience into a pitch of excitement almost unbearable."[6] An NBC News executive, William Corrigan, who had been sent to Watts for the emergency, was more explicit. "The copter," he said, "sent out some frightful reports that were totally unverified." He went so far as to say that "television sometimes has an instantaneousness that has to be repressed in the interests of responsibility."[7] Naturally, differences of opinion arose over television's effect on the disturbances.

Television cameras were an invitation to show-offs and troublemakers. Pictures of lootings and beatings caused a contagion of rioting. Cameras gave too much time to alleged "extremists," such as Stokely Carmichael of the Black Panther party, and H. Rap Brown, chairman of the Student Nonviolent Coordinating Committee. Rep. Harley O. Staggers, a Democrat from West Virginia and chairman of the House committee with jurisdiction over the communications field, said that statements by Brown and Carmichael were incitements to riot. Elmer Lower, president of ABC News, argued that an analysis of network logs before and during the Newark and Detroit riots showed that the views of responsible leaders, African American and white, were carried far more often than were utterances of Brown and Carmichael.[8]

Staggers also complained that television coverage of lesser disturbances blew them into full-scale riots. Don Oliver, an NBC reporter, disagreed. "Once a public disturbance has begun," he said, "cameras have very little effect on its progress."[9]

Lower shared this view. "In the major areas of trouble where ABC had reporters present this summer," he asserted, "I have been unable to find evidence that the presence on the scene of radio and television mobile units, tape recorders and cameras caused the demonstrations or seriously aggravated them."[10]

Robert Shafer, chief of the NBC News bureau in Los Angeles at the time of Watts, felt differently. It was clear to him that even the presence of television crews working in the streets, as distinct from filming by helicopter, was exacerbating the problem. At night television lighting attracted crowds and sometimes led to disturbances. "We were hampering the police in their efforts to get a grip on the rioting," Shafer said.[11]

"The blacks," Fred Rheinstein, an NBC producer involved in the Watts coverage, observed, "were caught up in something that was self-generating and out of control. None of us in the news business had any real contacts in the black community. We did not know how to cover the situation any more than the police knew how to control it."[12]

The near warfare in Watts continued for six days, from August 11 to 16, 1965. Thirty-four persons were killed; more than a thousand were injured. Nearly four thousand were arrested. Damage caused by fire was estimated at $175 million.

The assassination of President Kennedy was only two years in the past. The Vietnam War was growing grimmer. Outbreaks of rebellion on campuses startled and dismayed the country. In the next two years, especially during the "long, hot summer" of 1967, fifty-eight other American cities were shaken by riots. As a result, 141 persons were killed, and 4,552 were injured. The woeful climax of this wave of national disorders came in 1968 with the assassination, of Robert Kennedy, a former attorney general and a candidate for the Democratic presidential nomination, and civil rights leader Martin Luther King. A symbol of the lacerating grief in the African-American community caused by King's death was the dark smoke drifting over the White House and the sunlit magnolia trees the next day from fires set in African-American neighborhoods of the capital. All these events, beginning with Watts, spread on television a panorama of fire, destruction, violence, lawlessness, belligerence, and alienation that caused Americans to fear for the stability of their institutions and the quality of life in the future.

As a practical matter, Watts was a turning-point for television news. Each network devised guidelines for covering civil unrest, and they were much the same. In a potentially explosive trouble spot beware of live coverage: film or tape can be edited; live coverage cannot. Be as unobtrusive as possible in a riot. Ride in unmarked vehicles. If underlying causes of a disturbance are evident, report them in perspective. Avoid provocative language. Use compact equipment. In a tense situation do not turn on lights. If a helicopter is used, let pictures tell the story.

At a conference in Poughkeepsie, New York, two years after the Watts riots, representatives of the three networks agreed that the live coverage of Watts by helicopter had been inflammatory. During the height of the 1967 riots in Detroit, Newark, and elsewhere, Reuven Frank sent a memorandum to his NBC reporters and producers, saying: "We cover events. We report them, we do not arrange them, modify them, stage them or schedule them. We do not reenact them. . . . If a rally is to take place and the sponsors ask us when is the best time for us, we are to have no opinion."[13]

When the slowly developing Detroit riots began, local television stations, which inevitably had the jump on the networks, refrained from reporting violence for the first twelve hours. Ironically, the first person killed in the city was a woman who was shot while passing through a riotous crowd. If she had heard of the danger on television or radio, might she have avoided the area?

So frightening were the upheavals of that summer that on July 29, 1967, President Lyndon Johnson established the National Advisory Commission on Civil Disorders to study the causes of the trouble and recommend solutions. Chaired by former governor Otto Kerner of Illinois, the commission became most renowned for its warning that the United States was in danger of becoming two nations, one white and the other black.

The commission analyzed the effect of television news and the press on the riots and concluded that they "helped shape people's attitudes toward riots" but did not cause them. The report continued: "In some cities people who watched television reports and read newspaper accounts of riots in other cities rioted themselves. But the causal chain weakens when we recall that in other cities people in very much the same circumstances watched the same programs and read the same newspaper stories but did not riot themselves."[14]

In the riots everywhere except Detroit, the commission found that the time national and local television gave to reporting the event declined after the first day even though trouble may have worsened later. "These findings," according to the report, "tend to controvert the impression that the riot intensifies television coverage, thus, in turn, intensifying the riot."[15]

The report supported the contention of Elmer Lower and others that moderate African-American leaders were given more time on television than "militants" were. Most of the appearances were on local stations, where moderates were shown three times more often than militants.

Rioters were resentful that most reporters seemed to get their information from policemen and city officials. In the thick of disorders, the police and other officials *were* the principal, and sometimes the only, sources reporters could turn to. Reporters, the report said, "tend to arrive with the police and stay close to them—often for safety and often because they learn where the action is at the same time as the authorities." This tendency strengthens "the ghetto impression that police and press work together and toward the same ends"—an impression that may surprise many within the ranks of police and press.[16]

The report cited two related weaknesses of television news and the press at that time. One was that reporters, editors, and producers "too often do not achieve [a high] level of sophisticated, skeptical, careful news judgment. . . . The media report and write from the standpoint of a white man's world."[17] The other was that television and the newspapers

failed to report adequately on the causes and consequences of civil disorders and the underlying problems of race relations. . . . The media—especially television . . . failed to present and analyze to a sufficient extent the basic reasons for the disorders. . . . They have not communicated to a majority of their audience— which is white—a sense of the degradation, misery, and hopelessness of living in the ghetto. They have not communicated to whites a feeling for the difficulties and frustrations of being a Negro in the United States.[18]

The experiences of thirty years ago helped bring changes in the way print and television journalism approaches coverage of racial disturbances. The new generation of reporters and editors is more sophisticated, better educated in underlying causes, and more aware of the furies of ghetto life than its predecessor was. Furthermore, newsroom attitudes have been broadened by the influx of African-American reporters and editors since the 1960s.

7

Vietnam, 1965–1967

American combat troops entered Vietnam for the first time on March 8, 1965. Less than five months later CBS aired a report from the field by Morley Safer that infuriated President Johnson and aroused suspicion, which still lingers, of television's role in covering military action. Especially among the military and the political right, the feeling persists, as evidenced in the strict censorship of the Persian Gulf War in 1991, that television's coverage of the Vietnam War soured Americans' attitude toward involvement and thus contributed to North Vietnam's victory.

Safer's pictures showed U.S. marines setting fire, sometimes with Zippo lighters, to people's huts in the village of Cam Ne. The village was near the American air base at Da Nang. A patrol of the III Marine Amphibious Force had complained that, while protecting the base, it had received hostile fire from Cam Ne and other nearby villages that sheltered concealed fortifications. As a result, on August 3, the patrol set out on a search-and-destroy mission, and Safer and his crew went along to cover it.

A native of Canada, Safer had been a correspondent of the Canadian Broadcasting System, which had assigned him to cover fighting in the Middle East, Cyprus, and Algeria. After joining CBS, he was one of the first television reporters to be stationed permanently in South Vietnam. He liked being on the prowl, and, more than some of his colleagues, he knew what made good television.

His version and official accounts of the events of August 3 differ. In his memoirs Safer wrote:

I asked a lieutenant about our mission. "We are going to Cam Ne," he says. "Search and destroy. Especially destroy. We've been taking fire from there every time we go by, and the gook head honcho in these parts told us to go teach them a lesson. . . ." We walk into Cam Ne. . . . A black-toothed woman runs . . . toward me . . . pleading. The marines are rousting people out of the huts with their rifles, some with bayonets fixed. . . . As people stumble out of houses, marines, some with flamethrowers, others using matches, yet others with Zippo lighters, begin systematically to set fire to each hut.[1]

According to the official version, the marines were told their objective was to destroy all bunkers, trench lines, and huts concealing fortifications. Once they had reached the outskirts of Cam Ne, the official account said, the marines received occasional fire from an estimated one hundred Communist guerrillas (Viet Cong) deployed in and around the village. The marines responded with rockets and grenades, and some huts were burned or damaged by flamethrowers and by the demolition of bunkers and trenches. One ten-year-old boy was killed, and another was among three or four inhabitants wounded. After the marines entered the village, which reportedly had about four hundred huts that were surrounded by trenches and in some cases connected by tunnels, enemy fire slackened. But when the marines were leaving in the afternoon, they had to call in covering mortar and artillery salvos to silence renewed enemy fire.

At the first opportunity Safer sent a message to CBS News in New York. It said that an officer at the scene had told him that the marines had orders "to burn the village to the ground if [they] received even one round of enemy fire." An automatic weapon was fired at the marines, Safer recounted, and they retaliated with rockets, grenades, and machine guns. Despite the appeals of elderly inhabitants, the marines used cigarette lighters and flamethrowers to destroy 150 dwellings. The message concluded:

I witnessed the foregoing. . . . Prior to the burning, townspeople [were] urged to abandon their shelters in English. [Not understanding,] . . . they remained in their positions. This reporter offered services of South Vietnamese cameraman to give desired instructions in native tongue. . . . Defense Department says all our troops constantly reminded of need to protect civilians. Marines have lost men helping civilians in Danang area.[2]

Safer's message set off the fireworks at CBS. Reports were then surging around the world that American firepower was slaughtering civilians in Vietnam. CBS knew that showing the film could arouse passions. Scenes of a burning of common villagers' huts would accord poorly with America's claim to be in Vietnam fighting to save a vulnerable population from

Communist tyranny. The CBS night desk in New York awakened Fred Friendly, head of the news division, at home. He asked: Was Safer sure of his facts? CBS leased a special line to Los Angeles to preview the film. In their viewing room in New York, Friendly and Ernest Leiser, Cronkite's executive producer, watched the pictures of marines setting fire to thatched huts; none doubted the potential impact. One marine, his rifle hanging loosely at his waist, reached up and ignited a hut with his Zippo lighter. The picture conflicted with the official explanation that most of the huts had been destroyed in crossfire after the marines had encountered heavy opposition.

After its showing on the "CBS Evening News" on March 8, 1965, Safer's report became one of the most celebrated television performances of the war. His commentary was no less powerful than the pictures:

In Vietnam like everywhere else in Asia property, a home, is everything. A man lives with his family on ancestral land. His parents are buried nearby. These spirits are part of his holdings. . . . Today's operation shows the frustration of Vietnam in miniature. There is little doubt that American fire power can win a military victory here. But to a Vietnamese peasant whose home means a lifetime of backbreaking labor, it will take more than presidential promises to convince him that we are on his side.[3]

Safer later talked with marines who had fought at Cam Ne on August 3. The interview with one, which CBS aired, went as follows:

Q. You're up against a lot of women, children, and old men. How do you feel about it, corporal?
A. Well, this is what makes it hairy, being against these women and children, . . . but you treat everyone like an enemy until he's proven innocent. That's the only way you can do it.
Q. Yesterday, we were in that village of Cam Nanh [*sic*], we burned all the houses, I guess. Do you think that was necessary to fulfill the mission?
A. Yes I do. . . . We are the only company that went in there that hasn't had people [marines] killed . . . and I feel we . . . done a good job right there. And then we're going to have to show these people over a period of time that we're done playing with them. . . . These other companies moved through [on July 12] and left that stuff stand and they got people killed. . . . We went in and we done our job and destroyed the villages and we took four casualties. So I think we proved our point.[4]

The young marine's reference to previous engagements and casualties during the advance in that area provided another reason why marine officers criticized Safer's coverage. They believed that he should have emphasized in his report the previous firing from the village by the enemy.

In his interviews Safer asked a second marine if he regretted having left people homeless. "You can't have a feeling of remorse for these people," the man replied. "I mean, like I say, they are an enemy until proven innocent. . . . I feel no remorse. I don't imagine anyone else does. You can't do your job and feel pity for these people."[5]

Promptly, investigators from the Military Assistance Command, Vietnam (MACV) interrogated the marines who had talked to Safer. All of them pleaded that they had been enticed into indiscreet remarks by misleading questions. Lt. Gen. Lewis Walt, commander of the III Marine Amphibious Force, banned Safer from the I Corps Tactical Zone, where the marine operations were taking place. Col. Benjamin W. Legare, MACV chief of information, persuaded Walt to rescind the order. Disciplining reporters was the responsibility of MACV, Colonel Legare argued.

Marine officers were angered that Safer's broadcast emphasized the igniting of the huts rather than the Pentagon's policy of protecting civilians. In the marines' view the reporting of the Zippo incident helped give birth to the cliché that the way to save Vietnam was to destroy it.

In Washington Arthur Sylvester, assistant secretary of defense for public affairs, demanded that CBS recall Morley Safer. Before going to the Pentagon, Sylvester was Washington correspondent for the *Newark News*. As a reporter, Sylvester would have tolerated no interference with the rights of the press. He would have maintained that it was the job of a war correspondent covering a beleaguered village being set afire by cigarette lighters and flamethrowers to report the fact. But as assistant sec-- retary of defense, he demanded Safer's recall. He wrote a letter on August 12, 1965, to Fred Friendly, president of CBS News, reminding him that Safer was a Canadian by birth and, therefore, perhaps not sensitive to America's problems in Vietnam. Furthermore:

Canadian military friends of mine who know Mr. Safer personally . . . tell me he has long been known . . . as a man with a strong anti-military bias. They say the record shows that he shafted the Canadian defense establishment in the sense that he did not present a balanced account of controversial situations. That would be my complaint about his reports, picture and verbal, on Cam Ne.[6]

Secretary Sylvester's letter to Friendly drew only indignation. The president of CBS News retorted that it was "a matter of pure and simple character assassination." To suggest that an American might have been more sensitive than a Canadian to the situation at Cam Ne was tantamount to saying that an American would have been the "more sympathetic" to the official line, Friendly declared, adding:

The essence of our dispute is quite simple. You don't want anything you consider damaging to our morale or our worldwide image reported. We don't want to violate purely *military* security with reports which could endanger the life of a single soldier but, by the same token, we must insist upon our right to report what is actually happening despite political consequences. . . . In the long term, this, too, will help enhance our nation's position in the eyes of the world.[7]

Sylvester surely labored under great pressure from Johnson, who was boiling over the Safer affair. At a meeting in the White House, the president flung abuse at his old friend, Frank Stanton, president of CBS. Johnson questioned the loyalty to the United States of Safer and other CBS correspondents and threatened to release derogatory information about them. Barry Zorthian, the respected head of the Joint United States Public Affairs Office in Saigon, attended the meeting. He was asked later if Johnson attributed Communist backing to American reporters. "Oh, yes," Zorthian said. "He'd just fulminate against them, he'd get so goddamned mad."[8]

Zorthian also has recalled visiting Johnson in his bedroom in the White House during one of Zorthian's trips to Washington for consultations. When he entered the bedroom in midday, he found that Johnson, as was often his custom, had put on his pajama tops and climbed into bed for a nap before beginning what he called his second day in a twenty-four-hour period. The president immediately began roaring against journalists in Vietnam. He repeatedly demanded to know why Zorthian, who had no authority for such action, did not prevent reporters in Saigon from filing the stories they filed. Zorthian remembered:

But in the middle of this monologue—nonstop monologue—[he] threw off his bedcovers, got out of bed, walked around the room, not missing one word—he still kept talking—walked over to the john where the door was open, left open, relieved himself loudly, still talking, came back, got into bed, put the covers over him again, never stopped talking. And all the talk was about the press.[9]

Beginning in 1961 Kennedy enlarged Eisenhower's policy of granting political and economic support to the established regime of Ngo Dinh Diem in Saigon, the capital of South Vietnam, against the revolutionary government of North Vietnam. American reporters' coverage of Saigon provided sufficient information for attentive readers and viewers in the United States to understand that the Diem government was a rotting foundation on which to build a political or military alliance. For instance, "Vietnam:

The Deadly Decision," a documentary CBS broadcast from Saigon in April 1964, gave warning of pitfalls that would await American military intervention. Turning to this aspect, Bernard Kalb, a correspondent, said:

I think it's a good idea to keep in mind constantly . . . that it's exceedingly difficult, if not impossible, to beat an ideology with technology. . . . I think the enemy has patience . . . the fact that this is a long pull uphill should be remembered.

Charles Collingwood, his colleague, replied:

The Communists make no secret of their strategy. Their theory is that if they maintain the pressure long enough, either the South Vietnamese or the United States will weary of this inconclusive struggle and retire. . . . The only way this war can be won, if that's what we're bent on doing, is for the United States as a nation, as a people, to continue to accept the costs, the casualties, the frustration, and the uncertainty not just for a little while longer but perhaps for many years.[10]

When President Johnson committed combat forces to Vietnam in 1965, he furthered U.S. foreign policy in Asia of four of his predecessors in office: Roosevelt, Truman, Eisenhower, and Kennedy. Each had had a hand in fashioning a separate phase of that policy, but throughout, one purpose was clear: to prevent the spread of communism in Asia.

In the past American war correspondents had gone overseas to cover the adventures and ordeals of American forces and to report on American marches along the road to victory. A new generation of war correspondents was sent in ever greater numbers to Vietnam for the same purpose. If the new generation proved to be more skeptical and cynical than its predecessors, it was due in no small part to the errors, misconceptions, deceptions, and lies that had streamed from U.S. officials, civilian and military, in Saigon during the Diem period of the early 1960s.

One reporter who turned critic was David Halberstam of the *New York Times*. President Kennedy tried unsuccessfully in 1963 to nudge Arthur Ochs Sulzberger, then publisher of the paper, into transferring Halberstam out of Vietnam. Yet, at the time, Halberstam believed in the cause of stopping aggression in Southeast Asia. He and most of the other American correspondents in Vietnam in the early years of the conflict were of the generation of the cold war and the domino theory. They shared the prevailing view that Vietnam was vital to American security— an outlook that scarcely fit the mold of troublemaker intent on subverting U.S. interests. It is laughable to suppose that American newspapers and networks would have poured tens of millions of dollars into covering a war with a thought of frustrating an American victory.

In the beginning the American people believed their forces would conquer North Vietnam, and reporters did not think otherwise. Thus, for example, Safer said in one of his Cam Ne reports, "There is little doubt that American fire power can win a military victory here."[11] In August 1965, after marines routed the Viet Cong in another area near Da Nang, Safer praised the well-trained Americans—"the world's finest assault troops"—when he appeared on the Cronkite program. The battle, he said, was "rather historic. It marks the first time that American troops took on an aggressive role." From the State Department, Marvin Kalb observed that the marines' success might compel Hanoi to relent in its insistence that American forces withdraw before peace negotiations could begin.[12] Historian William M. Hammond spent ten years writing the official account, published by the army in 1988, of the relationship between the military and television news and press in Vietnam from 1962 to 1968. He confirms the view that reporters during the early years of the war were not trying to subvert U.S. policy. Reporters at that time "criticized U.S. tactics and strategy, but never argued about the wisdom of the American presence in South Vietnam."[13]

In the period that began with the commitment of combat forces in the spring of 1965, the war reporters were not imbued with pessimism. According to Lawrence Lichty, a historian, and Edward Fouhy, who was the CBS bureau chief in Saigon in 1967, reporters generally "reflected the optimistic news related by the military, the optimistic news they hoped for, and the optimistic news the American people thought possible, if not inevitable."[14] But like any large event a reporter might cover, a war takes on a life of its own. New and unexpected developments, inconclusive results, sacrifices that do not seem worth the cost can, and did, alter opinions. The Vietnam War was full of difficulties and inconsistencies, and reporters were intimately exposed to them. As the fighting dragged on month after month, a number of reporters became critical, partly because men in uniform whom they talked with in the field became critical. For the officials who set war policy and for those who tried to carry it out, the tasks were burdensome beyond description. Costs in blood and money soon exceeded expectations. Things seldom worked out as anticipated. Steadily the United States sank into the worst political, social, and moral conflict since the 1860s.

For all practical purposes Vietnam was the first war to have been shown on television in homes throughout America. This became a subject of vehement controversy, all the more so because of the unusual circum-

stance that television and press coverage was uncensored. South Vietnam
ostensibly was a sovereign nation, and U.S. forces were there by request
of the Saigon government. In such an arrangement censorship was im-
practical.

Technology permitted television news to cover the Vietnam War far
more insistently than it had Korea. In the Korean War black-and-white
film, much of it without a soundtrack, was flown to New York on pro-
peller planes, sometimes arriving almost a week after it was shot, for
editing and projection. By the time of the Vietnam conflict cameramen
used shoulder-held sound-on-film cameras that vividly caught whatever
action scenes film crews could get to. Footage was usually flown to New
York by jet, but after the introduction of satellite transmission coverage
of the 1967 Winter Olympics in Tokyo the networks shipped urgent film
to Tokyo for instant satellite transmission to New York. Beginning with
Tet in 1968 satellites were widely used for transmission of Vietnam War
coverage from Tokyo and also, later on, from Bangkok and Hong Kong.
Less urgent film was flown to New York, or occasionally to San Francisco, Los Angeles, or Chicago for land-line transmission to New York.

During the war, television coverage exasperated, to the point where it
became almost an obsession, presidents, generals, and some writers who
were firmly wedded to their opinions. Nixon, who succeeded Johnson in
1969 and took over responsibility for war policy, wrote later in his memoirs:

The American news media had come to dominate domestic opinion. . . . In each
night's TV news and in each morning's paper the war was reported battle by
battle, but little or no sense of the underlying purpose of the fighting was conveyed. . . . Whatever the intention behind such relentless and literal reporting of
the war, the result was a serious demoralization of the home front, raising the
question whether America would ever again be able to fight the enemy abroad
with unity and strength of purpose at home.[15]

Gen. William Westmoreland in his memoirs declared that "television's
unique requirements contributed a distorted view of the war." As seen
by the American people, he added, the war was "almost exclusively violent, miserable, or controversial."[16] Writing in the British magazine *Encounter* in August 1981, Robert Elegant, a sometime correspondent who
was long a resident of the Far East, did the tidiest summary of such viewpoints: "For the first time in modern history, the outcome of a war was
determined not on the battlefield, but on the printed page and, above all,
on the television screen."[17] James Reston wrote in the *New York Times*

at the end of the war: "Maybe the historians will agree that the reporters and the cameras were decisive in the end. They brought the issue of the war to the people . . . and forced the withdrawal of American power from Vietnam."[18]

On the contrary, since the war this conclusion has been rejected by the most thorough and respected historical studies, official as well as academic, that have been done on the subject. In a nutshell, they concluded that television news did not lead public opinion but reflected it. The memory of nightly scenes from Vietnam that still endures in the generation that watched television during the war testifies to its impact. On the whole, however, television and the press did not move ahead of public opinion. That would not have been characteristic of those mediums. Generally speaking, television and the press were supportive of the war as long as public opinion was supportive. And in 1965, public support was decidedly on the rise as more and more American troops went into action. In his study of public opinion in war, John E. Mueller of the University of Rochester found that 1965 was a time of "fairly considerable 'rally-round-the-flag' effect."[19] That summer, according to a Harris Poll, 62 percent of the American people approved Johnson's handling of the war.[20]

Only a few months after Johnson's commitment of combat troops, James L. Greenfield, assistant secretary of state for public affairs, called attention to the popular support in a speech in London. Greenfield, however, had been around long enough to remember what had happened in Korea a decade before. Heavy public support for that war declined as casualties grew, and this would happen again, Greenfield frankly told a meeting of the Joint United States–United Kingdom Information Group.[21] The Korean War had demonstrated that in a democracy the people are likely to support a limited war for only a limited time. Casualties plus stalemate were conditions that helped define the limits.

On balance, television coverage of the war from 1965 to 1968 was positive and fostered confidence about an ultimate American victory. Edward Jay Epstein wrote that before 1968 "the network searchlight tended to focus on the American military initiative—troop landings, air strikes, search-and-destroy operations and awesome new military equipment being deployed—and [to] present a picture of slow but sure progress in the war."[22] A study by George Bailey of the University of Wisconsin in Milwaukee concluded that the daily routine of the network anchormen was to read short news stories on the war "without much interpretation, certainly without challenging, adversary interpretation."[23] Of course, there were Cam Ne and reports on such matters as corruption in the South Vietnam government. "But these 'negative' stories," wrote Daniel C. Hallin, "were by no means typical of television coverage in the period before the Tet offensive. They were minor currents in a general flow of reporting that was strongly supportive of American actions in Vietnam."[24]

Nixon's complaint in his memoirs that news stories did not convey the reasons behind American participation in the war totally overlooked a principal part of the Vietnam coverage. This was the ceaseless flow of stories in his own administration, as in Johnson's, from the White House, the State Department, and the Pentagon on the rationale of policy and on the progress, or promises of progress, in the field. In August 1965 CBS ran a series of programs under the title "Vietnam Perspective," in which the participants included Secretary of State Dean Rusk; Secretary of Defense Robert S. McNamara; McGeorge Bundy, national security adviser to President Johnson; Gen. Earle G. Wheeler, chairman of the Joint Chiefs of Staff; Maxwell D. Taylor, U.S. ambassador to Saigon; and Arthur Goldberg, U.S. permanent representative to the United Nations. No critics of the war were invited to join this chorus of administration spokesmen, each of whom was allowed to review and edit tapes of his remarks before a broadcast.

In its issue of November 27, 1964, *Life* gave a large spread to interviews with American officials about the Johnson administration's aims and achievements in Vietnam. After examining more than a thousand evening news broadcasts and network documentaries on the war, Hallin wrote that roughly up to the time of the Tet offensive in 1968 "television coverage was lopsidedly favorable to American policy."[25] Lichty and Raymond L. Carroll of the University of Alabama surveyed more than three hundred documentary or television forum programs before 1965, which devoted time to Vietnam. Their finding:

Of those guests appearing on discussion programs such as "Meet the Press," "Face the Nation," and "Issues and Answers," 90 percent were "hawks"—arguing for the administration view: more support, more troops, escalation. It was not until 1968 that there were an equal number of "hawks" and "doves" on these interview programs. And not until 1970 was there a majority of "doves"—especially Democrats in Congress—who spoke against the Nixon policy of withdrawal tied to new aggression.[26]

In his official U.S. Army history, William M. Hammond wrote, "What alienated the American public, in both the Korean and Vietnam Wars, was not news coverage but casualties. Public support for each war dropped inexorably by 15 percentage points whenever total U.S. casualties increased by a factor of ten."[27] He alluded to the conflict between the military, on one hand, and television and the press, on the other. Many of those in uniform remembered that in earlier wars, especially World War II, the press had nearly always supported official policies. In that war, of course, the issues were far more momentous than in Vietnam, and the government had the overwhelming support of the people and the press. Furthermore, the press functioned under censorship. In Vietnam, where, apart from certain MACV operating guidelines, television and newspaper reporters were unfettered, the military still expected equivalent support. When, however, "the contradictions engendered by President Johnson's strategy of limited war led instead to a more critical attitude, the military tended increasingly to blame the press for the credibility problems they experienced, accusing television in particular of turning the American public against the war." Hammond concluded: "In so doing, critics of the press within the military paid great attention to the mistakes of the news media but little to the work of the majority of reporters who attempted conscientiously to tell all sides of the story."[28]

Although about half of the more than nine thousand television reports from Vietnam dealt with military action, including battles, most of them showed very little real fighting. Television coverage was "most often banal and stylized."[29] To read Westmoreland could lead one to suppose that nightly scenes from Vietnam resembled those on the Western Front in 1917. What viewers at home saw, he wrote in his memoirs, "were guns firing, men falling, helicopters crashing, buildings toppling, huts burning, refugees fleeing, women wailing. A shot of a single building in ruins could give an impression of an entire town destroyed."[30]

Many lasting impressions of television coverage of Vietnam are based largely on certain startling scenes such as the burning of Cam Ne. Most of the coverage, however, was not of gripping action. Michael J. Arlen, television critic of the *New Yorker*, remembered a "nearly total absence on the nightly network news broadcasts of any explicit reality of the war—certainly of any of the blood and gore, or even the path of combat." He added:

What television viewers of the Vietnam War saw—at least for the first two-thirds of its duration—was a nightly stylized, generally distanced overview of a disjointed conflict which was composed mainly of scenes of helicopters landing, tall grasses blowing in the helicopter wind, American soldiers fanning out across a hillside on foot, rifles at the ready, with now and then [on the soundtrack] a far-off ping or two, and now and then a column of dark, billowing smoke a half-mile away, invariably described as a burning Vietcong ammo dump.[31]

Television teams seldom became genuinely involved in combat, although they were under constant pressure from their offices to cover it. Between 1965 and 1970 "less than 5 percent of all evening news film reports showed 'heavy battle,'" according to Lichty and Fouhy. Heavy battle they defined as "actual combat seen close up with casualties." In their opinion "the view that TV reported a gory war every night in every American home is far, far off the mark."[32] "In fact," Hammond wrote, "the action scenes from any episode of the popular television dramas 'Gunsmoke' and 'Kojak,' carefully paced and filmed for effect, were probably more brutal than all but a few of the most explicit films from Vietnam."[33] In some instances worse scenes of bloodshed in Vietnam were carried in color in magazines than on television.[34]

The networks tried to shield dinnertime audiences from horror by rejecting shots of wounded American soldiers and suffering Vietnamese civilians. They also strove to withhold pictures of identifiable American casualties unless families had been notified. The very nature of the guerrilla war in Vietnam, however, made it hard for the networks to plan the news. Opposing front lines, which provided the focus for reporters in most wars, were a rarity in Vietnam. Skirmishes and battles were often spontaneous and localized. Early in the morning reporters and cameramen would set off by military transport from their headquarters in Saigon or Da Nang for areas where action was expected. Sometimes television crews would just wait until calls for medical evacuation helicopters came in from a field where fighting had erupted and then catch a ride to the scene. In Vietnam no facilities were available for developing and editing film. The task had to be done by technicians in New York and elsewhere to fit the sequence into a news program. As a result, stories as broadcast did not always come out with the nuances the reporter had intended.

Television crews seldom spent the night with the troops. For one thing, film had to be brought back to headquarters by nightfall to be speeded to New York; for another, cameras could not catch action after dark. Frequently, even in daytime, military action was out of range of a camera. In one typical month in 1968, Americans were involved in fifteen thousand small-unit operations, but in only seven hundred of them was contact made with the enemy, and many of these were at night.[35] For journalists as well as for soldiers and marines, Vietnam was a prowling kind of war. Prowling to find the enemy, men walked about in the jungle, wary of ambush, mines, and booby traps but often encountering no action.

"We helicoptered to a peak twenty-three hundred feet over a Vietcong-controlled valley," Peter Kalischer of CBS remembered, "but for the next seven hours we slid down the steep incline, hanging on to trees and struggling to protect our equipment. It was the most gruelling physical exertion I've ever encountered on a story. At the bottom we discovered the Vietcong had vanished."

"Near Chu Lai," Murray Fromson, another CBS reporter, recalled, "I walked for six hours in one-hundred-and-thirty-degree heat, but there was no significant contact with unfriendly forces, no story."

A marine major once apologized to Dan Rather, who was covering the major's mission, for having tramped about for four days without having found a single enemy soldier. The major said, however, that the next day looked promising, and Rather was game.

"We were up at 3 A.M.," he related afterward, "moved out before dawn, walked seventeen kilometers and reached a South Vietnamese army outpost which already had been wiped out. So all I got was one hundred feet of an aftermath story. No battle footage."[36]

Such experiences, of course, tell only part of the story. If most television teams did not find large battles to cover, many of them were exposed to danger. In October 1966 Lou Cioffi of ABC told *TV Guide*, "You begin wondering when the law of averages will catch up with you. I'm scared all the time, but I'm more scared now than when I first came out here."[37] His fear was justified. Thirty-one journalists were killed and twenty-three more were listed as missing in Vietnam, Laos, and Cambodia, the worst hazard.[38]

Reporters never were able to cover the air action over North Vietnam, one of the most important phases of the war. They were not permitted to fly in air force or navy planes.

While defending the press and television news from excessive criticism by the military, Hammond cited journalistic shortcomings. He found fault with reporters for accusing the military of attempting to mislead the public, as in the case of the clandestine bombing of Laos. "Yet even as they leveled this charge," he added, reporters

yielded far too readily to the pressures of their profession. Competing with one another for every scrap of news, under the compulsion of deadlines at home, sacrificing depth and analysis to color, they created news where none existed. . . . while failing to make the most of what legitimate news did exist. The good and bad points of the South Vietnamese Army and government, the wars in Laos and Cambodia, the policies and objectives of Hanoi and the National Liberation Front, the pacification program—all received less coverage in the press, positive or negative, than they probably could and should have.[39]

In criticizing the making of news "where none existed," Hammond cited one of the best reporters on the scene, Peter Arnett of the Associated Press. Arnett was awarded a Pulitzer Prize for his coverage of the war. Hammond faulted him for writing a story early in the war that South Vietnamese forces had twice used tear gas and nausea-producing gas against the enemy to facilitate the rescue of prisoners. He filed the story after an MACV information liaison officer in the field had declined to respond to his inquiry. Arnett pegged his lead to a Radio Hanoi report that the United States and South Vietnam had used "poisonous chemicals" and that a girl had suffered a swollen face. This casualty was not verifiable by an American journalist. Otherwise Arnett's story was correct. Such gases were regularly used in many countries, including the United States, for riot control and were considered more humane than bullets. It was memories of the horrors of mustard gas in World War I that made this story about two relatively minor incidents so volatile.[40]

Network anchormen described American attacks with enthusiasm more often than dismay. "American Air Force jets gave Communist Vietnamese their heaviest clobbering of the war, hurling almost half a million pounds of explosives at targets in the North," Cronkite declared on August 23, 1965. On January 10, 1966, Chet Huntley chimed in:

American and allied forces were on the offensive on three fronts today in Vietnam. An assault by units of the First Air Cavalry Division, kept secret for six days, wound up on the east bank of a river separating South Vietnam from Cambodia. The enemy was clearly visible on the other bank, but refused to fire. . . . [T]hree large camps and tons of equipment and supplies have been destroyed.[41]

Despite the irritation of certain officials who had their own ideas about what television ought to be reporting, there was no question as to whose side the reporters were on. North Vietnamese were repeatedly portrayed as fanatical and cruel, and in the matter of bombing pauses and other negotiating devices, the United States was invariably correct and Hanoi invariably and wrongly intransigent.

The principal source of hard news remained Zorthian's daily briefings, dubbed by journalists "The Five O'Clock Follies." Based on this infor-

mation, "combined with reporting from Washington on optimistic statements by the administration and a fair number of upbeat reports from
the field," Hallin wrote, the war militarily "appeared to be going very
well for most of 1965, 1966, and 1967."[42] The bulk of war reporting
reflected the official point of view.

"Until the mood of the country turned, or became ambivalent," Michael Arlen wrote in 1975, "the network news programs went out of
their way, or so it seemed, to portray the air war—the heavy, the light
bombing, the deadly 'gunships'—as romantic and enhancing."[43] The mood
of the country did change, as the next chapter makes clear. The "romantic" and the "enhancing," if such words could ever be applied to events
in Vietnam, withered before irrepressible doubts.

8

Vietnam, 1968–1975

Early on Tuesday, January 30, 1968, a presidential election year, the White House was stunned by news from Vietnam. Breaking a thirty-six-hour truce for Tet, Vietnam's principal holiday, nearly seventy thousand enemy troops had suddenly attacked more than a hundred towns and cities held by American and South Vietnamese forces. The cities included Da Nang, Nha Trang, and Kontum, all well north of Saigon. At the early hour in Washington there was no word of any attack on Saigon, which would have had especially grave implications for the Johnson administration. Since 5:37 A.M. President Lyndon Johnson had been in touch with the situation room in the White House basement, demanding to know the meaning and seriousness of the obviously coordinated enemy actions. Several blocks away at the National Press Club, Sen. Robert F. Kennedy of New York had arrived at seven o'clock for breakfast with a group of reporters. What happened there in the next hour symbolized the disruptive psychological effect the Tet offensive—as reported, interpreted, and understood in this country—was to have on American politics.

Kennedy and the reporters sat down to breakfast knowing nothing of what was happening in Vietnam that day. With the Democratic presidential primary election in New Hampshire only several weeks away, reporters asked Kennedy whether he would yield to the urgings of his liberal followers and become a candidate for president in 1968. For years Robert Kennedy and Lyndon Johnson could barely abide one another. Attorney general in his brother's administration, Kennedy had painfully continued in that post in the Johnson administration until 1964, when he ran for senator in New York. By 1968 Senator Kennedy had become a commanding figure among the forces insisting that the United States negotiate a withdrawal from the war. Hence, he was an obvious, though hesitant, rival to challenge Johnson for the 1968 nomination.

As reporters at the breakfast pressed him on the question, Kennedy's response was negative. "My running," he said, "would automatically elect a Republican by splitting the Democratic party, and Democratic candidates would be beaten all over the country." Were there any circumstances, the columnist Jules Witcover inquired, in which Kennedy would be a candidate against Johnson that year? "No, I can't conceive of any circumstances," the senator replied.[1]

Presently, someone from the *Chicago Daily News* bureau downstairs entered the room and handed the *Daily News* bureau chief, Peter Lisagor, a batch of copy from the Associated Press wire. The bulletins reporting the start of the Tet offensive startled Lisagor, and he passed them to Kennedy. Before the eyes of the reporters around the table, including one of the authors of this book, Kennedy's whole demeanor was changed by what he read. To watch him was to sense his gathering dismay that he had so flatly removed himself as a presidential candidate. In fact, his quick-thinking press secretary, Frank Mankiewicz, who was present, suggested that the senator temper his statement that he could not conceive of running against Johnson. Mankiewicz proposed that Kennedy change his position to one in which he thought his entry into the race "unforeseeable." Godfrey Sperling, Jr., of the *Christian Science Monitor*, who had arranged the breakfast, wrote long afterward, "Kennedy readily and, I thought, eagerly, accepted this softening."[2] Within weeks Kennedy announced his candidacy for the Democratic nomination in 1968.

After the early morning jolts from Vietnam, business seemed normal at the White House. Shortly after noon four journalists from the *Washington Post* arrived at the invitation of Walt W. Rostow, special assistant to the president for national security affairs. Rostow wanted them to read some documents, newly captured from the enemy, which he thought showed that the United States was winning the war—a theme the White House had been vigorously promoting for weeks. Rostow left the journalists in the hands of a briefing officer and departed to attend to his duties for the president. The reading of the document was interrupted by an aide who came in from the adjacent communications center and handed the briefing officer a piece of paper. The officer glanced at it and directed that it be taken to Rostow immediately. "Looks like some trouble in Saigon," he told the people from the *Post*.[3] Several more messages were brought in and then rushed to Rostow.

Later that Tuesday, Rostow attended Johnson's weekly high-level luncheon on Vietnam strategy. At 2:33 P.M., Rostow was beckoned to the kitchen to take an urgent call from Bromley Smith, head of the National Security Council staff. On his return to the table, Rostow asked to interrupt a discussion. "We are being heavily mortared in Saigon," he announced. He also reported that the Presidential Palace and the bachelor officers' quarters in the city were under fire.[4]

The president returned to the Oval Office. At 3:15 P.M. he received a typed memorandum from Rostow: "By direct telephone, NMCC [National Military Command Center] has learned that in an attack on the U.S. Embassy in Saigon, several Viet Cong got into the compound."[5]

Attack on the *embassy?* In the heart of the capital of South Vietnam? Near the headquarters of Gen. William C. Westmoreland's Military Assistance Command? Two years and ten months after American troops had entered the war? Two years and ten months after an American build-up in Vietnam to a current level of 492,000 soldiers, sailors, and airmen?

In Saigon exploding mortar shells and the rattle of small-arms fire sent hundreds of reporters and photographers racing for cover. Dumbfounded at being caught in the midst of a battle in the South Vietnamese capital, cameramen on the run filmed everything in sight. Dead bodies lay in the rubble. With the sound of gunfire being recorded on television's soundtracks, dazed American soldiers and civilians ran back and forth trying to flush out attackers. In one sequence the cameras caught a strapping American running with a pistol in his hand toward a villa behind the chancery. He was Leo Crampsey, civilian chief of the embassy guard. Reaching the villa, he tossed the pistol up to Col. George Jacobson on the second floor. Jacobson missed it, and Crampsey tried again and none too soon. The colonel shot and killed the last of the commandos, who was crawling up the stairs from the first floor.

The suddenness of the Tet offensive plunged the networks into wild logistical problems. As a result, raw and unedited pictures were flashed across millions of television screens, heightening the sense of chaos and terror. "There is a grim realization that the United States is in for a very rough time through all of Vietnam in the next few days and weeks," Frank Reynolds of ABC announced on the evening news.[6]

Film for satellite transmission had to be flown to Tokyo. NBC and CBS caught the same plane, but that did not end the scramble. Tokyo had only one laboratory that could develop their color film. CBS had a car waiting at Tokyo airport, yet still lost the race. The NBC courier drove a motorcycle. At NBC News in New York, the clock was ticking toward the start of the "Huntley-Brinkley Report" at 6:30 P.M. on January 30. Although they were constantly on the telephone with Tokyo, Robert J. (Shad) Northshield, the executive producer, and his assistant, Lester M. Crystal, could not learn how much film they would get or precisely when it would arrive. Huntley went on the air with only wire service still photographs to show:

The Viet Cong seized part of the United States embassy in Saigon early Wednesday, Vietnam time. Snipers are in buildings and on rooftops near the embassy and are firing on American personnel inside the compound. Twenty suicide commandos are reported to be holding the first floor of the embassy. The attack on the embassy and other key installations in Saigon, at Tan Son Nhut air base and Bien Hoa, north of Saigon, came as the climax of the enemy's biggest and most highly coordinated offensive of the war. There was no immediate report of allied casualties in Saigon, but they are believed to be high.[7]

Then Huntley switched to the signal arriving by satellite. Probably the most helter-skelter, exciting pictures of the Vietnam War appeared on television. No one in the control room knew how long they would run or what could come next. Like the original wire service bulletins and some newspaper leads, the Huntley report erred in relating that the attackers entered the chancery building. They blew a hole in a surrounding wall, killed five American soldiers, and then were slain. The error regarding the chancery was attributable, at least in part, to misinformation supplied on the spot by military police and by their exclusion of journalists from the compound.

The first rush of news was only the start of days of stories, columns, commentaries, film, and photographs of death and destruction in Saigon, Bien Hoa, Hué, Khe Sanh, and other places struck by the enemy. According to Hallin, the percentage of television stories in which reporters editorialized jumped from 5.9 percent before Tet to 20 percent in the two months after the offensive and then receded to 9.8 percent.[8] One of the severest criticisms of the coverage, made by Peter Braestrup, author and former war correspondent in Vietnam, was that it underplayed the enormous losses suffered by the enemy. Hence, the military setback to the United States and the South Vietnamese was exaggerated. The implication is that by portraying the enemy as being more powerful than he was, the stories and film discouraged vigorous prosecution of the war.[9] Clearly, on the other hand, the capability and endurance of the enemy in launching such an offensive as late as 1968 gave Americans, who were hoping for an early military victory, cause to lose hope. "The communists may not be winning the war," Robert Gorlaski of NBC said in a special report on February 1, "but they don't seem to be losing it either."[10]

On the same day on ABC, Joseph C. Harsch observed from Washington:

[The] best estimates here are that the enemy has not yet, and probably never will, run out of enough manpower to keep his effort going.

What this city yearns for is someone like a Winston Churchill, who would admit frankly the fact that after two years of massive American military intervention in Vietnam, the enemy has been able to mount . . . by far the biggest and boldest and most sophisticated offensive of the whole war.[11]

On CBS, Mike Wallace reflected the thinking among Americans in Saigon that "we are in for a long war."[12] In early February, Cronkite dwelt on the gravity of the situation and then went to Vietnam for his own assessment.

Tet wasn't the beginning of domestic discontent over Vietnam. As early as November 1965, polls indicated a decline in the previously strong public support for the war. Nevertheless, most people backed it. Sen. J. William Fulbright, a Democrat from Arkansas, was chairman of the Senate Foreign Relations Committee. In the summer of 1964, he had worked for passage in Congress of the Southeast Asia Resolution because he wanted to retain his close friendship with Johnson. Johnson's subsequent escalation of the war alarmed Fulbright, and on a prime-time CBS special on February 1, 1966, the senator apologized for the part he had played in winning passage of the resolution. Then he opened public hearings of the Foreign Relations Committee on military appropriations. During the hearings he questioned the legality of the president's use of the resolution to justify further escalation. The hearings produced testimony critical of war policy. The president, when he learned that they were to be televised, was horrified. He suddenly rushed off to Honolulu to take the play away from Fulbright by conferring with the South Vietnamese leaders, Gen. Nguyen Van Thieu and Air Vice-Marshal Nguyen Cao Ky.[13]

U.S. bombing of Vietnam began in 1965. It soon led to protests on college campuses and demonstrations by religious groups. In mid-April twenty thousand people gathered at the Washington Monument to show their opposition to war. The draft of more and more men drove many students to revolt. Public burnings of draft cards, which would have scandalized the American people during the Second World War, became commonplace. Some even flaunted the North Vietnamese flag. Martin Luther King, a power after his triumphs in the South, called for mass protests against the war. He linked the civil rights movement with the peace movement.[14] Vietnam was consuming money African-American leaders believed should be spent to relieve poverty. Protests spread. By early 1967 mistrust of the administration had gone so far that the president unwisely pressed General Westmoreland to return from Saigon to the United States to defend the government's war policy. Westmoreland's speech to a joint session of Congress on April 28, 1967, went off well enough. What he had said in New York at a meeting of the Associated Press Managing Editors Association on April 24, however, had caused a squall. Referring to an earlier antiwar flag burning in Central Park in New York, the general had said that he and his men had been "dismayed" by "recent unpatriotic acts here at home." Senator Fulbright complained that the administration likened dissent to treason. The *New York Post* described the speech as a form of domestic psychological warfare. Sen. George McGovern, a Democrat from South Dakota, accused military leaders of blaming their failures on their critics.[15]

During 1967, a number of major newspapers and magazines, most of which had supported American policy in Vietnam since the Eisenhower administration, either cooled in their support, as in the case of the *Los Angeles Times,* or joined the critics, as in the case of the *Washington Post* and *Newsweek.* Perhaps the most eye-catching turnabout was that of the Luce publications, *Time* and *Life.* The year after he had succeeded Henry R. Luce as editor-and-chief of Time, Inc., in April 1964, Hedley Donovan made his first visit to Vietnam. On his return he wrote, to Luce's high satisfaction, "Vietnam: The War Is Worth Winning," a preface to a thirty-one-page special section in the February 25, 1966, issue of *Life.*[16] Yet as months passed without decisive victories and as the antiwar movement reached disturbing dimensions, Donovan's doubts grew. Winning the war was "obviously harder, longer, more complicated than the U.S. foresaw" noted a *Life* editorial on October 20, 1967. "We are also trying to maintain a highly important—but in the last analysis not absolutely imperative—strategic interest of the U.S. and the free world. This is a tough combination to ask young Americans to die for."[17] Two other *Life* editorials in January 1968, written before Tet, called for a negotiated peace.

Late in 1967 President Johnson again called Westmoreland back from the war to deliver a speech of encouragement, this time at the National Press Club in Washington. On "Meet the Press," Vice-President Hubert

H. Humphrey managed to conjure up good news "on every front" in Vietnam. Johnson also welcomed home for a visit Ellsworth Bunker, then U.S. ambassador in Saigon. Bunker gave another report of progress and assured reporters that 67 percent of the population of South Vietnam was under Saigon's control. By staging this chorus of optimism about the war, Johnson unwittingly fashioned for himself a trap. Tet snapped it shut.

The American people were shocked to see on television the corpses and litter around their embassy. One death on February 2, 1968, was particularly loathsome. The killer was Brig. Gen. Nguyen Ngoc Loan, chief of the South Vietnamese national police. Fighting in the streets between the South Vietnamese forces and the guerrillas had been savage. It was reported that a guerrilla had killed a South Vietnamese colonel and murdered his wife and six children. Later, in Cholon, the Chinese sector of Saigon, the South Vietnamese randomly captured a guerrilla. They beat him, tied his hands behind his back, and marched him down a street to where Nguyen Ngoc Loan was standing near a pagoda. Eddie Adams, an AP photographer who would win a Pulitzer Prize for the photos he took that day, and an NBC team arrived on the scene. Climbing out of their car at the pagoda, they saw several South Vietnamese marines approaching with the diminutive captive, who was barefoot and wearing only a checked shirt and black shorts.

"He was not scared," Howard Tuckner, an NBC reporter, later recalled. "He was proud. . . . General Loan took one look at him and knew he was going to get no information out of him. Loan had been through this with many prisoners." The police chief had a pistol in his right hand. "Keep rolling," Tuckner whispered to his cameraman. "Keep rolling."[18]

"There was not one word," Tuckner said in recounting the confrontation. "Loan did not try to talk to him nor to scare him. He did not wave his gun at his face or his head. He did not put the gun to his temple. He just blew his brains out." The police chief turned to Tuckner.

"Many Americans have been killed these last few days," he said, "and many of my best Vietnamese friends. Now do you understand? Buddha will understand."[19]

The savagery of the Tuckner film shocked Robert Northshield, executive producer of the "Huntley-Brinkley Report," and John Chancellor when it arrived by satellite the next day. They saw the guerrilla, his head spurting blood, sagging to the ground dead. "It was too much for me," Northshield remembered. "I said to Chancellor, 'I thought that was awfully rough.' He could hardly speak. I said I was going to trim it off a little. So when it went on the air, you saw less. . . . That is, as soon as the man hit the ground we went to black."[20] Viewers saw the death but not the continuing oozing of blood.

Some 20 million people may have seen the film on NBC.[21] Many more than that would have seen the Adams photographs in newspapers and magazines in the United States and around the world. The sight of the summary execution of a man who had not been convicted of a crime horrified many Americans. It made them wonder all the more what their country was doing in such a war. Though perhaps not typical of justice as administered by the South Vietnamese, the pictures "legitimized the moral arguments of the antiwar movement."[22] Indeed, T-shirts emblazoned with the outline of the Adams photograph appeared on American streets.

"Well before Tet—in October 1967—a plurality of the public believed the United States had made a 'mistake' going into Vietnam," Daniel Hallin wrote. "Considerably earlier, at least by the beginning of 1967, a plurality were saying they disapproved of Johnson's handling of the war."[23] Washington politicians in general, who by 1968 were well on their way to being captives of television news, absorbed all the painful scenes and thrashed about trying to decide what should be done next.

Tet knocked the props from under Johnson. Once a president of the whopping gesture, the large response now failed him. At first he was reduced to tampering with public relations. Obsessed as always by television, he shoved aside the usual procedures to get Secretary of Defense Robert S. McNamara and Secretary of State Dean Rusk on "Meet the Press" together. Because of Johnson's ire at the coverage of Vietnam by the *New York Times,* he tried to have *Times* reporter Max Frankel excluded from the panel of questioners. Lawrence Spivak, the producer, refused. Although accounts of the program made front-page news the next day, McNamara and Rusk staged no great rescue mission for Johnson. McNamara did emphasize a fact about the Tet offensive that was favorable to the United States: the attack failed to ignite a general uprising in South Vietnam in line with the hopes of Hanoi. The secretary of defense, however, did not echo those in the Pentagon who tried to brush off Tet as a disaster pure and simple for North Vietnam. "I think there have been pluses and minuses psychologically," he admitted. "There's no question but that the people of the cities and towns of South Vietnam have been dealt a heavy blow. They must have been surprised, they must have been impressed by the weight of the attack." Rusk evinced discouragement over the prospect of early peace talks. North Vietnam did not appear to be "seriously interested at the . . . time in talking about peaceful settlement."[24]

Meanwhile, the president persisted in his quest for favorable news. He directed Westmoreland and Bunker to appear before reporters in Saigon every day with reassuring comments. In a message to the two officials, George Christian, the presidential press secretary, said, "We are facing, in these next few days, a critical phase in the American public's understanding and confidence toward our efforts in Vietnam."[25]

Back from his fact-finding trip to Vietnam, Cronkite made an appearance on CBS on February 27, 1968. What he said on that special program about the war was extraordinary. A patriotic journalist, Cronkite was naturally cautious about injecting his personal views into his reporting. But he felt, he explained later, that the country had been left confused by Tet and that he had a responsibility to say what he thought:

> To say we are closer to victory today is to believe in the face of evidence . . . optimists who have been wrong in the past. To suggest we are on the edge of defeat is to yield to unreasonable pessimists. To say we are mired in stalemate seems the only realistic yet unsatisfactory conclusion. . . . It is increasingly clear to this reporter that the only rational way out would be to negotiate—not as victims, but as an honorable people who lived up to their pledge to victory and democracy and did the best they could.[26]

Johnson was upset, angry. What he feared, he told Christian, was that Cronkite would change the minds "of middle-of-the-road folks who have supported the war all along."[27] Actually, the problem was more serious than that. Cronkite had not stepped out in front of public opinion. He reflected it. Many "middle-of-the-road folks" had already started changing their minds.

The administration itself was badly divided. Johnson and McNamara already had split over whether the United States could win the war as things were going. Clark M. Clifford, who on March 1, 1968, succeeded McNamara as secretary of defense, soon encountered the same conflict with the president. Indeed, Cronkite's views were in line with what the polls were beginning to show. In the first frenzy of Tet, polls indicated a spurt in American support of the war—from 56 percent to 61 percent, according to Hallin.[28] But this rally-round-the-flag effect didn't last. In a month or two, support declined "to levels significantly more dovish than prevailed in the days before Tet."[29]

On Sunday, March 10, 1968, the *New York Times* broke the story that the army was asking for an increase of 206,000 troops.[30] That evening NBC aired an unusual documentary. Without qualification Frank McGee, the moderator, made this statement: "The war is being lost by the Administration's definition." The administration's intent, he explained, was to halt the Communists until South Vietnam could secure the land and then form a stable government. McGee treated viewers to such stark films of desolation and homelessness created by Tet that Johnson's goal seemed more distant than ever.

In the *New York Times* the next day, Jack Gould discussed McGee's statement. "His comment," Gould wrote,

was further evidence that the influential mass media are steadily adopting a harder line in questioning the wisdom of national policy in Vietnam. . . . In general, the networks have allowed pictures from the battle scenes to speak for themselves; now it is evident that the [networks] feel a rounded assessment of Vietnam cannot be achieved without accompanying interpretation, particularly in certain phases of the conflict where no pictures are available.[31]

The networks were influencing the views of the White House insiders as well as those of the general public. One of the ablest men then in the White House was Harry C. McPherson, Jr., special counsel and a principal speechwriter for Johnson. Long afterward he tried to look as a social scientist might at his own experience during Tet. He had access to what he called an enormous panoply of intelligence-gathering devices, as well as to messages coming directly from the field in Vietnam. Yet, he said, "it is particularly interesting that people like me—people who had some responsibility for expressing the presidential point of view—could be so affected by the media as everyone else was." The truth of the matter was, as he stated it, that he trusted what television showed more than he trusted what Walt Rostow, the president's hawkish national security adviser, would tell him about the previous day's fighting. "Like millions of other people who had been looking at television the night before," he said, "I had the feeling that the country had just about had it, that they would simply not take any more."[32]

In the years since the Tet offensive, many have written about it but McPherson's simple words tell the essential story. As Neil Sheehan said in his book *A Bright Shining Lie,* "Tet had written a finis" to the war.[33] This was, of course, a case of taking the long view. For Americans, the fighting continued for five more years.

On March 31, Johnson surprised the nation by announcing that he would not be a candidate for reelection in 1968. In this televised address from the White House, he also announced a partial halt in bombing and new U.S. efforts for peace. His words, though memorable, brought no immediate tranquility at home. Avalanches of antiwar demonstrations soon surged through American streets, campuses, and even the grounds of the Pentagon.

Six months after Tet, masses of students and others descended on Chicago, site of the Democratic National Convention, to demand an eloquent peace plank and the nomination of an authentic peace candidate. With hopes for either one exhausted, demonstrators swarmed through parks and marched down Michigan Avenue toward the convention hall until stopped for want of credentials to admit them. Mayor Richard J. Daley's police were as primed for battle as the students. Afterward controversy lingered as to whether it was a student riot or a police riot. Of all times, telephone technicians in Chicago were on strike. This meant that the networks could not hook up with cameras in the streets, nor could they switch back and forth between the rioting and the convention. By late evening, however, the cameras had recorded reams of raw footage of street violence. These pictures, like those of the attack on the U.S. embassy during Tet, went on the air unedited. Pictures of police breaking up demonstrators taped by mobile units in Grant Park and along Michigan Avenue were brought in by motorcycle couriers and put on the air in the middle of nominating speeches. Scenes of unrelieved chaos, confusion, violence, and danger suddenly flashed from television screens scattered around the convention hall and caused bedlam. Viewers at home were no less shaken than the delegates.

In placing in nomination Sen. George McGovern of South Dakota, a favorite of the antiwar movement but not a leading contender for the nomination, Sen. Abraham A. Ribicoff of Connecticut exclaimed, "With George McGovern, we would not have Gestapo tactics on the streets of Chicago." This brought Mayor Daley of Chicago, a powerful Democratic boss, to his feet in the center aisle. Red-faced, puffed with rage, he shouted what appeared to be an epithet at Ribicoff, but the noise was so deafening that his words were lost.

As expected, delegates nominated Vice-President Hubert H. Humphrey to be their presidential candidate. On the eve of the November election, too late to assure victory for Humphrey, President Johnson finally stopped the bombing. The outcome of the election was surprisingly closc, but the drift of many Democrats to the antiwar movement and hence away from Humphrey helped Nixon win.

President Nixon pursued a policy of deescalation in stages, slowly withdrawing American troops and turning more and more of the fighting against the North over to South Vietnam. It was determination and stubbornness, reinforced by effective use of television, that enabled Nixon to keep American forces in action until 1973—five years after Tet had eliminated all prospect of winning the war.

According to a Twentieth Century Fund report by Newton N. Minow, former chairman of the Federal Communications Commission, John Bartlow Martin, journalist, biographer, and former diplomat, and Lee M. Mitchell, an attorney who specialized in communications law, President Nixon's televised speeches "played a significant role in maintaining public support for [his] position and in enabling him to withstand congressional attempts to limit his discretion in dealing with Vietnam developments."[34]

During the months from November 1969 through April 1971, Nixon preempted prime time on the networks seven times to explain and defend his war policy before huge audiences. According to the Fund's report:

Finding themselves the losers in the war powers debate with the president, members of Congress complained about the effectiveness of presidential television. "The President has used his prime time television series to present his position on the war, to discount the role of Congress in charting a course in Indochina and to criticize his Senate opponents and their position on the war." On the basis of this and similar complaints, the Federal Communications Commission found that President Nixon's first five preemptive television addresses had created a definite imbalance in favor of the president in network television's presentation of the Vietnam issue.[35]

Nixon's announcement on April 30, 1970, that American and South Vietnamcsc forces had entered Cambodia to attack Communist sanctuaries inflamed the student antiwar movement. On May 4 the Ohio National Guard fired on demonstrators at Kent State University. Four students were killed, and nine were wounded. The spread of protests closed, for all intents and purposes, a hundred colleges around the country. On September 21, 1971, Congress voted to end the draft in 1973. For protesters the wind began to subside. On January 23, 1973, Nixon announced an accord with Hanoi on ending the war.

The effect of tclcvised coverage of the Vietnam War was, as Lawrence

Lichty has observed, two-edged.[36] It provided encouragement for pro-
war and antiwar partisans. The more that was pictured on television, the
more the opinions of both sides hardened. Year after year television showed
scenes of the war to the American people and kept the argument going.
Much that might have faded into the background in previous wars continued to stir people as they watched television throughout the Vietnam
War. At a conference at the University of North Carolina ten years after
Tet, Westmoreland complained that if it had not been for television, no
one would have known about the war. To which Robert Northshield,
then with CBS, shouted in reply, "Then thank God for television!"[37]

The size, vehemence, and high visibility of the antiwar movement unquestionably encouraged Hanoi. The effect at home was profound and
long lasting. The conduct and attitude of many demonstrators so outraged many Americans that a backlash was all but inevitable. In 1968
the University of Michigan conducted a poll, asking the public to rate
groups and persons on a scale from zero to one hundred. At least one-
third of the respondents rated Vietnam War protesters zero. Only 16
percent of the respondents rated them anywhere in the upper half of the
scale. Other studies, wrote John Mueller of the University of Rochester,
"suggest that popular reaction to the disturbances surrounding the Democratic convention . . . was overwhelmingly favorable to the Chicago police and unfavorable to the demonstrators, despite press coverage that
was heavily biased in the demonstrators' favor." The protesters were associated, in many people's minds, with "violent disruption, stink bombs,
desecration of the flag, profanity, and contempt for American values."[38]

For the first time in its history, the United States lost a war. The reaction was delayed but inexorable. It helped elect Ronald Reagan as president in 1980. There was no doubt about the meaning of clouds of red,
white, and blue balloons wherever he went. It was "morning again in
America." The flag flew everywhere. Midstream America was "feeling
good" once more, or was supposed to be.

Captured in astounding television pictures, the final collapse of the anti-
Communist effort came on April 30, 1975, in Saigon two years after the
cease-fire and the departure of American troops from Vietnam. With North
Vietnamese forces closing in on South Vietnam, Graham Martin, the
American ambassador, his staff, and South Vietnamese assistants climbed
to the roof of the U.S. Embassy to evade their northern foe. Marine helicopters rescued them. Too few arrived to escort everyone. Frantically,

some who could not board a helicopter clung to its landing gear. Finally, the last of the helicopters pulled away from a sea of upraised arms of South Vietnamese trying to catch hold. On television screens in America the pictures caused a humiliation that was not to be assuaged until Iraq's surrender in the Persian Gulf War sixteen years later.

It has been said that television was so intent on action and immediacy that it never reported the full, true story of the Vietnam War. In other words, television news told what happened but not, broadly speaking, what was happening. Nevertheless, as Michael Arlen put it, "television news was crucial—in its commissions and omissions—to the American public's comprehension of our Indo-China involvement."[39] Arlen was right and so was historian William Hammond when he wrote that the reports on television and in the press "were still often more accurate than the public statements of the administration in portraying the situation in Vietnam."[40]

9

Nixon's presidency: a difficult time for television news and the press

Two years after his defeat by Kennedy in the 1960 presidential election, Nixon took a big political gamble and lost it. In spite of conflicting advice from friends and in the face of divisions within the Republican party, he ran for governor of his native California against the popular Democratic incumbent, Edmund G. (Pat) Brown. On November 7, the morning after election day, Nixon sulked in front of a television set in the Presidential Suite of the Beverly Hilton Hotel in Los Angeles. Unshaven and gaunt after having been up all night, he was surrounded by several of his associates, including Herbert G. Klein, his press secretary, who had just entered with a message that put Nixon in a still worse mood. Reporters had been waiting for hours to see him in the pressroom downstairs, Klein said.

"Screw them," Nixon retorted.[1] The latest returns from around the state had ended Nixon's chance of winning. Klein reiterated that reporters were waiting for a traditional concession statement from him. "Screw them," he said again. He instructed Klein to make a statement for him. But while Klein was in the act of complying, a rumpled Nixon suddenly appeared in the pressroom. "Good morning, gentlemen," he said. "Now that Mr. Klein has made his statement, and now that all the members of the press are so delighted that I have lost, I'd like to make a statement of my own."[2]

His words revealed a deep bitterness that seven years later would color relations between Nixon the president and the press and television. Interspersed were jibes and even some praise. He tossed laurels for fairness to one reporter present, Carl Greenberg of the *Los Angeles Times,* who without cause was embarrassed about it for years afterward.

"As I leave the press," Nixon declared, "all that I can say is this: for sixteen [fourteen] years, ever since the Hiss case, you have had a lot of fun . . . an opportunity to attack me, and I think I have given as good as I have taken."

He criticized some newspaper reporting of his campaign, offered thanks that television and radio had kept matters straight, and concluded: "I leave you gentlemen now and you will write it. You will interpret it. That's your right. But as I leave you I want you to know—just think how much you're going to be missing. You won't have Nixon to kick around anymore because, gentlemen, this is my last press conference."

On the evening news that night millions of television viewers caught the force of Nixon's stark appearance and grim language. His self-pitying "you won't have Nixon to kick around anymore" passed into political lore, not to mention popular idiom. The general reaction was that, barring a miracle, Nixon's public career was over. The performance, wrote Jules Witcover, author and columnist, "was the public act of harakiri of the century."[3] Such assessments erred. At that stage of his career, Nixon the politician was indestructible. Television news, the medium for indicating his early demise, soon became the medium that sparked an outpouring of public support.

Four days after the funereal scene at the Beverly Hilton, the weekly ABC program "Howard K. Smith News & Comment" had a show entitled "The Political Obituary of Richard Nixon." For this retrospective on Nixon's career, Smith had assembled four guests. One of them was Alger Hiss. He had been convicted of perjury, the statute of limitations on treason having expired by the time of his indictment. On the air, Hiss assailed Nixon for his role in the Un-American Activities Committee hearings: "He was less interested in developing the facts objectively than in seeking ways of making a preconceived plan appear plausible. I regard his actions as motivated by ambition, by personal self-serving."[4]

The program caused a howl. Whatever Hiss may have done wrong and whatever his motive, his name for a generation was a plague in the United States. He was the American outcast of his time. The Hiss case had been a prime tool for Republicans and conservatives to legitimize the frenzy of investigations that in the 1940s and 1950s distorted American lives and American government. And now Hiss was, in effect, testifying on national television against a former vice-president and candidate for president. Former president Dwight D. Eisenhower telephoned his erstwhile press secretary, James C. Hagerty, then an ABC News executive, to complain. In fact, even before the program ended, critical calls were flooding the ABC switchboard in New York. The *Chicago Tribune* reported the broadcast in a front-page story.[5] The Schick Razor Company threatened to break a million-dollar contract with ABC, and the Kemper Insurance Company considered cancelling half a million dollars in advertising. According to Nixon, more than eighty-thousand protesting letters and telegrams were sent. "The immediate uproar," he later wrote, "helped to turn me from the sore loser of the 'last press conference' into something of an injured party."[6]

On January 20, 1969, Richard Milhaus Nixon was sworn in as president of the United States. It had been a bumpy political journey—questions about his California fund in 1952, President Eisenhower's ambivalence about having Nixon as his running mate again in 1956, the defeat by John F. Kennedy in 1960, the shambles of his gubernatorial campaign in 1962 and, finally, the Beverly Hilton tirade—one pothole after another. But Nixon's second neck-and-neck presidential race, this one against Hubert H. Humphrey, had ended in victory. Controlled use of television to avoid reporters lay at the heart of Nixon's successful 1968 campaign. "Certainly," he told the National Association of Broadcasters a year later, "I am the world's living expert on what television can do for a candidate and what it can do to a candidate."[7]

Conflicts between presidents and the press are historical. They arise because the press invariably wants to know more than the government is willing to tell, and the government wants the press to report on a development or a situation the way the government prefers to have it seen. All these normal causes of dispute were present during the Nixon administration, but they were intensified on both sides by psychological and personal strains. The administration's internal memorandums, now part of the records of the National Archives in Alexandria, Virginia, only begin to reveal the suspiciousness and vindictiveness of Nixon and some of his assistants. Indignant about negative television coverage by the networks of his plans for developing an antiballistic missile system, Nixon in March 1969 wrote White House Chief of Staff H. R. Haldeman: "Give me a report from [Communications Director Herbert] Klein's outfit by noon today as to what we are doing to raise hell with NBC on this. [Same] for CBS."[8]

On June 10, 1969, Alexander P. Butterfield, deputy assistant to the president, sent a memorandum to John D. Ehrlichman, the president's counsel:

The President read in a recent news summary that many of his critics complain about the Administration's not being "as open as promised." His only comment, addressed to you, appears below:
John—Tell Herb [Klein] and Ron [Ziegler] to ignore this kind of criticism. The fact of the matter is that we are far *too* open. If we treat the press with a little more contempt we'll probably get better treatment.[9]

The margins of Nixon's notes were filled with his jottings, such as:
"Get our side out"
"Anti." (Next to John Chancellor's name, for example.)
"Cut him out."
"Knock this down"
"Get letters to editors"
"This buildup shows they're [the press] after blood."
"Who put this out?"
"Who leaked this?"
"Don't include him at WH functions."
A report to Nixon about television coverage in September 1969 said that NBC was determined to do a "hatchet job" on Lt. Gen. Lewis B. Hershey, director of the Selective Service, which was drafting thousands of young men for the Vietnam War. The president commanded Haldeman: "See that NBC gets a hard knock from Klein on this and *again* when are we going to have a system where this is automatically done and reported to me?"[10]
After reading a report in July on the PBS program "Washington Week in Review," Nixon observed: "I don't consider this program worth so much time. It is really a rehash of columns. What we need is more emphasis on the shows with big listening audiences." The White House staff prepared a four-hundred–page summary of television over the summer of 1969. On September 28, speechwriter Patrick J. Buchanan sent Nixon a memorandum on it, in which he said:

The one network where . . . on a controversial story the chances are greatest that *we* will come off badly is without question NBC. . . . There is always a market here for the Saigon-Washington rift type story; . . . they [NBC] do as much or more than any network on the Administration "confusion" over desegregation policy.
John Chancellor, we would estimate, is negative toward the . . . President's

position 90 percent of the time. Because of his frequency on the tube, and because of the time he commands on Huntley-Brinkley, we consider him perhaps the most offensive commentator on the air. A close second is [CBS reporter] Daniel Schoor [*sic*].[11]

On the margin of Buchanan's criticism of NBC, Nixon wrote an instruction to Haldeman and Klein, "Note and act accordingly."

From the time he entered politics after returning from naval service in World War II, or soon after, Nixon seemed implacably convinced that most reporters and columnists were untrustworthy, unfair liberal knaves. From what he read in the newspapers and magazines and heard in television commentaries, he appears to have concluded that many, perhaps most, journalists were either too stupid or too prejudiced to get a story straight when writing about himself or his policies. Frequently, Roosevelt, Truman, Eisenhower, and Kennedy fumed at the press, yet relations between those presidents and reporters were civil and manageable enough. By the time Nixon became president his cynical attitude had been formed, and his press relations only hardened under the rumblings of Buchanan, Haldeman, Jeb Magruder, Charles Colson, and others.

Mort Allin, a young conservative recently graduated from college, prepared a daily news summary for Nixon. "Reading the summaries with whatever objectivity twenty years can bring," Nixon's biographer Stephen E. Ambrose wrote in the late 1980s, "one is struck by the antipathy felt by Allin and Buchanan toward virtually all the big names in TV broadcasting, but most especially Dan Rather and Walter Cronkite of CBS News. They fed Nixon's idée fixe that the television newsmen, like newspaper reporters, were all his bitter enemies, men who hated him and would do anything to hurt him."[12] According to Ambrose, Herbert Klein tried to tell Nixon otherwise, but Nixon loved it all too much to listen to him. Klein, a level-headed, reasonable man, was not aggressive enough in dealing with reporters to suit the president. He did not fit the rough-and-tumble mode of the Nixon high command.

Although the memorandums that flew about the White House would not suggest it, some leading reporters in Washington thought that Nixon was smart, and they were not seriously put off by him. They were willing to grant that there was a good deal more substance to his presidency than wrangles with the press and television. Then there were others who could not stand him or trust him and who relished stories that embarrassed him. Their attitude, however, did not affect the general news coverage of President Nixon. It was Nixon's own obsession with journalism, amplified by certain arrogant advisers, that determined the course. Nixon's obsession drove the president beyond the bounds of common sense and led to his downfall, in the view of William Safire, Nixon's admiring speechwriter who later became a provocative columnist for the *New York Times*.[13] For most journalists, even those who voted for him for president, it was not easy to be comfortable with Nixon. Essentially, it was because they believed he mistrusted their motives. Of course, there were other reasons, too, for the difficult rapport between Nixon and those in the news business.

One was Nixon's manner. He forfeited the respect, for example, of Norman Chandler, owner of the *Los Angeles Times*, and Mrs. Chandler by using what they considered vulgar language at a dinner with them in Rome in the 1960s. Another was Nixon's tendency to lump all reporters together as a bad lot. As noted in Chapter 3, Nixon on the morrow of his defeat in California told reporters that ever since the Hiss case they had had "a lot of fun—a lot of fun . . . an opportunity to attack me."[14] But many at the press conference were California reporters who had been nowhere near Washington at the time of the Hiss case. Falsely, Nixon portrayed them as a group in sympathy with the national villain. Even if Nixon had said the same thing in Washington he would have been wide of the mark. Relatively few reporters in Washington in 1948 knew or personally cared about Alger Hiss, who had already left an inconspicuous job in the State Department for New York and the presidency of the Carnegie Endowment for International Peace.

While the assertion of Nixon and others that Washington reporters tend to be liberal is true, it is not necessarily pertinent. In his inquiry into Hiss in 1948, Nixon had the diligent cooperation of Bert Andrews, chief of the Washington bureau of the *New York Herald Tribune*. By 1950 Andrews was going around Washington touting Nixon as a future president and introducing him to friends. Furthermore, in the years of Nixon's rise, conservative newspaper bureau chiefs held sway in the capital. They were prominent, influential, and friendly to Nixon. The *Washington Post* and its cartoonist, Herblock, speared him. But the *Washington Star*, then the most powerful newspaper in the capital, was staunchly Republican.

If reporters, whether in television or print journalism, were not conspicuously with him, they were against him. This attitude became firmly implanted in Nixon's White House.

By October 1969, Nixon's tenth month in office, the tone of the memorandums had grown rougher. Jeb Magruder, of H. R. Haldeman's staff, had received from the president some twenty-one requests for specific action against so-called unfair news coverage. On October 16, Haldeman asked Magruder for a "talking paper" on "specific problems we've had in shot-gunning the media and anti-Administration spokesmen." There was no doubt. The administration was taking aim at its adversaries. It wanted to blast them away. The title of Magruder's paper was "The Shotgun vs. the Rifle." Some of Magruder's proposals, however, smacked more of brass knuckles:

1. Begin an official monitoring system [of television stations] through the Federal Communications Commission. . . .
2. Utilize the anti-trust division to investigate various media relating to anti-trust violations. . . .
3. Utilize the Internal Revenue Service as a method to look into the various organizations that we are most concerned about. . . .
4. Begin to show favorites within the media. Since they are basically not on our side let us pick the favorite ones as Kennedy did. I'm not saying we should eliminate the open Administration, but by being open we have not gotten anyone to back us on a consistent basis and many of those who were favorable towards us are now giving it to us at various times, i.e., Ted Lewis [of the *New York Daily News*] and Hugh Sidiy [Sidey].[15]

Nixon and his staff were absorbed in finding the best ways to use television. In press conferences Nixon used answers prepared for him. One problem with those answers, Haldeman wrote, "is that they are all in essence directed to the writing press, rather than taking into account the fact that what we are actually doing here is making a statement to the television viewer at home. The President emphasizes that we must get in tune with the fact that this is a TV operation and that that's all that really matters. The only thing that counts is the answer that a TV viewer at home will understand."[16]

In mid-October 1969 an antiwar movement known as the Vietnam Moratorium staged a massive demonstration in Washington. Nixon, who could view it from the White House windows, was rightly convinced that noisy protesters represented a minority view in the country at that time. On November 3 he went on national television to reject "precipitate withdrawal" from Vietnam and to solicit from what he called "the great silent majority of my fellow Americans" support for a more deliberate, negotiated settlement. Afterward he did not watch the summaries and commentaries that ensued on television. Members of his family who did told him that commentators criticized his words and motives and speculated on what he might better have said instead. The so-called instant analysis of major presidential speeches was a fixture of television news at that time. It was intolerable to Nixon when it thwarted him from getting an unchallenged message across to the American people.

As part of the speech he had read a private exchange of letters between himself and Ho Chi Minh, the late president of North Vietnam. Nixon's letter, dated July 15, 1969, argued that nothing would be gained by further delays in the peace talks then going on in Paris and said that the United States was willing to consider other proposals beyond those currently on the table. On August 25, three days before his death, Ho replied that he also wanted peace. First, however, he added, the United States must cease its "aggression," withdraw its forces, and agree to respect the rights of the Vietnamese people to enjoy peace without foreign influence. In his broadcast Nixon drew a conclusion from Ho's words. As he stated it, "The obstacle is the other side's absolute refusal to show the least willingness to join us in seeking a just peace."[17]

Marvin Kalb, then diplomatic correspondent for CBS in Washington, was assigned by his network to analyze the president's speech after delivery. Earlier in the year Kalb had covered the peace talks in Paris and had established news sources on both sides. On reading an advance copy of the Nixon speech, he was convinced that it overstated the obstinacy of the North Vietnamese about negotiations. After telephone checks with his sources and other experts in Paris and Washington, Kalb felt all the surer that Ho's language was not absolutely intended as a rebuff to Nixon.

Following the speech, Rather, as moderator, asked Kalb on the air what he thought the reaction would be at home and abroad. Rather conceded that such an analysis was a matter of a journalist's judgment and involved "guesswork." Kalb replied by casting doubt on whether the speech cut new ground.[18]

It was aimed, as the president put it, at you [the television audience] the great silent majority . . . presumably those who do not demonstrate, those who want an honorable end of the war but have difficulty defining what an honorable end is and are willing to trust the president to get it. Those who are not so willing will point out the absence of a new announcement on troop withdrawals or a definite timetable for total withdrawal of U.S. forces, and they may disagree with the president's judgment that the Ho Chi Minh letter was a flat rejection of his own letter. The Ho Chi Minh letter contained, it seems, some of the softest, most accommodating language found in a Communist document concerning the war in Vietnam in recent years.[19]

Kalb offered attentive viewers a different slant on a principal point made by the president. The White House was stung, not only because of this particular commentary but also because of the continuing practice of giving commentators the last word. Encouraged by Patrick Buchanan, Nixon decided to strike back. Under his eye Buchanan drafted the speech that Vice-President Spiro T. Agnew would deliver at a Republican gathering in Des Moines on November 13, 1969. For such a task, according to Safire, Buchanan was totally trusted to be antipress, though not beyond the point of having an occasional chuckle with reporters, from whose ranks he had come and to which he would return. Of the final draft of the speech, Nixon commented to Buchanan, "This really flicks the scab off, doesn't it?"[20]

The episode exemplified the administration's obsession with television and the press. In 1969 so firm was Nixon's command of his war policy of transferring more of the fighting to the South Vietnamese troops ("Vietnamization") and gradually withdrawing American forces that no instant analysis could dent it.

Attacking a national news medium on behalf of the White House was an unusual assignment for a vice-president, especially, it might have seemed, for the lumbering, solemn-looking former governor of Maryland. Nixon, however, had a sense of who could strike a blunt blow. Agnew was just the man because of his sharp tongue and critical attitude toward the press. "He had a strong feeling about the press, which went back to his days in Baltimore," Thomas Whiteside wrote. "He disliked the Baltimore Sun. When he was nominated [for vice-president] in 1968, the Washington Post compared that to the nomination of Caligula's horse and the press made him look like a fool in the 1968 campaign."[21]

Having received advance copies of the Agnew speech, the three major networks made the usual move of covering it live in Des Moines. Normally, they do not broadcast vice-presidential addresses, and it is unlikely they would have done so if Agnew's target had been, say, the automobile industry. The networks' decision was defensive: They wanted to appear fair in airing criticism of themselves. At the same time such heavy coverage built Agnew's attack into a major national story that stirred both friend and foe of television journalism.

Agnew's immediate targets were "instant analysis" and "querulous criticism," and he lost no time condemning Kalb, though not by name. The way he stated the complaint was that "one commentator twice contradicted the president's statement about the exchange of correspondence with Ho Chi Minh." And Agnew continued: "Another challenged the president's abilities as a politician. A third asserted that the president was now 'following the Pentagon line.' Others, by the expressions on their faces, the tone of their questions, and the sarcasm of their responses made clear their sharp disapproval." It was a case, he said, in which 70 million Americans pausing to listen to the president were quickly taken over by a small band of network commentators and self-appointed analysts, the majority of whom expressed, in one way or another, their hostility to what he had to say.[22]

The vice-president dwelt on a theme congenial to conservatives—namely, that commentators lived in Washington or New York, enclaves of liberal thought. "Worse," he said, "they talk constantly to one another, thereby providing artificial reinforcement to their shared viewpoints." He concluded that the commentary on Nixon's speech "emanated from the privileged sanctuary of a network studio and therefore had the apparent dignity of an objective statement."[23] Television stations operate under license of the Federal Communications Commission, Agnew also reminded his audience.

Agnew's speech struck a sensitive nerve. The White House switchboard was tied up all night, and thousands of letters followed, according to Nixon.[24] Many people wrote or telephoned their complaints to networks and local stations. The viciousness and profanity of some of these calls would have delighted the most fanatical critics of instant analysis.

The television industry also reacted. Agnew's speech stirred emotions, elicited rebuttals, and worried executives, especially after Nixon's newly appointed FCC commissioner, Dean Burch, endorsed it. "Nothing strikes terror into the hearts of broadcasters so quickly and leaves so profound a hurt," wrote Sig Mickelson, a former president of CBS News, "as a hint of government action." The threat of license cancellation, even though subtly delivered, is a deadly weapon aimed directly at the pocketbook of licensees.[25] (Years later the "terror" was greatly eased by the deregulation policies of the Carter and Reagan administrations.)

Frank Stanton, president of CBS, accused Agnew of intimidation. Julian Goodman, president of NBC, called the attack an appeal to prejudice. Without doubt, television and the press became scapegoats for many people who were troubled and bewildered by years of social revolution and stalemated war. On the other hand, a number of reputable journalists conceded that the hastiness of instant analysis could lead to rash conclusions or unfair criticism. Even before the Agnew speech Eric

Sevareid, then a senior commentator for CBS in Washington, had warned William S. Paley, chairman of the board of the Columbia Broadcasting System, that instant analysis could produce bad journalism, especially when reporters received no advance text or briefings and had to make judgments on the basis of the spoken word. Four years later, in 1973, Paley announced that CBS would dispense with instant analysis. Instead the network would make the time available for comment by leaders of the political opposition.

"Some of us at CBS rebelled," Daniel Schorr, then a member of the network's Washington bureau, wrote. "We thought it was a cop-out. We assumed that Paley was under some pressure, that he was yielding to the Nixon administration."[26] Schorr, later a commentator for National Public Radio, and other CBS reporters in Washington, including Bernard Kalb (Marvin's brother), Roger Mudd, and George Herman (but conspicuously not Dan Rather), wrote a joint letter of protest to Paley. Paley, however, did not change the new policy. Nevertheless, over the years and with changing administrations CBS has fallen into line with other networks in providing summary and commentary after major speeches and other developments.

The menacing tone of Nixon's and Agnew's attacks affected network executives. It had a "permanently dampening" effect on instant analysis, contends Marvin Kalb, later director of the Joan Schorenstein Barone Center on Press, Politics, and Public Policy at the John F. Kennedy School of Government at Harvard. "Agnewism," if not Agnew, succeeded. "Instant analysis today," Kalb explains, "is a brief, highly produced mini-documentary. Commentators know in advance the kinds of questions they will be asked by the anchor. This gives the impression the news is being analyzed in depth. Nonsense. The Agnew speech, Agnewism had a lasting impact on television news."[27]

This opinion is shared by Roger Mudd and other commentators of that period, who recall that the Nixon administration's hectoring of the networks did have a restraining influence. In a book, *The Chilling Effect in TV News,* Marilyn A. Lashner wrote:

Lawsuits, tax audits, FBI investigations, threats, subpoenas, license challenges, retaliation, and power plays became the hallmarks of [Nixon's] dealings with the press. By orchestrating a barrage of anti-media efforts, the Nixon White House was able to chill dissent in political commentary delivered on network television evening news programs—a feat it was not able to accomplish in nationally syndicated columns in newspapers.[28]

In sum, instant analysis is not the spontaneous, opinionated presentation it once was. The networks are not disposed to offer commentary that is as free-wheeling as it was twenty years ago. On news programs today the anchor routinely puts questions to reporters in the field. This is done to spice up the rhythm of the broadcast and to introduce a note of interpretation and commentary, albeit with queries carefully plotted in advance. Instant analysis is still alive, but it is less in vogue than it once was.

In the view of television news pioneers, now retired and scratching out their memoirs, this was another portent that broadcast news was no longer as weighty as in the golden years of the 1960s. Their catalog of disenchantment was long and growing. Control of the networks has passed to owners who did not consider news a serious, if unprofitable, mandate. Network news had responded to cost cutters by closing bureaus and laying off reporters, producers, and cameramen. News divisions were more and more becoming packagers rather than gatherers of news. Television news in the 1980s was not providing as much information. The serious documentary had become a dodo, the responsibility for providing it handed off to public television. Presentation of news had become personalized through the promotion of million-dollar anchorpersons. A surfeit of supermarket tabloid journalism fouled the airwaves, peephole fare dressed up to look like news. The satellite had ended the networks' monopoly on world news. By the time the nightly network news came on, viewers had seen it all on local programs.

As network news lumbered through its fifth decade, its viewers down, its durability in peril, one question was did it still have the skill to make the important interesting. Another was how could content keep pace with the dazzling advances in broadcast technology.

The uproar over the Agnew attack on the networks on November 13, 1969, gave fresh impetus to White House efforts to discredit the press and coerce television and newspaper coverage into line with administration wishes. In a speech in Montgomery on November 20, Agnew focused his condemnation on newspapers, in particular the *New York Times* and the *Washington Post* because of their power in their respective cities. Again catching a whiff of liberalism in printers' ink, he warned readers not to be deceived into thinking that the *Times* and the *Post* were neutral in their political coverage and editorials. He was especially critical of the Washington Post Company, which also owned *Newsweek* and television properties, including WTOP in Washington. The impact of the Montgomery speech was less than that of the speech ·in Des Moines a week earlier because newspapers have a constitutional right to publish and therefore are less vulnerable to charges of bias than are government-licensed television stations. Some newspapers may have made some changes in their editorial policy in response to Agnew's criticisms, but not the *Los Angeles Times*. Editor Nick B. Williams in an office memorandum asserted that at a moment when "the press is under violent attack it is essential, I think, that we persevere even more diligently along our present course, for any backing down will invite even more reckless and unreasoned assaults upon us."[29]

In 1970 Nixon's staff continued to try to keep him abreast of the attitudes of reporters and commentators. Some memorandums explored new ways to influence television coverage; others sought out new targets for the president to attack as he had television news. Four months after Agnew assailed the networks and the press, Buchanan argued that the time had come for Nixon "to focus a national spotlight" on the Brookings Institution of Washington and on foundations and universities "controlled by the liberal wing of the Democratic Party, that are being used to advance their causes politically and ideologically." Offering to do the research, he added: "We could initiate the same kind of national criticism of these hostile centers of power that we did with the networks, forcing them into the spotlight, where they might have to tread with more circumspection than in the past."[30]

On the front page of the *New York Times* on April 10, 1970, a subhead read, "President Bitter." The story, by Robert B. Semple, Jr., was about a statement Nixon had made to reporters, denouncing senators who the day before had refused to confirm G. Harrold Carswell for the Supreme Court. No longer was it possible, according to Nixon, to win confirmation for the Supreme Court of any appellate judge from the South who believed in strict construction of the Constitution. Carswell was the second nominee of Nixon's to fit this description. The Senate had earlier rejected his nomination of Clement F. Haynsworth, Jr., also a conservative southern judge. Nixon, Semple wrote, "talked rapidly and evenly in words that conveyed bitterness and anger."[31]

On April 21 Nixon sent a memorandum to Herb Klein and Ronald Ziegler in which, referring to himself as "RN," he disputed Semple's ascription of bitterness to him:

We had scores of letters from all over the country saying that they had seen me on television and that the Times was completely wrong in that assessment. This had led RN to the conclusion that all future press conferences will be televised and that none will be held without television cameras. The only time that RN will see any press without television will be when he has a private interview with a columnist who will not editorialize in his news writing.[32]

On August 14, 1970, the Federal Communications Commission ruled that the television networks must afford prime time for presentation of contrasting viewpoints to the president's Vietnam War policy. In a memorandum to Haldeman on September 25, Charles W. Colson, special counsel to the president, said that the networks were "terribly nervous" over the ruling. He added, "They are also apprehensive about us. Although they tried to disguise this, it was obvious. The harder I pressed them (CBS and NBC) the more accommodating, cordial and almost apologetic they become. Stanton for all his bluster is the most insecure of all."[33]

Nixon insisted that members of the White House staff closely monitor each network and every television program, day or night, on which political figures might appear. When anti-administration views were expressed, authorized officials on the staff were to get in touch with the news directors. "This must be done on a constant drumfire basis," Haldeman directed Alexander Butterfield. He then added: "The President also wants a similar monitoring program set up on the *New York Times,* the *Washington Post, Time* magazine and *Newsweek* for the same purpose."[34]

The appearance on NBC's "Tonight Show" of actress Shirley MacLaine, an antiwar activist, did not go unnoticed by the White House. In response Butterfield proposed "another letter-writing campaign to the network" to protest MacLaine's "diatribe."[35]

After the historian Barbara Tuchman made "strongly anti-Administration remarks" on the "CBS Morning News," the White House arranged for Rep. Donald Rumsfeld to appear on the program a day or so later. "Rummy was great," exclaimed the monitoring report, "and for 6 minutes went right down the line re our progress and current position on the Vietnam issue."[36]

On November 30, 1970, Nixon told Haldeman in a memorandum that it was time for Klein and Ziegler to bring up to date their listing on "media people"—"those who are for, those who are neutral, and those who are against [us]." Nixon added:

We must continue on a case-by-case basis to attack the press' credibility when it deserves such an attack, but blunderbuss, broad-range attacks should be avoided. . . . We should spend less time with columnists and others who are hopelessly against us and, as Jim Keogh [a special assistant to the president] suggested we should make more effective use of the calculated leak.[37]

Klein and Ziegler submitted their updated list on December 18. A brief random sample of the ratings, in descending order, follows:

Excellent—Victor Lasky, Ralph de Toledano, David Lawrence, and James J. Kilpatrick, all columnists, and Willard Edwards of the *Chicago Tribune,* and Jerry Greene of the *New York Daily News.*
Very good—Richard L. Wilson of Cowles Publications.
Good—Sol Kohler of the Philadelphia *Evening Bulletin.*
Moderate—James Batten, then of the Knight-Ridder Washington bureau, Thomas O'Neill of the *Baltimore Sun* and Alan L. Otten of the *Wall Street Journal.*
Disenchanted—John Pierson of the *Wall Street Journal.*
Getting worse—James Reston of the *New York Times.*
Can be helpful on specific plants—Jack Anderson, a columnist.
Poor, big on EMK [Sen. Edward M. Kennedy]—Robert Healy of the *Boston Globe.*
Anti-administration, inflammatory—Tom Braden, a columnist.
Bad, bad, bad—Stuart H. Loory of the *Los Angeles Times,* later an executive of CNN.[38]

On July 17, 1970, *Life* carried an article concerning the retirement of Chet Huntley, in which the old standby of the "Huntley-Brinkley Report" reminisced about presidents he had covered. Of Nixon he said, "the shallowness of the man overwhelms me; the fact that he is President frightens me."[39] To Lawrence Higby, Haldeman's chief assistant, the comment was one more proof of network bias. It was at this point that Higby wrote the secret memorandum to Colson, declaring, "We need to get some creative thinking going on an attack on Huntley for his statements. . . . The point behind this whole thing is that we don't care about Huntley—he's going to leave [NBC] anyway. What we are trying to do here is to tear down the institution."[40]

Even before the end of 1970, Haldeman brooded over relations with television and the press in connection with the next presidential election two years hence. "In our media relations," he said in a draft memorandum, "we should take the initiative to ease tensions a little by establishing good relations now to the maximum extent we can and then wait until late 1972 to start roasting them again."[41]

Good relations were not established. Nixon was ready to "fight." In a memorandum of January 5, 1971, he told Haldeman:

We have got to make a continuing fight on the fact that the networks are biased and that it always shows through in their inordinate emphasis on any negative stories in regard to the Administration. . . .

We have to start playing much more aggressively and much harder in knocking down false stories and building up our positive points and if our present staff doesn't have the stomach to take on this assignment we are going to have to find someone who does have it. Maybe we will have to give Colson a crack at it.[42]

Colson had a reputation as a "hit man."

On February 23, 1971, CBS ran a controversial documentary entitled "The Selling of the Pentagon" and narrated by Roger Mudd. With the fighting in Vietnam as a provocative background, the program gave a disconcerting portrayal of the large sums spent by the Pentagon on war propaganda. The program also delved into the comfortable relationship between the Pentagon and corporate contractors, echoing the admonitions against the military-industrial complex enunciated in President Eisenhower's 1961 farewell address. Although television critics praised the documentary on the whole, administration officials and conservatives in Congress excoriated it. The producers had skewed the context of certain interviews with military officials. A subcommittee of the House Committee on Interstate and Foreign Commerce subpoenaed the outtakes, or unused film segments. Frank Stanton, who was the main witness and the lightning rod for the network, refused to produce them. The full committee then recommended that he be held in contempt of Congress. The House refused to do so by a vote of 226 to 121. Between the time of the showing of the program and final action in the House, Nixon had invited several network officials in for what was sometimes referred to by the staff as the ongoing warfare. Afterward Nixon and Colson sat around laughing and engaging in tall talk about how the executives had had their arms twisted and been forced like cowards into a corner. Colson was convinced that Nixon and he had persuaded William Paley to tone down Rather's broadcasts. One of their biggest laughs, according to Colson's account, was how they had got Stanton to "squirm" and "cower" over "The Selling of the Pentagon."[43]

When critical articles on Nixon's twelve-month performance were published, around New Year's 1971, Magruder was instructed to initiate through the Republican National Committee letters to editors along the line that "TV has given the President his standing with the people and the print media no longer has the influence that it did."[44] Haldeman asked William Carruthers, president of a Hollywood television production company, who had been brought to the White House for just such a purpose, to help improve Nixon's appearances on television. "The President," Haldeman wrote in a memorandum on February 9, 1971, "would like you to give some careful thought to the question of colors and styles of suits, shirts, ties, etc., that would be best for his appearance on television. He will be buying some new spring suits and would like to know what kind of things he should look for." Evidently, this was not a matter to be taken lightly, for Haldeman added, "You may want to have some test runs on various things." Moreover, Haldeman said, "the president wants it clearly understood that before he moves into any event where there is camera coverage the TV men should come in and tell him what to do. . . . This would apply to getting off the airplane, walking across the garden or anything else where there is camera coverage."[45] Yet a month later in an interview with Barbara Walters on the "Today Show," Nixon declared, "The president, with the enormous responsibilities he has, must not be constantly preening in front of a mirror, wondering whether or not he is getting across as this kind of individual or that."[46] Nixon and his staff, however, were obsessed with wondering how he was "getting across." Indeed, preoccupation with Nixon's image had extended even to the tree-lighting ceremony the previous Christmas. The president was cautioned by Ziegler against letting a chosen child on the program get full credit in the press for lighting the tree. The president and the child should throw the switch together.[47]

Nixon was eager to have his staff plant ideas for columns favorable to the administration. While aboard Air Force One on January 14, 1971, he was pleased at the thought of how he might be pictured by a columnist as finessing the newspapers. In a memorandum to Haldeman he said: "For future columns, I think one on the theme of RN dismaying his critics by going over their heads on TV would be quite timely."[48]

Then he remembered having been told by Kissinger of a talk with James Reston, who asked, as Nixon remembered the story, "why RN did not get along better with the press in view of his handling of [an] interview and his ability to cope with intellectual subjects." The incident inspired Nixon to add to his memorandum: "Perhaps it is time that a column be written as to why the press doesn't get along with RN rather than constantly the subject being discussed on the basis that RN 'doesn't understand' the press and that somehow his press relations are responsible for the antagonism of the press."[49]

Nixon was pleased with the way a televised interview with network reporters came off early in January 1971, but then his enthusiasm faded. He told Haldeman:

I recognize that the problem we have is infinitely greater than that which confronted any President, except for possibly Johnson, in this century—a basically antagonistic television and press corps. What we have to do here is to play those few that are our friends and then just work as hard as we possibly can on those that are hopelessly against us but who, for pragmatic selfish reasons, will now and then give us a break if we give them a little tidbit.[50]

Unfortunately, Nixon seldom, if ever, mentions in his memorandums the names of the journalists to whom he is referring. This makes it next to impossible to assess the merits of his specific complaints. Neither do his memorandums of that period set the background for his difficult relationship with journalists. To a large extent it was the Vietnam War. The conspicuous difficulties between President Johnson and the press, which Nixon mentions, carried over into the Nixon administration because of the "credibility gap." The deceptions of the press by officials in Washington and Saigon during Johnson's conduct of the war left reporters more skeptical and more demanding. This attitude was intensified after Nixon's sudden thrust into Cambodia despite election campaign hints that he had a plan for ending the Vietnam War. Reporters' probing, as the memorandums indicate, was a constant irritant to Nixon and his staff. Needless to say, the kettle boiled after the story of the Watergate burglary broke in the fall of 1972.

Even the traditional ribbing politicians receive in the annual dinners of the White House Correspondents Association, the Radio-Television Correspondents Association, and the Gridiron Club was too much for Nixon. After the White House correspondents' dinner in 1971 he complained to Haldeman that reporters were "more bad-mannered and vicious than usual. This bears out my theory that treating them with considerably more contempt is in the long run a more productive policy."[51]

Nixon acknowledged that he had some friends among the journalists and did not wish to lose them through ill treatment of the others. The way to handle the problem, he told Haldeman, is

to deliberately invite our friends to events where it will be a compliment for them to come. For example . . . for White House Dinners, White House Receptions,

Church Services, or any other event in which I participate. I want *no one whatever invited* from the press or radio unless he is a friend of ours or, at the very worst, neutral (i.e., a wire service reporter). By friend, of course, I do not mean someone who writes positively all the time. I do mean someone who is not in the other corner.

Perhaps the best thing to do here is simply to submit the list to me because I'm afraid that even though our press boys [in the White House press offices] have been around for 2½ years, I should not expect them to know as much about these people as I have learned in 24 years.[52]

In a speech to the Knights of Columbus in New York on August 17, 1971, Nixon committed himself to financial aid to parochial schools, long an intensely controversial issue. Later, on CBS, Daniel Schorr, one of the network's most probing reporters and a recognized liberal, quoted sources in the administration and in Catholic circles as saying there were no plans for such a program. Haldeman later recalled what happened:

The president was furious. To his own detriment, he lapsed into old-time vindictiveness. "I want an FBI check on that bastard. And no stalling this time."

I called Higby who said no problem. Schorr had a White House pass which meant that he has been "cleared" for security by the FBI, so there must be a file. He called the FBI and asked for Schorr's file.[53]

Within a day or so, Schorr discovered that FBI agents were on his trail, questioning his employers and friends about his background. It was an outrage against the constitutional guarantees of freedom of speech and of the press. The *Washington Post* learned about it and reported the story on the front page. By Haldeman's own account, Nixon had asked for an FBI check but Haldeman only asked Higby for the FBI file. How the procedure came full circle has never been explained. Haldeman added:

We had to concoct a cover story one shade away from absurdity: the White House was considering Schorr for a federal job. Not one of our grander moments. But by then I was used to the trauma inspired by the hatred between Nixon and the press.

I can't remember all of the reporters and newspeople [the president] asked me to "go after" in one way or the other.[54]

On November 5, 1971, Colson sent a memorandum to John Scali, a former ABC reporter who had joined the White House staff as a consultant to the president. In the memo he revealed his true feelings about one network commentator, John Chancellor of NBC:

When I suggested you call the networks today regarding the unemployment story, you told me this was one we could rely on to give us a fair break. Chancellor's performance you should rerun. It's scandalous, yellow, shabby journalism (which as you know is pretty scandalous, yellow, and shabby). We should not bother to call him, we should break his goddamned nose. But, it's our fault because we rely upon the integrity of news broadcasters of which there isn't any.[55]

Television news—its programs, its executives, its reporters, its anchors—kept the Nixon White House in a stew. A respite of sorts came on January 21, 1972, doubtless the high point of Nixon's presidency, when he landed in Beijing to break ground for a new and friendlier relationship with China.

10

Nixon in China and Watergate

In the opera *Nixon in China* (music by John Adams, libretto by Alice Goodman) the character Richard Nixon steps from his plane in Beijing in February 1972 and sings to Chinese Premier Zou Enlai:

> It's prime time in the U.S.A. . . . .
> They watch us now;
> The three main networks' colors glow . . .

Later, in responding to Zou's toast in the Great Hall of the People, Nixon sings again:

> And millions more hear what we say
> Through satellite technology
> Than ever heard a public speech
> Before.

Indeed, one out of six people on earth could see it, according to the Communications Satellite Corporation (Comsat).[1] The opera also had it right about prime time. When Nixon arrived in China it was 7:30 P.M. on the American West Coast, 10:30 P.M. in the East. John J. O'Connor in the *New York Times* called the "impact and power" of television reporting of Nixon's trip "unique, perhaps still beyond full comprehension." He added that the future of diplomacy and history would no doubt . reflect the "profound change" introduced by "thrusting the main characters onto the central stage in homes around the world."[2]

As statecraft, Nixon's opening of a new era in Sino-American relations was his ultimate achievement in office. As public relations artistry, it was the "Sistine Chapel" of H. R. Haldeman, Nixon's chief of staff, or so someone remarked.

Although Nixon's visit turned a page of history, the agreements themselves represented only a modest beginning. The president pledged a gradual
withdrawal of American forces from Taiwan and a gradual increase in
contacts and exchanges between Washington and Beijing. What was truly
remarkable was not the diplomatic accomplishments, as important as
they were, but the television coverage of the visit. Preparations for the
television extravaganza went on for months. Nixon's staff worked with
network executives in New York and Washington. Gen. Alexander M.
Haig, Jr., then Henry Kissinger's deputy on the National Security Council, took a final survey party, including seven network representatives, to
China. Experts studied camera angles and lighting problems at Beijing
airport, the Forbidden City, the Ming tombs, the Great Wall, and other
national attractions. The air force transported across the Pacific Ocean
to China a television ground station and a twenty-four-foot dish an-
tenna—a load of forty thousand pounds. When Nixon arrived at the
Great Wall, Max Frankel of the *New York Times* reported that only two
of the two-story watchtowers along the length of the fifteen-hundred-
mile structure were adequate for network needs. Only those two, he wrote,
"can accommodate three rival network anchormen, with full crew, several tons of gear, including remote color cameras, several miles of cable
and several hundred camera-toting extras dangling from the battle-
ments."[3]

When Nixon's party, including Mrs. Nixon, Kissinger, and Secretary
of State William P. Rogers, arrived at Beijing airport the reception was
reserved. No balloons were flying, no flags fluttering. The Chinese were
playing in low key. The spectators included the arriving reporters, a small
company of interpreters, a few dozen Chinese officials, and a five-hundred-
man military honor guard. Nixon strode smartly forward and shook hands
with Zhou Enlai. The military band played "The Star-Spangled Banner,"
and Nixon and Zhou rode off together through uncrowded thorough-
fares. A day or so later Walter Cronkite attracted a mob when he was
filming on Hsi Dan Street. Nixon's talks with Zhou and Chairman Mao
Zedong were private, of course. But millions of Americans at their television sets avidly watched the public dinners and receptions, at which
Nixon ate with chopsticks, listened to a Chinese band play "Turkey in
the Straw" and "Home on the Range," and exchanged toasts.

Hatless but wearing a coat with a fur collar, Nixon arrived at the
Great Wall on February 24. In terms of the networks' master planning,
everything began to click. "Walter Cronkite had already filmed his 'Good

evening' from the Great Wall in the brilliant sunshine of a chill winter morn," Frankel reported. "Eric Sevareid had already pronounced an interpretation of the great conquest. Only ten minutes of Mr. Nixon's half-hour inspection tour were to be filmed before the film reels would be rushed back to Beijing for swift relay across the ocean."[4]

For several hundred yards Nixon moved sure-footedly past the firing slits on the wall, revealing, Frankel reported, that he had memorized the position of every major camera emplacement. At one point he introduced Barbara Walters, then of NBC, to his escort, Deputy Prime Minister Li Hsien-nien, explaining that she had been on television in the United States that very morning, describing a sports show in Beijing. Television coverage continued without a hitch until, of a sudden, the presidential party inadvertently cut off Cronkite's path to the film courier departing for Beijing. At the prospect of CBS going dark on Nixon at the Great Wall of China, Haldeman rushed to clear the way. With the aid of a commandeered vehicle, Cronkite made it to the studio in time.[5]

On the evening of February 28, 1972, Nixon returned to Andrews Air Force Base, where he was welcomed by members of the cabinet, Congress, and the diplomatic corps. The general reaction back home to his trip was favorable. Some Republican conservatives, still guided by the dictums of the China lobby and Gen. Douglas MacArthur, were angry at Nixon's commitment to withdraw troops from Taiwan. However, the president's *bête noir*, Sen. Edward M. Kennedy, was generous in his praise of the trip. Another nemesis, the *Washington Post*, described Nixon's visit to China as "a great event, which speaks for itself and speaks well for the President."[6] Obviously pleased with his reception, Nixon said that his talks in China had laid a basis "for a structure of peace."

One year later, on February 28, 1973, Nixon and John W. Dean III, counsel to the president, were closeted, searching for a way out of the Watergate morass. The break-in and bugging of the Democratic National Committee headquarters in the Watergate complex had occurred on June 17, 1972, but Nixon's deep trouble over Watergate did not begin until after the 1972 presidential election, in which he swamped Sen. George McGovern of South Dakota. Nixon ran away with the spoils partly because McGovern's campaign was a shambles almost from the start. His running mate, Sen. Thomas Eagleton of Missouri, was disclosed to have undergone psychiatric treatment and had little choice but to resign from the ticket. Nixon carried all the states except Massachusetts, as well as the District of Columbia. Seven hundred and fifty-three daily newspapers supported him, compared with only fifty-six for McGovern.[7]

Nevertheless, Nixon and Patrick J. Buchanan, one of his speechwriters and a voice of the right wing, were beside themselves over journalistic treatment. Before the start of the campaign, Nixon told Buchanan, "It is very important . . . that the media be effectively discredited."[8] After the campaign Buchanan warned Nixon that a "small, ideological clique has managed to acquire monopoly control of the most powerful medium of communication known to man." He insisted that "this ideological cartel" must "be broken up. Already the Sevareids, before their captive audience of this world, are doing dirt on the President's victory . . . [T]his must be viewed as a question of 'power.' " The Public Broadcasting Service must be purged "of that clique of Nixon-haters who have managed to nest there at taxpayer expense."[9] For such grand plans, however, time was growing short.

CBS scheduled two reports on Watergate by Walter Cronkite. The first was broadcast on the evening news on October 27, 1972, and ran for nearly fifteen minutes. The second apparently was to appear on October 30 but was delayed for a day and turned out to be shorter than the first. It was later confirmed that Charles Colson, the aggressive special counsel to the president, had complained about campaign coverage in calls to William S. Paley, chairman of CBS, and Richard Salant, then president of CBS News. The two of them denied that the calls had had anything to do with the delay and the shorter Cronkite report. But at a cocktail party shortly afterward, Colson taunted CBS reporter Daniel Schorr: "Well, Mr. Schorr, we didn't stop your goddam Watergate spectacular, but we sure cut you down a bit, didn't we?"[10]

Anyone connected, however tenuously, with CBS was suspect in Nixon's mind. After his reelection Nixon dropped from the cabinet his able secretary of commerce, Peter G. Peterson. Peterson wondered why, especially because Nixon had once told him that he was the greatest secretary of commerce since Herbert C. Hoover in the 1920s. Colson explained to Peterson in so many words that he had not properly distanced himself from CBS or from the *Washington Post*. Peterson had entertained, though never accepted, feelers about succeeding Frank Stanton as president of CBS. Colson also faulted Peterson for his attendance at parties given by Katharine Graham, publisher of the *Post*. Peterson had even been a weekend guest at her country home.[11]

It was the events of 1973 that dragged Nixon upon the stage of the

Watergate scandals. The seven men, agents of the Committee to Reelect President Nixon, who had been indicted for the break-in and bugging of the Democratic headquarters, were brought to trial. One of them, James W. McCord, Jr., confessed in a letter read in the courtroom by Judge John J. Sirica that political pressure had been applied to the defendants to plead guilty and remain silent. McCord also stated that perjury had been committed in the trial and that higher-ups, not named, were implicated in the crime. From that point on, the defense of the president began to crumble.

On May 17, 1973, the Senate Select Committee on Presidential Campaign Activities, chaired by Sam J. Ervin, Jr., opened nationally televised hearings on Watergate that continued for thirty-seven days. The three major networks devoted 319 hours to coverage. The hearings gave the Public Broadcasting System a great boost. At first some PBS station manages were hesitant about carrying the hearings because of that network's dependence on public funds. In the end, however, demands from viewers were so strong that 92 percent of the stations carried the hearings in the evening hours through delayed tape. These stations reported receiving 82,000 letters from their audiences, some bearing cash contributions. Membership drives on the air brought in another $1,250,000.

Fascinated audiences across the country heard testimony linking Nixon to an attempted cover-up of the break-in and to startling disclosures that many of his private discussions had been secretly recorded by him. After a series of court fights, tapes were released. They provided the basis for Nixon's ultimate downfall and shocked the public because of the profanity and the coarseness of his language. By mid-1973 a number of impeachment resolutions had been introduced in the House. Nixon wrote in his memoirs that he believed "the main danger of being impeached would come precisely from the public's being conditioned to the idea that I was going to be impeached. In the end, therefore, it would come down to a race for public support: in other words, a campaign."[12]

Nixon hoped that the public would tire of Watergate and pressure Congress, the press, and television to move on to other matters. The continuous heavy flow of television news and press coverage about Watergate frustrated Nixon. "The congressional and media assault and the controversy over the White House tapes had so embroiled me in Watergate that the public was increasingly seeing me as the roadblock, and their desire to move on to other things was affecting their willingness to have me removed. Unless I could do something to stem this tide, it would sweep me out of office."[13]

In his "campaign" to retain the presidency, Nixon turned to television. It had saved his career in 1952, and he hoped that it would again. Nixon formally addressed the nation about Watergate for the first time on April 30, 1973. In this prime-time televised speech he lamented the resignations of Haldeman and John Ehrlichman earlier that day. The very mention of the resignations, however, further undermined his public support. As Nixon was well aware, the departure of those two loyal assistants from the White House intensified public suspicion that the president knew about the Watergate break-in. In the speech Nixon pictured himself as a president who dealt with momentous issues and left the gritty chores of politics to subordinates. He did his best to convince the nation that he was not involved. Some believed him. At a cabinet meeting the next day he was given an ovation. Republican National Chairman George Bush assured him that "Republicans everywhere are strongly supporting you."[14] Such an assurance did not mean much. Polls indicated that his popularity was declining. The transcendent issue now was not the break-in at Watergate but rather obstruction of justice in an attempt to cover up the crime. If any Republicans were elated over the April 30th speech, Nixon was not one of them: "I gave the impression that I had known nothing at all about the cover-up until my March 21 [1973] meeting with Dean. I indicated that once I had learned about it I had acted with . . . dispatch to end it. In fact, I had known some of the details of the cover-up before March 21."[15] Nixon described the days that followed as "an increasingly desperate search for ways to limit the damage to my friends, to my administration, and to myself."[16]

Late in 1973, he made a campaign-style trip through the South, the last region where patches of support for his presidency remained. He appeared on national television in several cities. One stop that seemed especially appealing was Disney World in Orlando, Florida, but even that last refuge of fantasy turned into a trap. Managing editors of the Associated Press had assembled in Orlando for a meeting. As a clever way of holding what amounted to a televised press conference with reporters excluded, Nixon appeared before the managing editors on November 17 for a question-and-answer session. It was such a farce of meaningless interrogation that he felt obliged to ask himself a question about the scandals and answered as follows: "People have a right to know whether or not their president is a crook. Well, I am not a crook."[17] No national television audience ever listened to a more enduringly painful utterance by a president of the United States.

Perhaps the centerpiece of Nixon's defense was a performance he staged from the White House on the night of April 29, 1974. At nine o'clock he was ready, posed at his desk in front of a table with a bust of Lincoln and fifty books in pale green bindings stamped with the gold presidential seal. Never in the history of the presidency, he began, "have records that are so private been made so public." The books, he said, contained transcripts of White House tapes subpoenaed in the investigation by the House Judiciary Committee. He assured the American people that he was turning the material over in compliance with the subpoenas and that "everything that is relevant is included."[18]

Everything that was on the tapes was *not* included—only that which the president considered relevant. The subpoena had called for tapes, not transcripts. All the material on the desk would have filled a book about the size of the Manhattan telephone directory. One volume, however, would not have looked as imposing on television as fifty, even though the latter were loose-leaf binders, each containing an average of about twenty-five pages. Despite the careful stage management, the performance flopped. Nixon's good fortune with television news over the years had about run out.

The language of Nixon and his associates in the transcripts that were released to the public was atrocious and caused a hullabaloo. The transcripts became the reading sensation of the year. The Associated Press and United Press International flooded their wires with it. Fifty newspapers published the full text.[19] Television news was filled with quotes. Paperback publishers rushed out editions of the transcripts that overnight became bestsellers, with some 3 million copies in print. Senate Republican leader Hugh Scott of Pennsylvania called the transcripts "deplorable, disgusting, shabby, immoral." In the words of Joseph Alsop, long regarded as friendly to the administration, the language might have emanated from the "back room of a second-rate advertising agency in a suburb of hell." The evangelist Billy Graham, a friend of Nixon's, lifted his eyes to heaven, and the *Chicago Tribune* demanded that the president resign.

Ultimately, congressional investigators found a great deal more in the transcripts that they considered relevant than Nixon did. An example was a recorded discussion among Haldeman, Nixon, and Dean, threatening "damnable, damnable problems" to the *Washington Post* and its attorney, Edward Bennett Williams. Within a week it was obvious that the release had been, as J. Anthony Lukas wrote, "a massive miscalculation by the President, an unqualified disaster . . . in its impact on his standing in the country."[20] Needless to say, the "relevant" transcripts did not satisfy the House Judiciary Committee in its demand for sixty-four tapes. Nixon refused to release any more of the contents. With momentous consequences, the issue went to the Supreme Court.

Across the cover of the June 24, 1974, issue of *Time* slanted a banner: "Nixon's Trip. Seeking a Needed Lift." The cover photograph showed Nixon and Anwar Sadat standing in the rear of an open car as it moved through dense crowds in a motorcade in Egypt. The article set the trip in its true context, Watergate:

Like the prophets of old, the President of the U.S. demonstrated last week that he is not without honor save perhaps in his own country. From the moment Richard Nixon set foot on Egyptian soil, beginning his historic seven-day trip to four Arab nations and Israel, the huzzas and hosannas fell like sweet rain. For the President, coming out of the parched Watergate wasteland of Washington, the praise and the cheers of multitudes were welcome indeed, particularly since each stop was beamed in living color back to the living rooms of the U.S.[21]

In the increasingly depressing twenty-three months since China, Nixon had hoped that recognition of his role as a peacemaker might improve his standing at home. Congressional inquiry had moved from the Senate to the House. The House Judiciary Committee, chaired by Peter W. Rodino, Jr., was working its way in closed sessions toward a decision on whether to recommend the impeachment of the president. Because of the timing of the trip to the Middle East, Nixon's critics called it "video diplomacy" or "impeachment diplomacy"—a calculated attempt to convince millions of television viewers in America that Nixon's efforts for peace made peanuts of the allegations being pawed over by a bunch of congressmen, most of them Democrats. On his return to the United States, Nixon wrote in his diary:

We must have gotten some lift from the trip, although it seems almost impossible to break through the polls. . . . As I pointed out to [Ron] Ziegler, when he was telling me about the five or six minutes that we were on each network while we were away, I said, "Compare that with the eight or ten minutes that they have been hearing on Watergate for over a year!"[22]

Back in Washington for only five days, Nixon took off again, this time for Moscow. At the summit meeting, Soviet Party Chairman Leonid Brezhnev was friendly but uncooperative. Uncertainty about Nixon's tenure inhibited Brezhnev in negotiation. The question of Nixon's guilt, not diplomacy, remained the focus of national and international attention.

On July 24, 1974, soon after the president's return from Moscow, the House Judiciary Committee opened its doors to the public. Through them flooded the press and television for the final debates and the voting on articles of impeachment. Television lights were suspended on poles from the high ceiling. Two television cameras looked down from a one-story platform in the center of the room facing the two-tiered dais. Another camera stood in a corner of the room, and a fourth was positioned behind Chairman Rodino. At 7:45 P.M. he called the committee to order. Thirty-five hours and thirty-four minutes of hearings followed over the next several days. An estimated 90 million Americans watched all or part of the epic drama on television. What made it particularly gripping were the close-up shots of the members as they solemnly, thoughtfully explained their views. Political motivations were not absent, to be sure. But on the whole the higher purpose of the thirty-eight men and women on the committee was recognized all over the country. Historian Howard Fields wrote: "The committee's demeanor and impressiveness . . . probably did more than anything else had up to that point to convince citizens that considering impeachment of Nixon was not part of a vendetta after all."[23]

Until the hearings, none of the members of the committee was well known nationally. The words they spoke commanded respect. Rep. Jack Brooks, a Texas Democrat, told his colleagues:

We must put to rest the argument that the corruption we have witnessed in the last five years is only an extension of what has always been done. I do not share this view of those who hold that all our presidents have lied, have broken the law, have compromised the Constitution. And if George Washington accepted bribes, it would not make bribery a virtue, nor would it be grounds for overlooking such acts by his successor.[24]

Rep. William S. Cohen of Maine, a Republican who voted for each of the three articles of impeachment that were adopted, also addressed himself to the argument that other presidents besides Nixon had been guilty of misconduct, for which they had not been impeached. "The answer," Cohen said, "is that democracy, that solid rock of our system, may be eroded away by degree, and its survival will be determined by the degree to which we will tolerate those silent and subtle subversions that absorb it slowly into the rule of a few in the name of what is right."[25]

Rep. Thomas F. Railsback of Illinois, who attracted keen attention as the first Republican on the committee to vote for the first impeachment article presented for a vote, said:

I have agonized over this particular inquiry. . . . I regard it as an awesome responsibility, one that I did not relish at all, one that is particularly difficult for me because we are considering a man, Richard Nixon, who has twice been in my district campaigning for me, that I regard as a friend, that he only treated me kindly whenever I had occasion to be with him [who] has done many wonderful things for this country . . . and someday the historians are going to realize the contributions that he has made.[26]

On July 30, the committee by comfortable margins completed its votes recommending to the House articles of impeachment of a president for the first time since the case of Andrew Johnson, who was impeached by the House but not convicted by the Senate 106 years before. The articles against Nixon were based on obstruction of justice, abuse of power, and defiance of congressional subpoenaes. If the House approved the Judiciary Committee's recommendations, Nixon's ultimate hope was that the Senate would not judge him guilty. But before the Judiciary Committee had a chance to submit its formal report to the House, there was another calamitous revelation about President Nixon.

One of the Oval Office conversations on tape Nixon had agreed to surrender to Judge John J. Sirica was disclosed on August 5 to reveal that, contrary to his previous public statements, Nixon had ordered a cover-up of the Watergate break-in, an act of obstruction of justice, on June 27, 1972. That was six days after the Watergate crime. With this disclosure all remaining political support for Nixon collapsed, not only in Congress but in the country. In November 1972, 47,165,232 Americans had voted for Nixon—up to that time, the greatest number to back a presidential candidate in U.S. history. It is a telling commentary on the conduct of the hearings and the power of television to broadcast them to every corner of the country that twenty-one months later no body or faction of Republicans rallied against the recommendations of impeachment.

With its great reach television news had fueled the feeling, sparked by the press, that Nixon had abused the presidency and had to leave it.

The day Nixon left the White House he said farewell to his cabinet and staff. "Let the record show," he sarcastically commented, "that this is one of those spontaneous things we always arrange whenever the president speaks." Then he added: "and it will be so reported by the press."[27] A parting gibe of sorts but not his last word on the subject. In the January 14, 1989, issue of *TV Guide*, which appeared just before inauguration day, Nixon gave President-elect George Bush the benefit of his thinking on relations with the press and television. "Of all the institutions arrayed with and against a President," he wrote, "none controls his fate more than television." Newspapers and magazines were important, he continued, but only if their work is picked up and amplified by television. In his honeymoon period a new president might think reporters were his friends, but their relationship was "inherently adversarial."

TV reporters always claim to be "speaking for the people," but they are really speaking primarily for themselves. In many ways they are political actors, just like the President, mindful of their ratings, careful of preserving and building. A President must respect them for that power, but he can never entirely trust them.[28]

Nixon also urged Bush to regard television producers "with innate suspicion." As for television commentators, "Being more interesting is infinitely more important than being more responsible." Television, he told Bush, "is an entertainment medium, not an educational one. The combative, even obnoxious, personalities are the most successful."[29]

The president-elect was urged to be aggressive in his dealings with the press and the networks. The "media don't have to be convinced. They have to be outfoxed, outflanked and outperformed. Unless the President finds a way to use them to pursue his own agenda, they will use his failures to pursue theirs." Nixon had a lot to say about televised press conferences. They should be held at night, he insisted.

Daytime press conferences leave the decision about what makes the evening news solely in the hands of TV editors, who, unless there is a major news event, will always opt for the superficial, the entertaining, the embarrassing or the frivolous before they work their way down to the substantive. Prime-time viewers see the whole man and the complete performance. . . .

[Press conferences] have developed into revolting spectacles where reporters vie with each other to see who can play the best game of "Gotcha!" with the President of the United States. But a news conference is only in the President's interests when it achieves some purpose other than satisfying the media's insatiable thirst for confrontation.[30]

Finally, Nixon advised Bush "not to be reluctant to freeze out those whose pervasively unfair coverage goes beyond the pale. The only leverage he has for encouraging fair coverage is control over further access to himself and others in his Government."[31]

President Bush paid little attention. He didn't control access to himself and others in his government tightly. He didn't play "Gotcha" with the press, and the press didn't play "Gotcha" with him. On the whole his relations with newspaper and television reporters were friendly.

11

Infuriating pictures from Iran: television news, Jimmy Carter, and the Iranian hostage crisis

It was a Sunday morning in Tehran, capital of Iran, but, as usual, the U.S. Embassy was open for business. The date was November 4, 1979, an explosive time in Iranian history. The preceding February the monarchy of Mohammad Reza Shah Pahlavi had been overthrown by the followers of Ayatollah Ruhollah Khomeini, an Islamic religious leader of the Shi'ite sect. To the dismay of Americans, the shah, long their ally, had been forced into exile abroad. On this day he was a patient in a New York hospital, suffering from terminal cancer. An angry mob of Iranians, many of them students, gathered outside the embassy and chanted anti-American slogans. The recent admission of the shah to the United States infuriated them. The revolutionary government wanted him returned to Iran to stand trial for crimes against the people. The U.S. government knew this, but no one in the embassy or in Washington was prepared for what suddenly happened.

Instead of just standing in the street, chanting, a horde of militant "students" scrambled over the embassy walls and shoved their way into the first floor of the chancery building. Members of the staff and of the diplomatic corps barricaded themselves behind steel doors, but sixty-five of them were captured by the Iranians.

When the word reached the United States, Stan Opotowsky, director of ABC News, made a quick move that proved a bonanza for the American Broadcasting Company. He ordered Bob Dyk, a little known reporter for ABC radio in London, to fly to Tehran to handle television coverage. CBS and NBC hesitated just long enough to allow Iran time to close the gate behind Dyk. None of the three networks then had a bureau in Tehran—nor did American newspapers or magazines. During the next few days CBS dispatched five crews and NBC three, but all were turned back at the Tehran airport. ABC, which had long trailed its two rivals in the field of news, exploited its headstart in Iran. It provided the most extensive coverage of the hostage story. ABC also seized upon this major newsbreak to begin the first regular late-night news program. In a matter of months this effort evolved into a vital and enduring news program with a large audience: "Nightline," with Ted Koppel. With its established 6:30 P.M. news, ABC thus doubled the amount of news available nightly on any network.

On November 8, at about the time CBS and NBC were finally able to get crews into Tehran, ABC ran the first of its nightly special broadcasts titled "The Crisis in Iran: America Held Hostage." According to ABC, the program reached an average of 12 million viewers each night at 11:30 P.M. when it came on.[1] Also the late-night television audience as a whole increased by almost 4 million during the first weeks of the broadcast. The arresting scenes of the first program centered on one of the hostages, Barry Rosen, public affairs attaché at the embassy. A man of slight build, he was led before the cameras, blindfolded and looking very vulnerable. As Robert Seigenthaler, then vice-president of ABC News, put it, "Here's a guy paraded in humiliating fashion. The hostage-takers were rubbing our noses in it—*and getting away with it!*"[2]

These words fairly epitomized the reaction of the American people to what they were to see on television during the 444 days in which the hostages were in captivity. Evening after evening, television showed mobs of fanatical-looking Iranians, men and women, besieging the embassy, chanting anti-American epithets, shaking their fists, burning the American flag, and otherwise reviling the hostages and the country they represented. In no time hatred flowed back to Iran. Americans had never before experienced anything like the drama in Tehran and were quick to regard the actors as crazed disciples of the anti-Christ, Khomeini, a ghostly figure on television with fierce eyes and a gray beard. Nationalistic feelings surged in the United States. Cities across the country tolled church bells. New York and Washington taxicab drivers kept their headlights on day and night.

It was only six years since the last American forces were withdrawn from Vietnam. America had been in a resolutely antiwar mood. "No more Vietnams!" "Abolish nuclear weapons!" "Hell, no, we won't go!" But after a few weeks of watching Iranian demonstrations on television, many Americans freely speculated on how U.S. military power might smash Iran. Amateur strategists telephoned the White House with proposals, such as landing rescue helicopters on the embassy roof. Unfurled from a Princeton University dormitory was a bedsheet on which was painted "Nuke the Ayatollah." Fractional minority sentiment, of course, yet President Jimmy Carter would have had strong support at that point for military action to free the hostages.

"Instead of receding with time, eclipsed by fresh-breaking news," wrote Howard Husock and Pamela Varley in 1988, "the story of the 'hostage crisis' mushroomed, becoming a virtual fixation for the nation and its news organizations throughout much of the fourteen-month embassy siege."[3] During the first six months the three networks devoted nearly a third of their weeknight news time to it. In his column in the *Wall Street Journal* on December 19, 1979, Vermont Royster questioned whether "the news media were engaged in overkill." Perhaps they were, but because of the public anger and impatience, it was a hard story for newspapers, magazines, and television news to scale back. Fostered periodically in the coverage was the perception that the hostage-taking manifested a historic uprising of Islam. This intensified anxiety that Western civilization was confronting a serious and widespread menace. In the *Columbia Journalism Review,* Professor Edward W. Said described the networks' emphasis on Iran's anti-Americanism:

All the major TV commentators, Walter Cronkite and Frank Reynolds [of ABC] chief among them, spoke of "anti-Americanism" or more poetically of "the crescent of crisis, sweeping across the world of Islam like a cyclone hurtling across a prairie," as . . . Reynolds put it on November 21 [1979]; on December 7 he voiced over a picture of crowds chanting "God is great" with what he supposed was the crowd's true sentiment, "hatred of America." . . . Not to be outdone, CBS introduced its *Evening News* on December 12 with Marvin Kalb from the State Department quoting . . . "diplomatic and intelligence experts" as affirming that Palestinian guerrillas, Iranian extremists, and Islamic fundamentalists had cooperated at the embassy.[4]

The questions on the "MacNeil/Lehrer NewsHour," Said alleged, "tended to be looking for support of the prevailing national mood—outrage at the Iranians." "With very few exceptions," he concluded, "the news media seemed to be waging a kind of war against Iran."[5]

The history of American-Iranian relations was complex. The two countries drew closer together after World War II. Sometime after Richard Nixon took office, the shah became, in the words of William Safire, "about the President's favorite statesman in the world," his "anchor in the Middle East."[6] Iran stands between the Soviet Union and the Persian Gulf, the region with the world's largest oil reserves and an area long considered critical to the security and prosperity of the United States. Under Nixon the United States went to extremes in selling the most sophisticated weapons to Iran, and Carter went along. In turn, the shah accepted a larger responsibility than before for protecting American interests, including oil reserves, in the gulf.

Before the shah was overthrown, the plight of the Iranian population was not well understood by Americans. The press, some scholars allege, was blind to the oppressive and cruel conditions in Iran under the monarchy.[7] But then the White House was not much wiser. In American eyes, generally speaking, Iran was the shah, and that seemed fine until the shah was thrown out of power on January 16, 1979, causing the United States a stunning diplomatic defeat. The revolution was quickly taken over by what appeared to Americans as the strange religious movement around Khomeini. Through television and the press in 1979, the American people were confronted with an Iran they knew little about and quickly came to despise. For their part, the Iranians were enraged over Americans' lack of sympathy for their plight.

A crisis came in the fall of 1979 when the deposed shah asked to be admitted to the United States for medical treatment. Knowing that Pahlavi's admission was likely to create trouble with the Khomeini regime, Carter at first demurred. Various officials in the State Department supported this view. Opposing it was Zbigniew Brzezinski, national security adviser to the president. He was a hard-liner on dealing with Khomeini and a hard fighter for the president's ear. Also in favor of admitting the shah to the United States were the Rockefeller brothers, Henry Kissinger, their friend and sometime associate, and the Chase Manhattan Bank, which was headed by David Rockefeller and which had had huge financial interests in Iran under the shah. This group, including the lawyer, banker, and statesman John J. McCloy, had access to the president, Vice-President Walter F. Mondale, and members of Congress. The Rockefeller interests and their friends used this influence, stressing the humanitarian imperative for helping a dying ally.[8] Mondale also argued that this was the right thing to do. It would not have been an easy decision for any president. There were political as well as moral considerations. With the 1980 election on the horizon, Carter was not indifferent to the political influence wielded by the powerful private interests. He changed his mind and approved Pahlavi's admission to the United States, a decision that proved not to be in the national interest. The former shah arrived in New York on October 22, 1979; the embassy in Tehran was seized on November 4. In December the shah was "negotiated back out of the U.S." to Panama.[9] From there Pahlavi went to Cairo, where he died in July 1980.

In a nationally televised speech after the hostages were taken, Carter halted oil imports from Iran. Later official Iranian assets in American banks were frozen. Carter's decision to help the shah handed the ayatollah an issue to consolidate his own leadership. The provocative scenes at the embassy flashed all over the United States by television also served the ayatollah's interests. The more impassioned the Americans were by what they saw the easier it was for Khomeini to get the Iranian people to rally behind him.

The networks continued to give the hostage story heavy coverage. This was especially true of ABC. The story broke only a couple of years after the inventive Roone Arledge became president of ABC News. As it happened, Arledge was weighing the development of an 11:30 P.M. network news program with which to trump the opposition. On one side of him, NBC dominated the air at that hour with the "Tonight Show," with Johnny Carson. On the other side, CBS ran old movies and television series. When some big story broke late, all three networks would occasionally commandeer the 11:30 P.M. slot for news. The size of audiences was respectable. To exploit this slot, Arledge was considering starting a network news program. Then along came not only the captivity of the hostages but also the brief but precious ABC monopoly on the story with Bob Dyk alone in the field in Tehran. Working furiously with its bureaus at home and abroad, ABC kept "America Held Hostage" alive until it turned into "Nightline" on March 24, 1980.

In this ABC was helped by a White House practice of constantly moving President Carter into the forefront of the struggle to free the hostages. White House Press Secretary Joseph Lester (Jody) Powell, Jr., and Hodding Carter III, assistant secretary of state for public affairs, "made news even if there was none."[10] "The decision that was made," Hodding Carter (no relation to the president) later told Husock and Varley, "was for there to be a very visibly concerned president who said in effect that the hostages' fate is a primary concern of the president of the United States."[11] After retiring as editor-in-chief of Time, Inc., Hedley Donovan joined the White House staff as a senior adviser to the president and participated in much of the activity involving the hostages. "Carter discussed their plight," he wrote in his book *Roosevelt to Reagan,*

with literally thousands of people in briefings and meetings in the White House, he assured the country he prayed for the hostages every night, he received delegations from their families. . . . It was an admirable humane reaction, and it weakened Carter's bargaining position vis-à-vis the Iranians and eventually hurt him with the U.S. electorate. Carter people began to accuse the media of overplaying the hostage story, especially ABC. . . . But Jimmy Carter himself did at least as much as the networks to keep the country—and his administration— lacerated by the hostages.[12]

Of their plight, Jimmy Carter said long after he had left the White House, "It was an obsession with me." But on the other hand, he observed, "The publicity focused on the hostages made it more unlikely that an individual hostage would be tortured or executed. So there was, I would say, a mixed effect of television coverage."[13]

In the months before the seizure of the embassy in 1979, Carter's political standing had been in decline. In part, this was due to an oil shortage and daily long lines of cars waiting for gasoline. Another cause was Carter's suggestion in a televised speech that the nation had sunk into malaise. Polls also indicated that he was perceived as weak. His approval rating jumped from 30 percent to 61 percent, however, in December 1979, the month after the hostages were taken. The public saw Carter acting in his role as commander-in-chief to resolve the crisis in Iran. According to *Newsweek,* this was "the sharpest one-month leap in presidential popularity since Gallup started polling 41 years ago."[14] Certainly, this did nothing to discourage the White House from trying to keep Carter in the center of the stage in the hostage drama. The tactic had its perils. His critics, of course, were intent on finding signs that the commander-in-chief was playing politics with the crisis. Carter's popularity depended on his bringing the hostages home quickly. As that prospect faded, so did his high standing in the polls.

Carter's difficult situation was compounded by the presidential election a year away. Sen. Edward M. Kennedy already had announced that he would challenge Carter for the nomination. The likely candidate for the Republicans was Ronald Reagan. Inevitably, the hostage situation, for however long it lasted, would be entangled in politics.

Years later a task force on crisis management faulted Carter's strategy of heavy journalistic coverage of activities in the White House because it "can limit or preempt the government's options."[15] Carter, however, had little choice. "We certainly did not downplay our own reaction to the crisis," Hamilton Jordan, Carter's chief of staff wrote, "but we never had a chance to 'control' the news, as many critics contended, and put the hostages on the 'back burner.' "[16] The holding of American hostages is searing news in the United States. Highly competitive television networks, newspapers, and magazines will pursue it tirelessly.

"Whatever influence ordinary coverage would have had on the crisis," Warren Christopher, Carter's deputy secretary of state, wrote, "was magnified because the coverage was so intense. It was also magnified by the phenomenon of television, with its capacity to display news graphically, or bring it alive into the American home. . . . Coverage that reinforced a national sense of outrage and frustration put heavy pressure on the government to act swiftly and visibly."[17] The pressure was relentless. Vice-President Mondale, who worked closely with Carter, later spoke of "the horror of that evening news guillotine dropping every night."[18]

In January 1980 Walter Cronkite adopted a new sign-off of his evening news program on CBS: "And that is how it was on January ——, the —— day of the hostages' captivity." Night by night he checked off the number until it finally reached 444. "It was purely my idea," Cronkite recalled long afterward.

As an old-time newspaper man and broadcaster I knew how stories lose their prominence, how they fall back page by page and section by section. I said to myself, "This should not be allowed to happen with the hostage story. They are denying us a chance to report what is happening there. They are kicking our correspondents out. This story has got to be kept alive. There have to be reminders."[19]

On January 14, 1980, the Iranians, irked by news coverage, ordered American reporters to leave the country. Each of the three television networks, however, maintained an international crew in Tehran, so the pictures kept flowing. Apparently feeling the loss of communications with the West, the Iranians lifted the ban on reporters after seven weeks.

Cronkite's nightly sign-offs took on a drumfire effect, and some listeners at least regarded them as a goad, a form of pressuring Carter to do something. In the *New York Times* James Reston quipped that Carter's actions under pressure "came as much in response to the 'Ayatollah' Cronkite as to the Ayatollah Khomeini."[20] "I had no intention," Cronkite said, "of making a political statement or attempting to incite early action,"[21] but anything that served to keep the hostage problem conspicuously before the public for months invariably had political effect. Troubled though they were by this new pressure, White House officials never complained to Cronkite or CBS. After leaving office, however, Carter once ran into Cronkite and remarked, "That announcement of yours every day didn't help."[22]

"Outside the American Embassy," Arlie Schardt wrote in *Newsweek*, "the mob plays to the television cameras. The well-drilled chants of 'Death to the Shah!' 'Death to Carter!' were rendered in Persian, English, and French at one point for the benefit of a Canadian TV crew. In contrast to the tense, swirling anger Americans saw daily on their home screens, the masses off camera were far less menacing." When no camera was around, the scene outside the embassy was something like a carnival. When cameras appeared, good times vanished. "Fists are waved," Ray Vicker, a *Wall Street Journal* reporter wrote. "The mood changes. Fierce expressions are adopted."[23]

Hamilton Jordan was right that the Carter administration could not control news from Iran. Iranian officials were quick to discover that television was a way for them not only to speak to the American people but also to send messages, however meaningless, to Washington. Sadegh Gotzbadeh, the American-educated Iranian foreign minister, was a clever television strategist. On "America Held Hostage" he appeared seven times to plead his side of the dispute. He also appeared on "Today" and on the "CBS Morning News." Gotzbadeh even counseled demonstrators on when and how to stage marches in front of television cameras for best effect abroad.

Gotzbadeh was not the only Iranian who used television and the press to influence public opinion. During the hostage crisis Iranian officials invited American reporters to a luncheon on Thanksgiving Day and a showing of a patriotic film. Afterward, Abol Hassan Bani Sadr, soon to become president of Iran, told them: "We need to convey our message to the world. For this we must use the press. . . . Don't you want this world problem to be the first one that is solved by reporters?"[24] Indeed, with no direct diplomatic contact existing between Tehran and Washington, the Iranians tried to use reporters as if they were diplomats. In an interview with John Hart of NBC, Bani Sadr sought to get a message to Washington about how certain processes for release of the hostages might work. "Help us," Bani Sadr urged Hart, "so that reason may reign." Hart tried to explain to him that reporters were not diplomats.[25]

To further its course, the Iranian government granted three reporters—Hart, Mike Wallace, and Peter Jennings—interviews of a sort with

Khomeini. In each case the reporter had to submit questions in advance, which Khomeini might or might not answer, and to agree that the interviews would be aired in prime time. No progress toward resolving the hostage crisis was made. Wallace, who was given much the longest session, a full hour for "60 Minutes," was ready with his daunting look, but the ayatollah glanced in his direction only three times, an average of once every twenty minutes. Wallace conceded that "in some respects it was an unsatisfactory interview."[26] Khomeini droned on with slogans, demands, and ultimatums such as, "Carter must return the shah. . . . Unless he is returned, the hostages will not be freed."[27]

On April 24, 1980, more than six months before the voters would decide whether to elect President Carter to a second term, Vice-President Mondale wearily told his wife, Joan, that the Democrats had already lost the election.[28] Carter's fortunes were unmistakably in decline, symbolized by Cronkite's continuing count of the hostages' days in captivity. As their imprisonment lengthened, the popularity enjoyed by Carter as commander-in-chief in time of crisis waned. His campaign strategy didn't help. Preoccupied with freeing the hostages and dealing with the Soviets' recent invasion of Afghanistan, he decided against campaign traveling. The kind of speeches he might have made on the road he delivered instead before television cameras at the White House, many of them in the Rose Garden. The "Rose Garden campaign," as it became known, resulted in charges, then and since, that Carter was playing politics with the hostage crisis. Certainly, the tactic was likely to founder if the commander-in-chief could not get the hostages home.

By the end of March, television news programs were often troubling to the White House. Off to a lusty start, "Nightline" was playing up the hostage story, replete with Koppel's challenging interviews with informed and opinionated guests. On "60 Minutes" Mike Wallace and the producer Don Hewitt put their heads together on a story that the president himself asked to have kept off the air. It was a story attempting to explain the bitterness and hatred of the Iranians for the Americans. The focus was on the cruelties of SAVAK, the shah's secret police. In 1953, early in the Eisenhower administration, the United States took part in a successful plan to oust Iranian Prime Minister Mohammad Mossadegh, a challenger to the shah's rule. The plan was coordinated by Kermit Roosevelt of the Central Intelligence Agency. In the "60 Minutes" script Wallace alluded to a Senate report stating that the CIA and other arms of the government had been aware that SAVAK had tortured thousands of Iranians.

The program was objectionable to Carter and his advisers because they thought it would impede negotiations with Tehran. Lloyd Cutler, special counsel to the president, called Hewitt to ask that it be withdrawn, but Hewitt refused. Next Cutler telephoned Bill Leonard, then president of CBS News, with the same request only to get the same answer. "You may get a call from someone else," Cutler warned. Shortly, the president called Leonard. "He was polite," Leonard remembered. "I was polite. He said the program would not be in the national interest. I said I would give it [his opinion] every consideration." This was formidable pressure for a network to resist, but Leonard decided that viewers had a right to understand Iranians' grievances against the United States. He did not consult anyone else in CBS about the White House objections. "The buck stopped with me," he said.[29] The program went on the air.

The time was tense for Carter. In the administration's view a prerequisite for release of the hostages was their transfer from the hands of the "students" to the Iranian government. For weeks a remote possibility of such a step flickered in a labyrinth of secret negotiations through third parties. On March 25 Bani Sadr, now president of Iran, received a message from Carter. It said that unless the transfer occurred by March 31 the United States would impose further nonbelligerent sanctions. Just when all was beginning to seem futile, an announcement came that Bani Sadr would make a speech on April 1 at 4:30 A.M., Washington time. If there was a chance for a break in the impasse, this might have been it.

Carter, surrounded by advisers, waited at his desk. It was before dawn. The text of Bani Sadr's speech began coming in by wire. Line by line it said everything but what they wanted to hear, until the very end. If Washington would make certain moderate concessions, the revolutionary government "will accept to take control of the hostages." The men in the Oval Office were tentatively encouraged. The White House issued a statement saying that in view of Bani Sadr's speech, "we will defer imposing further sanctions at this time." Then at 7:20 A.M. President Carter invited reporters and television crews to his office. He told them:

This morning the president of Iran has announced that the hostages' control will be transferred to the government of Iran, which we consider to be a positive step. . . . We will monitor the situation very closely. We would like to see this positive development continue, and our foremost consideration and our constant effort will be devoted to the earliest possible release of the American hostages and their return to this country and to freedom.[30]

This early morning statement on April 1 burst a bubble of cynicism that had been rising in the political community. Commentators castigated Carter for underhanded political trickery in the timing of his statement. "Diplomacy as Politics" read a headline in the *Washington Post*.[31] And in the *New York Times:* "Iran's Shadow on the Primary."[32] April 1 was not only the day of the Bani Sadr speech; it was also the day of the Democratic primary in Wisconsin. Voters heard the president's moderately encouraging words before they went to the polls. Carter won by such a wide margin—57 percent of the vote to 32 percent for Edward Kennedy—that it would stretch matters to say that his restrained statement on television that morning decided the outcome. A man in a trap, Carter was liable to be criticized, fairly or unfairly, for almost anything he did, except bring the hostages home.

Now a much worse rap than outraged political columns was in store for Carter. By a vote of eight to three, the Revolutionary Council in Tehran approved Bani Sadr's recommendation for accepting custody of the hostages, but Khomeini vetoed the action. Negotiations were moribund. Seven months before the election Carter could see only one option remaining.

Years later, when asked about the degree of pressure television news exerted on Carter to launch a military mission to rescue the hostages, Walter Mondale said, "Tremendous." Speeches and newspaper stories, editorials, columns, and cartoons added to this pressure, and, of course, as Mondale acknowledged, Congress was running out of patience. "I remember what I told the president one day," the former vice-president recalled. "I said, 'Boy, I was just up on the Hill, and they want you to do something.' He said, 'I know it.' "[33]

On April 24, 1980, eight helicopters took off from the carrier *Nimitz* in the Arabian Sea. On their way to Tehran they landed in the Iranian desert to refuel. A refueling aircraft on the ground burst into flames when struck by a helicopter maneuvering in a blizzard of dust sucked up by the rotor blades. Eight members of the aircraft crew were killed, five others were injured. Waiting in the White House, Carter first received news that the secret mission to rescue the American hostages had been aborted. Then, at 6:45 P.M., Gen. David Jones, chairman of the Joint Chiefs of Staff, called to tell him about the accident. Television screens and the front pages of newspapers were soon filled with pictures of the sorry wreckage in the desert. It was after the meetings in the White House broke up following General Jones's call that the vice-president, on returning home, told Mrs. Mondale that the Democrats had lost the election.

Carter put the Rose Garden behind him and campaigned around the country. What most worried the Reagan entourage, curiously, was that the president might pull off an "October surprise," a last-minute deal to free the hostages and thereby win the election. In fact, Reagan had television commercials ready to go in such a contingency, one of them reportedly accusing Carter of insincerity with the people. In an unhappy coincidence for the Democrats, the weekend before election day was the first anniversary of the taking of the hostages. Television observed the occasion by rerunning highlights of a year of painful films. By that time Reagan was not in danger of losing the election, but around Carter the replays were judged a disaster. "The wave of stuff on television had a major impact," Ray Jenkins, former deputy press secretary to Carter, said. "Lots of recapitulation, parading the whole nightmare before the public. The anniversary shows were a calamity."[34]

All the way it was a bitter story for Carter. If the rescue mission had succeeded, he would have been a hero. The failure heightened the feeling of futility in the land. When Khomeini decided that the hostages were of no further use to him, he let them go. It was immediately after Reagan became president in January 1981. Carter's presidency ended on an empty note and Reagan's started on a joyous one.

"I never have understood, and never have tried to understand," Carter said a decade later, "why the ayatollah refused to let the plane [with the freed hostages] depart until after I left office. Whether it was just a personal animosity toward me, or something else, I've never understood."[35]

The "something else" clearly referred to an allegation stoutly advanced by a number of Democrats. The charge—still alive in 1991—is that Khomeini held the hostages just long enough to glorify Reagan's inauguration in conformity with a secret deal with the incoming Republican administration or its agents.

Carter's statement was made on a November 1989 television program (fittingly, ABC's "Nightline" with Ted Koppel), commemorating the tenth anniversary of the hostage crisis. Gary Sick, an assistant to Brzezinski, who took part in the program, explained that soon after Reagan became president, the United States shipped arms from Israel to Iran, the pro-

ceeds surreptitiously to be used for strengthening the Nicaraguan con-
tras. The implication was that this transaction was compensation for the
holding of the hostages until after President Reagan took the oath of
office.

"Have you ever had any kind of suspicion up to and including this
moment," Koppel asked Carter, "that there was some kind of a deal that
had been struck between the Reagan administration, or the Republican
party, and the Iranians?"

"Yes, I've had suspicions," the former president replied, "but I don't
have any evidence. President Bani Sadr, who was the leader of Iran then,
working under the Ayatollah Khomeini, has made public statements on
several occasions to responsible news reporters that there was a deal made.
I've never tried to find out if this allegation is true."[36]

Television news influences international conflicts. During the Vietnam
War it hastened the rise of domestic opposition after the Tet offensive.
In the Iranian crisis scenes on television of hostile mobs before the U.S.
embassy as they burned the American flag and screamed anti-American
slogans ripped the bonds of public patience and undermined confidence
in Carter's ability to free the hostages. In the Persian Gulf War, by contrast, pictures of attacking allied aircraft, rolling tanks and convoys, and
massive surrender by enemy soldiers raised support at home to the point
of euphoria.

12

The call: relief for the Ethiopian famine, 1984

On October 23, 1984, the British Broadcasting Corporation called the NBC bureau in London with an urgent message: "We have something here you will want to see." It was gripping film shot by Visnews, an organization owned by the BBC and NBC. Donna Mastrogelow Ryan, the NBC producer in London that morning, took a cab to BBC for a preview of the footage before the film appeared on the BBC 1:00 P.M. news program. What she saw struck her as so exceptional that she got in touch with Joseph Angotti, general manager in Europe for NBC, and Frieda Morris Williamson, the NBC bureau chief in London. They watched the one o'clock news. "I was stunned," Angotti recalled. He immediately called Cheryl Gould in New York, the foreign producer of "NBC Nightly News," and told her the BBC material was "stronger than anything I had ever seen." Nevertheless, the word that came back to London was that the Brokaw program was not interested, at least for that day. "There was too much other news."[1]

Stunned again, Angotti went home from work. Aware that the film would be rerun on the BBC nine o'clock news, he watched it again. "I knew I could not let it lie," he said afterward. The difference in time between London and New York still allowed leeway for getting the film on the Brokaw program that night. "I phoned the bureau," Angotti continued, "and instructed the night producer to feed the material [to New York] on the regular evening satellite at 10 o'clock. Then I called Paul Greenberg, the man who succeeded me as executive producer of the *NBC Nightly News*. I told him we were feeding the BBC report whether he wanted it or not. All I wanted him to do was watch it when it came in on the satellite."[2]

153

Greenberg gathered together Brokaw and some others. "There are a few times," Greenberg later observed,

that a newsroom can be brought to a complete silence, and this was one of those occasions. All the side talk and worried preparations for the evening broadcast, all the gossip and talk of political campaigns and concern for the night's stories just stopped. Tears came to your eyes, and you felt as if you'd just been hit in the stomach.[3]

The film, as it rolled, was harrowing. The scene was a desert in Ethiopia with mountains far in the distance. Withered trees dotted the brown landscape. No water was to be seen and only a trace of parched foliage. In the forefront of this tableau of desolation stretched thousands of drought-stricken people, some of them nearly skeletons. Naked babies huddled next to mothers with dry breasts. Most of the multitude sat or lay in the sand. Beyond, wizened men carrying sticks for walking trudged aimlessly. Now and then at a rumor of food, groups of children would scamper off, but many others were too near death to move. At one point a three-year-old, last of one mother's children, died before the camera's lens. Thirty-seven others reportedly had perished during the night. Nothing was more revolting than the unrelenting scourge of flies. Swarms of them preyed on the eyes and mouths of the bloated, bony children, too weak to brush the tormentors away.

Greenberg and Brokaw decided on the spot to use the story that night. With minutes running out, they made room in the "Nightly News" line-up.

The earlier decision of New York producers on a busy day to reject a film they had not seen was not unusual. After all, famine in Ethiopia was old hat. For at least two years it had been known by governments, international organizations, newspapers, and network newsrooms that one of the greatest disasters in recent human history, as *Time* described it, was developing in the sub-Sahara region of Africa.[4] In the months before the call to NBC, the Associated Press had filed 101 stories on the famine. In 1984, prior to October 23, the *New York Times* had published twelve articles on the subject and the *Washington Post* six, three of them on the front page. In a story filed from Addis Ababa, the Ethiopian capital, and published in the *Post* on September 18, 1984, David B. Ottaway attributed some of the misery to "donor fatigue." This was in spite of forecasts that millions of people faced imminent starvation and in spite of an Ethiopian appeal before the United Nations Security Council on May 11, 1984. By then it was known that the spring harvest in Ethiopia had failed.

Because the Soviet-supported Marxist regime in Ethiopia made political use of food, the Reagan administration was reluctant to send funds.

In the summer of 1983, when millions of persons already were destitute in the Ethiopian drought, NBC decided to send its senior foreign correspondent, John Cochran, and a crew to report. Senegal and Kenya granted them visas, but Ethiopia, ruled by a hostile Marxist regime with close ties to the Soviet Union, refused. The regime was not interested in drawing attention to the plight of its people. Political considerations were a serious obstacle to outside relief and to news coverage. The Reagan administration had distanced itself from the Ethiopian government; no ambassadors were exchanged between the two countries. As for the famine, Washington suspected that Addis Ababa was using human suffering as a pawn in a long civil war and that American-donated goods would wind up in the black market.

Despite these problems, Cochran filed two reports from Senegal and Kenya on the spreading devastation of the drought in Ethiopia. NBC broadcast the reports in September, and they did not evoke a murmur. Bill Blakemore, the ABC correspondent in Rome, wanted to take a shot at covering the famine, but New York turned him down because of the cost of such an assignment. CBS for the time being limited itself to gathering available material in Europe and elsewhere.

In the eyes of network producers, the famine was a distant event, and the people involved, of course, were African natives. Television news, and most Americans for that matter, were given to a certain sense of doom about Ethiopia: men, women, and children had starved there for ages and probably always would. "We'd all seen the pictures hundreds of times before," Angotti commented.[5]

Perhaps because London is nearer Ethiopia than is New York, or because British broadcasting had made a stronger commitment to covering Africa, the BBC was in a state of alert. The BBC and NBC were part owners of Visnews, an organization that gathered pictures all over the world. Mohammed Amin was the African bureau coordinator and cameraman for Visnews. In July 1984 he teamed up with Michael Buerk, BBC correspondent in Johannesburg, and the two of them managed to get into Ethiopia. When the film they shot there ran on the BBC, viewers were so appalled they contributed to relief organizations the equivalent of $10 million. In the fall, Buerk and Amin decided to return to Ethiopia but were at first refused visas. Amin, who lived in Kenya, made such a row over the refusal that Addis Ababa yielded, and the two journalists were flown into Ethiopia by World Vision, an international Christian relief and development agency. Three weeks later in London word came that Buerk and Amin were on their way back with an incredible story. And now, on the evening of October 23, NBC was broadcasting part of their film.

Brokaw called it *The Faces of Death in Africa*. To viewers whose experiences were limited to Western civilization, it was a nightmare. The Ethiopian famine of the mid-1980s put at risk 10 million lives. One million Ethiopians died. To reach the fields of death shown on television in the fall of 1984, men, women, and children had dragged themselves across tens, even hundreds, of miles. In stifling days and cold nights, they desperately searched for food and water. World Vision estimated that by 1984 two thousand Ethiopians had died of famine every day. With pitifully little imported food available, workers from voluntary organizations who were on the scene had to decide who would live and who would die. What was most heart-rending about the sight of the dying perhaps was their appearance of having been abandoned by the rest of humanity. Then, of a sudden, something marvelous and unexpected happened.

This happening, as Peter Boyer characterized it in the *Washington Journalism Review*, was "The TV Accident That Exploded."[6] When the "Nightly News" broadcast ended, thousands of viewers called NBC wanting to know how they could help the starving Ethiopians. The next night NBC carried a second segment of the film. Awareness of the crisis seemed to roll across the country, gathering force as the other networks picked up the story in their morning and evening news. A segment appeared on "60 Minutes." American relief agencies told the *New York Times* that they had not been so overwhelmed with offers of assistance in years.[7] Staff members and volunteers worked after midnight and through the weekend to handle the deluge of telephone offers. Reacting to the popular mood, the U.S. government made a fourteenfold increase in annual relief for Ethiopia. Abroad, the wide penetration of BBC programs in many countries generated more waves of charity. That pictures on television could have fired up people's sympathy was perhaps not surprising. What was truly extraordinary was that the television coverage created a self-sustained movement of global scope.

The spectacle was hailed as unquestionable proof of the might of television news to influence masses of viewers. If the BBC program could have been meticulously transformed into a newspaper article, who could imagine a comparable reaction? "The famine has been going on for a long time and nobody cared," Steve Friedman, then executive producer of "Today," remarked. "Now it's on TV and everybody cares."[8] Joanne Omang wrote in the *Washington Post* that the popular response "is a lesson in the relatively feeble power of anything but television to galvanize the U.S. public—and, thereby, to overcome political squabbling in the U.S. government."[9] There was, as will be seen, another side to this phenomenon, but for the time being the outpouring was a wonder to behold.

A fat ledger would be needed to itemize the contributions and governmental appropriations around the world. Indeed, no one really knows how much came from piggy banks and wallets, checkbooks and rock concerts. The sums ran into the equivalent of hundreds of millions of dollars. The money was spent on food, seed, fertilizer, trucks, and use of airplanes and helicopters. Parishes, schools, and even jails sent money. In the first seven weeks after the broadcast, Catholic Relief Services received ninety-one thousand letters containing a total of $13 million. The total raised by that organization in 1984 and 1985 for famine in Africa was $50 million. In the period ending December 31, 1987, USA for Africa (United Support of Artists for Africa), of Los Angeles, raised $91 million, of which $54 million came from the sale of the record *We Are the World*. In less than eight weeks after the broadcast, the Save the Children Federation of Westport, Connecticut, took in $2.7 million. At Harvard some undergraduates raised cash by fasting. In Canada's Northwest Territories two Eskimo villages were reported to have raised $7,000 for Ethiopia. In Great Britain, Oxfam (the Oxford Committee for Famine Relief) reported receiving contributions at a rate equivalent to $1 million a month. A woman at the Oxfam America office in Boston was surprised to receive $100 from a childhood friend. The friend wrote: "The inclosed check is for Ethiopia. I think of Ethiopia every time I look at my fat happy baby."[10] According to Peter Davies, president of the American Council for Voluntary International Action, in New York, the total contributions in the United States was of the magnitude of $250 million.[11] Appropriations by Congress, the United Nations Food and Agriculture Organization, the European Community, and other public bodies more than doubled it.

In May 1983 the State Department and its arm the Agency for International Development (AID) had determined that there was a disaster in Ethiopia. According to a Government Accounting Office report of May 1985, seven requests for famine relief had been submitted by AID in fiscal 1983 and 1984 by voluntary organizations, primarily Catholic Relief

Services. The requests took five to six months, "considerably longer" than usual to be approved.[12]

The NBC broadcast on October 23 drastically changed the administration's policy. Suddenly, AID had to battle "a public perception—and political criticism—that the Reagan administration has not been doing enough."[13] Within days of the broadcast, the White House authorized the use of two cargo planes to ferry grain to remote areas and sent $51.2 million worth of food. Restrictions that complicated and hampered efficient provision of relief were lifted. In 1984 AID had provided $21.1 million in assistance to Ethiopia. In 1987 the figure soared to $305.7 million.[14]

"On most big issues the government leads and public opinion follows," former ambassador Robert J. McCloskey, then senior vice-president of Catholic Relief Services, wrote in the *Los Angeles Times* on January 29, 1985. "Certain gut issues have the capacity to turn that process around. We are now witnessing a singular example."[15] And not only in the United States.

Three days after the Amin-Buerk film was aired on the BBC, Great Britain pledged the equivalent of $6 million plus three month's service from two military transport planes to carry food into central Ethiopia. Within a week Italy announced a pledge of the equivalent of $10 million. From the Netherlands to Pakistan, Western and non-Western countries alike, made pledges of grain. When Joseph Clark, Canadian minister of external affairs, was asked why most Westerners had paid so little attention to the gathering crisis in Ethiopia, he first replied that most people do not read the United Nations Food and Agriculture Organization reports. On second thought, he said, "But they do watch television."[16]

NBC ran another broadcast about the famine on November 12, 1984. "If ever there were an example of the saying, 'out of sight, out of mind,' " Garrick Utley reported, "it is what is happening in Ethiopia. Until three weeks ago, most Americans didn't care about starvation because we didn't know about it."[17] Ethiopia had more famines after 1984. A cruel one occurred in 1988. This one television news covered extensively at first. The horror was not "out of sight, out of mind." But this time the pitiful scenes caused no explosive public reaction. No relief organization is known to have complained of being deluged by offers of money. Being a medium of emotion, television is fickle. In 1984 its pictures from Ethiopia sent other peoples rushing to their checkbooks. In subsequent years they did not.

Television's capacity to support a sustained response proved to be limited. Once the visual impact of the first response wore off, people turned to their other concerns. By the fall of 1987, an international effort to prevent another famine in northern Ethiopia failed, and large numbers of drought victims were again trudging the hot sands in search of food. Though an estimated 2 million people were reported to be threatened with starvation, the delivery of food was slowed by Ethiopian rebel attacks on truck convoys in the Tigray and Eritrea regions. Could television help to save innocent victims again? The networks tried. They carried fresh pictures of the devastation. To many viewers, however, these looked like a replay of 1984. The American public seemingly could not comprehend why, after pouring money into Ethiopia in 1984 and 1985, it had to dig into its pocket again. America looked inward at the economy and the presidential election. The plight of Ethiopia receded into the shadows. The level of donations to some relief organizations was actually lower than it had been before Ethiopia flared on the television screens in 1984. The program manager for the relief organization Africare cited the problem: compassion fatigue. Television was no cure for that, not at that moment at least.

II

Ongoing impact

13

‹◦●◦

The White House in the television age

Television news has been an irresistible force for change in the conduct of the presidency. Because of television, the task of managing the White House is more complex. Presidents must act in a much greater glare of public attention than they did forty years ago. Day after day the White House is the big story. Gerald Rafshoon, communications director for Jimmy Carter when he was president, aptly described the presidency today as "an ongoing series for television."[1]

When times are going well for a president, this attention is a blessing. Television has brought undreamed of opportunities for presidents to communicate with people and hence to lead. Not only White House staffs but also government departments and agencies have been enlisted to assist presidents in exploiting this new instrument of political power. When, on the other hand, things are going badly for a president—for example, Lyndon Johnson during the Vietnam War, Richard Nixon during Watergate, Jimmy Carter during the hostage crisis, and Ronald Reagan during the Iran-contra scandal—television makes a president more vulnerable because it heightens emotion.

When Lloyd N. Cutler became the White House counsel in the Carter administration, it came as a surprise to him how much television news intruded into the timing and the substance of the president's policy decisions, especially on foreign policy. For one thing, television news "vastly increases the number of people who get interested in an issue and care about the outcome." This can have good and bad effects. "The most harmful effect of TV news," Cutler declared,

is its tendency to speed up the decision-making process on issues that TV news is featuring and to slow down and interrupt the process of deciding other important

163

issues that get less TV attention. Whatever urgent but less televised problem may
be on the White House agenda on any given morning, it is often put aside to
consider and respond to the latest TV news bombshell in time for the next broadcast.[2]

Fortunately, during the Cuban missile crisis in October 1962, the Kennedy administration was not distracted, as it would be today, with "the
latest TV news bombshell." For thirteen days, beginning with confirmation that the Soviet Union was placing missiles and atomic weapons in
Cuba, President John F. Kennedy and his high command were remarkably insulated from outside interference while they decided how to handle the crisis. Secretary of Defense Robert S. McNamara did not even
look at a set during those thirteen days. There was nothing compelling
to see. There was no Cable News Network (CNN) carrying news twenty-
four hours a day. The regular network news shows ran for only fifteen
minutes. There was no "MacNeil/Lehrer NewsHour" with discussions of
the missile issue by panels of experts every night. Unborn also was
"Nightline," which would have aired endless questions about what Kennedy should do. The press reported such news of the crisis as was available, and there is no assurance that television reporters could have found
more. But television could have made a bigger noise. Assorted newspapers cannot keep the kind of glare on the White House that national
television can. If a missile crisis were to occur today, television would
distract the White House with words at all hours from all parts of the
world, stirring up greater public agitation in the process. By the late 1970s,
in Cutler's time, there surely would have been more clamor. A president
would have felt the pressure of noise that Kennedy escaped.

If as recent a president as Harry Truman or even Dwight Eisenhower
could see the working quarters of the White House today, he would be
amazed at the enlargement of facilities and the installation of technology
needed for a president to take full advantage of television. When television news began in 1948, the year the polls indicated that Thomas E.
Dewey would be elected president in a landslide, the White House pressroom occupied 574 square feet in the northwest corner of the West Wing.
Today there is a combined pressroom and television studio, built in the
Nixon administration by flooring over the swimming pool, that occupies
3,280 square feet in the colonnade between the White House residence
and the West Wing, the workplace of presidents. The sixfold increase in
space for reporters, camera crews, television equipment, and technicians

is one measure of how the presidency has changed in the pursuit of image-making for political advantage.

The transition to the new era in the White House hit its stride in the television-conscious Kennedy administration, although the first steps were taken under Eisenhower and his wide-awake press secretary, James C. Hagerty. In his father's footsteps, Hagerty had been a political reporter for the *New York Times* before his appointment as press secretary to Governor Dewey in Albany. Through his close contacts with Madison Avenue advertising agencies, Dewey was aware of television's potential, and he capitalized on it to win reelection as governor of New York in 1950. Hagerty was intimately involved, of course. When he became press secretary to Eisenhower, after the general entered the 1952 presidential campaign, he brought with him an understanding of and enthusiasm for television as a political tool. By 1952 the television industry was thriving. Like Hagerty, Eisenhower was close to big advertising executives and big publishers. He had a sense of what television might do for him, although he was never captivated by it the way Kennedy, Johnson, Nixon, and Reagan were to be.

Television cameras were brought to the White House for the first time on October 5, 1947, to cover a speech by President Truman. When, two years earlier, he succeeded to the presidency upon the death of Franklin Roosevelt, radio was the medium of instantaneous broadcast of speeches. With his midwestern twang and too-rapid delivery, Truman was no virtuoso on the microphone, although he was to use radio regularly throughout his nearly eight years in office. Because of poor eyesight and thick glasses, he was even less accomplished on television. For him, television was an extension of radio. On major occasions after 1947, he spoke before cameras, more or less because they were there. Truman's use of television was light years from where President Reagan's would be in the 1980s. Television was the stage upon which Reagan, an actor by trade, played his presidency.

During his first year in office, Eisenhower continued Truman's and Roosevelt's news conference policy: no photographs, no film, no live television or radio coverage, and no direct quotations. Then, at Hagerty's urging, he made an important move toward the modern use of electronics by a president. Eager to make the best use of the bully pulpit provided by the White House news conferences, Hagerty began to allow them to be recorded for use on radio, but only after he had cleared the text. This would cause a delay in the broadcast but would insure against a presidential misstatement going out over the air. After Eisenhower consented, the radio coverage went well. Indeed, Hagerty soon relaxed the procedure on clearance and told radio reporters they could air the tapes as soon as news conferences had ended. Eisenhower's words were thus heard by millions of listeners.

Encouraged, Hagerty moved on. He asked network television reporters if they could film the president at the conferences without using glaring lights. They assured him that they could because of the sensitive Tri-X film recently developed by the Eastman Kodak Company. With that problem out of the way, Hagerty turned to the question of noise and commotion if television cameras were admitted. He called in Harry Tugander, an old-time newsreel cameraman assigned to the White House. Hagerty asked him to demonstrate how his battered hand-held camera worked. Because it sounded like a coffee grinder, Hagerty decided it would not be suitable for a news conference. The network cameramen, however, assured Hagerty that they could shoot without the clatter of changing film magazines. Their cameras were equipped with twelve-hundred–foot film loads that ran continuously for thirty-three minutes, three minutes longer than the half-hour limit Eisenhower had established for the conferences. Still, the president was cautious about permitting televised coverage of his news conferences. He remembered that Truman had made a couple of slips in answering reporters' questions. One such occasion had caused an explosive reaction around the world during the Korean War, when Truman intimated, contrary to his own good sense, that Gen. Douglas MacArthur had authority to use the atom bomb, if things got worse. Early in 1955, however, Eisenhower agreed to permit filming of his news conferences for television, subject to review of the transcript by Hagerty for possible errors. This was the last step before live coverage was introduced by Kennedy.

When, on January 19, 1955, Eisenhower entered the Indian Treaty Room in the Executive Office Building, where news conferences were held then, the scene had changed. A narrow wooden platform along the back wall held stationary television cameras, and cameramen and soundmen crowded around them. The platform displaced two rows of seats for reporters. The room glowed with bright lights mounted on steel stanchions. "Well," Eisenhower commented, "I see we are trying a new experiment this morning. I hope it doesn't prove a disturbing influence."[3] Despite the displeasure of some newspaper reporters over the further aggrandizement of television news, it did not. As for the release of the film, consequential errors proved to be so rare that clearance became practically automatic. Eisenhower never would consent to live coverage. Nevertheless, for the first time the public could turn on the evening news and see a White House news conference filmed that day. Eisenhower eschewed theatrics, yet came across as businesslike, informed, dignified, and likable. He kept his temper in check except, most notably, in his press conference of March 27, 1957, when his face turned incandescent. A question by William McGaffin infuriated him.

Q. William McGaffin, Chicago Daily News: Mr. President, sir, do you feel that there are any economies that you can make in the executive branch of the government to help cut government spending? For instance, would you be willing to do without that pair of helicopters that have been proposed for getting you out to the golf course a little faster than you can make it in a car?
The President. Well, I don't think much of the question, because no helicopters have been procured for me to go to a golf course.
Q. Mr. McGaffin: Well—
The president. Thank you; that is all.[4]

Eisenhower experimented with other forms of television presentations. On one occasion, after Secretary John Foster Dulles had returned from a trip overseas, the president and the secretary of state sat before cameras in the Oval Office to review issues confronting the United States abroad. Then Eisenhower staged a couple of televised meetings with his cabinet. The first, in 1953, was a roundtable discussion of current problems and what the administration was doing to solve them. A television specialist from a Madison Avenue advertising agency, Batten, Barton, Durstine and Osborne, had come down for a rehearsal to try to create an illusion of spontaneity in the discussion. The show, however, was a bore. Eisenhower concluded that it was overly glutted with issues for a thirty-minute program. The following year, without much better luck, Eisenhower put another session with cabinet officers on the air, but again with more or less memorized lines. Cabinet meetings can be tedious enough even when the talk is spontaneous.

In the closing days of the 1958 off-year election campaign, Eisenhower tried unsuccessfully to use television to help the Republican party. On Sunday, October 26, Sig Mickelson, the head of CBS News, got a call from the network's president, Frank Stanton. Stanton asked Mickelson if he would be interested in live coverage the next day, at 7:00 P.M., of a regular cabinet meeting led by the president. Mickelson had some doubts, yet found the offer too tempting to resist. Stanton suggested that Mick-elson call Hagerty immediately to confirm the broadcast. When he did, it was evident to Mickelson that Hagerty was waiting to hear from him. Uneasy about the arrangement, Mickelson thought it was a questionable use of commercial television for political gain. After the broadcast he regretted not having pointed out to viewers that carrying the cabinet meeting was an act of favoritism toward the Republican party. He need not have worried. The dull broadcast, with Eisenhower calling on differ-ent members for perfunctory answers, "did not help" the Republicans noticeably, Mickelson concluded. The Democrats handily retained their hold on the Senate and the House.[5]

In the summer of 1959, Eisenhower became the first president to have a jet plane. He was quick to sense the significance for his presidency. The jet opened the world to him and to television viewers. His last year and a half in office was filled with long, colorful trips to Europe, the Far East, and South America. Television cameras always went with him, filling screens throughout the United States, day after day, with pictures of the president at his best. In Rome he met with Pope John XXIII. In New Delhi he and Prime Minister Jawaharlal Nehru addressed a throng of a million people. In Tehran the president lunched with the shah. In Madrid he breakfasted with Generalissimo Francisco Franco. At home, television presented Eisenhower as the outstanding leader of the world. An Ameri-can Marco Polo, he visited the Taj Mahal, watched rifle-bearing Berber tribesmen in Morocco, and beheld an exhibition of tent-pegging by mounted lancers in Karachi. The image of a president grandly carrying the colors around the globe was not lost on Kennedy, Johnson, Nixon, Reagan, and Bush. The newsworthy combination of television and the jet plane changed the presidency forever.

Assuming office in 1961 at the age of forty-three, John Kennedy was a true member of the television generation. In 1946, two years before tele-vision news began, he had run successfully for the U.S. House of Repre-sentatives. What the ensuing fourteen years in Congress did not teach him about the influence of television in politics, the debates with Nixon during the 1960 presidential campaign did. After the staid Eisenhower years, the life in the White House of Jack, Jackie, Caroline, and baby "John-John," together with a pony named Macaroni, fascinated Ameri-cans hungry for glamour. During Kennedy's early months in office, each of the three networks aired its own hour-long documentary on the president, his family, and his staff, something that had never been done before. Kennedy gave his views on the importance of television to a president in a nationally televised interview on NBC with one of the authors. Kennedy observed:

The presidency is an office which, in a sense, is shared by all the people. I would say the more we can communicate successfully beyond the White House and the more we can take back the more effective this office will be administered—so that everybody has a piece of the White House. Everybody's lives and security are affected by the judgments that are made . . . here, and I think everybody ought to know about it as much as possible.[6]

At the very start of his presidency, Kennedy moved the White House news conference all the way into the television age. Despite some hand wringing in the State Department and grumbling by certain newspaper reporters, he opened his first news conference on January 25, 1961, to live television coverage, and that has been the rule ever since. Kennedy had the self-confidence to submit to questions without requiring a staff check on his accuracy prior to release. Eager to be seen, he held his first news conference at 6:00 P.M. when television audiences were larger than in mid-morning or mid-afternoon. Furthermore, for theatrical effect he moved the site to a large auditorium in the State Department. One day at a news conference, a group of nuns turned up and applauded some of the president's replies to reporters' questions. Originally restricted to a few reporters clustered around Franklin Roosevelt's desk without a camera in sight, the White House press conference under Kennedy took on the air of a matinee, the idol in solitary command of the wide stage. What was once an intimate institution—a quiet gathering of reporters, faceless to the public, questioning the president the way members of a parliament might interrogate a prime minister—ended forever with the dynamic combination of live coverage and star performer. Kennedy's first news conference was attended by 418 reporters. Today television reporters have become celebrities, vying with each other and, as a group, dominating the questioning during news conferences.

If Eisenhower cultivated television cautiously and if Kennedy's was a maestro's approach to the camera, Lyndon Johnson made a Texas-sized grab for the whole apparatus. He burst into programs that were already on the air to make news himself. Once for political advantage he tricked the networks into switching suddenly from covering one important event somewhere else to cover a virtual nonevent he staged in the White House.

To try to keep him within bounds, the networks spent a quarter of a million dollars converting the motion picture room in the White House into a small television studio. Three cameras were installed. The studio was staffed with directors and technicians. For five and a half days each week, they kept the cameras "hot," ready for almost instant use. Then, typically, Johnson had his own ideas. He seldom used the facility and after months of costly maintenance, the networks closed it.

Although Johnson was never comfortable performing on television, and he never found a format to his liking, television seemed to obsess him. Near him he kept hand-held remote-control switches to operate the three television sets (one for each network) in his office and in his bedroom. Attached to his bed he even had electronic levers to raise or lower the windows behind the sets. Although he probably realized that his appearance on television sometimes hurt rather than enhanced his image as president, he could not stay away from cameras. Indeed, the addiction extended to all kinds of cameras. Thirty years earlier, when the only cameras he saw in Washington were those of newspaper photographers, he was in torment over which profile, right or left, he should present to the lens. When he moved into the White House with television cameras on all sides, he tormented his staff, demanding arrangements that would have cameras catch his right profile, which he had settled upon as the better. During his first twelve months in the White House, his face was seen on television more than Kennedy's had been in thirty-five months. In his first two years as president Johnson made more television appearances than had Eisenhower in both terms. Johnson's pace was frenetic. "In the course of a single breathtaking, nerve-shattering, totally impossible week," said an article in *Time* in 1964, "the president of the United States made nearly two dozen speeches, traveled 2,983 miles, held three news conferences, appeared on national television three times, and was seen in person by almost a quarter of a million people."[7]

A man in a rush, Johnson once gave the networks apoplexy in 1964, when he decided suddenly to go on the air. Ebullient that a national railroad strike might be averted, Johnson commanded negotiators for both sides to stay in the Executive Office Building west of the White House and bargain until they reached an agreement. The tactic worked. At 6:23 P.M. the White House telephoned the networks to say the president wanted to go on the air at once. Since the networks did not at the moment have live cameras in the White House, the president needed to race to the studio of WTOP-TV on upper Wisconsin Avenue several miles from the White House. This CBS affiliate could then feed all the networks.[8]

"Let's go! Let's go!" Johnson yelled. In two minutes Chet Huntley and David Brinkley would come on NBC and in thirty-two minutes Walter Cronkite would follow on CBS. The negotiators and Secretary of Labor William W. Wirtz were shoved with the president into a limousine, which took off into Washington rush-hour traffic. Johnson was in such a panic over making the two big news shows that he spurred the driver into roaring past all four motorcycle officers assigned as an escort. Breathless, he arrived with his company while the Huntley-Brinkley program was on the air. A Secret Service man grabbed a lectern and hung the presidential seal on it. The usual tightly scripted program was pulled apart to make time for the president. How much time the agitated producers did not know. Johnson proudly informed America that the trains would keep rolling. He did it his way, of course. Taking up valuable time, he read a letter to himself from Cathy May Baker of Chicago. In it she pleaded for a settlement of the strike so her grandmother could attend her confirmation. The negotiators also spoke their pieces. The segment took several minutes to report what otherwise probably would have been a ninety-second item. Instead of taking prompt leave of his jittery hosts, Johnson hung around to watch the Cronkite show.

During the 1964 Democratic National Convention in Atlantic City, President Johnson used his influence with the networks to keep viewers from seeing something he did not want them to see. One of the few live issues at that otherwise tedious convention (Johnson was sure to be nominated) involved two rival delegations from Mississippi. One was the delegation of Mississippi regulars, eight of whom, unpledged, had bolted the ticket in 1960 over Kennedy's commitment to a civil rights bill. In 1964 these regulars were sympathetic to Barry Goldwater, the Republican candidate, who had voted earlier that year against the Civil Rights Act. To displace the regulars, civil rights groups had established another delegation, the Freedom Democratic Party of Mississippi. Composed of blacks and whites, it was pledged to support the Democratic ticket on election day.

To decide which delegation should be seated at the convention, the credentials committee heard arguments by both of them. It was a lively session, and television news covered it, much to the displeasure of Johnson, who watched at the White House. He wanted to carry all southern states on election day, and he regarded the fight of the Freedom delegation as unnecessarily provocative to the South. He knew that whatever happened he would get the black vote.

The more Johnson watched the more emotional the session became. The vice-chairman of the Freedom delegation, Mrs. Fannie Lou Hamer, was called as a witness. A sharecropper since the age of six, she had a grim story to tell about brutal beatings she had suffered for opposing the regulars. Fearful that the convention might be swept into a controversy over civil rights, Johnson moved quickly to preempt national television. His staff notified the networks that he was about to address thirty Democratic governors in the East Room. Because the governors would later be on their way to the convention, the networks, lured by the prospect of a big story, "stopped rolling in Atlantic City."[9] In his speech to the governors, however, Johnson said next to nothing. As doubtless would have happened, even without his intervention, the regulars were seated at the convention, and Goldwater carried Mississippi.

Lyndon Johnson was the nearest thing to perpetual motion in the history of the presidency, and television spurred him on. When, for example, he ordered marines to the Dominican Republic in a civil war (caused by "a band of Communist conspirators," as he said), he simply could not wait an extra few minutes to tell the American people all about it. If it had been Normandy, he could hardly have been more insistent in his demands on the networks to break into prime time on a Sunday evening, of all moments. Shortly before nine o'clock, the audience watching the popular show "Bonanza" suddenly found itself face to face with the president talking about the Dominican Republic.

Johnson was a man of enormous personal force and energy, a figure almost too outsized for a television screen to accommodate well, some thought. For years he had been renowned for his capacity for persuasion in Congress. Indeed, he showed himself to be a powerful president in getting his Great Society programs enacted. And from 1964 to 1967 he managed to hold public support for his war aims in Vietnam. Although he found it hard to be himself on television, he did, at least on November 17, 1967, steal the show.

Things were going badly for him in Vietnam, and so his advisers convinced him to try a different news conference style, one that unchained him, liberated him from a podium. Johnson hoped to be as persuasive with millions of television viewers as he was one on one with a few people in a room. For the conference of November 17, a lapel microphone was pinned to his jacket. Instead of standing and talking to reporters and to the cameras beyond them as he usually did in a news conference, Johnson strode back and forth as in the old days in the Senate, gesturing, answering questions.

What about criticisms of the war?

There is a difference between constructive dissent and storm trooper bullying, howling [a reference to antiwar demonstrations] and taking the law into your own hands.

How about domestic programs?

We have much farther to go, as you can see from our education and health and city statistics and farm statistics. As long as there are four people out of every ten in the world who can't spell cat or can't write dog, we have much to do.

Was progress being made in Vietnam?

Our American people, when we get in a contest of any kind—whether it is a war, an election, a football game, or whatever it is—want it decided and decided quickly—get in or get out. . . .
The time came when we had to put up or shut up. We put up. And we are there. We don't have a big battle each day in a guerrilla war. It is a new kind of war for us. So it doesn't move that fast. . . . We are making progress. We are pleased with the results that we are getting.[10]

The performance impressed a lot of people. A headline in the *Chicago Daily News* read, "His Best Press Conference: Real LBJ Finally Cuts Loose."[11] The same night as the conference, NBC broadcast a half-hour special on the "new" Johnson.

Johnson, somewhat inexplicably, abandoned the new style. But no news conference style, old or new, could salvage his presidency. With the Tet offensive and the decline of Americans' support for the war, television offered Johnson no way out of his difficulties, especially the "credibility gap" between what he said about Vietnam and what the public believed. His decision not to run for reelection in 1968 removed him from the center of the news. A man who loved center stage, he ended his presidency, sadly, in the wings.

The importance and vitality of the White House news conference, which had waxed from the earliest days of the New Deal through most of Johnson's term in office, began to wane, at least until the Bush administration. The form seemed outworn. The soaring number of reporters in Washington destroyed the closeness of earlier conferences. The novelty was gone. During his presidency from January 20, 1969, to August 9, 1974, Nixon held thirty-nine news conferences, fewer for such a time span than recorded by each of his predecessors, including Franklin Roosevelt. Nixon handled his first several news conferences in 1969 adroitly, but then a heavy sarcasm crept in. Nixon became more and more hostile to the press and to television news.

On June 29, 1972, Nixon's sarcasm was aimed at Dan Rather. On that day, when Rather rose to ask a question, he identified himself, as was the custom then. "Mr. Rather," Nixon said, "I remember your name." Rather quickly replied, "Thank you, Mr. President. I remember yours, too."

At a press conference on October 26, 1973, in the midst of the Watergate crisis, Rather drew a gasp in the East Room when he asked Nixon to "share with us your thoughts, tell us what goes through your mind when you hear people, people who love this country, and people who believe in you, say reluctantly that perhaps you should resign or be impeached."

"Well," Nixon sarcastically retorted, "I'm glad we don't take a vote in this room."

Peter Lisagor reminded the president that before the election he had said that too many shocks can drain a nation. Had the nation, the *Chicago Daily News* reporter inquired, now reached that point?

"I have never heard or seen such outrageous, vicious, distorted reporting in twenty-seven years of public life," Nixon said, yet added, "I am not blaming anybody for that."

In the same news conference Robert Pierpoint of CBS told Nixon he was puzzled to know what it was about television coverage that had so aroused the president's anger.

"Don't get the impression you arouse my anger," Nixon said.

"I'm afraid, sir, that I have that impression," Pierpoint responded.

"You see," Nixon said, delivering the *coup de grace,* "one can only be angry with those he respects."

Afterward, trying to make amends for a remark that was badly received in the room by those who knew Pierpoint and his work, Nixon said that he did not wish to leave the impression with "my good friend from CBS over here that I don't respect the reporters."[12]

"From that news conference on," wrote Helen Thomas of United Press International, "everything was downhill for Nixon."[13]

Vice-President Gerald Ford became president as Nixon stepped down.

Ford's imprint on the evolution of presidential television was a modest one, more a change of tone than of method. His straightforward manner and lack of artifice were a plus at the sudden beginning of Ford's presidency when he spoke to Congress and the nation to bring the country out of its "long nightmare."

Ford's relations with television and the press corps were easy and low key. During the two and a half years of his presidency he held twenty-nine news conferences—about one a month. Although he was no dazzler as a television performer, Ford was video-minded. He was the first president to choose as news secretary a television correspondent, Ron Nessen, plucked from the reportorial ranks of NBC News in Washington, when his original choice, Gerald Ter Horst of the *Detroit News*, bowed out in the wake of Ford's pardon of President Nixon. The choice of Nessen was still another signpost that television had assumed the dominant role in presidential communication. Ford and Nessen made one significant addition to the formal news conference format, the provision for a "follow-up" question.

Jimmy Carter and his Georgians came to the White House determined to use television in every way they knew to project the new president as a man of the people. In the early days they had a fair degree of success. Television had propelled Carter to national prominence in the Iowa primary. His walk down Pennsylvania Avenue on Inauguration Day was designed to show him on the home screen as something different. Another common touch came when, dramatizing the need to conserve energy, Carter spoke to the nation clad in a cardigan sweater and seated in front of a crackling fire.

More than any president before him Carter made effective use of local and regional television. The Carter White House rounded up citizens in various locales around the country and gathered them in high school auditoriums for town meetings, an old Nixon format updated and enlarged on. Carter was at his populist best in such situations, friendly and personal as he rolled up his sleeves and answered questions, usually soft ones from the natives. He held forth at some thirty of these town meetings, covered by regional television. The networks taped these sessions and occasionally they provided the lead story for the evening news.

As the years ground on and Carter fell into the grip of high inflation and the Iranian hostage crisis, the fresh, man-of-the-people quality that television magnified at the beginning of his presidency came across differently—an ordinariness, a fecklessness, a helplessness in the face of events. Television had helped put Carter in the White House, but at the end of his four years in office he no longer found the tube a reliable friend.

All this was prelude. As Nixon's standing deteriorated, as Ford came and went, as Carter ran aground, the governor of California was eyeing the presidency. In truth, the television age did not reach full bloom in the White House until Ronald Reagan moved in on January 20, 1981.

14

The television president: Reagan on prime time

Before they entered the White House, some presidents were lawyers, others were governors, senators, representatives, or generals. Woodrow Wilson was president of Princeton University. Engineering was Herbert Hoover's field. Only Ronald Reagan had an extended career as an actor. It was an improbable path to the presidency, yet what a schooling it proved to be. If most of Reagan's films were grade B, the experience gleaned for later political use was grade A: a sense of timing, a knack of nod and gesture, a knowledge of where to stand, a feigning or hiding of emotion, an aura of likableness, brightened by a disarming grin. Reagan had an actor's skill before cameras—so important today because Americans are accustomed to being entertained by television news.

On the president's staff were bright, clever politicians with a shrewd grasp of public relations. Like Reagan, they understood how to mix politics and show business. Three of them, as former members of the presidential staffs of Richard Nixon or Gerald Ford, had learned a great deal about the potentialities and pitfalls of television news. They knew that the mass-marketing techniques that sell hamburgers on television can be applied to promoting a president and his policies.

Reagan projected a winning image on television and, in the main, enjoyed very favorable coverage in the press. This was not entirely attributable to his communication skills or those of his staff. The political climate had a lot to do with it. In Reagan's favor were the debilitated condition of the Democratic party after the Carter administration and a long-gathering conservative surge in America. Vietnam, Watergate, and Iran's imprisonment of American hostages had left a large residue of bitterness and discouragement in the country—tinder waiting for a buoy-

177

ant, confident president to ignite on prime time surrounded by flags and red, white, and blue balloons.

Another circumstance contributing to Reagan's success in communicating with the people was the generally passive mood of the American press in the 1970s. For some thirteen years in the Vietnam-Watergate period, the press had borne down on two American presidents, Lyndon Johnson and Richard Nixon, and helped force them out of office. For its pains the press found itself in a very unpopular position with the public. This was all the more true because of Nixon's success in branding reporters and editors as puppets of liberalism. Thus, when Reagan rolled into the White House on a wave of popular sentiment, the press was unaggressive. Owners of many newspapers were worried about public hostility. Many editors did not want their papers to be seen as attacking someone; they did not wish to have it appear that they were liberals lying in wait to get their hands on a conservative administration. As a result, they went easier on Reagan than on Johnson, Nixon, and Carter. Blunders and culpability in the new administration did not get quite the treatment they would have received previously.

"No question at all about that," recalled Benjamin C. Bradlee, executive editor of the *Washington Post,* which had taken the initiative in investigating Watergate.

One, the less aggressive stance was a natural reaction to Watergate. No matter what our right-wing critics used to say, we on the *Post* had no idea, none at all, that investigation would lead to the impeachment of Nixon. Two, Reagan was the first real conservative Republican president in a long time. We were sensitive to the reaction of the right, even though it would have been easy to give the president a hard time of it by judging him according to the standards by which we judged Kennedy and Nixon.[1]

Generally speaking, the reporters who covered Reagan, all supposedly captives of liberal doctrine, liked him personally. This contributed to the favorable coverage he received.

Television news was so basic to Ronald Reagan's career as a politician, a leader, and a president that he was as much absorbed in watching it as in using it. And just as using it conveyed a carefully cultivated image of himself to win support for his policies, so watching it sometimes led him directly to unshakable decisions about programs. On weekends and at night he and his wife Nancy passed hours together, switching from program to program.

"Boy, they watched them," recalled Michael K. Deaver, Reagan's television mentor and deputy chief of staff in the White House.

They were very affected by television. The president learned a lot from television about how what he was doing affected people. After he had seen something on television, for instance, in spending cuts in the welfare area, he would come in to me and say, "I want you to check this out—a guy out there in Virginia whose social security, or medicare, has been cut." He'd say, "We can't be doing that." I'd always get an answer that same day because he would either want to call the cabinet secretary or the person he'd seen on television. He wanted to follow up, and in some instances he changed policies.[2]

Television coverage of the hijacking of Trans World Airlines flight 847 in Athens in 1985 left Reagan so much distressed over the plight of the American hostages that Secretary of State George Shultz had difficulty restraining him from offering concessions to obtain their freedom.[3]

Reagan was especially affected by tales of tribulation afflicting an individual. One day following his reelection in 1984, the press reported that David A. Stockman, director of the Office of Management and Budget, planned to take advantage of the Republican landslide by, among other things, eliminating the nearly two-billion-dollar-a-year program to subsidize heating bills for the poor. Upon reading the story, Mike Jensen, NBC's chief financial correspondent, obtained the name of a random recipient of the program who lived in Pennsylvania. With a crew Jensen set off to interview him. On the "NBC Nightly News" of November 28 he introduced his segment of the program:

James Bradshaw of Philadelphia is retired on social security. His wife is disabled with a stroke. Last winter the Bradshaws got $465 from a federal program for people who can't afford to heat their homes. But he still owes the gas company money, and now it's threatening to shut off his gas. Bradshaw says if the federal program ends, he's in deep trouble.

The camera then turned to Bradshaw for his reaction: "That would be terrible. I wouldn't be able to heat our house, and I wouldn't be able to heat no water. I wouldn't be able to do anything."[4]

At a later meeting in the White House Stockman brought up his proposal. Reagan flatly waved it aside. The president said that he had seen an old fellow on television telling what the end to the subsidy would do to him and that he, Reagan, could not let it happen.

One administration official arranged to have an utterly obscure event covered by CBS for a national program she knew the president rarely missed—"Sunday Morning" with Charles Kuralt. The purpose of this astonishing stratagem was to effect a change in policy, and it worked.

From the early days of the administration in 1981, Secretary of Transportation Drew Lewis sought an increase in the gasoline tax to finance repair of the country's infrastructure of bridges, highways, and tunnels. Whenever he would bring the matter up in the cabinet, however, James A. Baker III, then the White House chief of staff, would remind him that the president had been reelected after pledging no increase in taxes. Meanwhile Linda Robinson, director of public affairs at the Department of Transportation, kept feeding stories to television reporters about an "infrastructure crisis." CBS finally asked for an interview with Lewis on the subject. Mrs. Robinson said she had a better idea, one made to order for the Kuralt show. CBS took her up on the suggestion and sent a crew to the western Pennsylvania town of Lilly. As a result, on Sunday morning, November 21, 1982, the Kuralt show opened with a commentary on the need for a public works program. A school bus appeared, heading for a bridge in Lilly. "This happens twice each school day," said the CBS reporter Jed Duvall.

A school bus stops at the approach to an old, worn bridge over railroad tracks. The children disembark and walk across the bridge. The driver is willing to risk only himself and the bus on the dangerous span. Fixing that bridge could provide many jobs. Fixing thousands of other bridges and thousands of miles of highways could provide many more jobs.

Later, to the strains of the "St. Louis Blues," the scene shifted to St. Louis. "The city has a clean, bright, open appearance," Duvall commented. But "underneath, St. Louis, like so many cities, is literally falling apart." Next a scene of a fire in a New York subway. Then back to the bridge in Lilly and Duvall's conclusion: "The little bus stops at each end of the bridge each morning and each afternoon. . . . And all the buses will stop at all the bridges, eventually, if the bridges aren't fixed."[5]

The next morning, November 22, the president informed Baker that he had watched a Sunday television program and thought the staff should take a fresh look at Drew Lewis's proposal for an increase in the gasoline tax.

On November 23 Rather reported on the "CBS Evening News": "Today, before heading off for a Thanksgiving holiday in California, President Reagan tried to signal 'no change' in his principles, but as [CBS correspondent] Jerry Bowen reports, he did endorse a tax increase and a jobs bill [in practice]."[6]

Congress promptly voted to increase the federal tax on gasoline by five cents a gallon. Probably neither the driver of the school bus in Lilly nor old Mr. Bradshaw in Philadelphia gave a great deal of thought to the influence of television news, but it was considerable.

Television also had an effect on U.S. foreign policy in Lebanon. Israel's invasion of Lebanon in 1982 and the carnage spread by the invaders' artillery and planes brought grim scenes nightly to American television screens. Among the millions who watched, although separately, were Reagan and Deaver. Each became increasingly incensed. After the extremely heavy bombing of Beirut August 12, Deaver by his own account found it intolerable to stay in the White House while an ally of the United States was killing many innocent people. As he tells the story in his memoirs, he walked into the Oval Office and startled Reagan by saying, "Mr. President, I have to leave." Deaver recalls explaining, "I can't be part of this anymore—the bombings, the killing of children—it's wrong. And you're the one person on the face of the earth right now who can stop it. All you have to do is tell [Israeli Prime Minister Menachem] Begin you want it stopped." Deaver continued:

Reagan rang his secretary and asked her to get Menachem Begin on the phone. In the meantime, George Shultz had joined us and added his endorsement of the president's intervention. When the call came through, [Reagan] told [Begin] in the plainest of language that the shelling had to stop. . . .

Twenty minutes later, Begin called him back and said he had just issued the orders. . . . The bombings had ceased. There were no planes over Beirut. When he hung up the phone, Ronald Reagan looked up and said, seriously, "I didn't know I had that kind of power."[7]

Evidently, he didn't, quite. According to the best available history in the field, *Israel's Lebanon War*, by Ze'ev Schiff and Ehud Ya'ari, cessation of the bombing already had been ordered before Begin was awakened from a nap in his office in the Knesset by Reagan's call.[8]

Among the television programs Reagan had a habit of watching were Sunday talk shows. The president once told former Secretary of Defense Caspar W. Weinberger "that more policy is made on Sunday morning than at any other time." Reagan was in a position to know. Weinberger himself was a guest on these shows a number of times. He preferred being interviewed on television to putting out stories through newspapers. He said that newspaper stories were often in error or were distorted by the judgment of the writer. On television the secretary could be seen saying what he said. He concluded that the availability of such direct contact between government officials and the public lent greater influence to television news.[9]

Reagan had been president for only sixty-nine days when, after lunch on March 30, 1981, he rode to the Washington Hilton Hotel to address a labor convention. Suddenly, at about 2:30 P.M., television programs everywhere were interrupted. Viewers saw videotape of an astonishing scene of gunplay outside the hotel, as Reagan was leaving it. Secret Service agents slammed the president to the floor of his waiting limousine. Behind them, lying face down on the sidewalk, was White House Press Secretary James S. Brady, gravely wounded with a bullet hole in his forehead. Two law enforcement officers also had been hit. As the limousine sped away, dazed spectators on the scene and minutes later others in front of countless television sets were relieved at least that the president had escaped being hit. It was not until the speeding White House limousine reached George Washington University Hospital a few minutes later that the world learned that one of the bullets fired by John W. Hinkley, Jr., had hit the president. It had entered below Reagan's left armpit and then been deflected by the seventh rib into his left lung. The lung collapsed. When his wife rushed to his bedside, he said, "Honey, I forgot to duck."[10]

Surgery was successful. By evening the public was reassured about his chances for complete recovery. Upon regaining consciousness, the president scribbled a note to the surgeons, "All in all, I'd rather be in Philadelphia."[11] When he awoke the next morning, Mrs. Reagan told him, "You'll be happy to know that the government is running normally." "What makes you think I'd be happy about that?" he retorted.[12] People admired such wit in circumstances so trying. After a month of often painful recuperation, Reagan addressed a joint session of Congress in prime time on April 28. His purpose was to speak on the economy but the atmosphere was better suited to a coronation. The gallery was ecstatic. On the floor of the House chamber, members of both parties tried to outshout each other in acclaiming a fallen hero who had risen to fight again. Tens of millions of television viewers witnessed about the most joyous scene in Washington in years. And, to be sure, Reagan knew exactly how to send the decibels crashing against the ceiling by reading a letter from a seventh-grade student in New York. "I hope you get well quick," the student wrote, "or you might have to make a speech in your pajamas."[13]

Surely, no president would wish to be shot in the lung. If he were hit by a bullet and recovered, however, he would have reason to be thankful for the invention of television. Before the shooting, Reagan's popularity, even though he had been in office little more than three months, had dipped somewhat. Concern that he might commit U.S. forces in Nicaragua or El Salvador was part of the problem. After the shooting, his overall favorable rating rose 19 points to 77 percent.[14] The political effect of the national outpouring of good will and sympathy for Reagan was unmistakable. The "honeymoon" traditional for new presidents has different time spans in different administrations. The televised acclaim Reagan received in the House chamber guaranteed him a long one.

Television, however, had exactly the opposite effect on the public standing of the secretary of state. Permanent political damage was inflicted on Alexander Haig because of a too hasty, ineptly worded statement he made before the cameras while the doctors were still treating Reagan.

The shooting and the rush to the hospital threw the staff in the White House into dismay and confusion. In the atmosphere of crisis Haig hurriedly joined a group of senior officials in the situation room in the White House. A television set was tuned to network news. Vice-President George Bush, who had been in Texas, was flying to Washington. At a time when the president's fate was still unknown, reporters were urgently questioning Larry Speakes, the assistant White House press secretary, on certain points. If the president went under anesthesia, would the vice-president automatically become acting president? Who would determine the president's condition?

Haig was watching on television with his colleague, Richard V. Allen, national security adviser to the president, as Speakes replied to the questions by saying he had no information on such matters. Allen was perturbed about the doubt left by the replies. According to Haig, Allen said to him, "This is very bad. We have got to do something." With that, the two darted from the situation room, which is in the basement, up the stairs to the newsroom on the ground floor. The place swarmed with reporters; since the shooting, the networks had been on the air continuously. In no time Haig took the podium. Again reporters pressed to know who in the government was making decisions. His answer:

Constitutionally, gentlemen, you have the president, the vice-president, and the secretary of state in that order, and should the president decide he wants to transfer the helm, he will do so. He has not done that. As of now, I am in control here, in the White House, pending the return of the vice-president and in close touch with him. If something came up, I would check with him, of course.[15]

To begin with, Haig was making up the law. Nothing in the Constitution deals with a situation such as existed that afternoon, with the president still alive. If the president had died, Vice-President Bush would have become president, with the power under the Twenty-fifth Amendment to name a vice-president, subject to approval by a majority vote of both houses of Congress. What Secretary Haig should have said, simply, was that he was on hand as the senior cabinet officer by virtue of the fact that the State Department was the first government department established. In light of Speakes's inarticulateness and the horror and confusion spread by the shooting of the president, it may have been a good idea for Haig to assure the country that the senior cabinet officer was taking charge in the White House until the vice-president's arrival. Circumstances, however, overrode good intentions. Many highly concerned viewers mistakenly got a whiff of something resembling usurpation in the former general's urgent manner, heightened by his breathlessness from having rushed up the stairs. Worse, the networks celebrated the event by rerunning it hour after hour into the night, sometimes trimming his statement to a brusque "As of now, I am in control here." On television the image hit a lot of people the wrong way, and they did not forget it, as Haig found when he was trounced in the Republican presidential primaries in 1988. Not even his self-deprecatory jokes about his statement moved voters. He likened the effect of his damaging experience on television on March 30, 1981, to the effect of Nixon's awkward appearance in his first televised debate with Kennedy in 1960.

"The one clear American policy revolution in this decade," David S. Broder wrote in 1989, "was engineered by Ronald Reagan when he came to power intent on reversing the almost half-century growth of the welfare state. He succeeded to a significant degree in realizing that ambition."[16] In this effort and others television news helped Reagan. He was able to influence members of Congress because of his popularity with their constituents, and his popularity sprang largely from his skill on television. Through television he identified himself with the values and traditions of millions of American voters. Day in and day out, on a scale never before seen in the White House, Reagan and his assistants meticulously planned how they could use television to build support for the president's programs in Congress. To keep abreast of how his programs were faring, Reagan often watched the broadcasts of congressional sessions on C-SPAN. After listening to a member make a speech on the floor, he was apt to telephone him or her to express his pleasure or, if the member opposed the administration, his displeasure. In such cases the president would proceed to review his reasons for having sent up the program.

After five years as a sports announcer on radio in Des Moines, Reagan went to Hollywood. During his twenty-seven years as an actor, he appeared in fifty-four movies. He played the parts of doctors, lawyers, cowboys, musicians, soldiers, and crooks. His role in *Knute Rockne—All American* as an unfortunate football hero, George Gipp, enabled Reagan afterward to make the sentimental appeal to his supporters to "win one for the Gipper."

When it came to political persuasion and leadership, could Reagan address the public on television and in person as effectively as he had performed in Hollywood studios? On October 27, 1964, seventeen years before he was elected president, he answered the question overwhelmingly in the affirmative. Practically on the eve of the 1964 election, Reagan spoke on national television for Barry Goldwater, who by then had no chance of defeating Johnson for reelection and, of course, did not. Reagan's performance, however, was a revelation to Republican conservatives—the most successful political debut since William Jennings Bryan electrified the 1896 Democratic convention with his "Cross of Gold" speech. Reagan's speech brought in a million dollars for Republican candidates. "Most of Reagan's address," wrote his biographer Lou Cannon,

was standard antigovernment boilerplate larded with emotional denunciations of communism and a celebration of individual freedom. His statistics were sweeping and in some cases dubious. His best lines were cribbed from Franklin Roosevelt, and he quoted from nearly everybody else as well—Plutarch, Alexander Hamilton, James Madison, Sumner Schlichter, Karl Marx, Joseph Clark, Harry Byrd, James Ramsey McCulloch, and Howard K. Smith, to name a few.[17]

In their despair over the 1964 campaign, conservative Republicans asked why Reagan had not been nominated instead of Goldwater. Why, they lamented, had not Goldwater enunciated conservative aims and values as Reagan did? Reagan not only had high style and a friendly air on television, he also had convictions stubbornly held on the limitations of government. In the end, the combination of style and principles was unbeatable.

"The Reagan White House more than any before it, established the

Presidency as theatre," wrote Elizabeth Drew in the *New Yorker* in 1989.[18] Ronald Reagan intended it to be that way. He once told someone on his staff, "Politics is just like show business. You have a hell of an opening, coast for awhile, and then have a hell of a close."[19] For this performance Reagan had the stage and equipment he needed. The enlarged newsroom/ television studio built during the Nixon administration was fully equipped for the big time. It little resembled the old pressroom in the West Wing of the White House, which was crowded if fifteen journalists were there all at once, handling a good story; twenty of them would turn the place into a madhouse. The only publications available were the District of Columbia telephone directory and a few newspapers. No more than ten reporters regularly had special telephones connected directly with their offices. Those who did not were well advised to have a nickel handy for the two pay phones.

In the new newsroom/television studio, a portion of which is duplex, eight rows of permanent seats, six to a row, occupy the center. They face a podium and a microphone always awaiting the president. The Oval Office is only several steps away. Two rows of television cameras stand focused on the podium with its blue backdrop decorated with the White House logo. Banks of lights hang from the ceiling. At the far end of the room from the podium are glassed-in booths for broadcasters. During Reagan's presidency the networks regularly kept two and sometimes three reporters and camera crews on the job at the same time. When news broke, a network could be on the air from the White House within minutes, either from the newsroom or from a camera position on the North Lawn. In the early days of television news, eight hours of advance notice was required for live coverage from the White House. A TV truck as large as a moving van had to be parked outside and hundreds of feet of heavy cable fed to a camera position.

With their computer terminals, fax machines, modems, and television monitoring systems, the reporters covering Reagan had access to more information storage capacity, it is said, than was available to the entire government when Harry Truman was president. By punching the right keys a reporter could call up reports from the Associated Press, United Press International, and Reuters News; a reporter could even communicate directly with a fellow correspondent in a news bureau in London, Frankfurt, or Tokyo.

Much has been made of Reagan's apparatus in the White House for releasing news and, as many would say, propaganda. The term "managing the news" originated in the Kennedy administration and was mastered by Reagan and his presidential staff. Their success revolved around planning ahead, controlling the flow of information, keeping the administration on the offensive, stressing issues favored by the president, limiting reporters' access to the president, speaking for the administration in one voice, and, for good effect, repeating the same message again and again. However vaguely, another element was there, too, perhaps caught best by Hedrick Smith in his book on the workings of Washington. Reagan understood, Smith wrote, "that politics for the millions—in the television age—is not rational but emotional."[20]

When Reagan entered politics, rivals dismissed him as just another actor, as if drama was a liability in public office. After watching the discomforts of Richard Nixon, Lyndon Johnson, Jimmy Carter, and Gerald Ford on television, skeptics changed their minds. Reagan's talent was a golden asset in the new politics of image. He was always at ease on the stage. He loved it. Ritual and ceremony came naturally to him. He was never more appealing than when he was comforting the families of men and women who had died in a combat zone or in accidents in space.

At the outset Reagan's news apparatus was managed by James Baker, Michael Deaver, and David Gergen. Richard G. Darman also took an important part. Baker was the White House chief of staff. A Texan who had graduated from Princeton, Baker brought to the White House a background in law and politics. Deaver, a public relations man, had been a confidant of Reagan throughout most of Reagan's political career. A former speechwriter for President Nixon, Gergen was Reagan's communications director. One thing all of them had learned through previous experience, Gergen said, was that Watergate demonstrated the dangers of extreme partisanship.[21]

A typical day in the White House during Reagan's first term began with Baker, Deaver, and Edwin Meese III, counselor to the president, sitting down to breakfast to range over new developments, keeping an eye out for topics that might lend themselves to newsworthy remarks or actions by the president. Then, following Baker's senior staff conference at eight o'clock, the "line-of-the-day" meeting would tackle the question of how the White House could make the best showing on television that evening. Gergen and Larry Speakes were present for this, one of the day's most challenging tasks. "If we could dictate as much of the sound bites on the evening news as possible, and dictate it so that we got our story [out]," Deaver explained years later, "we could continue to be at fifty

plus in the public opinion polls. That's all that really mattered to someone like me or the politicians."[22] The substance of the sound bites was
the responsibility of members of the staff who dealt with policy. An informal press briefing at 9:15 A.M. was of particular interest to the network television crews. The "line of the day" would be revealed, along
with instructions on what pictures of the president could be taken and
under what conditions. For the longer perspective (anywhere from two
weeks to three months) Deaver held staff luncheons every Friday in Blair
House. As nearly as possible he wanted to keep the flow of White House
stories in line with a coherent scenario that presented a favorable impression of what Reagan was doing.

Since the beginning of the Republic, presidents have not made news
of significance every day. Far from it. Even in the 1940s and 1950s there
were periods when a reporter covering the White House would have felt
fortunate to have a front-page story once or twice a week. But by the
time of the Reagan administration and the banks of television cameras at
the ready, television was so much driven by hunger for pictures of the
president that practically anything he might say or do that could be filmed
was treated on the evening news shows as a newsworthy event. The networks needed Reagan, and Reagan needed the networks.

Although Reagan had a good press and favorable television coverage,
it would be a long step to conclude that his news apparatus was the
reason for it. Actually, the Reagan system was not original. Much of it,
according to author Mark Hertsgaard, had been devised by Nixon, or
more exactly by the men around him, and adapted by the Reagan staff.[23]
And Nixon did not have a good press, or so he often lamented. Presidents
Franklin Roosevelt, Dwight Eisenhower, and John Kennedy, in particular, got their stories out very effectively without an array of procedures
and quasi committees. In Reagan's case the master key to success was the
combination of his personality, convictions, training, and theatrical talent.

Hertsgaard and other critics have faulted the press and television for
not adequately exposing the difference between the administration as
portrayed by Reagan and his experts and the administration as it really
was. Like other trades and professions, journalism never does its task as
well as it might. It never probes deeply enough, never launches enough
of its own initiatives, never achieves the originality it ought to. Journalism, to a large degree, is necessarily reactive to government's pronounce-
ments, decisions, and actions. The press and television cannot cover a

National Security Council meeting; television and the press do not have the power to subpoena officials. Secret documents are protected by law. Government holds the high ground. It is the government, not the press and television news, that sets the so-called national agenda. It is true, of course, that journalistic exposés and stories based on leaks can cause a certain upheaval in government and compel government for a time to concentrate on the issue at stake. Government may even be required to submit to reform. But basic policy and action continue to reside with government, not with journalism. In a 1988 review of Hertsgaard's *On Bended Knee*, the historian and biographer Stephen E. Ambrose wrote:

Of course, the Government lies; one would have to be deaf and dumb not to know that. Of course, President Reagan and his aides manipulated the press. Of course, reporters concentrate on scoops rather than depth, on polls rather than issues, on personalities rather than events. But in 30 years of doing research on recent American history, much of it in newspapers, I've become convinced that the American press is not only the best and freest in the world, but the most critical, thought-provoking, thorough and diverse.[24]

As a case of staging a presidential appearance for best effect on television probably nothing up to that time excelled Nixon on the Great Wall. With Reagan, however, such stagings under Deaver's direction were commonplace. At one of the morning conferences, Deaver elected for prominent play in the news a report showing a rise in housing starts, always cheerful news on the business page. But Deaver did not want it on the business page. He wanted people who never read the business news to know the good tidings. Let the president get out and about to demonstrate what was happening. Fort Worth, Texas, was chosen as the theater. Air Force One was wheeled out. An accompanying press plane had the usual number of customers. And soon there was Ronald Reagan surrounded by hard hats, making his way before television cameras through the halls of a half-finished frame house. It was just something to make people feel a little happier after turning on the evening news.

Deaver loved putting the old movie actor in roles in which he looked strong and heroic. In picking the settings, Deaver was meticulous. An outstanding performance was staged in 1983 at the Demilitarized Zone separating North and South Korea. Deaver arrived a day in advance to choose the best point for Reagan to stand for a distant but bold look at the Communist defenses. When the president arrived to sweep the scene with field glasses, he was wearing a flak jacket. "It was great television," Gergen related. "I think every White House would rather see its President in what amounts to a heroic situation . . . and it sure is a hell of a lot better picture than a guy like Carter, stumbling up in Camp David when he's jogging around up there, falling down. One picture builds support for the President. The other, I think, destroys him."[25]

In 1984 Reagan went to Normandy to commemorate the fortieth anniversary of the Allied invasion. Probably not since General Eisenhower's staff planned the cross-Channel attack did the Normandy coast undergo such scrutiny as it did from Deaver in search of the perfect spot for Reagan's speech. It was at the Omaha Beach Memorial on a cliff overlooking the sea in Pointe du Hoc. While preparations were in progress, Deaver got his hands on a letter that twenty-eight-year-old Lisa Zannatta Henn of Millbrae, California, had addressed to Reagan after his trip had been announced. Her late father, Peter R. Zannatta, had fought at Normandy with the Thirty-Seventh Engineer Combat Battalion. He had always intended to return to the scene but died before he had a chance. In her letter Mrs. Henn told the president that she was determined to make a pilgrimage to France for her father. To make this possible Reagan paid her way to France for the commemoration. When he spoke on the cliff, which had been captured by American rangers on D-Day, she stood close by. At a poignant moment he read from her letter, which said: "I'm going there, Dad, and I'll see the beaches and the barricades and the monuments. I'll see the graves and I'll put flowers there just like you wanted to do. I'll never forget what you went through, Dad, nor will I let anyone else forget. And, Dad, I'll always be proud."[26] Mrs. Henn wept. The president practically did.

Reagan seemed to be as successful with the ridiculous as with the sublime. During his reelection campaign in 1984, the air force wanted him to take part in a rollout of the controversial new B-1 bomber at the Rockwell International Corporation plant in southern California. Deaver, however, preferred to have him avoid military events because of old concerns about Reagan's supposed proclivity for getting the country into war. On the other hand, Deaver knew that some forty thousand persons in southern California were employed in the work on the B-1. He compromised by scheduling the president to participate but with a large sign reading "Prepared for Peace" erected in front of the bomber, almost screening it from view. This was about on a par with Reagan's earlier visit to an Irish saloon in Boston to hoist a beer or two with some workmen. This much televised drink with the workers was on the same day

Reagan appealed to corporate executives by calling for abolition of the income tax on corporations.

A phenomenon about Reagan, the one that earned him the sobriquet "Teflon president"—the president to whom criticism did not stick—was that he could scandalize the sophisticated with his errors and misstatements at press conferences and other forums, yet leave most of the public indifferent. The explanation must lie in the affection for the man among the millions who watched him on television. With them, his gaffes did not seem to register. People were not particularly bothered, for example, when the president said, incorrectly, that the Soviet Union had most of its strategic nuclear weapons on land-based missiles. When Reagan said that he had reached a compromise with congressional leaders to retain the MX missile, but later could not recall for reporters the terms of the compromise, few seemed to care. Reagan also said that Israel did not know that the United States was secretly shipping arms to Iran when it did know. The assorted incorrect and contradictory statements Reagan made about the insidious Iran-contra affair were a reflection of his porous management style, emphasized in the Tower Commission report on the scandal in 1987. Chaired by retired senator John Tower, a Republican from Texas, the commission found that Reagan's way of conducting the presidency was "to put the principal responsibility for policy review and implementation on the shoulders of advisors."[27]

Compassion for American hostages seized at the U.S. embassy in Iran led Jimmy Carter in 1980 to a heap of wrecked helicopters in a desert. It cost him the confidence of the electorate. Five years later an urgent desire to free American hostages in Lebanon agitated Reagan. Public pressure on him to get them home was never as great as it had been on Carter. Nevertheless, the hostage situation was an emotional stress for Reagan. His resolve to free the hostages, whose fate he believed was controlled by Iran, was an extenuating circumstance in an otherwise foolish decision to sell arms to that country. He escaped blame for responsibility for the sometimes criminal wrongs of the initiative as well as he did because, for one thing, nobody could abide the thought of investigation carried to a point where it might have led to another impeachment proceeding, especially against the most popular president since Eisenhower.

Reagan's appearances on television were staged to show him on the move, making speeches, visiting schools, striding for his helicopter on the South

Lawn. Thus, a passive president was perceived by the public to be an active one. To admiring television viewers he seemed gregarious, accessible; to reporters in the White House he seemed inaccessible, almost reclusive. Even the reporters were used as props to convey an image of presidential activity, as in the scenes of their shouted questions to Reagan when he was on his way to his helicopter. Many people thought shouted questions to a president were rude. In fact, the White House often set up the event, preparing the president with answers that were not only like telling sound bites but also safe against challenge from follow-up questions because Reagan was on the move. If a question was asked that he did not wish to hear, he grinned and held his hand cupped to his ear, seemingly helpless, as he continued on his way. Reagan held few formal news conferences—forty-four in eight years. Reporters were eager to ask him questions under any circumstances.

The nickname "great communicator," conferred on him because of his adroitness on television, suited Reagan least well in handling details in news conferences. The familiar scene of President Reagan striding like a conqueror through the main foyer of the White House on a red carpet to face reporters and cameras waiting in the East Room conveyed a sense of serene confidence. It was staged to do so. What it concealed was the apprehension of the president and his advisers over his making errors and misstatements, like those mentioned earlier.

Before press conferences all modern presidents have been briefed by their staffs for information and guidance in answering anticipated questions. As a former actor, Reagan went one step farther: he held dress rehearsals. The date of a Reagan press conference was usually chosen about ten days in advance by Larry Speakes, Baker, Deaver, and Meese, often after they had been assured as to its propitiousness by Mrs. Reagan upon consultation with Joan Quigley, her astrologer.[28] Government departments and agencies were solicited for hunches about what reporters might ask. All such material as well as recent newspaper clippings were assembled in a briefing book for the president. After he had perused it, the first rehearsal was held in the moving picture room, equipped for the occasion with podium, television lighting, microphone, and public address system to make him think of the East Room. "We would fire questions, we would follow up, we would try to trap him, we would try to play the exact role of the press,"[29] Speakes wrote. After about forty-five minutes of this Baker, Deaver, and Meese would critique his perfor-

mance. On the afternoon of the day of the prime-time conference the
White House press office would rehearse him again, whereupon he would
go upstairs for a nap. By the time the appointed hour arrived, he and
Mrs. Reagan talked together tensely, seriously.

"There would be this long farewell between the two of them," Speakes
recalled. "Sometimes their goodbys would last so long that I would be
afraid we'd be late for the news conference. She would hold his hand, tell
him to do well. . . . Then they would kiss and he would be off to his fate,
waving to her as he got on the elevator."[30] He gave the impression of a
man heading for combat. Then when he reached the foyer and the television cameras, he looked as calm as if he were walking up to get a
medal. Just before Reagan stepped up on the podium in the East Room
to take reporters' questions, Deaver would give the president's military
aide a note to slip into Reagan's hand.

"It was always a note to be a last-minute mind-setter for him," Deaver
recalled.

There would be all kinds of things I wrote. Quotes from the Bible. Quotations
that would remind him of the greatness of other presidents. There were warnings
how not to get into trouble. When Ed Meese was in trouble [as attorney general
in Reagan's second term], I put down: "If you are asked to comment on Ed
Meese, Answer number 1: No. Answer number 2: No. Answer number 3: No.
Answer number 4: No." . . . Ninety-nine percent of the time the notes were to
affect his mood. To get him *up* when he walked in there. To get him feeling good
about himself. To remind him of something that he and I or Nancy and I knew
about him that would bring him up.[31]

Despite all this flutter over details, Reagan was no amateur at using
televised news conferences and speeches to marshal support for his programs in Congress. "The president was not much on the details of legislation," wrote the then Speaker of the House, Thomas P. (Tip) O'Neill,
Jr., "but he was great at fighting for it."[32] In his first two years in office,
Reagan won passage of tax and budget legislation that reversed decades
of federal policy. In fact, he was so successful that Speaker O'Neill got
the Congressional Research Service of the Library of Congress to study
the fairness of the president's access to the television networks.

Published in August 1984, the report drew no startling conclusions on
the issue of fairness. Within reason, presidents since Truman have had
ready access to network television. But the report left no doubt about the
power of television in Reagan's hands. "Throughout his Presidency," it

said, "many political observers have perceived Ronald Reagan as a formidable communicator in network television broadcasts."[33] The report
added:

As with his predecessors, access to network television has proved valuable to Mr.
Reagan in winning public support for Administration policy. Perhaps even more
valuable to President Reagan has been the impact which his various broadcasts—
addresses to the Nation, speeches before joint sessions of Congress, and news
conferences—have been seen as having on the outcome of policy issues before
Congress.[34]

In buttressing its conclusion, the report cited a number of polls and
surveys. For example, early in 1982 Reagan broached an initiative for
expanding international commerce in the Caribbean area. A survey by a
two-way interactive cable television system in Columbus, Ohio, found
that 35 percent of the viewers supported the proposal. After the president
made a televised speech on the plan on February 24, 64 percent of the
viewers favored it. On April 27, 1983, Reagan addressed a televised joint
session of Congress on problems in Central America. ABC conducted a
network call-in on viewer reaction; it received 336,462 calls. Of these,
258,943 calls agreed with Reagan's assertion that events in Central America
threatened the United States.[35]

Reagan's television broadcasts, the report noted, influenced legislation
in Congress. "On three occasions, the simultaneous access to the three
commercial television networks which the President used for addresses
on his economic program was followed days later by passage in the House
. . . of Reagan-backed budget or tax measures over the opposition of the
House Democratic leadership."[36]

On May 9, 1984, the day before a House vote on economic and military aid to El Salvador, Reagan went on television to urge passage of a
Republican bill instead of one approved by the Democratic-controlled
Committee on Foreign Affairs. On May 10 the House approved the Republican bill by a vote of 212 to 208. "Various observers," the report
said, "credited Mr. Reagan's address as being a key, though not the only
factor behind the narrow Administration victory. . . . Of the President's
televised address, the Chairman of the House Foreign Affairs Committee,
Rep. Dante B. Fascell (D-Fla.), said, 'Obviously, it had to be a plus. It
was a masterful performance.' "[37]

When President Eisenhower attended the summit conference in Geneva in 1955, Secretary of State John Foster Dulles admonished him not
to smile while being photographed with the Soviet representatives, Nikita

S. Khrushchev and Nikolai A. Bulganin. Dulles did not want Eastern Europeans to conclude that the Republican party's 1952 plank calling for their liberation from the Soviets was collapsing in good will in Geneva. It would be hard to imagine any adviser telling Ronald Reagan not to smile on television. Throughout most of his eight years in office he seldom lost his buoyancy and lightness of touch before the camera. Like President Franklin Roosevelt with his tilted cigarette holder, he had an optimistic smile, a country jauntiness that people liked to see. Almost every day he was on television—a glamorous figure wearing a business suit in the Oval Room, or white-tie attire for a state dinner, or riding clothes at Camp David, or a sport shirt for cutting brushwood on his California ranch. If he was not making a speech, he was shaking hands. If he was not shaking hands, he was standing before the Statue of Liberty, or attending the Olympic Games in Los Angeles, or reviewing troops somewhere in the world. Television pictured him in every light. It caught his words and gestures, moods and movement. In the final analysis, though, television never penetrated the man behind the performer.

15

-0➡0➡0➡0➡0➡0➡0➡0➡0➡0➡0➡0➡0➡0➡0➡0➡0➡0➡0➡0➡0➡0➡0➡0➡0➡0➡0

The television occupation of Capitol Hill

The stream of television pictures that flowed from the White House in the fifties and sixties swept away, in the late seventies, years of opposition to televising Congress. The resistance collapsed for one main reason. Legislators feared that the incessant appearances of presidents on the nation's television screens were pushing them into the shadow of the executive branch.

Complete television coverage of the House began in 1979. Worried that televising their House colleagues might put *them* in the shade, senators voted to allow complete coverage in 1986. All congressional sessions are regularly covered by C-SPAN, the Cable Satellite Public Affairs Network. It carries other public affairs programs when Congress is not meeting. Since the Senate and the House control the broadcasting system, other networks and stations may pick up episodes for their own use if they choose. No commercial station, however, would dream of providing the gavel-to-gavel coverage carried by C-SPAN.

During the rising craze over radio in 1922, Rep. Vincent Brennan, a Republican from Michigan, had what he thought was a good idea for Congress. In order to enable citizens around the country to hear the debates and speeches, he introduced House Joint Resolution 278, providing for the "installation and operation of radiotelephone transmitting apparatus for the purpose of transmitting the proceedings . . . of the Senate and the House of Representatives."[1] Proof of the practicality of this proposal accumulated over the years as the Canadian House of Commons and most state legislatures opened their sessions to coverage by radio. H. J.

Res. 278, however, died for lack of support. So did a number of later resolutions, which substituted television coverage for radio coverage.

From its beginnings in the late 1940s, television news was regarded as such a brash junior medium that it had to wage a prolonged fight just to join newspapers, magazines, and radio in having its own quarters in the Capitol and gallery rights for its reporters in the House and Senate chambers. This was, of course, long before televising regular sessions was permitted. Television struggled to get into the Capitol to do interviews and stories about what was happening in Congress. A good deal of hit or miss characterized its early operations on the Hill.

Major hearings in the Senate office buildings were sometimes televised. (Speaker of the House Sam Rayburn, however, banned coverage in the House office buildings.) But in the Capitol itself the large studio-type cameras were seen only on special occasions. The ceremonial opening of the Eightieth Congress on January 3, 1947, was the first telecast of Congress assembled as a body. This debut was nearly a disaster. A heavy lens fell off a camera in the gallery and plunged steeply to the House floor, just missing one of the members.[2]

When Truman fired Gen. Douglas MacArthur on April 11, 1951, and television reporters covering the Senate sought angry reactions, they rightly brought before the camera the Republican floor leader. He was Kenneth S. Wherry, a licensed embalmer from Pawnee City, Nebraska, who once referred to Southeast Asia as Indigo China. When the camera started rolling, Wherry was still in such a rage at Truman that he could do little more than splutter. To celebrate Alfred M. Landon's ninetieth birthday in 1977, a group of Republicans gave a luncheon for him in the Capitol. The party's presidential nominee in 1936, and former governor of Kansas, Landon liked journalists, and they liked him. After lunch the guest of honor agreed to go to the television gallery to reminisce. When he got there he sat down in front of the camera and fell asleep. A brief nap refreshed him and the interview proceeded.[3]

By the late 1970s, television cameras wheeled into the Capitol for newsworthy events were so ubiquitous and the marble floors so much resembled snake farms of cable that the situation was intolerable. Hence, the architect of the Capitol and a consortium of television news organizations joined hands to rewire much of the historic building so that cameras could be plugged in almost anywhere. Installing miles of fiber-optic cables capable of carrying ninety circuits was a task that involved circumventing abandoned chimneys and pipes and cutting through old walls, some as much as twelve feet thick. Ultimately, the spider web of lines converged in a hub in the Capitol basement, whence pictures could be flashed to a number of destinations.

In 1979, three years after he became speaker of the House, Thomas P. (Tip) O'Neill, Jr., authorized live coverage of House sessions. It "turned out to be one of the best decisions I ever made," he wrote later.[4] His immediate predecessors in office, Speakers John W. McCormack and Carl Albert, had adhered to Rayburn's precedent. For years Speaker Rayburn had been an insurmountable bar to television in the House chamber. According to Tip O'Neill, Rayburn "used to say that microphones and cameras would detract from the dignity of the House."[5] Furthermore, Rayburn was suspicious that hacks could make themselves look like statesmen on television.

Rayburn was particularly outraged at the soaring popularity the rather lumpish Estes Kefauver had won during the much-televised Senate committee hearings on organized crime in 1951. After the hearings ended, Kefauver, the chairman of the committee, informed President Truman, whose term was nearing an end, that he was considering running for the Democratic nomination in 1952. Privately, Truman persisted in pronouncing the senator's name "Cowfever," and he was not enchanted by the senator's presidential aspirations. Nothing came of them in 1952. But the huge exposure on television from the hearings did help Kefauver win the vice-presidential nomination in 1956, the year of Adlai E. Stevenson's second futile campaign against Eisenhower.

Rayburn's opposition to television in the House was later shared by Leo Ryan, a Democrat from California. In 1978 he warned his colleagues that television cameras could transform the House from a forum to a theater. He pleaded for resistance to pressures "to change this [body] from a place where reasonable men and women may debate to the kind of place which the Roman Senate became."[6] In the U.S. Senate Howard Baker, a Republican from Tennessee, was a leading champion of televised sessions. He countered such arguments by saying that if members wanted to cavort to attract attention, they could always do so before television cameras on the Capitol steps, if denied the opportunity in the Senate.

By the late 1970s television had become too big a force in American politics to be excluded from either the House or the Senate floor. Worn thin were the old arguments that Congress would not make good television because of parliamentary diversions, that television would make Congress look dull, that broadcasters could not be trusted for accuracy and that cameras would encourage demagoguery. The elevation of the presidency in relation to Congress, heightened by television news, had become a serious concern to Speaker O'Neill, one that many representatives shared. And so in 1979 the House—and seven years later the Senate—permitted live television coverage.

If the televising of every session of the House and Senate is the centerpiece of the broadcasting of Congress, there is an extraordinarily busy periphery. Indeed, the periphery may be more important to many individual members because it is there that they broadcast their messages to constituents at home.

Members have access to radio-television galleries on the Senate and House sides of the Capitol. Until recent years the Senate television headquarters in the Capitol was the Senate document room. To meet the growing needs of broadcasters, it was expanded into a spacious studio with rows of booths for the networks and independent companies and with a theaterlike chamber in which members may be interviewed on camera. In 1989 the House also revamped its gallery to accommodate the increasing number of members intent on making television appearances.

C-SPAN and the bureaus of various regional television networks are located in an office building on North Capitol Street near Union Station. Correspondents of independent television stations and freelance producers who work on Congress-related programs also use this building. The roof is wired for cameras. For members broadcasting to the folks at home this is a favorite setting and a mite scary at night, some say. "You're standing up there on the roof with the Capitol dome in the background, and there is no guardrail," Rep. Daniel Glickman, a Democrat from Kansas, related. "The Occupational Safety and Health Administration would go crazy if they could see how close you are to falling off down on North Capitol Street."[7]

On South Capitol Street is the Harriman Communications Center. It is owned and operated by the Democratic Congressional Campaign Committee and is available to Democratic members of both houses.

The House and Senate have their own recording studios where members of both parties can tape video recordings, satellite feeds, and other television services. The House studio is in the Rayburn House Office Building. Nearby is an adjunct of the House radio-television gallery in the Capitol. It has a large television studio that can be booked by individual representatives or by broadcasters. The Senate recording studio is in the subbasement of the Capitol. Republican senators also can use a studio on the fourth floor of the Hart Senate Office Building.

Room H-137 in the Capitol, part of the House Ways and Means Committee quarters, can be used by members of both parties, especially at busy times, to televise remarks to their districts and states. In his book on the workings of Washington, Hedrick Smith tells of watching forty rank-and-file Democrats lined up there, waiting to give constituents their reaction to Reagan's 1986 State of the Union address.

Most were quietly rehearsing little set pieces . . . nervously teasing each other about performing on cue. Each had forty-five seconds to a minute—no time for fluffs or retakes. The entire operation had to be completed within ninety minutes, if they were going to hit the eleven o'clock local news in New Haven, Cleveland, or San Francisco. . . .

The room had the bare rudiments of a set: an American flag as backdrop and a camera mounted on [a] tripod and focused toward the flag at a spot where a "T" had been marked off on the carpet with gray masking tape. Each member would stand on the "T" facing the camera and a young woman holding a microphone who gave the cue line: "Congressman, your reaction?" [8]

If all the television facilities mentioned should prove insufficient, members may find three other broadcasting sites in the Capitol wired for television cameras: the Rotunda, Statuary Hall, and the South Door. Outside, the "swamp" and "elm tree" sites on the east lawn are popular for filming because of the Capitol dome in the background.

It is but a mild exaggeration to say that the whole of Capitol Hill has become something of a huge television studio. Old customs and practices, especially those affecting communication between legislators and constituents, have been radically changed with unmistakable political consequences. Most senators and representatives use television to present themselves, often daily, to their constituents. This has made it harder to defeat them. Incumbents enjoy, frequently at government expense, access to voters that their challengers at the polls can seldom afford to match.

Television has loosened party discipline in Congress. Instead of depending on organizational support, members can use television to build their own followings and attract funds. Members with little seniority in Congress can make themselves experts on certain issues—Central America, Southeast Asia, savings-and-loan institutions—and sometimes beat their "elders" in the rush to the national networks.

"The presidential-congressional struggle for publicity," Ronald Garay wrote, "has been central to the legislative history of congressional television. . . . The struggle is rooted in what has been perceived, either rightly or wrongly, as an erosion of congressional prerogatives that tipped the executive-legislative balance of power towards the President."[9] In this competition the nature of theater works against Congress. The president of the United States as a single actor playing his part on a narrow stage is usually more dramatic than 535 legislators spread out before the footlights. Historically, a president has been given access to network airtime virtually upon request. For his opponents, access is harder to win. On television the president can be terse, interesting, surprising, entertaining. Sometimes what he has to say is dramatic and eagerly awaited. Events in Congress, by contrast, often develop over a period of weeks or even months. To the uninitiated, procedures may be bewildering. Routine roll-call votes, quorum calls, and points of order slow the pace. "The drama, the immediacy, and, most important, the mass audience that television can deliver," Rep. Robert Michel of Illinois, the House Republican leader, said in 1989, "has little room for Congress."[10] C-SPAN executives maintain they are not concerned about the size of their audience; for the congressional sessions it is small by the standards of commercial television ratings.

Sen. Daniel Patrick Moynihan, a Democrat from New York, has observed that C-SPAN's coverage of the regular sessions has less impact on viewers and members of Congress than does its coverage of committee hearings, which were usually ignored by the public in the past. Since the basic work of Congress is done in committees, viewers are now able to obtain through television a clearer picture of how decisions are reached. Moynihan sees this as a mixed blessing at times because decisions require compromise. With television cameras staring down on them in committee rooms, members may find it more difficult to work out compromises.[11] In Moynihan's view,

as government becomes more open, it becomes less flexible. Our deliberations are more and more open and, in theory at least, our bargaining processes are open but that paralyzes things. . . . A senator can never say before the cameras, "I'll give you this, if you will give me that." Television has made it very hard to negotiate. You can't say, "I give up on the hog farmers, if you give up on the commuters."[12]

Even more than C-SPAN programs, the satellites above the Capitol and the ring of broadcasting facilities around the Capitol have helped members of Congress win votes back home. The satellite broadcasts from Capitol Hill are readily picked up by local news programs at individual television stations around the country. Some of these stations run local news for two or three hours every day, and they need all the good items they can get. This need has led to close relationships between many local producers and the press secretaries of members of Congress from the producers' states and districts. The producers know what newsworthy events are coming up in Congress, and the press secretaries are alert to the interests of local producers. From the satellites the local stations can pick up these carefully scheduled appearances on Capitol Hill. This high-tech form of communication is the modern equivalent for members of typed press handouts and franked letters to constituents.

"We find this the most effective way to get our message across," said Representative Glickman, a quintessential television communicator.

I'm never too busy to talk to local television. Period. Exclamation point. I believe local television is the number one priority. Even if Tom Brokaw is calling me on the line and one of my local stations wants me on the other, I'll always talk to the local station first. Of course, it would kill me to have to turn Tom Brokaw down.[13]

As soon as the satellite broadcasting technology appeared on Capitol Hill, most members were eager to try it. After all, new members had used television in their campaigns and swore by its influence. Some older members who were skeptical at first changed their minds. Sen. Howell Heflin, a Democrat from Alabama, had to be talked into experimenting with the satellite by his press secretary, Jerry Ray. At first the senator used the satellite feed from Washington to Montgomery, Alabama, to talk on local television programs. Heflin found the response so favorable that within a year he had practically created his own network, beaming his comments to twenty-two Alabama stations. Before joining Heflin's staff, Ray had worked for WSFA in Montgomery and was struck by the importance of symbols, like the Capitol dome, in television pictures.

"That Capitol out there—that says power," he declared. "You have the senator talking from the Rotunda with this great painting behind him and this white statue looking down on him, blessing him. That gives the senator a statesman's image. That is what I am trying to say with my pictures."

The senator caught on. Once in the early days of the satellite era, Ray got an urgent message to meet Heflin in the rotunda of the Russell Senate Office Building. When the press secretary arrived, he found Heflin, a stout man, standing next to a great marble pillar in the fading afternoon sunlight. "I've just found a great new spot to shoot the satellite feed," Heflin announced. "The senator, who started as a skeptic," Ray remarked later, "wound up as a television director."[14]

16

From Dulles to Gorbachev:
diplomacy and terrorism in the television age

In the fall of 1985, the government of President Ferdinand Marcos of the Philippine Republic tottered in a crisis of confidence. A friendly relationship with the Philippines was vital to American interests in the Far East, and the possible consequences of a collapse in Manila were understood in the United States. During the autumn William J. Casey, director of central intelligence, visited the islands. He and Marcos pondered the idea of Marcos's calling a special election, or snap election, as the Filipinos say, to reestablish his authority in an insurrectionary atmosphere. When no favorable response came from Marcos, President Ronald Reagan sent Senator Paul Laxalt of Nevada, a close friend, to Manila as his personal emissary, but again Marcos ducked the suggestion of a special election. After Laxalt's return to the United States, however, Marcos telephoned the senator to say he had reconsidered.

On Sunday, November 3, 1985, editors of progovernment newspapers in the Philippines were alerted to keep their front pages open for a late announcement. Television stations carried bulletins notifying viewers to stay tuned for important news. When the moment came, Filipinos seated in front of their sets saw George F. Will, a Washington columnist, asking President Marcos a prearranged question about Marcos's declining credibility.

"Some people wonder," Will continued, "if it would not be possible for you to call an early election to set a new mandate."

"I understand the opposition has been for an election," Marcos said. "In answer to their requests I announce that I am ready to call a snap election."

A barrage of questions from other American reporters followed.

"If all these childish claims to popularity on both sides have to be settled," Marcos declared, "I think we had better settle it by calling an election right now."

After proposing a sixty-day campaign, he exclaimed, "I'm ready, I'm ready."[1]

For what was coming he was not ready, no readier than were the Filipinos to see George Will setting the stage for a momentous event in Philippine history. The wonder of it was that Marcos was not broadcasting to his people. Rather, he was speaking as a guest by satellite on ABC's "This Week with David Brinkley," airing from Washington at 11:30 A.M. Sunday, eastern standard time. After Marcos told Laxalt that he would call a special election after all, the senator advised him: "It would be very dramatic for you to make that announcement on the Brinkley show. That would be very effective for American consumption."

Television news can play a significant role in diplomacy by conditioning American opinion. Nixon understood this when he began a new relationship with China. Laxalt understood it, too. His strategy was designed to quiet Marcos's critics in the United States.

The interplay of television and international relations began in the 1950s. Dwight D. Eisenhower and John Foster Dulles were the first president and the first secretary of state to have continuing access to television, and they were very sensitive to its possible effect on diplomacy. In fact, Dulles hired a television coach and manager, David J. Waters, a former NBC director-producer in Chicago. As television news expanded rapidly in the 1950s, Eisenhower and Dulles became concerned about how the Soviet Union could use it in the United States to contest the administration's views. They were particularly upset by Nikita Khrushchev's appearance on the CBS program "Face the Nation" on Sunday, June 2, 1957. After two years of negotiation, he agreed to be a guest on the program. The interview was filmed in Moscow four days before the show was to air. Stuart Novins was the moderator, and Daniel Schorr and B. J. Cutler, the Moscow correspondents, respectively, of CBS and the New York *Herald Tribune,* asked questions. At a news conference on June 4, Eisenhower bristled at what he considered the opportunity granted to the Soviet leader to spread propaganda in the United States. Referring to a Khrushchev statement on proposed withdrawals of U.S. troops in Europe, the president implied that Khrushchev was trying to drive a wedge between the United States and its European allies. Eisenhower suggested that an interview with a Soviet leader in Moscow was not as free and honest a proceeding as a White House news conference. On a note of disapproval, he ventured that the program was a case in which "a commercial firm in this country, trying to improve its own commercial standing, went to unusual effort to get someone that really made a unique performance in front of our people."

This comment disturbed Charles von Fremd, the CBS White House correspondent, who then questioned the president at the news conference. Von Fremd's desire to explain that the program was an unsponsored, noncommercial "sustaining" program touched off this exchange:

Q. You referred to a commercial firm trying—
The president. I meant it was not governmental.
Q. —trying to improve its commercial standing, sir. The CBS News and Public Affairs Program was *Face the Nation*, which is a sustaining program. I just did want to get this clear, sir.
The president. Well, isn't the CBS a commercial firm?
Q. Yes, but the program on which he appeared is a sustaining program. I just did want to get this straight, Mr. President, and that is you don't believe, do you, that CBS was remiss in its news judgment in seeking to get Mr. Khrushchev to appear on the program?
The President. Well, I am not willing to give an opinion on that one.[2]

The conference erupted in laughter. "Chuck should have quit when he was behind," James Reston said when the reporters were leaving.

During the Kennedy administration NBC was caught in a serious dispute with the State Department, which feared that a documentary being readied for showing might bring danger in Germany at a very tense time. It was 1962. Reuven Frank, then an executive producer for NBC News, wanted to do a news special about East Germans who escaped to the West, bypassing the Berlin Wall by crawling through makeshift tunnels, leaping from roof to roof, or wading through sewers. He asked his Berlin staff to take whatever pictures they could find of escapes of that kind.

In Berlin, Piers Anderton, the NBC correspondent, and Gary Stindt, the bureau manager, were approached by three German engineering students. They proposed that for twenty thousand dollars they would tunnel under the wall and grant NBC rights to film their digging and the escapes made after the project was completed. Anderton flew to New York with their proposal. NBC investigated. Convinced of the good faith and capabilities of the students and of the likelihood that they would dig the tunnel with or without NBC support (the three were bent on rescuing friends and relatives trapped in East Berlin), NBC agreed to pay the students twelve thousand, five hundred dollars.[3] "Only a few at NBC were told of the project, and these carried on in cloak-and-dagger fashion," Erik Barnouw wrote.[4]

On September 14, 1962, NBC filmed the last shovelful of dirt being tossed from the tunnel. The cameras also caught that day the escape of twenty-six persons, including five babies. Altogether the filming depicted the escape of fifty-nine. After twenty hours editing the complete film, Reuven Frank in Berlin told New York that it was worthy of ninety minutes on the air. Clandestinely, he carried the film back to New York on the plane as hand luggage. The program was scheduled for October 31.

Then problems descended. Somehow the State Department got wind of the project, as it had earlier learned of a similar undertaking by CBS. The department had warned CBS that involving American personnel in clandestine tunnel operations was dangerous and irresponsible. Fearful in any case that the East Germans knew what was afoot, CBS had never used its tunnel. After the State Department discovered what NBC was up to, "all hell broke loose," Robert Kintner, then president of the network, related. He said the dispute was the "worst encounter" with the government that the network had experienced up to that time.[5] In late October the country was gripped in the Cuban missile crisis. "With peace hanging by a thread it is no time for adventurous laymen to turn up in the front lines of world tension," wrote Jack Gould in the *New York Times*.[6]

Despite the objections of the State Department, "The Tunnel," as the Berlin documentary was called, was broadcast by NBC on December 10, 1962. Viewers were not driven off. On the contrary, helped by the controversy, "The Tunnel" received the highest ratings ever recorded up to that time for a public affairs program.[7] The audience even matched that for the popular "Lucy Show." Awards followed and so did surprises. The State Department allowed the U.S. Information Agency, one of its arms, to show the documentary abroad.[8]

With "The Tunnel," television news made itself a part of the story of the breaching of the Berlin Wall, a volatile issue in the heart of Europe. Other dramatic cases of participation in critical events lay ahead, notably, in cases of terrorism. "In terrorist incidents," Michael J. O'Neill, former editor of the New York *Daily News,* wrote in 1986, "television is now overwhelmingly the dominant medium. It mobilizes public emotions, influences government policies, and even shapes the events themselves."[9]

O'Neill is the author of *Terrorist Spectaculars,* a study of the subject for the Twentieth Century Fund.

Terrorism, a form of warfare, must have an audience to succeed. What larger one exists than that of viewers of television news carried around the world? Terrorists create their own news in order to communicate to the general public their grievances and goals. The taking of hostages abroad has caused perplexing problems for television. Televised coverage of Americans in captivity abroad releases strong emotions at home. Viewers are horrified—and fascinated. Sympathy for captives' families swells. Families exert open pressure on Washington to bring about the release of their loved ones. International relations and good will suffer. Terrorists are often skillful at manipulating news coverage for their own advantage. There is a saying—probably nothing more—that a terrorist admonished a compatriot, "Don't shoot now. We're not in prime time." The combination of terrorism and news coverage can cause difficulty for a democracy. News coverage is likely to make the U.S government more vulnerable to the emotions stirred by television pictures and newspaper stories. The coverage may not only enhance the power of the terrorists but also intensify Washington's political problems and complicate possible methods of operations for thwarting the terrorists.

This was the case with the hijacking of TWA flight 847 at Athens International Airport on June 14, 1985, by militant Lebanese Shi'ites of the Hizballah, or "Party of God."[10] Thirty-nine Americans were held hostage for seventeen days. One American passenger was murdered savagely. A small band of gunmen commandeered the Boeing 727 with 153 passengers, 104 of whom were Americans. They forced the plane to fly from Athens to Beirut to Algiers and then back to Beirut again, where it remained until the thirty-nine were released. Other hostages on flight 847 had been let go earlier. The price demanded for the freedom of the thirty-nine was the release of several hundred Shi'ite prisoners being held by Israel.

When the TWA plane made its second and final landing in Beirut, after stopping in Algiers, the pilot, Captain John L. Testrake, radioed the control tower to report the act of a hijacker. "He just killed a passenger!" Testrake cried. "He just killed a passenger!"[11]

The victim was Robert Dean Stethem, twenty-three years old, of Waldorf, Maryland. The hijackers asked him for his identification card. It showed that he was enlisted in the U.S. Navy. He was returning home after serving as a frogman on a navy project in Greece. The hijackers then beat him, as they had beaten other passengers. One of the captors shot him, and his body was flung out the door of the stationary plane.

The problems posed for the Reagan administration by news coverage of the hijacking became evident quickly. Apparently, the hijackers had intended to remain in Algiers, but they decided to return to Beirut because of what they learned on the radio. The U.S. Army Delta Force, the radio reported, had taken off for the Mediterranean. To some Washington officials, the reporting of the departure by American newspapers and networks bore the stigma of publicizing troop movements in advance. Network executives countered that the existence of the antiterrorist Delta Force was well known and its deployment surely anticipated by the hijackers. In any case the hijackers inconveniently ordered the plane back to Beirut.

While it was standing on the runway after the return, an ABC cameraman and two ABC reporters, Charles Glass and Julie Flint, approached the front of the aircraft. Captain Testrake was leaning out of his cockpit window, but a pistol was brandished very visibly beside his head by a hijacker. The picture on television was sobering.

"Captain," one of the reporters asked, "many people in America are calling for some kind of rescue operation or some kind of retaliation. Do you have any thoughts on that?"

"I think we'd all be dead men if they did," Testrake answered, "because we're continually surrounded by many, many guards."[12]

The statement was bound to strengthen any second thoughts in Washington about a rescue mission. The next day the hijackers staged a televised news conference with five of the hostages. Allyn Conwell of Houston, who had been elected as spokesman for the thirty-nine, read these words: "We as a group most importantly beseech President Reagan and our fellow Americans to refrain from any form of military or violent means as an attempt, no matter how noble or heroic, to secure our freedom. That would only cause in our estimation unneeded and unwarranted deaths." The hijackers also used this news conference to pressure Israel. "We sincerely ask and pray," Conwell declared, "that Israel expeditiously release Shi'ites."[13] Unfortunately in this case, television news and newspapers, owned by companies in a land that championed democratic freedoms, helped terrorists who had captured and murdered Americans communicate their demands.

In negotiations involving the hijackers and the United States and Syria, the role of middleman was assumed by Nabih Berri, head of Amal, the principal Shi'ite Moslem militia in Beirut. If Yasser Arafat personified a terrorist, the English-speaking Berri was the picture of a sophisticated Lebanese entrepreneur who combined his lawyer's skills, familiarity with the United States, and study of television to guide him. "For two tumultous weeks . . . Berri and his lieutenants stage-managed the crisis with Madison Avenue skill—arranging photo opportunities, laying on press conferences, supplying hostages for interviews, and hawking tips, inside information, and tapes," said Michael O'Neill in a 1986 speech on terrorism and the news. The terrorists "even arranged news pools. . . . With full network cooperation, Berri used American television to broadcast his litany of Shi'ite grievances, sent messages to Ronald Reagan and to [Israeli Prime Minister] Shimon Peres, negotiated with Dan Rather of CBS and David Hartman of ABC, chatted with anchormen and other media celebrities and even offered fatherly assurances to the worried wife of Allyn Conwell." [14]

Tom Brokaw later recalled that he was taken to Berri's headquarters the first day he arrived in Beirut, and "was given a kind of VIP escort because I was an anchorman. . . . An awful lot of manipulation was going on there." [15]

The three networks devoted from 62 percent to 68 percent of their evening news shows to the hostage story.[16] Richard C. Wald, senior vice-president for news at ABC, conceded to O'Neill that, as the latter wrote, "the volume of reporting was so staggering that it became tasteless." [17] On the second day of the crisis, for example, CBS carried thirteen special reports, according to a survey by Edwin Diamond and his News Study Group at New York University. The group's analysis of sixty hours on the three networks revealed a pattern of "individual journalistic achievement and collective news mindlessness." Television news "went wrong," the study concluded, transforming "moderate television into terror-vision." [18]

L. Paul Bremer III, former State Department ambassador-at-large for counterterrorism and later a member of Kissinger Associates in New York, believes other terrorists in Lebanon may have been encouraged to take and kill hostages because the perpetrators of the 1985 crime went unpunished.[19] Kissinger himself wrote that it was indecent to show Americans on display under the control of terrorists, enabling the latter to "spread their propaganda." [20] In this regard the *pièce de résistance* was the question David Hartman, then host of ABC's "Good Morning America," asked Nabih Berri: "Any final words to President Reagan this morning?" This was one of several instances in which a journalist came close to adopting the role of negotiator. Six months after the hijacking, Katharine Graham, chairman of the Washington Post Company, cited the "unbridled" journalistic competition that may develop in incidents such as the TWA crisis. She warned that unrestrained competition can reduce journalism to the lowest common denominator, which was the case, certainly among the networks, in 1985.[21]

As usual, there is another side to the matter of intense television coverage of terrorism. At the time of the Beirut affair, Robert B. Oakley, predecessor to Paul Bremer, was ambassador-at-large for counterterrorism. In the beginning, he conceded, the television coverage complicated the situation by heightening the pressure on the Reagan administration to make concessions. "But the coverage was a two-edged sword that cut both ways," he added. "Once Berri and Amal accepted responsibility for the hijackings, the media may have been a help. They put Berri on the hook. He was then identified with the hostages and, in a way, he was stuck."[22]

This was the same point Jimmy Carter had made, it will be recalled, in the case of the Iran hostages—to wit, whoever identifies himself as a captor is burdened with responsibility for the captive's life. In both instances the hostages were released unharmed. The terrorists had got about all the publicity for their causes that they could have expected. And, in the case of the TWA hijacking, Israel freed some Shi'ite prisoners it had reportedly planned to let go anyhow.

During the hostage crises of the 1980s, White House officials followed events closely on television. President George Bush often kept abreast of developments in a crisis by watching the Cable News Network. His press secretary, Marlin Fitzwater, told Maureen Dowd of the *New York Times:* "CNN has opened up a whole new communications system between governments in terms of immediacy and directness. In many cases, it's the first communication we have."[23] In the Gulf War of 1991, CNN proved to be a valuable source of timely information for the president as well as the public.

When Ferdinand Marcos announced on the Brinkley show that he was calling a snap election in the Philippines, it was only the beginning of the role television news would play in U.S. relations with that country. Heavy coverage of Marcos's defeat by Corazon Aquino had powerful impact in the United States and the Philippines—indeed around the world—because it was superb drama. In the pictures that dominated news programs an attractive, upright, American-educated heroine, widow of an assassinated rival to Marcos, vied for votes with a dictatorial, wily, corrupt, superannuated villain. Good opposed evil. For millions of viewers it would have been unbearable if "Cory" had lost.

Stanley Karnow described the drama as a morality play, one in which the actors used American television to influence Filipinos:

> For the U.S. news media the event was irresistible: A morality play in an Americanized setting with the principal characters speaking English. . . . The candidates knew all about prime time and ratings—so much so that Marcos insisted on being interviewed on CBS only by Dan Rather. Cory craved attention in the United States in the realization that American validation made them credible to the Filipinos, who distrusted their own news media.[24]

Richard G. Lugar, then chairman of the Senate Foreign Relations Committee, called Marcos's use of American television "prophetic. I had no idea then that most Americans and hundreds of millions of other television viewers around the world would spend tens of hours in February 1986 watching an election and a revolution in the Philippines."[25]

Marcos and his wife, Imelda, enjoyed a warm friendship with Ronald and Nancy Reagan. In fact, through the years, American presidents, fearing that the only alternative to Marcos was Communist rule in the Philippines, had accepted him as an ally. However ruthlessly, he was entrenched and could assure the United States of continuing access to naval and military facilities in the islands, an issue of rising intensity among the Filipinos. Increasingly, however, his autocratic rule had been losing popular support. This posed the question whether the United States could retain its traditional close relationship with the Philippine Republic without a renewal of democracy there. A serious turn in the other direction occurred in 1972 when, in the face of unrest, Marcos imposed martial law. He also jailed thousands of Filipinos, including the politician who was considered most likely to succeed him—Benigno S. Aquino, Jr., Corazon's husband. Later Aquino went to the United States to live for a time. On his return to Manila on August 21, 1983, he was assassinated as military guards escorted him from the plane. The crime intensified the growing distrust of Marcos in the United States. Mrs. Aquino announced that she would run for president in her husband's stead. With concern about Marcos's unpopularity rising, Reagan sent Laxalt to the Philippines, and plans for the election were set in motion.

So cocksure of the outcome was Marcos that he invited a congressional delegation to observe the propriety of the election. John P. Murtha, a Democrat from Pennsylvania, headed the House group, and Lugar, an Indiana Republican, was the leading senator. Because he was chairman of the Foreign Relations Committee, Lugar became the preeminent American on the scene. Using television rather copiously himself from Manila and Washington, he was as influential as any other American in Aquino's ultimate victory. This was because of his convincingly stated case of wholesale fraud at the polls.

As election day, January 17, 1986, approached, Marcos followed the advice of Senator Laxalt and retained the Alexandria, Virginia, public relations firm of Black, Manafort, and Stone, which had been involved in a number of Republican campaigns including President Reagan's. Soon the Philippine president was on so many television programs in the United States it was as if he were campaigning for the White House. Indeed, he was seeking public confidence in the United States as well as votes in the Philippines. But the questions Ted Koppel and others put to him were far from helpful, even in the Philippines, where some of his answers were reported in the press. Aquino appeared less often on American television. She needed it less because, as Michael O'Neill commented, "Marcos with his pewter face and autocratic manner could not compete with Corazon Aquino's telegenic image, attractive, articulate, spunky."[26]

The major American networks opened election bureaus in Manila. "It wasn't just the American public being influenced by foreign elections," said Mark Helmke, press secretary to Lugar. "It was the electorate in a foreign country being influenced by the American coverage bouncing to them back from the United States. To me, it showed the incredible power of the American network system."[27]

As the vote count went on, interminably, the Marcos government stole votes, and the national legislature under Marcos's domination declared him the winner. To press her claim Aquino took to the streets. Television cameras caught the spectacle of huge crowds rallying behind her. When Marcos's armored cars tried to disperse them, the Aquino forces wearing the yellow ribbons of her cause stood their ground. "Scenes of violence, injury and death were abundant," Lugar wrote afterward. "Cardinal [Jaime] Sin and the Catholic Church were outspoken in their criticism of fraud and violence."[28] As the crisis approached, Lugar, back in the United States, and Aquino and Marcos in the Philippines made one television appearance after another. The senator was struck by what a remarkable time diplomacy and politics were experiencing. "It was all being played out live and in color," he observed, "with all the participants discussing the fate of each other over the television."[29]

On the "MacNeil/Lehrer NewsHour" on February 17, the senator declared that Marcos should either call a new election or resign, an opinion Lugar was instrumental in spreading in Congress. Marcos had hoped that through television he could bring Reagan, the Congress, and the American press to his side. "But those who saw the Marcos interviews," Lugar noted, "had also seen violence in fashionable Makati, nuns being chased by masked men with clubs, funerals of election-related victims, and critical comments by informed and trusted journalists and scholars from many countries."[30]

The climax came February 24, 1986. Reagan decided that the United States could not support a government that used armed force against its own people. With Reagan's assent, Senator Laxalt telephoned Marcos and said, "Mr. President, my advice is to cut and cut clean."[31] Within hours a U.S. plane arrived to take Ferdinand and Imelda Marcos to Guam en route to Hawaii, leaving the government of the Philippines in the hands of Corazon Aquino.

No foreign leader since Winston S. Churchill has made such an impression on American opinion as has Mikhail S. Gorbachev, and he did it largely through television. In 1984 Gorbachev and his wife, Raisa, visited Prime Minister Margaret Thatcher in London. He was then a rising young figure in the Politburo and the Secretariat in Moscow. To Americans watching on television, as well as to Londoners, the Gorbachevs had the comforting look of a well-groomed, cosmopolitan Western couple. Stylishly dressed, Raisa looked as though she had arrived from the Via Veneto or the Champs Elysées rather than from Red Square. Like his wife, Gorbachev was at ease before the cameras. He had an agreeable face and a reasonable and unintimidating manner. Thatcher felt she could do business with him, and the world took note of this new breed of Soviet politician.

After becoming the national leader in March 1985, following the death of the general secretary, Constantine Chernenko, Gorbachev attached maximum importance to the need to expand television in the Soviet Union. To him, television and radio were all-embracing mediums for conveying information and propagating moral and cultural values. Abroad, Gorbachev used television to impart a less authoritarian image of Soviet rule.

For audiences at home he conducted himself at international conferences in a way that showed his people that he was a major figure on the world stage.

Gorbachev attended four summit conferences in the 1980s—in Geneva, Reykjavík, Washington, and Moscow. Because the novelty of Gorbachev's participation attracted special attention, it was easy to overlook the critical role Reagan filled. This was all the more surprising because of his almost ostentatious anticommunism; but there he was at the summits, pumping Gorbachev's hand, putting his arm around his shoulders, negotiating, smiling, laughing, playing the good friend, urging that they call one another Ron and Mikhail. Such a display of good will and good cheer is infectious. It was as if Reagan were certifying Gorbachev to those Americans who would soon be telling pollsters of their approval of the Soviet leader. When half a world apart, the two men were unalike, yet when they came together they were companions. To some it was incomprehensible that Reagan, the man who had poured billions into weapons to challenge the Soviets, should then celebrate the presence of their general chairman. To others, like Reagan's biographer Lou Cannon, who have known and studied Reagan for a long time, the president's conduct was in keeping with his conviction that the purpose of rearmament is to cause negotiation.

The extravaganza of the Washington summit meeting of 1987 could be compared only to Khrushchev's visit to the United States in 1959, and television was not nearly as ubiquitous then as it was when Gorbachev came. A week before Gorbachev left Moscow, NBC broadcast a fascinating hour-long televised interview with him by Tom Brokaw. As the two of them talked easily at a round table in the Council of Ministers building in the Kremlin, Gorbachev was firm about his own policies but conciliatory on the whole and said he was ready to negotiate arms reduction. He said that eighty thousand Americans had written to him. As he described the thrust of the correspondence, the writers asked, "Now why can't we be allies? We were allies at one time. Why can't we be allies now?" In words that were a suitable prelude to his trip to Washington, he commented, "We need mutual understanding, and I believe that we must display greater respect for each other and try to understand the history of our nations better." [32]

On Gorbachev's arrival in Washington, no more talk was heard about the "evil empire," as Reagan had once referred to the Soviet Union. The Marriott Hotel renamed its coffee shop Café Glasnost. At the Ritz-

Carlton Hotel "summit cookies" along with conciliatory quotations from
Reagan were left on guests' pillows at night in place of mints. TV news
anchors had moved into the city. Near the White House the networks
had set up elaborate temporary studios. Everywhere Gorbachev was
scheduled to go cameras were awaiting him. Television was ready to "go
live" whenever and for as long as Gorbachev or Reagan was in view.
Dinners, luncheons, meetings with congressional leaders, exchanges with
business executives were to be carried on the networks. For all of this
Gorbachev had his own special television advisers, former Ambassador
Anatoly F. Dobrynin, who had spent twenty-four years in Washington,
and Alexander N. Yakovlev, chief propagandist for the Soviet Union and
a member of the politburo.

At a televised ceremony December 9, 1987, Reagan and Gorbachev
signed a treaty committing their governments to abolish midrange missile
systems. Although only a small step on the road to disarmament, it was
the first decision by the two nations to reduce the size of their nuclear
arsenals. "Admit it," Tom Shales of the *Washington Post* wrote of the
ceremony, "it was thrilling."[33] A free spirit, Gorbachev jumped out of
his car during one motorcade trek through downtown Washington to
shake hands with astonished spectators. "If a spaceship had landed in the
middle of Washington," Maureen Dowd wrote in the *New York Times,*
"it could not have caused more commotion."[34] In between toasts and
linking arms with Vice-President Bush while waving to crowds on Connecticut Avenue, Gorbachev scored a *tour de force* with a televised news
conference that lasted nearly two hours. The first seventy-three minutes,
however, were taken up with a speech. Even so, veteran reporters did not
conceal their admiration for his forcefulness and understanding of issues.
Gorbachev spoke well of his meeting with Reagan: "Our dialogue is more
businesslike. There is more of a constructive approach, and I'll even venture to say that I think we trust each other more."[35]

Their fourth and last conference in Moscow in May and June 1988
did not produce any significant new agreements. The importance of the
event, as Gorbachev said, was Reagan's very presence in the Soviet capital, where he did not hesitate to offer ringing public praises for political
freedom. In terms of the new climate in Soviet-American relations, the
best of the occasion was what Peter Jennings described as "The Ron and
Mikhail Show" in Red Square. Their televised camaraderie in the shadow
of the Kremlin was an arresting sight for Soviet and American citizens,
who had been conditioned since 1946 for a much different atmosphere.

Reagan threw his arms around Gorbachev's shoulders. From there it was only a step toward the Muscovite version of political baby-kissing as when Gorbachev scooped up a youngster and bounced him in his arms. Reagan moved in, but Gorbachev would not let go. It was a case, Walter Goodman wrote in the *New York Times,* of "the world's preeminent arms negotiators competing for the attention of a child in arms—Soviet arms."[36] For all practical purposes, this incident and the summit in general were staged for television news.

Polls confirmed the high standing of Gorbachev in the United States. In a June 1988 survey by the Boston company Marttila and Kiley, 67 percent of respondents answered "more" to this question: "Do you think we can trust Gorbachev more, less, or about the same as past Soviet leaders?"[37] By the early 1990s, however, the Soviet people trusted him little. Gorbachev's magnetism in front of television cameras was little help to him at home.

When Gorbachev was vacationing in the Crimea on August 19, 1991, a coup d'état was attempted by reactionary Communists seeking to crush the movement toward democracy. While Gorbachev was held under house arrest in his dacha, Boris Yeltsin, president of the province of Russia, became a hero by facing down Communist tanks in Red Square. When Gorbachev returned to Moscow on August 21, Yeltsin was the unmistakable national leader. On August 24, Gorbachev resigned as general secretary of the Communist Party Central Committee. The collapse of the coup and Gorbachev's abandonment of the party apparently spelled the end of communist rule in the Soviet Union. The events left Gorbachev's future almost as much in doubt. His popularity, generated largely by television outside his country, was no great bulwark at home.

17

Television and the transformation
of American politics, 1952–1984

As a young reporter for the *Richmond Times-Dispatch,* Charles Mc-Dowell was one of the first persons to witness from the inside television's impact on politics. By sheer chance he observed at the Republican National Convention in Chicago in 1952 how people's reaction to what they saw on television influenced political decisions—a phenomenon that would profoundly change the workings of the political system.

The Republican convention in 1952 was the first at which television news had the technical resources and the large audience to enable it to exert significant political impact. In 1940 NBC had broadcast scenes of the Republican convention in Philadelphia to a few stations. That year the network also made newsreels of the Democratic convention in Chicago and sent them to New York for broadcast the next day on a small scale. Although the Democratic and Republican conventions of 1948 in Philadelphia were fully covered by television, the number of people around the country who had sets was small and the networks' reach from Philadelphia was limited mainly to the East.

McDowell was in Chicago in 1952 as a member of his newspaper's convention bureau covering the fight between Gen. Dwight D. Eisenhower and Sen. Robert A. Taft of Ohio for the Republican nomination. Although it seemed unlikely that the Republicans would reject a war hero of Eisenhower's stature, the Taft forces nominally controlled the party machinery. Before the convention Taft had more delegates committed to him, on paper at least, than had Eisenhower. Sentimentally, most delegates probably preferred Taft, "Mr. Republican," as he was called. A critical issue at the convention was whether pro-Eisenhower or pro-Taft delegations from Texas, Louisiana, and Georgia should be seated. In the three states pro-Eisenhower delegates had been chosen by precinct conventions. The respective Republican state committees, however, brushed these actions aside, alleging that Democrats had been allowed to vote. The committees selected alternative slates of delegates favorable to the Ohioan and demanded that they be seated at the convention. The whole nominating process thereupon descended into a labyrinth of charges, countercharges, negotiations, and proposed compromises.

Much in need of a decisive issue, the Eisenhower camp seized the moral ground in the delegate dispute. Shrewdly Eisenhower's people used television to tell the whole nation that the general was the victim of those who would spurn fair play. On the eve of the convention Eisenhower said that the dispute over southern delegates was "a straight-out issue of right and wrong." He accused the Taft campaign of "chicanery."[1]

According to Edward R. Murrow, one of the CBS staff covering the proceedings, the Taft people wanted to keep the whole convention off television. This would have included a hearing in which the credentials committee took up the question of the disputed delegates. In a news broadcast from Chicago, Murrow reported that Eisenhower's staff sided with broadcasters in favor of having television cameras at the credentials committee hearing. This was not, Murrow said, because the Eisenhower camp liked television cameras but rather because "a full airing of these proceedings" would be to the advantage of their candidate.[2] At a prior meeting of the Republican National Committee in Chicago, in which the issue was to be discussed, the Eisenhower people had lights and cameras in place, but the Taft forces balked and had the meeting moved to another room.[3] Nevertheless, Eisenhower's supporters kept talking to television crews wherever they could find them. In the end they succeeded in getting the credentials committee hearing on television.

When the hearing opened in the Gold Room of the Congress Hotel, McDowell came to listen. Well known in later years as a stalwart on the PBS television program "Washington Week in Review," he was then a junior member of the *Times-Dispatch* convention staff. Lacking the proper credentials for this particular event, he slipped unnoticed into a kitchen just off the main room in the hope of being able to hear what went on. Soon strategists for the Taft side ducked into the kitchen to assess the progress of the hearing. Meanwhile preoccupied hotel employees shuffled in and out of the kitchen, ignored by the politicians. If the politicians noticed McDowell, they evidently assumed he was one of the help and made no effort to keep their voices low. McDowell's listening post proved to be a good one. He learned that "the Taft managers were talking about conceding the Louisiana delegates to Eisenhower."[4] From what the Taft managers were saying, McDowell also learned that the television coverage of the hearing was affecting viewers' opinions of the two candidates. Specifically, it was undermining Taft's support.

Never before at a national political convention had television been such a force. With a nationwide audience in 1952, television was having a transforming effect on the nominating process.

"What was happening," McDowell later wrote, "was that people back home, following the debate on television, were telephoning and telegraphing their delegates to say that Taft's case was coming through as weak. Republicans of consequence were saying that a steamroller approach would look bad on television and hurt Taft more than yielding the delegates." At one point Warren E. Burger, a Minnesota delegate supporting Harold E. Stassen as a dark-horse candidate, entered the kitchen to join in a discussion. "He rested an elbow on a dishwashing machine as he talked," McDowell recalled about the man who would later be the chief justice of the United States. "He was earnest and deep-chested and had a big, hollow voice, and there was no trouble hearing him tell the Taft people that they could ruin their candidate if they insisted on arrogantly running over Eisenhower."[5]

The credentials committee awarded the Louisiana delegates to Eisenhower. Taft's position crumbled. Eisenhower was nominated on the first ballot. Television contributed to the outcome. Over a period of days it conveyed the impression that the conqueror of Normandy was getting a raw deal from the Republican Old Guard.

Beginning in 1952, television caused structural as well as superficial changes in politics. That year delegates of both parties were warned that the probing television lenses could capture every movement they made in their chairs, including manifesting boredom by reading newspapers. They were admonished to be careful about what they said to one another lest lip readers pick up the conversation from the television screen. Women delegates were cautioned against affronting blue collar viewers by wearing showy jewelry. Television even affected their attire, as John Crosby wrote in the *New York Herald Tribune*: "Already television has made one large contribution to the nation's taste. The ladies are being asked to abandon, for God's sake, those large floral print dresses which have been the tribal costume of the political committeewoman since forever."[6] Another change was so startling that CBS put out a news release on it in Chicago: the bald, gruff Sam Rayburn, chairman of the Democratic convention in 1952, agreed to wear makeup from gavel to gavel.

Memories of the 1948 convention convinced broadcasters to change convention coverage. The traditional style—with the endless nominating speeches, the proliferation of seconding speeches, and hours of parades and whoopee in the aisles—was boring for television viewers. At the disorderly Democratic convention in 1948, the nominee, Harry S. Truman, did not begin his acceptance speech until 2:00 A.M. In 1952, when events on the rostrum became boring, the networks simply diverted their cameras to cover interviews or important meetings in downtown hotels. For the first time, television producers, not party officials, decided what aspect of the convention would be shown throughout the nation at any given time. Advances in electronics enabled NBC anchormen to converse with their reporters and cameramen roving the aisles with hand-held portable cameras then called "creepie peepies." This gave coverage a new range and mobility. Any delegate or other politician trying to strike a deal on the convention floor was fair game for an interview. The television audience was provided a broader look at how the politics of conventions worked. The unfavorable side was that in future years roving reporters and cameramen began to clog the aisles in their search for pundits, charlatans, and celebrities of all kinds, as well as delegates. Unfortunately, this generated competition among the networks for often meaningless, not to say misleading, scoops on the floor, sometimes blurring the true picture of the convention proceedings.

When the Democratic convention opened in Chicago in 1952, the party cooperated with the networks. The Democrats limited nominating speeches to fifteen minutes and individual seconding speeches to five minutes (with a ten-minute limit for all seconding speeches for a candidate). Floor demonstrations were limited to twenty minutes for each candidate placed in nomination. At the start, five candidates were in the running for the party's nomination. Almost before the rap of the opening gavel had faded away, however, the field narrowed. It was customary for the governor of the state to give an opening speech on the first day. The governor of Illinois was then Adlai Stevenson. Truman had once favored Stevenson for the nomination, but the president later backed away. The governor had not tossed his hat in the ring and had no pledged delegates. His welcoming speech, however, was so exciting, so filled with music and good sense, that the convention was over almost before it began. The delegates were thrilled. Television viewers around the country sent tele-grams. Truman threw his support to Stevenson.

Before the week was out Stevenson was on his way to a hopeless cam-paign. The Democrats had been in power for twenty years. The Korean War had shredded Truman's popularity. The electorate was hungry for change, and the voices of the people said, unmistakably, "I like Ike." Stevenson never succeeded in recapturing the magic of the welcoming speech, and it was the Eisenhower campaign that grasped the new tech-niques of the television age. Indeed, in their desperation for a winning issue, the Democrats charged that Madison Avenue had taken over Ei-senhower. Stevenson said: "I don't think the American people want pol-itics and the presidency to become the plaything of the high-pressure men. . . . [T]his isn't Ivory Soap versus Palmolive."[7] One of his leading advisers, George W. Ball, lamented that Stevenson "obstinately refused to learn the skills of the effective television performer."[8]

Eisenhower, however, did learn. In fact, his campaign used the first spot television commercials in the history of presidential politics. When Eisenhower was president of Columbia University after the war, he be-came friends with Bruce Barton and Ben Duffy. During the 1952 presi-dential campaign, Eisenhower trusted Duffy, president of the large ad-vertising agency Batten, Barton, Durstine and Osborn, and followed his advice and that of professional Republican politicians. They told him that the formal set speech of earlier campaigns could not convey the warmth of Eisenhower's public personality. Of course, some such speeches would have to be made, but the new emphasis should be on informal television productions in which the candidate appeared to be talking to Americans individually. Where a set speech was necessary, it should be part of a large drama, a rally staged for paid political television and glittering with all the hoopla of a Hollywood premiere.

In city after city the Eisenhower campaign rolled into auditoriums bathed in spotlights. Arms overhead in his famous V-for-victory sign, he stepped out of the wings as a band was blaring. Mrs. Eisenhower beamed from a box, the crowd roared, and the television cameras caught it all.

Television speeches were held to twenty minutes, with frequent pauses for applause. On the road Eisenhower cut a handsome figure in a double-breasted camel's hair coat and brown fedora. At airport rallies or on the rear platform of a campaign train, he often would pull an egg from his pocket and ask the crowd, "Do you know how many taxes there are on one single egg?" If no one answered, he would cite a list of levies that would make any good Republican shudder. At other times an aide passed him a thin, two-foot long piece of wood, scored down the center so it would break easily. In what amounted to an early demonstration of how to produce a visual for television, Eisenhower held up the wood while inveighing against the alleged shrinking value of the dollar under the Democrats. "This is what is happening to your hard-earned dollar," he declared, snapping the wood in two.

The men behind Eisenhower's television commercials were Rosser Reeves, Jr., of Ted Bates Advertising, and Michael Levin, a former Bates associate. In the early days of television, Bates had pioneered the clustering of spot advertisements before and after entertainment programs. Reeves was confident that television could market a politician as well as it marketed toothpaste. In a memorandum to the Eisenhower staff, he suggested this "no risk" strategy for buying advertising time on television:

A big advertiser . . . puts on a one-hour television show. It may cost him $75,000—for that one hour. Immediately after, another big advertiser follows it with another big expensive show. Jack Benny! Martin and Lewis! Eddie Cantor! Fred Allen! Edgar and Charlie McCarthy! . . . THESE BIG ADVERTISERS SPEND MILLIONS—WITH TOP TALENT AND GLITTERING NAMES—TO BUILD A BIG AUDIENCE. But—between the two shows—comes the humble "spot." If you can run *your advertisement* in this "spot," for a very small sum YOU GET THE AUDIENCE BUILT AT HUGE COSTS BY OTHER PEOPLE.[9]

When he started to work on the campaign, Reeves first watched an Eisenhower political speech in Philadelphia on television. Reeves counted thirty-two separate points Eisenhower made and then dispatched a research team the next morning to ask people at random what Eisenhower had said. None of those questioned could say. Reeves then read all of Eisenhower's speeches and extracted a dozen important issues, but found them too diverse for sharp focus. From George Gallup he learned that the issues that most bothered Americans were the Korean War, corruption in Washington, and rising taxes and inflation. Thereupon, Reeves drafted twenty-two scripts and, in mid-September, joined Eisenhower in a Manhattan studio to have him read them from cue cards. What Eisenhower was reading were ostensibly his own answers to questions that had been written by Reeves. Reeves later insisted the answers were framed in words from various Eisenhower speeches. But who would ask the questions? They would be asked by randomly chosen citizens, reading in front of a camera from the same cue cards. The respective questions and the respective answers would be spliced together. The questioners would never see Eisenhower, nor would Eisenhower see them. On the television screen, however, it would appear that they were face to face. "To think that an old soldier should come to this," Eisenhower commented in the studio, as his brother, Milton S. Eisenhower, cleared the scripts.[10] The questioners were selected from among patrons, many of them tourists, emerging from Radio City Music Hall in New York.

For example, a woman holding a shopping bag complains: "I paid twenty-four dollars for these groceries—look, for this little." Eisenhower answers: "A few years ago, those same groceries cost you ten dollars, now twenty-four, next year thirty—that's what will happen unless we have a change." An elderly woman in a hat says that "high prices are just driving me crazy." Eisenhower replies: "Yes, my Mamie gets after me about the high cost of living. It's another reason why I say, it's time for a change. Time to get back to an honest dollar and an honest dollar's work."[11]

Executives of NBC and CBS at first hesitated to run such simplistic material, arguing that the commercials were not up to the standards of a presidential campaign. Under pressure from Batten, Barton, Durstine and Osborn, however, they yielded. Beginning in mid-October, twenty-eight of the commercials were broadcast in forty states. Commercials faking conversations between a candidate and citizens would be unacceptable today. But compared with ugly commercials of later campaigns, the Eisenhower spots were mild fare. The general was embarrassed by the "circus barking" that went on during his campaign tours, yet he did not betray his dismay on camera. His campaign was a moderate one. He never attacked Adlai Stevenson or Harry Truman. The general was the great crowd-pleaser of his time, and his consultants strove to capture this magnetism in the televised events they staged. Eisenhower surely did not need to rely on theatrics to defeat the Democrats in 1952. Unquestionably, the stagings and the commercials enlivened his campaign. More than that, they were harbingers of a style of politics that Eisenhower could not have foreseen and would not have liked.

Edwin Diamond and Stephen Bates thus described the significance of Eisenhower's spot campaign in 1952:

[It] raised the major, disturbing—and continuing—questions about politics, advertising, and television. Should presidential campaigns be run by marketing principles and [advertising executives] or by political tactics and party professionals? Do thirty-second or sixty-second spots ignore issues and content in favor of image and emotion? Does the best man win, or the more telegenic performer?

Can money buy enough media to buy elections? Every four years since 1952 these questions have reappeared.[12]

The year 1952 was a pivotal one in modern American politics, although changes inspired by television were just beginning. Television networks for the first time covered state primaries. The coverage attracted national audiences. In January 1952 President Truman, a product of an era of political bosses and machines, had told a news conference, "All these primaries are just eyewash when the conventions meet."[13] But he was wrong. The victory of the Eisenhower forces over Taft in New Hampshire, the first primary of the year, provided strong impetus for the general's drive at the Chicago convention. In the years that followed, primaries and caucuses multiplied as a result of democratizing reforms and the decline of party organizations. And to an extent Truman would not have believed, television coverage turned the primaries into crucial stepping-stones for candidates.

Instead of being eyewash, primaries determined the outcome of the nominating process. Once decisive, national conventions were reduced to gaudy gatherings that ratified decisions already made. When the selection of delegates to the conventions was largely in the hands of state party bosses, television had little to cover. But in 1952 the presidential aspirants began to campaign openly for delegates, and television moved in and covered the events for the public to see. The new development was not without its drawbacks.

For years early primaries were held in small states, and these states exerted a disproportionate influence on the selection of presidential nominees. As primaries increased in number, the costs of running for office soared. With incalculable effect on the health of the political system, television advertising required candidates to raise vastly more money than ever before. In 1948 Truman's supporters had to pass the hat to collect enough cash to move his campaign train out of the station in Oklahoma City. By 1990 the amount of money spent just on political advertising was $227.9 million.[14] "In Washington today," Richard L. Berke wrote in the *New York Times* in 1989, "raising money takes nearly as much time as legislative work."[15] An incumbent's war chest helps make him or her nearly invincible on election day. In 1948, 79 percent of House members seeking reelection won.[16] In 1990 the figure was 96.3 percent.[17]

After 1952 the next stage in the magnification of television's role in elective politics came with the televised debates between John F. Kennedy and Richard Nixon in 1960. The impact has already been discussed in an earlier chapter. Aside from the superior image he projected in the first debate, Kennedy's most influential performance that year was his appearance in Houston before the Protestant Ministerial Council. In a superb presentation he met, head-on, the issue of whether a Roman Catholic could properly serve as president of the United States. The only televising and videotaping of the event was local. The Kennedy campaign acquired a copy of the tape and bought spot time for broadcasting sections of it in other areas where Kennedy planned to campaign. The purpose was to saturate these communities with scenes from Houston immediately before his campaign entourage arrived. "The technique demonstrated for the first time," Sig Mickelson wrote, "that television could be used as a rapier rather than as a blunderbuss." [18]

It had the effect of a blunderbuss at the tempestuous Republican National Convention of 1964 at the Cow Palace in San Francisco. As television news and the press accurately reported, the convention was a cockpit of wrath and bitterness. "I'd Rather Fight Than Switch" was the slogan of the right-wing conservatives supporting Arizona senator Barry Goldwater. Under no circumstances were they going to switch to his opponent, Gov. Nelson A. Rockefeller of New York, the favorite of such moderates and liberals as could be found in the Cow Palace. Republican conservatives were desperate to nominate their candidate. Since Roosevelt's defeat of Herbert Hoover in 1932, the only Republican to sit in the White House had been Eisenhower, from 1953 to 1961, and once again, in 1964, the Republicans were the underdogs against Lyndon Johnson. Not surprisingly perhaps, a mood of loathing for the liberal repute of television and newspaper reporters and commentators saturated the convention hall. Suddenly and probably unintentionally, the smoldering heap was set ablaze by, of all people, Dwight Eisenhower. As a general and then as president, he had enjoyed years of overwhelming backing and favorable treatment by television and the press. His incendiary comments about columnists were all the more surprising because he generally tried to avoid unnecessary controversy. In an otherwise traditional speech by a former Republican president, he said: "Let us particularly scorn the divisive efforts of those outside our family, including sensation-seeking columnists, because, my friends, I assure you that these are people who couldn't care less about the good of our party."

Uproar. Bedlam. "Down with Walter Lippmann!" screamed a North Dakota delegate. Other delegates shook their fists at the television booths and the press stands. This fury "seems to me to have marked the emergence of 'the press' as an issue in American life and politics," wrote Tom Wicker of the *New York Times*. He continued:

So far from being "observers" . . . reporters, by 1964, were coming to be seen by millions of Americans as players in the game itself. Those fists raised in anger at . . . the "commentators" and "anchor men" bore this message, too: "the press" had become inextricably linked with television in the public mind.[19]

To avoid this linkage, the misleading term *news media* is not used in this book.

Unmistakably, the mud-slinging at the Cow Palace in 1964 revealed a new bitterness and cynicism seeping into American politics. Anger at "the press," especially among right-wing conservatives, was part of it. Less than a year away was the commitment of American forces to combat in Vietnam and the resultant spread of distrust to institutions of all kinds.

After winning the nomination and delivering his parting credo—"Extremism in the defense of liberty is no vice. . . . Moderation in the pursuit of justice is no virtue"—Goldwater set forth on the 1964 campaign.[20] Eager for exposure on local and regional television, he designed his schedule to get it, even though this meant grueling days of flying from time zone to time zone. "They would schedule Goldwater with a breakfast rally on the East Coast, then follow the sun and the time zones to the Midwest for lunch and the Mountain States or the West Coast for dinner or a nightly rally," Jack W. Germond and Jules Witcover wrote.[21]

The frenetic effort could not rescue Goldwater. Johnson's Great Society programs were popular, and American ground troops had not yet been committed to combat in Vietnam. "American boys," Johnson promised, would not be sent across the Pacific Ocean to do what ought to be done by Asian boys. Moreover, Goldwater was vulnerable on the issue of defense. His suggestion that nuclear weapons were just another asset in the American arsenal made some people fear he was trigger happy.

On September 7, 1964, the Democrats decided to attack Goldwater in a television spot unlike the one in which Eisenhower said that Mamie, too, was worried about the cost of groceries. This hard-hitting spot showed a pretty little girl plucking petals from a daisy. As she plucked, a doomsday voice did a countdown to fire an unseen intercontinental ballistic missile. The scene dissolved into a mushroom cloud and a voice said, "Vote for President Johnson on November third. The stakes are too high for you to stay home." Viewers then heard Lyndon Johnson say, "We must either love each other, or we must die."[22]

Another spot was aimed at Goldwater's opposition to the test ban treaty. Again a little girl appeared, this one licking an ice cream cone outdoors while a motherly voice was heard lamenting that without a test ban treaty the atmosphere might be poisoned by Strontium-90. Still another spot attacked Goldwater on social security. He had suggested that it might be better if the social security system, among other things, was taken over by private institutions. The spot just showed a social security card being torn up.

When the film of the little girl plucking the daisy was first viewed at the White House, jubilation was aroused by its power. On second thought, however, came the realization that the use of it in the campaign would evoke criticism that it was unfair, even an example of dirty politics. "So we evolved a strategy," Richard N. Goodwin, a speechwriter and adviser to President Johnson, wrote. "We would saturate prime-time viewing hours for a few days (or more, if we could get away with it) and then respond to the inevitable protests by withdrawing the spot." [23] The first showing drew a chorus of criticism. The spot was withdrawn. But the voters who saw it on television got the idea.

It was Nixon's campaign against Hubert Humphrey in 1968 that produced a radical turn toward reliance on television. From his disastrous debate with Kennedy in 1960, Nixon concluded that "I had concentrated too much on substance and not enough on appearance. I should have remembered that 'a picture is worth a thousand words.' " [24] Surrounded by advertising men, consultants, lawyers, and speechwriters, Nixon centered his campaign in 1968 not just on television but on controlled, manipulated television. In this way it foreshadowed the election strategies of Ronald Reagan and George Bush. Nixon's daily appearances were carefully staged to project a certain image of himself and his programs. Vestiges of old-style campaigning, still pursued by Humphrey, were largely swept aside by Nixon. Only four years earlier Johnson and Goldwater had stumped the country tirelessly. Four years before that Nixon in his race against Kennedy had been so obsessed with the importance of stumping that he wore himself out visiting all fifty states. For Nixon in 1968, endless motorcades were out. Long weeks of whistlestopping in the style of the 1940s or of the airport-hopping of the 1950s and early 1960s were out. Dedications of American Legion halls were out. Local press conferences were out. Nightly speeches in civic auditoriums along the way were out. As far as Nixon was concerned, that kind of campaigning was as far gone as the torchlight parades for William McKinley in 1896.

Germond and Witcover described the new tactics:

Throughout most of the campaign, the Nixon managers limited him to a single carefully staged event each day. . . . The events were held relatively early in the day and, as often as possible, near an airport with frequent service to New York, because in those days before satellites network reporters had to ship their film . . . to get it on the air. Producers in the home office might have two or three possible pieces of film to use on Humphrey, but the one piece they had on Nixon was nearly always the one his campaign arranged for them to have.[25]

The Republican party purchased air time for ten live regional television broadcasts. Nixon's consultants would set the stage. They would decide what film would be shown. Republican organizations would screen the audiences beforehand, and the Nixon staff would select particular men and women to ask the candidate questions. Most questions, not surprisingly, turned out to be amateurish; Nixon could have answered them in his sleep. Reporters were excluded and had to cover the farces from television screens in anterooms. Consultants would signal the audiences when to applaud. They also would arrange for the audiences to mob Nixon in admiration as the programs ended.

At various stops across the country in earlier days, presidential candidates would discuss strategy with county and state chairmen of their political party. By 1968 the power of the parties had run down too far for much of that kind of diversion. Roger Ailes, later ringmaster of Bush's 1988 campaign, devised Nixon's strategy with other consultants, pollsters, "media experts," advertising executives, and speechwriters. After his inside view of the Nixon campaign, the writer Joe McGinniss observed in his *The Selling of the President 1968:* "With the coming of television, and the knowledge of how it could be used to seduce voters, the old political values disappeared. Something new, murky, undefined started to rise from the mists."[26] A candidate's image superseded issues.

One of the ablest and most reputable men around Nixon was Raymond K. Price, formerly chief editorial writer for the New York *Herald Tribune.* Price was much concerned with how the campaign could overcome Nixon's reputation as a loser. After all, Nixon was making a run for the presidency in 1968 after having lost to Kennedy in 1960 and to Edmund Brown in the California gubernatorial election of 1962. In a memorandum of November 28, 1967, Price emphasized the importance of voters' image of Nixon:

We have to be very clear on this point: that the response is to the image, not to the man, since 99 percent of the voters have no contact with the man. It's not what's *there* that counts, it's what's projected—and carrying it one step further, it's not what *he* projects but rather what the voter receives. It's not the man we have to change, but rather the *received impression*. . . .

All this is a roundabout way of getting at the point that we should be concentrating on building a *received* image of RN as the kind of man proud parents would ideally want their sons to grow up to be: a man who embodies the national ideal, its aspirations, its dreams, a man whose *image* the people want in their homes as a source of inspiration, and whose voice they want as the representative of their nation in the councils of the world, and of their generation in the pages of history.[27]

Nixon's campaign staff read excerpts from Marshall McLuhan's book *Understanding Media.* "The success of any TV performer," one of the excerpts said, "depends on his achieving a low-pressure style of presentation."[28] Lowering the intensity of Nixon's earlier political behavior was a crucial part of the strategy for Nixon in the 1968 campaign. Reliance on controlled appearances on television facilitated this. He would not debate Humphrey. He avoided reporters. And the interrogation of him on camera by prudently selected persons was practically guaranteed to keep him out of sharp controversy. A memorandum to Nixon on November 16, 1967, from Leonard Garment, another of the bright and reputable persons on his staff, said that Nixon must try to get "above the battle, moving *away* from politics and *toward* statesmanship." To this end Garment advocated "a fundamentally philosophical orientation, consistently executed, rather than a program-oriented, issues-oriented, or 'down-in-the-streets' campaign."[29]

The availability and lure of television completely transformed Nixon's customary manner of running for office. Unlike in previous campaigns, in 1968 he eschewed open forms of campaigning and marketed himself in a closed, controlled environment. This strategy was followed even more rigidly four years later in his reelection campaign. Watergate was not yet a major issue, George McGovern was a weak rival, and Nixon was reelected by a landslide. His style of campaigning in 1972, however, was far from the ideal of democratic dialogue, as David Broder noted in his syndicated column:

There is a wall a mile high between Mr. Nixon and the press. Mr. Nixon travels in isolation. . . .

His major speeches on the trip—to Republican fund-raising dinners—were watched by reporters from separate rooms, via closed-circuit television. In Los Angeles, it took personal intercession by a White House press aide for a few reporters to gain access to the banquet hall—the same room in the same hotel where reporters had freely interviewed guests at a McGovern fund-raiser the night before.

The only sound television cameras in the room when Mr. Nixon spoke were the closed-circuit cameras controlled by the White House itself. The scenes of the dinner you saw on television—and that most of the reporters saw—were exactly what the White House wanted you to see, and nothing more.[30]

Likening Nixon to "a touring emperor" rather than a candidate for president, Broder declared that "the Nixon entourage seems to be systematically stifling the kind of dialogue that has in the past been thought to be the heart of a presidential campaign."[31]

Well before the presidential election of 1976, Jimmy Carter received an insightful memorandum from his assistant Hamilton Jordan. Recently retired as governor of Georgia, Carter was thinking about running for president. Jordan gave him this advice: "We would do well to understand the very special and powerful role the press plays in interpreting the primary results for the rest of the nation. What is actually accomplished in the New Hampshire primary is less important than how the press interprets it for the rest of the nation."[32]

If recognition of that kind was important to Dwight Eisenhower and John Kennedy, both nationally recognized figures when they ran for president, it was surely valuable to Carter, unknown to most of the country in the mid-1970s. Grasping this reality, he made a shrewd decision to focus first on the Iowa Democratic caucuses of 1976, which would precede the New Hampshire primary. It was a testing ground that had been largely ignored by presidential aspirants in previous years.

In quest of a surprising early victory that would propel him into New Hampshire, Carter began cultivating Iowa Democrats in 1975. His strategy clicked. On October 27, the Iowa Democrats held a Jefferson-Jackson Day fund-raising dinner at Iowa State University in Ames, on which a straw vote was to be taken. Jimmy Carter and his wife, Rosalynn, were on hand. Carter's staff, especially pleased that R. W. Apple, Jr., of the *New York Times* was covering the affair, did their best to pack the place with Carter supporters. When Carter won a definite victory— 23 percent of the 1,094 respondents, the largest individual share—Apple filed a story about the Georgian's "dramatic progress." Carter, he reported, "appears to have taken a surprising but solid lead" in the race for Iowa delegates.[33]

On January 19, 1976, the day of the caucuses, Carter flew not to Iowa but to New York City, where he talked about his victory on the late-night television specials and the next morning's network news shows. At one point Roger Mudd said on CBS: "No amount of badmouthing by others can lessen the importance of Jimmy Carter's finish. He was a clear winner in this psychologically important test."[34] This was exactly what Hamilton Jordan had had in mind. Carter went on to win the New Hampshire, Florida, and Ohio primaries and was nominated at the Democratic National Convention in New York in July.

Seldom had there been a better time for a Democrat to run. In the previous four years Vice-President Spiro Agnew had resigned in disgrace, Nixon had resigned to avoid impeachment, and Watergate had horrified the country. In 1976 the Republican nominee was Gerald Ford, who had succeeded Agnew as vice-president and then Nixon as president. As president he had soothed the nation's shock over Nixon and Agnew. Yet he damaged himself with a sudden, surprising, and ill-prepared announcement that he had granted Nixon a presidential pardon. The way this was done led to innuendoes that Ford had secretly promised Nixon a pardon in advance as the price of his being appointed vice-president by Nixon when Agnew left. Such innuendoes have not been proved to this day, but the granting of the pardon became a political liability for Ford. On top of that, in a televised campaign debate with Carter, Ford blundered by asserting, "There is no Soviet domination of Eastern Europe." In answer to a question by Max Frankel, he said, "I don't believe . . . that the Yugoslavians consider themselves dominated by the Soviet Union. I don't believe that the Roumanians consider themselves dominated by the Soviet Union. I don't believe that the Poles consider themselves dominated by the Soviet Union."[35]

Such a statement by a president of the United States in 1989 or 1990 would have been understandable; the president's comment in 1976 seemed idiotic. Run and run again on the networks, in the familiar way television magnifies an incident, it caused people to say, in effect, what Ford himself was to say thirteen years later: "I blew it."[36] Carter won the election.

A great deal of public criticism was heard after the campaign about television's failure to report on the issues involved. Writing in the *Columbia Journalism Review*, James H. McCartney, a national correspondent for the Knight Newspaper Group, said:

What we have witnessed has been the emergence of the dominance of television ... and its influence on both candidates and journalists. The candidates were trying to cater to what they thought they had to do. And many journalists were confused about what their proper role should be in a campaign so totally dominated by television. The candidates, both Ford and Carter, ran their campaigns almost totally as media events, designed for television, scheduled for television. The writers were left to pick up the leavings.[37]

Richard Kaplan, a producer for the "CBS Evening News with Walter Cronkite," was assigned to Carter throughout the campaign. McCartney quoted Kaplan as saying that television "just can't handle issues the way a newspaper can." Kaplan added: "We have to have something on that film. And you've got ninety seconds to tell it." During the campaign Carter had a press briefing to discuss his proposal to make the term of the chairman of the Federal Reserve Board coterminous with that of the president. The seriousness of this proposal was that it could lead to presidential influence over the Federal Reserve, an independent body. Nevertheless, the Cronkite show never reported Carter's briefing. "We couldn't figure out a way to do it on television," Kaplan said. "What do you show, people sitting around a table?"[38]

In campaigns played out on television, as they are, any conspicuous misstep or misstatement can do lasting damage to a candidate. On November 4, 1979, almost on the eve of Sen. Edward Kennedy's announcement of his candidacy for president, CBS broadcast a special on interviews the senator had granted to Roger Mudd. Of course, Chappaquiddick came up, which was no help to Kennedy, but he had nothing new to say on the subject. Then Mudd asked a bromide quadrennial question that all candidates expect and prime themselves to answer to their advantage.

"Why do you want to be president?" Mudd inquired.

Kennedy answered:

Well, I'm—were I to—to make the—the announcement and—to run, the reasons that I would run is because I have a great belief in this country, that it is—has more natural resources than any nation in the world, has the greatest educated population in the world, the greatest capacity for innovation in the world, and the greatest political system in the world. And yet I see at the current time that most of the industrial nations of the world are exceeding us in terms of productivity, are doing better than us meeting the problems of inflation, that they're dealing with their problems of energy and their problems of unemployment. And it just seems to me that this nation can cope and deal with its problems in a way that it has in the past. We're facing complex issues and problems in this nation at this time, but we have faced similar challenges at other times. And the energies and the resourcefulness of this nation, I think, should be focused on these problems in a way that brings a sense of restoration in this country by its people to—in dealing with these problems that we face—primarily the issues on the economy, the problems of inflation, and the problems of energy. And I would basically feel that—that it's imperative for this country to either move forward, that it can't stand still, or otherwise it moves back.[39]

That night ABC captured 57 percent of the audience then watching with the first television showing of the movie *Jaws*. The fact that the Mudd program drew an audience share of only about 16 percent was first seen as a lucky break for Kennedy. "Which, of course, missed the point," Jeff Greenfield wrote. He added:

While the audience's numbers were small, it is fair to say that every political writer, every political and campaign official, every "opinion maker" watched *Teddy*. And the impact of such a program is hardly confined to the original audience. As with many political events on television, most especially debates and speeches, the press—print and broadcast—acts as a mediator, explaining to the country at large what it is they have seen. And the unanimous verdict, among Kennedy's staunchest friends and most unremitting foes, was that his performance was a disaster.[40]

Mary McGrory wrote in her syndicated column: "Away from the prepared text, the face-to-face encounter, Kennedy is halting, rambling and uncertain when he starts a sentence, where will it all end? He could, in a debate, the White House must be thinking, do the impossible. That is, make murmuring Jimmy Carter sound crisp and forceful."[41] Kennedy won the New York and Connecticut primaries, but then faltered, and Carter was renominated.

At the Republican National Convention in Detroit in July 1980, television had an extraordinary effect. Reagan had the presidential nomination in his hands long before the convention. The unanswered question was who his running mate would be. For weeks the political community had been fascinated by reasonably well founded reports that Reagan was thinking of standing history on its head by selecting former president Ford for vice-president. In the middle of the convention it nearly happened.

With all suspense gone from the nomination of the presidential candidate, the only big spot news in sight was the race for vice-president, in which George Bush was also a serious contender. Newspapers were as much interested as television in the story. But television was on live for hours on end. Newspapers could thoughtfully wrap up a day's events around midnight; television had to deal with them somehow as they happened, or seemed to be happening. The result of this, inevitably, was a constant outpouring on the air of tips and speculations passing between the anchors and reporters throughout the hall. It added up to a breaking story intriguing to viewers and nerve-wracking to the assembled politicians. Several weeks earlier Reagan had called on Ford at Palm Springs, but Ford told reporters that Reagan should look elsewhere for a running mate. Clues of a different import kept turning up. Then on the opening night of the convention, Monday, Ford delivered the traditional former president's address.

"This Republican," he said, "is going to do everything in his power to elect our nominee to the presidency of the United States. . . . This country means too much for me to comfortably park on a park bench. So when this convention fields the team for Governor Reagan, count me in."[42]

According to Jeff Greenfield, Reagan's advisers interpreted Ford's words as a sign of willingness to run. The next day Reagan was putting out feelers to his own backers about a Reagan-Ford ticket. Then came Wednesday, July 16—for television a date that will live in fervidity. With the networks in a caldron, the morning began with a tip from a reliable Republican official that it looked as though Ford would be on the Republican ticket. At noon Ford had a previously scheduled luncheon with *Newsweek* reporters and editors. He indicated to them an interest in an arrangement in which the president would be the chairman and chief executive of the government and the vice-president the chief operating officer.

The balloting for president was scheduled for that night. Ford had a standing agreement with Cronkite to drop by the CBS booth at seven o'clock.

"What would happen," Cronkite asked him at that meeting, "if [delegates] got out there on the floor tonight or tomorrow and said, 'It's got to be Gerald Ford'?" Ford's answer to Cronkite must have struck the Reagan headquarters like a bolt of lightning:

If there is any change it has to be predicated on the arrangements that I would expect as a vice-president in a relationship with the president. I would not go to Washington, Walter, and be a figurehead vice-president. If I go to Washington—and I'm not saying that I'm accepting—I have to go there with a belief that I will play a meaningful role across the board in the basic and the crucial and the important decisions that have to be made.

Perhaps something like a "co-presidency"? Cronkite asked. The term was his, but it did not appear to give Ford pause. "That's something that Governor Reagan really ought to consider," Ford replied, adding, "For him not to understand the realities of some of the things that might happen in Washington is being oblivious to reality."[43]

Astonishment spread through the convention hall, and reporters descended on the CBS booth to catch Ford. "Reagan, we would learn the next day," wrote Broder, "had been equally nonplussed."[44] But at 10:10 P.M. Cronkite was on the air with a sensational bulletin:

CBS has learned that there is a definite plan for Ronald Reagan and the former President of the United States, Gerald Ford, who will be his selection as running mate, an unparalleled, unprecedented situation in American politics . . . to come to this convention hall tonight to appear together on the platform for Ronald Reagan to announce that Gerald Ford would run with him.[45]

The other networks followed with stories that were more tentative. The Associated Press and a number of newspapers carried stories about an impending "dream ticket." The convention meanwhile had settled down to the real, if rather tedious, ninety-minute task of choosing the only effective candidate for president in the field. When the balloting was over, the expectation was that Reagan would appear and tell the delegates that his preference for running mate was Ford. Instead, the former president took himself out of the picture, and Reagan aides burst onto the floor shouting that Bush was the choice for vice-president. When Lesley Stahl, a CBS reporter, relayed the word to Cronkite, he said, "It's hard to believe."[46] Bush must have been thinking the same thing. If it had not been for television, his political career might have ended in Cobo Hall. Instead, Cobo Hall witnessed the dawn of the Reagan-Bush era.

In transforming American politics, television raised a critical challenge to the parties and to their candidates. To benefit the most from television, one has to know how to use it more effectively than does one's opponent. Beginning with Eisenhower in 1952, the Republicans—Nixon (except in 1960), Reagan, and Bush—have gotten the better of their opposition on television. These Republican candidates were not necessarily better men or more honest than their Democratic opponents, but their appeal to television audiences was somehow more compelling. In experts such as Michael Deaver, Roger Ailes, and Lee Atwater, the Republicans enlisted more skillful but not necessarily more noble tacticians than the Democrats employed. Certainly, the Republican edge was clear in the 1984 campaign between Reagan and Bush and Vice-President Walter Mondale and Geraldine A. Ferraro of New York. In his book on the campaign, Martin Schram wrote that President Reagan had "skillfully mastered the ability to step through the television tubes and join Americans in their living rooms." Schram called Reagan and Deaver "pols who understand TV better than the TV people themselves."[47]

Indeed, by 1984 television news executives strove to keep their news programs from being manipulated by image-makers. In a picture medium, however, this is not always possible to do. "If Ronald Reagan makes a speech in front of the Statue of Liberty, and the speech has news in it," Joseph Angotti, then an NBC political director, said, "there is no way we can show Reagan without showing the statue behind him."[48]

On July 4, 1984, the best shot Mondale could offer the television evening news was of himself at home in Minnesota, talking with Mayor Henry Cisneros of San Antonio, a potential vice-presidential nominee. Reagan, aboard Air Force One, was on his way to the annual Daytona Beach 400 stock car race and a picnic with twelve hundred of the fans. As the plane, equipped with television cameras inside to catch the president, swooped down, he picked up a radio-telephone, sang out the traditional, "Gentlemen, start your engines," and then set the cars thundering down the track. Furthermore, after he arrived at the stands, packed with eighty thousand spectators, he sat in for a while as guest commentator on the racing circuit radio network. It was all lively fare on the network evening news.

Labor Day, when the campaigns should have been off like the stock cars, was even a worse calamity for Mondale and Ferraro. Anyone who had been with President Truman on Labor Day in 1948 had to wonder what was the matter with the Democratic party in 1984. At noon Truman had addressed an estimated one hundred thousand people in Cadillac (now Kennedy) Square in Detroit. Then tens of thousands more turned out to cheer him on an afternoon-long motorcade through Hamtramck, Royal Oak, Pontiac, Flint, and Grand Rapids. On Labor Day in 1984, Mondale, Ferraro, and a small, loyal contingent kicked off the national Democratic campaign by marching sixteen blocks up Fifth Avenue in New York at 9:30 A.M. The streets were practically deserted at that hour on a holiday. The pictures on the networks that night were pathetic. The grotesque planning grew out of the kind of scheme Goldwater had used ten years earlier of campaigning in three time zones on a single day to exploit three different television markets. A Labor Day parade *was* scheduled in New York. But it was a *midday* parade. It *did* draw a crowd and *would* have made a good launching vehicle for Mondale and Ferraro. But by then the candidates' plane was in, or approaching, their next stop, Merrill, Wisconsin. To get there on time they had had to make their own sad parade in New York. Unfortunately, by the time they arrived in Merrill for another parade and rally, it was raining. Then delays of one kind and another caused the candidates to arrive late for what was intended to be their climactic appearance of the day in Long Beach, California. But the crowd had already dwindled, and the public address system conked out. On television news Mondale was shown tapping on a microphone, asking, "Does this thing work?" With no television to worry about, Harry Truman had a hell of a Labor Day. Driven to squeeze the last drop out of television, Walter Mondale had a day of hell.

By October 7, 1984, the date of the first televised debate in Louisville between the candidates, Mondale was trailing so badly in the polls that practically his only hope lay in this confrontation with Reagan. So much aware of it was Mondale that he practiced in the dining room of his house in Washington, which, for the purpose, had been converted into a mock television studio with two podiums. Under bright lights members of his staff fired questions at him before a camera. His answers were played back until he had memorized them. Then, to almost universal surprise, he went to Louisville and so unmistakably carried the day that the polls indicated an incipient turnabout in the campaign. It was not the dining room rehearsals that changed things. Rather, for the first time the Gipper, at the age of seventy-three, blew it on television. He was worn. He was confused. He was not himself. "Reagan is really old," Mondale told an aide after the debate. "I don't know if he could have gone another fifteen minutes."[49]

What was seen on television suddenly changed the overriding issue of a campaign. Two days later a headline in the *Wall Street Journal* read: "New Question in Race: Is Oldest U.S. President Now Showing His Age? Reagan Debate Performance Invites Open Speculation on His Ability to Serve."

Other newspapers and the networks took up the question. Some television news programs spliced scenes from the debate with shots of the president dozing during an audience with Pope John Paul II. The White House cried foul.

By the time of the second debate, on October 22 in Kansas City, the drama centered on Reagan's appearance and the state of his alertness. Beforehand, his technicians went to the studio and changed lighting angles and candlepower to give him more of a glow. When the two contenders appeared, the president was poised and wide awake. He seemed more rested than before. His self-confidence was palpable. "They pumped him up with sausage and he looked okay," Mondale recalled long afterward. Reagan knew what pitch was coming. His eye was on the center field stands when, sure enough, a reporter on the panel reminded him of the youthful John Kennedy's ordeal over the Cuban missile crisis and asked Reagan if he himself was "too old to handle a nuclear crisis." Crack went the bat. "I am not," the president replied, "going to exploit, for political purposes, my opponent's youth and inexperience." The whole country watched the ball sail over the fence. "When I walked out of there," Mondale said, "I knew it was all over."[50]

The waves of changes that began with the televising of the national conventions in 1948 had, by 1988, transformed the mode, mechanics, and theater of elective politics. To be sure, television has not eliminated ethnic, religious, and racial preferences among voters, or the ancient division between left and right, or people's tendency to vote their pocketbooks. The effect of television is secondary to what Jeff Greenfield has called "the shaping influences of American political life . . . embodied in political realities."[51] Politicians, more than political scientists and journalists, have exalted the importance of television. They have done so not only in words but in actions. For more than forty years they have not been able to stay away from television. It is the one thing that matters most to them. By their own words it is possible to judge where the dividing line lay between what politics was before 1948, when television news was born, and what politics has been since. The day after his dramatic victory over Dewey in 1948, Truman articulated the essence of the "old politics" when he said, "Labor did it."[52] A mere twelve years later, after defeating Nixon in 1960, Kennedy's comment went to the heart of the "new politics." "It was TV more than anything else," he said, "that turned the tide."[53] While not the only determinant of a candidate's popularity, television has become an unavoidable threshold to political power.

18

1988

The 1988 presidential campaign was the culmination, often the degradation, of practices, strategies, manipulations, and distortions that had been multiplying in elections almost since the advent of television news. Television spots, or commercials, were more numerous and, on the whole, more unpleasant than in any previous campaign. Discussion of issues was more than ever reduced to sound bites measured in seconds. Mostly, the blame for the tone fell not on the loser, Gov. Michael S. Dukakis, but on the winner, George Bush, whose campaign, nevertheless, was the more effective.

Bush advocated, among other things, a day care program for children. He promised a vigorous attack on the drug scourge. But after he was inaugurated on January 20, 1989, it was evident that the more conspicuous issues with which he had saturated the campaign—which candidate liked the flag better, which disliked murderers more—had little to do with governing the country.

Short on content, long on bile, the Republican campaign often seemed less commanded by the candidate than deputed to handlers and consultants like Roger Ailes, Bush's media adviser, and Lee Atwater, Bush's national campaign manager. They may have wanted it to seem as if they were calling the shots. But an erstwhile campaign consultant, Mark Shields, who became a syndicated columnist for the *Washington Post*, wrote: "That was Bush's campaign. To fault Ailes and Atwater for the 1988 campaign while endowing Bush and Baker [James A. Baker III, the campaign chairman] with a form of moral Teflon is frankly dishonest. . . . For what's wrong with American politics, you have to look beyond the consultants to the candidates."[1]

240

The year of the campaign was barely three weeks old when, on January 25, 1988, Bush appeared on the "CBS Evening News" in an interview with Dan Rather. The program shook the political stage and offered a foretaste of the mean spirit of '88. Both men entered the arena encumbered by recent difficulties. Particularly because of an appearance of meekness as Ronald Reagan's vice-president, Bush had a certain reputation as a "wimp," a slang word of unknown origin but one carrying a connotation any candidate would gladly relinquish. Rather, four months earlier, had stunned the television industry by stalking off a set in a huff, causing CBS to transmit a blank signal for seven minutes, a serious embarrassment to the network and to Rather. He'd been riled by word that a late match at the U.S. Open tennis tournament would preempt the evening news. When the match ended suddenly and the network switched to Rather, the screen was black without explanation to affiliated stations.

CBS had requested the interview, and Bush agreed. He insisted, however, that the interview be carried live so that nothing he said could be edited out as might be the case in a taped interview. Negotiations ensued. CBS said that the interview would be substantive, oriented to issues, and replete with tough questions. It was agreed that the two participants would not be face to face, though it would appear on television sets that they were. Rather would be on the air from New York, Bush from Washington. In its own preparations Rather's staff concluded that the most newsworthy issue was Bush's role in the Iran-contra scandal, a matter on which the vice-president had been rigidly reticent. The advertisements for the program said the interview would deal with Iran-contra.

As the day of the interview approached, both sides rehearsed assiduously, with Bush's staff becoming increasingly suspicious of ambush at the hands of Rather. The bewhiskered Ailes, in girth and gusto the Falstaff of the sound-bite, photo-op era, coached Bush. Characteristic of Ailes's volcanic personality, he insisted on having Bush ready with a counterpunch. If Rather hit the vice-president hard with the Iran-contra scandal, Bush must react with a blow about Rather's embarrassing CBS by plunging the network into darkness. Mary Martin, deputy news director for CBS in Washington, recalled what happened in Bush's office in the Capitol before the interview. "Ailes was waving his arms and telling Bush, 'He's gonna sandbag you.' "[2] In that case, Ailes instructed, Bush was to exclaim, "This is outrageous!"[3]

As an introduction to the interview, CBS ran a five-minute film on the Iran-contra affair, with intimations that Bush's part in it had been more important than he had acknowledged. Seated before the camera in Washington, Bush watched the opening film with increasing anger. He barked, "That's not what I'm here for." If he was going to be grilled on this subject, he added, CBS was going to experience another "seven minute walk-out." The interview was not yet on the air, but an open microphone picked up Bush's words. Rather thus knew Bush was angry. Undaunted, when the interview began, he hit Bush with Iran-contra. A clash ensued. Bush wasted no time calling the introductory film "outrageous." Rather moved on, citing a poll indicating that one-fourth of the respondents "believe you're hiding something" on Iran-contra.[4] "I am hiding something," Bush retorted. "You know what I'm hiding? What I told the president, that's the only thing, and I've answered every question put before me." Sarcastically, he asked Rather if he had a question.

> Rather: You have said if you had known . . . this was an arms-for-hostage swap . . . that you would have opposed it.
> Bush: Exactly.
> Rather: You also said that you did not know—
> Bush: May I answer that?
> Rather: That wasn't a question, it was a statement.
> Bush: It was a statement and I'll answer it.
> Rather: Let me ask the question if I may, first.
> Bush: The president created this program . . . he did not think it was arms for hostages.
> Rather: That's the president, Mr. Vice-President.
> Bush: And that's me. Because I went along with it, because you know why, Dan? Because—
> Rather: That wasn't a question, Mr. Vice-President.

Rather proceeded to push in the direction Bush's handlers feared. He asked questions about the vice-president's recollection of specific incidents in the Iran-contra scandal. At Bush's end, Ailes, out of range of the camera, scribbled on a yellow pad for Bush to see, "not fair to judge career—yours."[5] The time for the counterpunch was nearing.

> Rather: I don't want to be argumentative, Mr. Vice-President—
> Bush: You do, Dan.
> Rather: No, sir, I don't.
> Bush: This is not a great night because I want to talk about why I want to be president, why those 41 percent of the people are supporting me. And I don't think it's fair—
> Rather: Mr. Vice-President, those questions are designed—

The time for the counterpunch had come. "I don't think it's fair," Bush told Rather, "to judge a whole career—it's not fair to judge my whole career by a rehash on Iran. How would you like it if I judged your career by those seven minutes when you walked off the set in New York?" (The incident took place in Miami.)

Watching Rather shake off the punch brought relief to Bush's advisers.

Rather: Mr. Vice-President—
Bush: I have respect for you, but I don't have respect for what you're doing here tonight.
Rather: Mr. Vice-President, I think you'll agree that your qualifications for president and what kind of leadership you'd bring to the country, what kind of government you'd have . . . what kind of people you'd have around is much more important than what you just referred to.

With both of them talking at the same time, Rather managed to cut through with a comment on Iran-contra. "Mr. Vice-President," he said, "you've made us hypocrites in the face of the world. How could you— how could you sign on to such a policy? And what does this tell us about your record?" Again a rush of words, this time with Rather getting frantic signals from the control booth to end the program. Harried, he asked Bush if he would be willing to hold a news conference before the forthcoming Iowa caucuses. While Bush was trying to explain his schedule, Rather cut him off with an iciness that made even some loyal Democrats wince.

"I gather the answer is no," he said. "Thank you very much for being with us, Mr. Vice-President," he said. "We'll be back with more news in a moment."

Bush looked nonplussed. He glanced at some of the CBS staff and said: "The bastard didn't lay a glove on me. . . . Tell your goddamned network that if they want to talk to me, to raise their hands at a press conference. No more Mr. Inside stuff after that."[6]

Telephone calls, most of them critical of Rather, poured into CBS and some of its affiliated stations. Bush was encouraged, and his advisers were satisfied that the feisty engagement lessened the "wimp factor." In the *Washington Post*, Mary McGrory lamented, "Dan Rather has probably nominated the Republican candidate and may even have elected the next president."[7]

As anticipated, Bush was defeated in Iowa by Sen. Robert Dole, of Kansas, his principal opponent for the presidential nomination. The Reagan administration was not popular in Iowa. Worse news for the vice-president was that he ran third in the Iowa Republican caucuses behind television evangelist Pat Robertson. This poor showing made the New Hampshire primary, only eight days after Iowa, a critical test for Bush. As a native New Englander, he was a logical favorite. The Reagan administration was highly esteemed in New Hampshire, and Bush had influential backers in the state, most notably Gov. John Sununu. Nevertheless, Bush's defeat in Iowa created at least an illusion of a tight race, and the polls were oscillating.

Bush was quick to seize opportunities to get on local television news shows in the state. At a plant in Manchester he shook hands with arriving workers. In a lumberyard he operated a forklift. At a truck stop he climbed into the cab of an eighteen-wheeler and drove it around a parking lot. In a snowstorm he cleared out a patch of roadway at the wheel of a snowplow. But it was in the home stretch that Bush outdid Dole through the use of television commercials.

In Hollis, New Hampshire, on the Thursday evening before the election, Bush staged and filmed a New England–style town meeting. Then on Saturday night he bought thirty minutes on three nearby Boston television stations and on the important New Hampshire outlet, Channel 9 in Manchester, to run the film in an effective political program titled "Ask George Bush." The hardest-hitting commercial that Bush ran the weekend before the primary attacked Dole principally on taxes. New Hampshire is a state with perennially inadequate revenue, and the inhabitants keep it that way because of their hostility to taxes. Any presidential campaigner entering the state is well advised not to yield an impression that he favors raising them. Dole had no intention of proposing higher income taxes, but he did not flatly promise, on his arrival in New Hampshire, to hold the line on all taxes.

In the week before the primary, confidence ran high in Dole's staff. The polls were encouraging, and no last-minute aggressive television spots were aired. But Ailes the last week produced what came to be known in the Bush camp as the "straddle ad." Sununu and others pulled strings to get it on stations in New Hampshire and Boston after normal deadlines for acceptance of advertising had passed. Dole was accused of straddling ratification of the intermediate-range missile treaty and other questions, mainly taxes. A picture of Bush appeared with a caption, "Won't Raise Taxes." An announcer repeated, "George Bush says he won't raise taxes period." Then two faces of Dole, with a caption, "Straddled." Then the words "Taxes—He can't say no." And the announcer again: "Bob Dole straddles, and he just won't promise not to raise taxes. And you know what that means."[8]

Bush won the primary with 38 percent of the vote against 29 percent for Dole. The road to Bush's nomination looked smooth. Dole seemed shocked and bitter. In an interview after the returns were in he used television in exactly the wrong way. On NBC, Tom Brokaw asked him if he had anything to say to Bush, who was also on the program but from another studio. Dole snapped, "Stop lying about my record."[9] The heated answer revived the image of the senator as an acerbic man and mean campaigner. Two years later he was asked at a trade convention what had caused the downfall of Gen. Manuel Noriega, the Panamanian strongman. Dole grumbled, "He had the same pollster I had in New Hampshire."[10]

In June Michael Dukakis, the Democratic frontrunner, swept four states, including California and New Jersey, on the last primary day. A *Wall Street Journal*–NBC survey taken June 9–12 showed Dukakis leading Bush for the presidency, forty-nine to thirty-four. A Gallup Poll of June 10–12 indicated a Dukakis lead of fifty-two to thirty-eight.[11] Then the lead sagged. Dukakis did not do much to sustain it. Bush managed to make more news. In a breeze Dukakis was nominated in Atlanta in mid-July by a well-unified party. As best he could, he finessed the ambition of Jesse Jackson and, hoping the choice would help him in the South, selected Sen. Lloyd Bentsen of Texas as the vice-presidential nominee. As a climax, Dukakis delivered a good acceptance speech. The Democrats seemed to know how to pummel Bush. In the keynote address Ann Richards, state treasurer of Texas, poured ridicule on "poor George" who "was born with a silver foot in his mouth." And Ted Kennedy got the delighted delegates chanting after him, "Where was George?" as he ticked off Reagan's alleged mistakes over the previous four years.

Watching all of this on television, Ailes concluded that he had problems ahead. His worries were unnecessary. For the Democrats it was uphill from Atlanta. Probably the elements made it a Republican year, willy-nilly. Bush was riding a tide of peace, prosperity, conservatism, and enduring resentment in some regions of the country against the civil rights reforms of past Democratic administrations. A sharp Republican team knew the rough way to play, and the Democrats did not know how to, or preferred not to, fight back. Republican veterans were ever quick to go with television commercials and photo opportunities on emotional subjects like blue-collar crime, prisons, patriotism, and the welfare state. Dukakis considered himself a political moderate, but the Republicans branded him a 1960s-style liberal and, *ipso facto*, "soft" on crime, committed to heavy civilian public spending, and niggardly on defense appropriations. For all the vulnerabilities of the Reagan administration, Dukakis failed to frame a winning issue against Bush.

The Bush team had no such trouble. Well before the conventions Lee Atwater asked Jim Pinkerton, the chief researcher, to make a list of issues that might help bring Dukakis down. Pinkerton returned with a three-by-five card on which he had noted Dukakis's positions on taxes and national defense, his veto of a Massachusetts bill requiring the pledge of allegiance to the flag in classrooms, the state of pollution in Boston Harbor, and Dukakis's opposition to the death penalty. The list also contained something Pinkerton had discovered in the text of a debate among Democratic contenders before the April presidential primaries in New York. Sen. Albert Gore of Oklahoma had questioned Dukakis about a Massachusetts prisoner-furlough program. Pinkerton went on to discover that an imprisoned convicted murderer named William (Willie) Horton, Jr., an African American, had received a weekend pass under the program and had then raped a woman. After this atrocity Gov. Dukakis had the procedure changed to exclude convicted murderers from furloughs. Nevertheless, the Bush campaign seized on this tragedy as a way to accuse Dukakis of being soft on crime.

To make, in effect, a market test of issues, Bush consultants had two so-called focus groups of voters organized in Paramus, New Jersey. The participants chosen were Democrats who had voted for Reagan in 1984 but who, four years later, intended to vote for Dukakis. Out of sight behind two-way mirrors, the Bush experts watched with increasing jubilation the reactions of these voters as moderators in each group introduced them to the issues on Pinkerton's card. According to later reports, 40 percent of one group and 60 percent of the other said they would switch to Bush. "I realized right there," Atwater was reported to have said, "that we had the wherewithal to win . . . and that the sky was the limit on Dukakis' negatives."[12] A conference was held the following weekend at the Bush home in Kennebunkport. According to a report in *Time,* Bush was hesitant about a negative campaign of attacks on Dukakis, but then yielded.[13]

Most states had a prisoner-furlough program. The one in Massachusetts had been enacted under former Gov. Frank Sargent. The fact that Sargent was a Republican did not bother Ailes, who proceeded with work on a commercial showing prisoners exiting jail through a revolving gate. A voice said, "[Dukakis's] revolving-door prison policy gave weekend furloughs to first-degree murderers not eligible for parole. While out, many committed other crimes like kidnapping and rape and many are still at large. Now Michael Dukakis says he wants to do for America what he has done for Massachusetts. Americans can't afford that risk."[14] This first commercial did not use a photograph of Horton, but one Bush state committee in Illinois "circulated fliers bearing his picture and an accusation that Dukakis's election would set murderers and rapists free across the country."[15]

At a Republican state convention in Illinois in June, Bush accused Dukakis of having allowed "murderers out on vacation to terrorize people" and added: "I think Governor Dukakis owes the American people an explanation of why he supports this outrageous program." Democrats, he concluded, "can't find it in their hearts to get tough on criminals."[16]

Ironically, the Republican spot had been produced by a midwestern advertising man who, in 1985, had been sent to jail for a hit-and-run accident while driving when drunk. He had collided with a motorcycle carrying two teen-agers. One suffered brain damage.

On October 30, 1988, the *Washington Post* carried an article under the headline "For Television Mendacity, This Year Is the Worst Ever." The piece was written by Kathleen Hall Jamieson, an authority on campaign advertising, who later became the dean of the Annenberg School of Communications at the University of Pennsylvania. She wrote, in part:

Never before in a presidential campaign have televised ads sponsored by a major party candidate lied so blatantly as in the campaign of '88. . . .

Here's [one] from the Bush image mill: A procession of convicts circles through a revolving gate and marches toward the nation's living rooms. The ad invites the inference—false—that 268 first-degree murderers were furloughed by Dukakis to rape and kidnap. In fact, only one first-degree murderer, Willie Horton, escaped furlough in Massachusetts and committed a violent crime—although others have done so under other furlough programs, including those run by the federal government and by California under the stewardship of Ronald Reagan.[17]

It was a second prison-furlough commercial, sponsored by the National Security Political Action Committee, that used a glowering photograph of Horton. "Bush and Dukakis on crime," an announcer said. Then a photograph of Bush and the comment, "Bush supports the death penalty." Next a photograph of Dukakis and the observation, "Dukakis not only opposes the death penalty, he allows first degree murderers to have weekend passes from prison."[18] Finally, a mugshot of Horton. The commercial appeared throughout the country on cable television for twenty-eight days. Network news programs replayed it as an example of the deteriorating tone of the campaign. The *New York Times* assigned three reporters to get the story of the production of this commercial. According to the investigation, the National Security Political Action Committee claimed the quiet support of the Bush staff. During his own campaign, Lloyd Bentsen was among the first to label the commercial racist. The Bush people earnestly retorted that Horton was not chosen because of his color. Notwithstanding, as a symbol of white fear of African American criminals, his menacing visage could scarcely have been improved upon. At an early point Pinkerton told Atwater, "The more people who know who Willie Horton is the better off we'll be."[19] As a commentary on where American politics stood at the end of 1988, Russell Baker observed, "1988's Most Famous Man You Never Heard of until after 1987: Willie Horton."[20]

In the history of the Republic, political campaigns have at times been so full of strife, libel, nastiness, and brawling that the political exploitation of Willie Horton's crime does not stand alone on the horizon by any means. The resonance and impact of political attack, however, have been magnified beyond measure by the technology that brought the menacing image of Willie Horton into millions of American homes simultaneously. Reaction to people and events can be massive nowadays. In their book on the 1988 campaign, Peter Goldman and Tom Matthews likened television "in the hands of the new managers" to what napalm might have been in General Sherman's hands. "You could scorch a lot more earth with a lot less wasted time and motion."[21]

When the Massachusetts legislature passed a bill requiring teachers in their classrooms to lead the pledge of allegiance to the flag, Governor Dukakis could not have imagined the consequence for him. The legislation was promptly challenged in the court. An advisory panel of the state supreme court informed the governor of its opinion that the measure was an unconstitutional abridgement of the First Amendment right of free speech. Dukakis thereupon vetoed the bill. His response was perhaps overly legalistic. In 1988, however, the Bush campaign was not interested in legalism; it was interested in an issue of patriotism and resurrected the veto as a litmus test of which candidate was the more patriotic. Bush made a point of ending his acceptance speech at the Republican convention by leading the pledge of allegiance. To dramatize the difference between his own patriotic ardor and Dukakis's veto, he visited a flag factory during his campaign.

Bush also succeeded in attracting television cameras when he made a theatrical excursion in a boat around Boston Harbor. His purpose was to call attention to the polluted water. Alleging delay by Massachusetts in cleaning it up, he said of its governor, "I don't call that leadership, and I certainly don't even call it competence." Twice Dukakis had sought waivers from the Clean Water Act to defer construction of sewage-treatment plants; the program was involved in fiscal and jurisdictional disputes. But it was Dukakis who ultimately came forward with a plan for cleaning the harbor. Not mentioned that day was the Reagan administration's weak record on enforcing the act. The Bush campaign's television spot on the pollution of Boston Harbor showed sludge near a sign reading, "Danger/Radiation Hazard/No Swimming." But the sign had nothing to do with the Massachusetts governor or his record. It was a warning to navy personnel not to swim in waters that had once harbored nuclear submarines under repair.

Seeking to be fair in their stories about the harbor pollution, reporters tried to question the Republican nominee about his own record on improving the environment. Bush flatly refused to respond, explaining that his message would come at a later appearance. With the network evening news programs in mind, he had his own well-prepared political "message" of the day and wanted nothing else, especially of an unfavorable nature, to distract viewers' attention.

It was hard for reporters, especially fast-working television reporters, to avoid being set up by contrived events. On October 28, 1988, Brit Hume of ABC described, as the camera rolled, Bush's visit to a California highway patrol academy. To some familiar with journalism, the report sounded as if Hume was trying to remind viewers that the event was staged. Hume said:

We see patrol cars driving in formation. Cut to Bush. Then cut to new scene of candidate surrounded by cheering uniformed cops, receiving plaque from beefy officer. Officer: "America's number one crimefighter award!" Finally, we hear Bush's attack line: "The [Democratic] leadership, much of it, is a remnant of the sixties, the New Left, those campus radicals. . . ."[22]

These words by a reporter made far less of an impression on viewers than the pictures they saw. Such is the nature of television.

If Bush's strategy exemplified how television can help a campaign, a blunder and an incomprehensible lapse by Dukakis screamingly heralded the opposite. The blunder occurred when, on the defensive on the question of national military strength, Dukakis made a campaign stop at the General Dynamics plant in Warren, Michigan. At one point he donned an oversized helmet and drove an M1 tank around the plant. What appeared on television was a pathetic picture of a faltering candidate. The inexplicable lapse occurred before a huge television audience just when some superficial signs were indicating a possible turnabout in the campaign in his favor. In the second debate with Bush, held at the University of California at Los Angeles, Dukakis fell victim to a question that was irrelevant in a presidential election because it would have involved state, not federal jurisdiction. Asked by the moderator of the debate, Bernard Shaw of CNN, the question was: "Governor, if Kitty Dukakis were raped and murdered, would you favor an irrevocable death penalty for the killer?" Before the broadcast the other reporters chosen to ask questions (Ann Compton of ABC, Andrea Mitchell of NBC, and Margaret Warner of *Newsweek*) met with Shaw to make sure the four of them did not broach the same opening subject. When the three women panelists inquired of Shaw what he would ask Dukakis, he said a question about crime. When they pressed him to be specific, he balked at telling them. Then, under further pressure, he did. By all accounts, they were shocked, found it hard to believe, and considered the question very tough. Shaw was unyielding. The women urged him at least to modify the question by leaving Kitty Dukakis's name out of it and saying instead, "your wife." He refused, and the question was asked.

Evidently, since the question was entirely hypothetical, the point was to tap Dukakis's emotions. How would Roosevelt, Truman, Johnson, or Kennedy have managed the treacherous footing spread by this question? If, before an audience of seventy million or more, a reporter had asked General Eisenhower how a rape of Mamie Eisenhower would have affected his attitude on crime, the response would almost surely have been one of frozen fury, especially over the use of her name in such a context. How greatly such a response would have served Michael Dukakis! The nature of Bush's campaign had compelled Dukakis to be ready with set responses to questions on crime, yet at the critical moment they remained bottled up inside him. He simply left the whole country limp with a business-as-usual reply. He rambled on about his long opposition to capital punishment, the reduced crime rate in Massachusetts, and the need to halt drug traffic. So many theories have been advanced about the cause, or causes, of the lapse that it is obvious no one knows, maybe not even Dukakis. Hope for a miracle on election day drained out of the Democrats. Sometime later Dukakis told Shaw he considered the question fair and reasonable. In the *New York Times,* Walter Goodman called it "repulsive."[23]

Bound for certain nomination at the Republican convention in August 1988, George Bush arrived in New Orleans aboard the paddle-wheeler *Natchez* on the second day of the proceedings. After his cruise down the Mississippi River, he was welcomed at the dock by a crowd. Waiting there was a handsome young man of forty-one with sandy hair and large blue eyes. He was about to provide the country with the biggest political surprise since Thomas E. Dewey lost the 1948 election. Little known to the public and practically unheard of abroad, Dan Quayle, the junior U.S. senator from Indiana, was on hand at the request of Bush, who was, it turned out, very comfortable with his company. With glee at fooling the political cognoscenti, Bush introduced Quayle as his choice—almost totally unanticipated—for the nomination as vice-president. When, at the Republican convention in 1968, Nixon chose Gov. Spiro Agnew of Maryland as his running mate, the reaction fairly leaped up the Richter Scale. Agnew was but a tremor, however, compared with the jolt caused by Bush's announcement.

After Bush introduced him, Quayle, bouncing up and down, grabbed Bush by the arm and shoulder and exuberantly cried to the crowd: "Let's go get 'em! All right? You got it?"[24] From that moment on the dock, every movement Quayle made in public, every word he uttered in public was captured by television cameras. For such scrutiny and mass attention he had no adequate preparation. For the hazards of a parade of interviews on national television, he had little experience. He had not even had a chance to benefit from training by Bush's consultants because they had been kept as much in the dark as everyone else about the vice-presidential selection.

Because of the secrecy of Bush's choice, reporters in New Orleans were caught with practically no information about Quayle. This led to a barrage of questions. One question answered prompted a dozen more asked. In the frantic convention pressrooms and television studios, conflicting reports circulated about Quayle's abilities as a senator. Some who had known him in Washington ventured that he was a lightweight and often played golf instead of attending hearings. Others had found him good-natured, accommodating, quick to master issues that interested him—a Republican regular who nevertheless sometimes went his own way on roll call votes.

On the morning after the docking of the *Natchez,* Bush and Quayle held a televised news conference in an atmosphere already swirling with controversy. A reporter commented that Quayle had been a staunch supporter in Congress of the Vietnam War yet in the 1960s, when he was of draft age, had not served in the war. This sounded a jarring note in the patriotic exhibitionism of the Reagan-Bush era. With the Quayle candidacy already the biggest running story on television and in the press, talk about whether the prospective vice-presidential nominee had been a draft-dodger spread furiously. While a student at DePauw University in Indiana, Quayle had been exempt from selective service. After graduation he joined the Indiana National Guard. This meant that he would not go to a war zone unless his unit were deployed there. It was not.

The news conference was a deplorable spectacle for the Republicans. Then, during the convention, stories out of Indianapolis raised the question of whether family influence had enabled Quayle to get into the already crowded national guard. He denied it, and nothing of consequence has turned up in later investigations. In response to questions about his studies at the University of Indiana Law School, Quayle acknowledged low grades but refused to authorize release of his record.

At the convention James Baker insisted that Quayle promptly make the rounds of the NBC, CBS, ABC, and CNN anchor boxes for individual interviews. Confusion was compounded because Quayle made somewhat different statements in his different appearances. All this gave rise to short-lived speculation that the convention would select another vice-presidential nominee. Perhaps Quayle's most damaging remark came on the day after his selection by Bush, while answering questions about his entering the shelter of the national guard instead of the army. "I did not know in 1969," he said, "that I would be in this room today."[25] The implication was that if he *had* known, he would have hastened to enlist, not out of patriotic duty but out of political discretion.

The Democrats may have had hopes for help on the draft issue, but they melted quickly. Vietnam was not the great patriotic war, and everyone knew it. Many young men had gone to lengths to avoid fighting. No enduring damage could be wrought out of Dan Quayle's roughing it in the national guard. An ABC News poll released on August 18 asked whether, if it turned out that influence had been used to get Quayle in the national guard, he should remain on the Republican ticket. Fifty-five percent of the respondents said yes, 37 percent said no.

After the convention, according to a CBS News poll released on August 21, 50 percent of the respondents did not think Quayle had sufficient experience to be a good president in the event the office was vacated; 22 percent thought he did. With some variance shown in polls, an unfavorable opinion of Quayle as a vice-president persisted.[26] In his campaigning around the country, Quayle had more and more trouble. His statements became so embarrassing that the Bush team had him specially managed and for a time shunted to the whistlestops. Ironically, the youthfulness that Bush thought would make Quayle attractive on television to the baby-boom generation was the very thing that hurt him. Quayle's boyish looks and manner made him seem immature for the vice-presidency.

Quayle's handlers could not keep him from one scheduled debate with Lloyd Bentsen, the Democratic vice-presidential nominee. Even the ablest politician of the day would have been sobered by the prospect of debating Bentsen on national television. The sixty-seven-year-old Texas senator was courtly but tough. His appearance was commanding, as befit the powerful figure he cut in Washington as chairman of the Senate Finance Committee. Because of his age, Quayle needed to be able to convince voters that he had the qualifications and experience to be vice-president. Someone finally hit upon what seemed a perfect argument: by 1988 Quayle's combined service in the House and Senate was about the same as John Kennedy's when he was nominated for president in 1960. What better answer could there be, it was asked, to challenges about Quayle's qualifications? His wife, Marilyn, reportedly subscribed enthusiastically to the idea of such a response, and so it was included in his bag of tactics without awareness of one potential danger.

As the debate in Omaha on October 5 moved along, the question of Quayle's qualifications came up. Leaping before he looked, Quayle said: "It's not just age; it's accomplishments; it's experience. I have far more experience than many others that sought the office of vice-president of this country. I have as much experience in Congress as Jack Kennedy did when he sought the presidency." Judy Woodruff of the "MacNeil/Lehrer NewsHour," who was the moderator, looked at Bentsen for a response, if any. There was: "Senator, I served with Jack Kennedy. I knew Jack

Kennedy. Jack Kennedy was a friend of mine. Senator, you are no Jack Kennedy." The audience in the Civic Auditorium exploded with applause, cheers, even some screams. Quayle looked dazed, as he managed to reply, "That was really uncalled for Senator." Bentsen would not be checkmated. He insisted on the last word: "You are the one that was making the comparison, senator, and I'm the one who knew him well. And, frankly, I think you are so far apart in the objectives you choose for our country that I didn't think the comparison was well taken."[27]

If the result of the 1988 election had come down to balloting between Bentsen and Quayle, the White House might have been returned to the Democrats for the first time since Carter departed on January 21, 1981. On election day, however, the people are accustomed to voting for the presidential candidates, not for their running mates.

The sad thing about Bush's style of campaigning was that it was unnecessary. On August 27, nine days before Labor Day, the Op-Ed page of the *New York Times* carried an article under the headline "Maybe Bush Has Already Won." Written by Henry F. Graff, professor of history at Columbia University, the piece began, "The presidential campaign, only now formally set to begin, is in fact virtually finished . . . the die is just about cast." That week's Gallup Poll indicated that Bush was leading Dukakis by four percentage points. Graff contended that voters make up their minds by Labor Day. Time proved Graff's reasoning correct: Bush was in the lead for good. With all the advantages going for him, he did not have to descend into two months of mean-spirited television advertising.

A headline on the front page of the *New York Times* on October 30, 1988, read: "TV's Role in '88: The Medium Is the Election." In other words, television news not only shaped the campaign but also in many fundamental ways *was* the campaign.

During the fall an important ritual occurred at 6:30 every evening in both the Dukakis and Bush headquarters. Staff members gathered around television screens to see how their respective candidates had performed that day in the campaign's most competitive arena: the network evening news. The networks were aware of the rituals and less than happy about their meaning. "We have all been led around by the nose by the handlers of the candidates," Roone Arledge, head of ABC News, complained afterward. "Access [to the candidates] has been restricted. Commercials have taken the place of thoughtful interviews. It is a very serious problem that keeps us from doing the job we should be doing [and] has led to a lack of interest in the political process and a disillusionment."[28]

After the election NBC called in its campaign reporters and producers for a critical reassessment of the problems of covering the campaign for television. The names of the participants were not disclosed, but here is what one Washington-based reporter said: "The great ugly secret of campaigns is this: not much happens. The candidates give the same speech over and over again to different audiences. Because we won't report the same speeches over and over again, we are left to do the photo-ops and the inner workings of the campaign." Another reporter complained about the problems of logistics. "[Airplane] coverage involves so much shlepping around from baggage call to staged events and then a frantic race to the television feed-point [that] there is little time and less energy for the kind of research and reporting that shapes a thoughtful report, and that's when it's very easy to accept balloons and sound bite candy."

The tendency toward an ever more pivotal role for television in presidential campaigns reached new and troubling heights in 1988. The trend began in the Kennedy-Nixon debates of 1960 and accelerated in 1968 with the Nixon campaign's skillful play for exposure on the evening news. Twenty years later the candidates' so-called media managers had become masters of getting their messages across in television commercials and in events staged for television. For the television industry this produced the deep dilemma of how to use the pictures without becoming entrapped in stagecraft. Television techniques all but displaced old-time political campaigning as the focus of coverage. Reporters began to sound like drama critics.

Another change in the way television covered politics in 1988 was what one study called "the case of the shrinking sound bite." In 1968, it was not uncommon for candidates to speak on the evening news without interruption for more than a minute. By 1988 the average sound bite for presidential candidates ran 9.8 seconds. The Harvard study declared that "television's growing impatience with political speech raises serious questions about the democratic prospect in a television age. What becomes of a democracy when political discourse is reduced to sound bites, one-liners, and potent visuals." News departments, the study noted, become the "unwitting conduits of the television image the campaigns dispense." This is especially true in instances where campaigns buy commercials on the news programs.[29]

Another insidious problem occurs when the networks run political advertisements on news programs for the very purpose of exposing and criticizing them. In a study of this dilemma, Kathleen Jamieson concluded that the results of these endeavors were quite different from the intentions. The showing of the advertisements magnified their impact. The pictures overrode spoken criticisms and gave the advertisements new life.[30]

Because television is now the medium of the election, as the October 1988 headline said, candidates and their managers continue to hold the high cards. Some candidates will fall victim to their own commercials, and some voters will turn on them. Deplorable as they may be, however, commercials that attack an opponent have proved too effective for politicians to abandon. For the country the sad thing is the widening gulf between what it takes to win a campaign and what it takes for the winner to govern well.

19

○➤○➤○➤○➤○➤○➤○➤○➤○➤○➤○➤○➤○➤○➤○➤○➤○➤○➤○

Profound change in print journalism: the invasion by television news

When the World's Fair opened in New York in 1939, its theme was the world of tomorrow. Sightseers could view the General Motors exhibit of a model city of the future and then walk a short distance to an RCA exhibit of a primitive television set. The first was fantasy and the second was real, but both at the time seemed equally unbelievable. After the United States entered the Second World War in 1941, all technical development on the new invention of television was suspended. Newspapers, radio, and magazines continued securely as the staples for the communication of news, opinion, and entertainment.

More than most people realized, however, large sums of money had been invested in the development of television before the war. One of the executives in the newspaper business who understood this was Norman Chandler, then publisher of the *Los Angeles Times*. While the war was still being fought, Chandler wrote to a number of fellow publishers. He urged them, as he recapitulated, "to get into television business because newspaper advertising revenue from department stores and national advertisers was sure to take a big dip as soon as TV got going."[1] Wisely, Chandler followed his own advice. By 1948, the advent of television news, Douglas Edwards of CBS was regularly broadcasting nightly news. Several months later NBC followed with John Cameron Swayze. Both networks televised the 1948 Democratic National Conventions in Philadelphia. By the early 1950s television was competing with newspapers not only for advertising but also for stories.

"In the beginning," recalled John Seigenthaler, editor of the *Nashville Tennessean*, "many editors had a vague but none the less certain sense of antagonism toward TV. Some ignored it. Some openly waged war against it. Still others whose newspapers owned TV stations treated it like an illegitimate cousin who had come into a lot of money."² The feelings of print reporters and still photographers also were far from friendly. John W. Finney of the *New York Times* remembered the antagonism of reporters on Capitol Hill to the new competitor. "We suddenly found ourselves jostled by TV people and their heavy gear. We were like Luddites. We used to carry little metallic crickets in our pockets and at press conferences reach in and snap them to interfere with the TV sound equipment."³

After the Republican National Convention in Chicago in 1952, Felix R. McKnight, then managing editor of the *Dallas Morning News*, declared: "Television must learn some manners if it is to enter the reporting field. It was big, rude and somewhat of a bully at . . . Chicago."⁴ Four years later the Republican convention met in San Francisco. When Jay G. Hayden, Washington bureau chief for the *Detroit News*, rose to ask a question at a news conference at the convention, a member of a television crew behind him tugged his jacket and whispered, "You're in the way of the camera." In language certain to keep the film off the air Hayden retorted, "Then turn the goddamn thing off." He hated television and believed, not without reason, that it would ultimately degrade press conferences. He refused to budge.⁵

When television with its own power and techniques shouldered its way in beside newspapers to cover the American scene, the very novelty of the new medium gave it a special force and appeal. This wonderful invention, free of charge, brought plays, romances, the World Series, roller-skating derbies, Notre Dame football games, Howdy Doody, national political conventions, and nightly news into Americans' living rooms. Little wonder that journalists found it hard to compete. Ben H. Bagdikian, dean of the School of Journalism at the University of California at Berkeley, recalled what it was like in the early 1950s when he was a young reporter on the *Providence Journal*. "I made what seemed to me a significant discovery. People were talking about what they had seen on television, not, as previously, about what they had read in the newspapers."⁶

Since early in the 1920s, newspaper executives had been disgruntled by the competition of radio in delivering headline news and selling advertising. When television news began hitting its stride in the 1950s, however, the wisest of them knew they would have to react.

The American Society of Newspaper Editors (ASNE) first addressed the advances of television at its annual convention in Washington, D.C., in 1951. Television news was then barely three years old. The main speaker was E. C. Hoyt, editor of the *Cedar Rapids Gazette*. Hoyt warned the other editors: "Yes, the battle is on whether we like to admit it or not. It is a battle over the time it takes to watch television and the time it takes to read a newspaper. It is a battle for the revenue we need to keep our newspapers free and prosperous." Even though television was a newcomer, Hoyt said, it was a factor in causing a decline in newspaper street sales in Detroit. Furthermore: "Already some newspapers report that they are being hurt by the increased use of television by advertisers."[7]

Vintage 1948 television news does not seem a likely cause for worry by the nation's leading newspaper editors. CBS news with Douglas Edwards and the "Camel News Caravan" with John Cameron Swayze on NBC were simple black-and-white programs. For fifteen minutes these two former radio newscasters read the news that would make the next morning's headlines. The stories were supplemented by film, much of it purely feature material. News film from out of town had to be flown to New York, and often it arrived at the studio too late to be used the same day the story was broadcast. Film from abroad was sometimes days late in being aired. The film features were like the old semiweekly newsreels that had long been popular in the motion picture theaters. Viewers attracted by Edwards and Swayze thus saw their share of bathing beauty contests. By modern standards the studios were crude. Purposefully visible on Swayze's set was a carton of Camel cigarettes. He urbanely urged his audience to give Camels a thirty-day trial. To be sure, not many persons then were aware of the possible consequences of a thirty-year trial.

Although television news in its early days was limited, newspaper editors sensed its potential. Gradually, the news shows became more substantive, and Edwards and Swayze were provided the facilities for switching to Washington and other cities for news. In time the networks produced their own film distinctive from the newsreels. On January 14, 1952, NBC inaugurated the first televised morning program offering news—the two-hour "Today Show," hosted by Dave Garroway. As the laying of the coaxial cable moved westward, more and more stations were hooked to the networks. One of the first shows to be telecast from coast to coast was "See It Now," a seminal news program with Edward R. Murrow as the reporter and Fred W. Friendly as the producer. Then as now, however, television consisted of much more than news. Its entertainment programs and sports broadcasts drew large audiences.

"Newspaper publishers and editors must recognize television and radio for the competitors they are," Hoyt warned the editors at the 1951 convention. "They must not be complacent; they might wake up some day and find the props washed out from under them. They must not embrace too fondly this new medium, television."[8] Hoyt argued that neither radio nor television was "qualified to do the thorough job of reporting that is needed to let the people know how their city councils, county boards, and state legislatures are operating." Nor did they, he declared, have the reportorial resources to provide for viewers the range of public services that newspapers could offer.[9] His position that television news did not regularly offer the breadth and background that good newspapers provide is as unanswerable today as it was then.

Newspaper editors' talk in 1951 about television's shortcomings had little effect. By then television was exuding an aura of power, success, and excitement. Television news had recently aroused extraordinary attention by broadcasting two unusual events. One was Gen. Douglas A. MacArthur's address before a joint meeting of Congress on April 19, 1951. Because of differences between them on war policy, President Harry S. Truman had relieved MacArthur of his command in the Far East. MacArthur went to Congress to say his farewell in a speech long remembered: " 'Old soldiers never die; they just fade away,' . . . I now close my military career and just fade away." According to Ralph E. McGill, editor of the Atlanta *Constitution,* MacArthur's address "had a radio play certainly as large as any previous story, and it had the greatest television coverage of any news story in the history of television."[10]

The other event was the televised hearings of the Senate Special Committee to Investigate Organized Crime in Interstate Commerce, chaired by Estes Kefauver, a Democrat from Tennessee. As many as twenty million viewers tuned in to hear the testimony of notorious racketeers and gamblers. In New York dinner parties were held for watching the broadcasts. John Crosby, radio and television critic of the *New York Herald Tribune* and one of the speakers at the ASNE convention, recalled that "you couldn't get work out of anybody—your wife or your secretary or anybody else. They sat glued to that machine."[11] About the hearings Jack Gould, radio and television critic of the *New York Times,* wrote on March 18, 1951:

Television displayed a social impact of such enormous potentialities that undoubtedly the politicians, broadcasters, and educators will be studying and debating its impact for days to come.

From the standpoint of public enlightenment the union of television and [the]

Committee . . . has been uniquely timely and beneficial. Television's qualities of intimacy and immediacy have made the experience so personal that the TV viewer is actually closer to the scene than the spectator in the courtroom.

The last week has demonstrated with awesome vividness what television can do to enlighten, to educate and to drive home a lesson.[12]

The editors invited Senator Kefauver to speak at one of their sessions. He was introduced by Hamilton Owens, editor-in-chief of the Baltimore Sunpapers, as "a man who probably has been looked at by more people than any man in American history up to today." Kefauver's words about the role of the press in his investigation also apply to notable investigations by Congress in later years.

Television and radio, of course, added a great deal of interest to our hearings. They brought the hearings into the homes of the American people and made them feel that they were participating in government to an extent that I think they have never felt before. But let me say that while television and radio did this, had it not been for the press of America, there probably never would have been a Senate investigation, because the press had been exposing and asking for the prosecution and the cleaning up of criminal conditions for a long, long time.[13]

In retrospect, the 1951 editors' session sketched a rough outline of what was to be the response of newspapers to the challenge of television for the next forty years. Hoyt quoted Dale Stafford of the *Detroit News* as saying, "Too many newspapers are being presented in the vintage of 1902. They must wake up!"[14] Hoyt followed this advice later by urging editors to modernize their newspapers. Simply to compare the graphics, color, layout, topics, and special sections of newspapers today with those of the traditionally styled newspapers of that time is to begin to understand the revolution that has transformed newspapers in the second half of the twentieth century.

Ralph McGill predicted that "newspapers will step up the use of pictures and of color, because it will not be long, I assume, before TV is using color."[15] He was right. Another change prompted by television also was predicted at the ASNE convention: less traditional, "objective" reporting. "Newsmen have got to see," Hoyt admonished, "that they produce a more interpretive, a more accurate, and a more easily read product."[16] Turner Catledge, managing editor of the *New York Times,* agreed: "It isn't enough for us to say that we printed the news and now it's up to the reader to figure it out. We must make the intake for him easier."[17]

Should newspapers lean more heavily toward features or persevere with coverage of breaking news? Editors in the early 1950s didn't agree on the answer. Rebecca F. Gross, editor of the *Lock Haven* (Penn.) *Express,* chided newspaper executives for "trying to meet radio and TV competition by throwing more and more features into their columns, apparently trying to make their papers so fascinating that they can keep children from TV and old men from the radio dial." She wrote in 1955:

This is not an argument that entertainment has no place with the news in the press, nor that other forms of mass communication do not do a useful job in helping to disseminate the news.

It is an argument, however, that TV is bringing a new type of entertainment, a new channel of information and a new medium of advertising into the American home, which challenges the owners and editors of newspapers to reevaluate the performances of their chief—and still undisputed—function of telling news in the most useful and practical way.[18]

Through the years the Associated Press Managing Editors (APME) has scrutinized the problems posed for the press by television news. An association of managing editors of newspapers that subscribe to AP services, the APME in the early 1950s appointed a permanent committee on news innovations. In a report at its 1955 convention in Colorado Springs, the committee noted an "impressive trend" in reporting in depth. "Reporting in depth bears many labels—interpretation, illumination, background, analysis, comment, opinion," the committee said. "What it stands for is complete and thorough coverage to the satisfaction of the reader and *the requirements of the competitive situation.*"[19] Examples cited by the committee left little doubt that at least some serious newspapers were changing through experimentation.

For its coverage of negotiations between the United Automobile Workers and the automobile manufacturers in the summer of 1955 the *Detroit Free Press* won the approval of the APME committee on innovations. Along with its straight news coverage of the labor disputes, the paper frequently ran a front-page column called "A Look Behind the UAW-Auto Curtain." It was a potpourri of individual items about issues, personalities, speculation, background and similar information not likely to be reported by television.

Another front-page series in the *Free Press* that summer ran during the Big Four conference in Geneva under the heading "Sitting in at the Summit Meeting: How the Talks at Geneva Shape up for You." The breezy effort was intended to give readers fresh insights into the talks among the United States, Great Britain, the Soviet Union, and France. While the APME committee commended the series as a new approach, the articles turned out to be little more than contrivances to entertain. Coverage of the meetings of the heads of state began on July 19, 1955:

The talks at the summit have thrown a lot of people for a loop because it's not very clear what summit is meant.

There are a lot of summits around Geneva, Switzerland. . . .

In full view of Geneva is Mont Blanc (15,782 feet) and not far away are the Matterhorn, the Weisshorn, Dent Blanche and a variety of other hazards of life and limb.[20]

The next day readers were informed: "Bulganin Extended the Other Chiefs of State a Sack of Bonbons Loaded with Cocked Mouse Traps."[21] On the third day: "Tuesday's meeting of foreign ministers was widely touted as a big victory for the West, but some of the observers at the scene felt that Russia just didn't care."[22]

At Colorado Springs another APME standing committee, one on news features, also reported. It counseled that television news was "making rapid strides in reporting international conferences, so-called live meetings of the cabinet [staged by Eisenhower], national political conventions, etc. Furthermore, TV has added its great influence to that of radio, magazines, and freer travel in bringing national interests closer together."[23] This development added greatly to the demands on AP Newsfeatures. In response to the changing needs of newspapers, the AP broadened and deepened its coverage in the 1960s. It produced magazine-style features and conducted long investigations, such as Bernard Gravzer's inquiry into the case of James Earl Ray, the assassin of the Reverend Dr. Martin Luther King, Jr. One forty-thousand–word story, then an extraordinary length for a wire service, reconstructed the tragedy of Comdr. Lloyd M. Bucher, skipper of the USS *Pueblo,* an intelligence ship seized by the North Koreans in January 1968. The AP also formed special assignment teams. One team, headed by Gaylord Shaw, traveled across the country interviewing officers and men who had been aboard the American destroyers *Maddox* and *C. Turner Joy* in the Gulf of Tonkin in 1964. The AP interviews were conducted after questions—never satisfactorily answered—had been raised as to whether attacks on the destroyers by the North Vietnamese were unprovoked, as the Johnson administration claimed. The AP material was used by J. William Fulbright, chairman of the Senate Foreign Relations Committee, in support of his futile effort to have the Southeast Asia Resolution, popularly called the Gulf of Tonkin Resolution, repealed by Congress.

In listing interpretive and analytical writing as special instruments for newspapers in combatting television competition, E. C. Hoyt had neglected to mention a third tool, namely, investigative reporting. Bob Woodward and Carl Bernstein's exposé of the Watergate scandal in the early 1970s touched off a contemporary fad of journalistic investigation, but American newspapers had been digging into fraud and corruption for years. On some papers investigative reporting became institutionalized. On the *Washington Post,* for example, Woodward was made an assistant managing editor for investigative reporting. Almost all newspapers of consequence, however, have intensified their investigative reporting—not only on the old target of official corruption but also on schools, hospitals, hazardous waste, airline safety, shelters for the homeless, and other places and institutions affecting human lives.

The *Philadelphia Inquirer* has won Pulitzer prizes for its investigations into various Pennsylvania state bodies. Nevertheless, Eugene Roberts, its executive editor, dislikes the term *investigative reporting* because "to many people it means catching a crook." He explained:

I think where many papers go astray in investigative reporting is defining it as unearthing criminals. This immediately casts reporters as cops rather than as gatherers of information. Society will get along quite nicely without newsrooms that view themselves as police forces. But society, especially our democratic society, tends to falter when it doesn't get adequately informed. Here lies the opportunity and the obligation for newspapers.[24]

Ironically, in light of their competitive relationship, television advertises in newspapers and newspapers advertise on television. By the mid-1950s it was not uncommon to see a full page in a newspaper devoted to listings, television advertisements, and stories about television. In recent years some newspapers have gone to two television pages daily. By 1980 the *Los Angeles Times* had eleven reporters assigned full time to covering television. Because much of television entertainment is produced in Hollywood, it is a local story for the *Times.* Television critics, many of them highly paid, are employed by many other papers as well. On the *Washington Post,* for example, critic Tom Shales gets as much or more exposure than any other writer on the paper. The *Post*'s much read Style section devotes a large amount of space to news and commentary about television, its programs, its stars, and its business troubles. In the mid-1950s, managing editors around the country, complaining that the magazine *TV Guide* seemed to have monopolized such material, were pressing AP Newsfeatures to furnish more of it. To millions of persons, television brought into intimate view actors, singers, politicians, athletes, and other celebrities. On a scale without precedent, newspapers were enticed into writing about them. Special sections, like Style, not only served as a vehicle for such articles but also attracted new advertising. Most Sunday newspapers now carry television magazines. In sum, television sells newspapers.

As has been noted, the experience of the 1952 election, particularly the Eisenhower campaign, startled editors and reporters with the realization that a powerful competitor stood in their midst. In June 1952 General Eisenhower traveled to Abilene, Kansas, his hometown, to announce over national television his candidacy for the Republican nomination. At the open-air rally a cloudburst came close to ruining his performance. Luckily, a scheduled press conference the next day offered him a second chance. The television cameras were in town, of course, and the networks set about to cover the conference. The battalion of newspaper reporters and columnists present raised such a protest against an intruder that would beat them in the delivery of news that the Eisenhower staff yielded and excluded television. CBS and NBC decided the time had come for a showdown. They informed the candidate's staff that the cameras would be in the hall ready to shoot and that the responsibility for removing them would rest with the Eisenhower staff. This démarche was carried to Eisenhower. "We had better leave them there," he ruled.[25] Sig Mickelson, then head of CBS News, later wrote, "For the first time in its short life, television had insisted on equal rights with the printed press and won. . . . The new boy on the block had stood up to his peers and had signaled a demand for respect."[26] In a commentary well borne out in the history of journalism, Jack Gould admonished in the *New York Times*, "Remember Abilene!"[27]

John H. Carter, editor of the *Lancaster* (Penn.) *New Era*, was indignant at the way politicians swarmed to television cameras at the Republican National Convention in Chicago. "The politicians," he complained, "are carried away with the idea of a TV audience of sixty million, being allowed to forget that twice that many people read newspapers every day. On the whole the press got pretty shabby treatment at Chicago. When will we ever learn to present a united front?"[28]

Mr. Carter forgot an old lesson and failed to grasp a new one. Newspapers are born competitors, and almost never present a united front. To do so covering a political convention would surely result in a fiasco. The new lesson he failed to discern was that television was becoming the prime medium of communication in national and international politics.

Today newspaper reporters still become exasperated over the way politicians swarm to television cameras, and politicians are still carried away with the idea of a television audience. When he was secretary of state, Henry A. Kissinger often briefed newspaper reporters under a rule prohibiting the identification of himself as the source of the stories. Then, upon leaving, he would sometimes espy waiting television cameras in the corridor and eagerly report substantially the same statements he had just made to newspaper reporters off the record.

When Clifton Daniel, who had been abroad for the *New York Times*, returned to New York in the mid-1950s, to become managing editor, he was surprised to turn on television news and see a film of President Eisenhower's press conference that same day. If a reader could watch a news conference the day it was held, Daniel wondered, what freshness would remain in a story in the next morning's paper? "I knew then," he recalled, "that we would have to start doing things differently."[29]

Since the end of the Second World War James B. Reston, who had become the *Times* Washington bureau chief in 1953, had been writing for the news columns occasional interpretive articles that clearly reflected his own judgments. Eventually labeled news analysis, these pieces, which ran under a distinctive italic head, caused dispute among *Times* editors. The prevailing rule was that the news columns be restricted to fact while the editorial page alone voice opinions. Nevertheless, Reston's initiative caught on, and in time similar articles were written occasionally by other *Times* reporters. "There is no doubt," Daniel said, "that television news accelerated acceptance of the news analysis articles."[30]

The *Times* had long been accustomed to the universal recognition it received as the preeminent American newspaper. It had the largest staff. Its best reporters and columnists were renowned within the profession. It provided not only more news but more exclusive news than any other paper. When events warranted, it covered them on the grandest scale. But then the networks—their talent, their huge audiences, their financial resources, their worldwide reach, their complete coverage of major events— brought shock and confusion to Times Square.

In a history of the *Times* published in 1966, Gay Talese wrote:

The Times had to move along, to keep pace with a faster life in the Fifties. Now the newspaper industry had a serious new threat, television, and Catledge knew that the formula that had worked so well would require some adjustment. . . . Television reporters, with few exceptions, were really skimming the headlines, hitting the highlights of a few top stories. Newspaper reporters would now have to dig more deeply into more areas and to inform the public more thoroughly; they could no longer merely report all the facts, but they would often have to interpret the meaning behind these facts.[31]

The *New York Times* did far more than "move along." It drastically changed and modernized. A. M. Rosenthal, the powerful executive editor of the 1970s and early 1980s, instituted magazine-style weekday special sections on science, sports, and "living." Writing and editing became sharper, livelier, more knowledgeable. Change continued under Rosenthal's able successor, Max Frankel. Departments dealing with news of law, health, journalism, and education were set up. The paper moved into heavier coverage of national trends and greater coverage of the poor.[32]

In the early 1990s the *Times* essentially reversed the direction it took in 1980 when it established a national edition. With that edition the *Times* gained many readers only to find that businesses preferred to advertise locally and regionally. To stem the loss of profits, the *Times,* while continuing the national edition, dramatically turned the attention of the New York editions toward city and suburban coverage. In competing with the New York tabloids and strong suburban newspapers, the tone of the *Times* became less elite. A key to the popularization of the paper was a 50 percent increase in the sports section. Like all papers, the *Times* tackled afresh the task of appealing to men and women under thirty-five who did not read newspapers regularly. The local news section was expanded. Bigger headlines appeared. Color was on the way. Like *USA Today,* the *Times* began to use graphics for the convenience of the television generation. It also introduced on Sundays a second main news section aimed at college-age readers. A senior editor told Thomas B. Rosenstiel of the *Los Angeles Times,* "The trick is how to do [all] this and still be the New York Times."[33]

For decades, newspaper publishers have been preoccupied with staying solvent. When television rallied from the halt in production during World War II, there was considerable speculation, especially in intellectual circles, that newspapers would be driven out of business. "All that talk scared the owners," recalled William D. Rinehart, vice-president for technical matters for the American Newspaper Publishers Association. "In the face of television they knew they had to do something, especially to cut costs, which were hurting them badly."[34] At that time newspaper establishments were largely labor-intensive manufacturing plants. Phalanxes of well-paid union printers were the heart of the operation. Drastic reduction of costs depended on production of newspapers without printers, or at least with many fewer of them. Since the war this has largely been accomplished through the development of photocomposition, offset printing, and computers, to mention the principal inventions. Contributing to the impetus for this revolutionary change was one of the major long-term effects television exerted on newspapers.

To make money, many newspaper owners have acquired licenses to operate their own television stations. In 1949 the *Washington Post* purchased WTOP, which was then the CBS television outlet in Washington. When Sam Zagoria, a senior reporter on the *Post,* asked Philip L. Graham, the publisher, for a raise during a lean time for the paper in the early 1950s, Graham countered with a question. "Sam," he asked, "did you get a check last week from the *Post?*" Zagoria said he had. "The funds for that came from WTOP," Graham continued. "We lost money here." Zagoria did not get a raise. J. Russell Wiggins, then the editor, was told by Graham, "There is simply no available money to award merit increases, except on the most extraordinary cases, and I hope none of these will arise."[35]

Deep changes in American society following the war often bedeviled newspapers just as television news was moving in. By the millions, middle-class families moved from cities to suburbs. In turn, whole neighborhoods in cities like New York, Chicago, Los Angeles, and Miami were taken over by members of minority groups who had neither the education, the money, nor the motivation to buy newspapers. In many of their neighborhoods, newsstands could not be maintained because of vandalism and looting. The *Chicago Tribune,* to cite one case, tried to reach out for African-American readers by sending an interracial reporting team to Africa in search of interesting articles, but the response at home was disappointing.[36] To survive in these circumstances, metropolitan newspapers had to make deliveries in the suburbs and even then faced aggressive competition from new and improved suburban papers. As decay spread through urban areas, crime made it safer for people to stay home after dark and watch the popular new television shows than to stroll out to buy street-sale editions of morning newspapers. In New York the sharp drop in these sales owing to the exodus to the suburbs, crime, and the popularity of television hurt not only the tabloids but also the once distinguished *Herald Tribune*, which misguidedly started its own 8:00 P.M. early bird edition in 1950. In a changing industrial pattern New York lost hundreds of thousands of manufacturing jobs, dispersing blue-collar workers, who were the most dedicated readers of the tabloids. The *New York Daily Mirror* folded in 1963. The *New York Daily News*, which after the war had a circulation of 2.3 million on weekdays and 4.7 million on Sundays, was caught in a fight for survival. In 1988, the paper's circulation was 1.2 million on weekdays and 1.5 million on Sundays.[37]

For some midwestern morning newspapers, especially the *Chicago Tribune*, the disintegration of railroad passenger service after the war was a blow to regional circulation. Chicago, Burlington & Quincy trains used to carry bundles of the *Tribune* to points as distant as Omaha, Nebraska. Other trains served the *Tribune*'s circulation network throughout Illinois, Indiana, Wisconsin, and Iowa. As rail service declined and as railway mail cars were pulled off trains for lack of business, the *Tribune*'s circulation fell. While other factors were also involved, between 1950 and 1970 weekday circulation dropped from 944,133 to 775,416. As a substitute for trains, trucking was tried but proved too slow and too expensive.

By late in the 1950s, of course, newspapers encountered serious competition from television news in the reporting of the first phases of the civil rights revolution in the South. Speaking from the vantage point of one who had covered some of the marches and clashes for the Atlanta *Constitution*, William R. Shipp concluded that television forced a change in newspapers' methods. "It made us see more and more," he recalled, "that . . . we were not the primary source for immediate information. Therefore, we had to do a better job of telling why it occurred and how it occurred and setting it in the proper context of the time and place."[38]

20

●━○━●━○━●━○━●━○━●━○━●━○━●━○━●━○━●━○━●━○━●━○━●━○━●━○━●━○━●━○━●━○━●━○━●━○━●━○

Newspapers in the age of television

Television transfixed the American people for four days in November 1963—from the official announcement in Dallas that President John F. Kennedy was dead to the lighting of the eternal flame at his grave in Arlington National Cemetery. Six years later, on July 21, 1969, millions of television viewers heard the exciting words from outer space "The *Eagle* has landed" and watched in wonderment as the astronauts in white space suits and dark sun visors walked on the moon. These two events of such moment, emotion, and novelty demonstrated television's power to communicate. Even in the coverage of lesser happenings, the reality was the same: television could bring live pictures of events into people's homes. To survive and prosper newspapers would have to react to such competition. But how? Recalling his reaction to the televising of the Kennedy funeral, Sam S. McKeel, then chairman and publisher of the *Philadelphia Inquirer,* said, "It seemed to me very clear that we could not compete in the same way."[1]

The imperative for change by newspapers was all the greater because the advent of television news occurred right after World War II, a time when the whole world was changing drastically, with or without television. The demands on newspaper coverage were sterner in the postwar period than before. Newspaper readers were more sophisticated. Also, as a rule, young reporters and editors, especially on small and middle-sized newspapers, were better educated than their elders, like Jack Setters, city editor of the *Nashville Tennessean.* After atomic bombs were dropped on Japan in 1945, he was understandably excited to learn that work on the bombs had been done at Oak Ridge, Tennessee. Then an announcement that the plant would be open for a look by the press galvanized him to summon a reporter and photographer for instructions on the coverage. As a former *Tennessean* reporter, Richard Harwood, later assistant managing editor and ombudsman of the *Washington Post*, recalled, Setters said: "I want a picture of an atom before they split it and a picture of the two halves after they split it. We'll run them at the top of page one."[2]

Newspapers in the 1960s, the second decade of television news, were as far from the Jack Setters breed as they were from the newsroom in *The Front Page*, a famous newspaper play of the 1930s. The new compulsion for more interpretive, analytical, and knowledgeable writing instead of routine news stories narrowed the line between the good newspapers and magazines. The change, of course, was gradual and uneven. In 1965 Don Carter, managing editor of the now defunct *National Observer*, noted the trend: "Almost imperceptibly we are seeing some of our better newspapers change in their emphasis from hot spot news to what we like to call the daily magazine concept."[3]

A magazine concept was, of course, a more natural development for a national weekly newspaper like the *National Observer* than for a daily newspaper. No daily paper then or now would be mistaken for a magazine. On the other hand, numerous articles now appear in the news columns of newspapers that undoubtedly would have been published by the *Saturday Evening Post, Life, Look,* or *Collier's.* Moreover, many newspapers have been redesigned since the sixties and seventies with special sections having definite magazine characteristics. For example, Science Times, a section that runs in the *New York Times* on Thursdays, qualifies as a science magazine in a newspaper format, even though it also carries breaking news on scientific developments. The news essays, called "takeouts," in *Time* and *Newsweek* also appeal to newspaper editors and reporters seeking change. These articles sometimes fill a magazine page or close to it. They are newsy without always being dependent on an immediate event. They are bright, tightly written, focused on one subject, reasonably comprehensive, and often reflect a point of view. Their purpose is to give the reader the kind of background he or she would not ordinarily get in a fast-breaking news story, and the best of the takeouts are made piquant by offbeat research.

The newspaper that tried most spectacularly in the 1960s to adopt a news magazine style and format was the *New York Herald Tribune*. Though once one of the greatest newspapers in the world, it was perennially underfunded and trailed the *New York Times* in circulation and advertising. The *Herald Tribune* lost money after the Second World War. Already hurting from competition by radio for advertising, the paper was then hit by television. Together, radio and television "drew away the profitable national advertising—automobiles, brokerage houses, refrigerators etc.," explained George A. Cornish, the managing editor through some of the paper's greatest years.[4] At the urging of President Dwight D. Eisenhower, who did not want the voice of an important Republican newspaper silenced, John Hay (Jock) Whitney, then Eisenhower's ambassador to the Court of St. James's, bought the *Herald Tribune* in 1957. Four years later the editor of *Newsweek*, John Denson, an engaging old scoundrel and erratic genius, was appointed editor. In a desperate effort to find a new niche for the *Herald Tribune*, he jettisoned its once distinguished format. With a grin he said that news magazines had hornswoggled newspapers into thinking that *Time* and *Newsweek* were able to do what they did only because they had a week to work on each issue. The *Herald Tribune*, Denson promised, would expose that flimflam by showing that the job could be done in a day—every day in the week. He and his intense executive editor, James G. Bellows, made a mighty effort.

"People at *Newsweek* didn't like what Denson did at the *Tribune*," Mel Elfin, Washington bureau chief for the magazine, remembered.[5] *Newsweek* was sufficiently concerned about the competition of television without having to contend with rivals on another front. But then, exhausted and engulfed in controversy, Denson departed, and Bellows took the helm. Financially starved, the *Herald Tribune* soon went out of business. The lively writing, crisp headlines, sweeping layouts, and dominating photographs of the Denson-Bellows period, however, had a lasting influence on other papers. On one occasion Clayton Kirkpatrick, the editor of the *Chicago Tribune*, found the flamboyant style of the *Herald Tribune* irresistible. The night the *Eagle* landed he set aside the paper's standard make-up of the first page, one of the most rigid in the business then, and filled the entire page right up to the logo with a photograph showing a man's footprints in the crust of the moon. "Denson was somewhere in the back of my mind," Kirkpatrick acknowledged years later.[6]

Nevertheless, it was not primarily Densonesque capers or magazine articles that were to find their way then into most newspapers seeking a better vehicle for giving readers something different from television news. Rather, the model was the deceptively easy-looking but well-researched and informative "leader" that the brilliant editor Bernard Kilgore had developed on the *Wall Street Journal* before his death in 1967.

With a gift for stating complexities in simple language, Kilgore moved, step by step, up the ladder from reporter on the *Journal* to chairman of the board of Dow Jones, the parent company. As a lad in Indiana he had once entered a Boy Scout contest for building birdhouses. Striking out in his own direction, he built an owl house on the hunch that no one else would think of doing so. He was right, and he won the sole prize in his category. Later in life his owl house was the innovative leader, which still regularly appears on the front page of the *Journal,* usually in column one or column six. Narrative in nature, the article, or leader, might deal with a social trend, the latest controversy at Yale, Jimmy Carter and the neutron bomb, heroin, or the menace of the rising water level in the Great Lakes. The article is not wedded to an event that occurred the day before. Generally, therefore, it makes no difference which day in the week a particular leader runs. The point is that it must immediately strike the reader as an interesting topic. Such an article might take a reporter days or weeks to research and write. When it is finished it is turned over to a group of senior editors to revise in the accepted style, though under the reporter's byline. The senior editors work at making the start of the story simple and easy to read, using quotes and anecdotes. What they cherish most is an opening sentence that will surprise a reader, a quest that sometimes produces leads that are too coy. Explanation of every phase is a requisite. In keeping with this standard, veterans on the *Journal* recall, an article once identified Moses as "a Jewish leader." The finished product, however, is invariably first-class journalism, an article that may well justify the price the reader paid for the paper.

"The lesson of the *Wall Street Journal* has not been lost on a lot of editors," observed Benjamin C. Bradlee, executive editor of the *Washington Post.* Each day his paper has three or four "nonhard" news stories on the front page. These "groundswell stories," he said, "look at courses rather than results."[7] In 1988 Bradlee succinctly summed up a basic fact about the change that had occurred in newspapers since the coming of television journalism: "We no longer write as if our stories were breaking the news for the first time."[8]

The changes in news writing in recent years have been reflected in the altered categories for the Pulitzer prizes. No longer is a prize awarded for the best local story written under pressure of a deadline. What was once a newspaper's quintessential function—delivering the news before anyone else did—has been usurped by television. Three more pertinent categories were added for best criticism, best feature, and best explanatory writing.

The *Wall Street Journal's* leader is not limited to large national and international issues that traditionally have dominated newspapers. The articles often deal with smaller things in people's lives. Gordon Hanna of the Memphis *Commercial Appeal* observed in 1957:

To a large degree, the *Wall Street Journal* has shown us the way. I've recently read in that newspaper about new crayons that won't mark on wallpaper, about new gimmicks used in selling homes, that girls are spending less at college than boys—but actually cost their dads more—that there's a boom in skim milk as more folks count their calories.

There's not a big story in the bunch. But they're all interesting. And I wish I had read them in my own newspaper first.[9]

To its credit, the *Wall Street Journal* is not dependent on daily "occurrences." The problem of relying only on breaking news is that the developments may be dull. In retrospect, the 1955 APME report captured a significant turning point in newspaper journalism. The committee found evidence "that newspapers generally are moving away from dependence on . . . what comes over the wire or off the beats. They are getting away from being nothing more than daily bulletin boards or panting competitors of the breathless broadcasters."[10]

Reg Murphy, successively editor of the *Atlanta Constitution*, editor and publisher of the *San Francisco Examiner*, and later publisher of the *Baltimore Sun*, saw television competition as the cause of drastic changes in newspapers. "In the 1960s there was surprise at the success of television, and a feeling that newspapers were not improving themselves fast enough," he said. "The *Baltimore Sun* was still delivering to homes morning papers that only covered the stories of Orioles' night games to the seventh inning. They didn't understand what TV had done."[11]

Two of the country's largest and most influential morning newspapers, the *Los Angeles Times* and the *Chicago Tribune*, independently underwent change in the 1960s that was downright astonishing in view of their respective histories. Change on the *Los Angeles Times* began earlier than on the *Tribune*, and because of the burgeoning wealth of the *Times* in the rich southern California market, the change was much greater and costlier. In 1957 publisher Norman Chandler moved Nick Williams from his rounds on various news desks to the post of managing editor and later editor. He instructed him, as Williams has recalled, "to do what is right," to give readers a fair account of what was happening in southern California. Williams interpreted this to mean, among other things, hiring new reporters qualified to give the same kind of coverage to Democrats as to

Republicans—a revolutionary development on the *Times* of that era and a task Williams undertook with relish.[12]

One of a company of remarkably fine journalists who had broken into the profession working on newspapers in their native South, Williams, the founding editor of the modern *Los Angeles Times*, was a man of compassion and laughter. He was a thinker and a good writer. He understood writers' problems. He had a devotion to and an understanding of art. His boldness of decision was tempered by a sure sense of how fast change could and should be made on a newspaper. And he never disguised the fact that his interest in Gutenberg was secondary to his interest in Lady Godiva.

When thirty-three-year-old Otis Chandler succeeded his father as publisher in 1960, it was more than a generational change. He was well aware that the state of journalism on the *Times* then was not in a class with that of the best American newspapers, and he was too ambitious and competitive to accept this. Hence the *Times* was taken in hand by an unusual combination of a young publisher with the resolve and the resources to remake a large newspaper and an editor with the experience to carry out this vision. Southern California had the highest saturation by television of any comparable area in the country. Off and on in the 1950s, the *Times* had experienced loss of national advertising to television. The decision to do something about it was not half-hearted. "TV," Williams recalled, "had the effect of pulling the *Times* into broader coverage."[13]

Theretofore the paper had relied on wire services for most of its national and international coverage. In the 1950s the *Times* had one bureau abroad, in Paris, where one roving reporter was based. At the end of the 1950s it had three reporters in Washington. In the 1960s Williams began opening bureaus around the world. Today the paper has thirty-two reporters in twenty-seven foreign bureaus, including the United Nations.

In 1973, Chandler shocked California Republicans by announcing that the *Times* no longer would use its editorial page to endorse candidates of any party for election to public office. In a private memorandum to the other owners of the paper, he explained: "The newspaper of the past, with its narrow point of view, one-sided presentation of the news and provincial outlook cannot succeed *against the competition of more sophisticated media in today's society*" (italics added).[14]

James E. Bassett, the gentlemanly editor of the editorial pages and an active Republican in earlier days, had already been moved to other duties on the *Times*. He was succeeded by Anthony Day, a graduate of Harvard and former Washington bureau chief of the Philadelphia *Evening Bulletin*. What caused far greater commotion in southern California was the selection of Paul Conrad as the political cartoonist of the *Times*. This was viewed as a thunderbolt aimed directly at the right wing. The hostility of many conservative readers created such pressures at the *Times* that Conrad's job would have been at risk without Williams's stubborn protection.

The most significant part of Williams's plan for rebuilding the *Los Angeles Times* was soon overtaken, he found, by the onrush of television news. His first goal had been to follow the course of the *New York Times* by greatly enlarging the Washington bureau and establishing regional bureaus around the United States and foreign news bureaus around the world. In a memorandum of August 16, 1968, to Frank Haven, the managing editor, Williams explained, "The crux of this concept was that our own people, selected for their superior capabilities, not only would give us exclusivity . . . but also a calibre of writing that we would not get from other newsgathering agencies."[15] All too soon, however, Williams's satisfaction faded. Expansion of foreign and domestic bureaus did not solve the problem then confronting all newspapers. In the same memorandum to Haven, Williams concluded that "complete and exclusive coverage of the news is not enough; the 'complete newspaper' is not enough." He explained:

The reason for this is as obvious as the 6 o'clock newscast. Television not only has preempted the printed media's role as the source of instant news—it has also gone increasingly (and very skillfully) into interpretive and situation and anticipatory reporting. It has compelled the print media, if they wish to retain the public's interest, to search for nonduplicative methods of reporting, analyzing, and writing.

The *Times*, therefore, must move to a new level of reporting and editing. Determined to hold the public's interest, Williams told Haven that the paper must continue to run important news. But each day it must also give readers "articles containing information that has not surfaced on television or other media, or at the very minimum each day we must collate information and interpret it in so provocative a manner that it seems new." He added: "More specifically, we must begin printing on Page One *each day,* at least one story of this kind that has not surfaced anywhere before we print it. For demonstration to your editors and re-

porters, simply point to the article each day in column one of the Wall
Street Journal—although most days now the WSJ has two such stories
on its front page. When we can offer two or three, we should do it. . . .
And what we are doing on Page One with these stories ought to become
a model of what we do in reporting throughout the paper."[16]

The column one story on the front page is still a popular feature in the
Los Angeles Times.

Williams's concern about the competition of television news was focused more on the long term than on the next day or the next week. He
took it none the less seriously for that. He personally told the Washington bureau that it should consider its main competition to be not the
Washington Post or the *New York Times* but network television news.
Robert Gibson, then foreign editor of the paper, recalled similar advice
from Williams:

> Nick took me aside and said in so many words, "I know you want to compete
> with other papers..But here in Los Angeles our big competitor is television. Be-
> cause of it, people are going to know the spot news every morning. We have got
> to go beyond the facts. Television is easy to look at and listen to, so we've got to
> give readers something else. Emphasize good features."[17]

Such instructions implied a marked change in the approach to foreign
and national reporting particularly. When the veteran Tom Lambert was
assigned to Israel by the *Los Angeles Times* in 1970, he was not asked to
cover day-to-day military events, which the AP, Williams believed, could
do just as well. "We have asked him to take a deeper look at Israel itself,
its people, its archaeological richness, its economy and the general thrust
of its history," Williams wrote a friend.[18] This kind of coverage, Williams hoped, would give a *Times* reader more than the reader would get
on the same day's television news programs.

Whereas Chandler and Williams could proceed with change at their own
discretion without hindrance, Kirkpatrick had to struggle at the *Chicago
Tribune* against the potent legacy of its late owner, Col. Robert R.
McCormick, who died in 1955. McCormick was ultraconservative, nationalistic, and isolationist. The legacy was cherished by the board of
trustees, to whom the colonel had bequeathed control of the paper and
who considered it their responsibility, according to Kirkpatrick, to keep
the *Tribune* as it was when the colonel died. "You will never know,"
Kirkpatrick said, "how many meetings I had to go through to change the

nameplate of the paper from the *Chicago Daily Tribune* to the *Chicago Tribune*. When the change was made we hardly heard a murmur from the outside."[19] Appointed executive editor of the *Tribune* in 1967 and editor in 1969, Kirkpatrick set about to rid his paper of its partisan trappings and its boastful slogan "World's Greatest Newspaper." "Television opened a window on the world," Kirkpatrick recalled, "through which people could see there were all sorts of good papers."[20]

For years the paper's most conspicuous fixture was a front-page cartoon more often than not ridiculing Democrats, liberals, and internationalists. "One day," recalled Russell W. Freeburg, then managing editor, "Kirk said to me, 'If you don't want the cartoon on page one, throw it off.'" Gradually, Freeburg relegated it permanently to the editorial page, to the dismay of the old sentinels.[21] "It was a credibility thing," Kirkpatrick observed later. "You couldn't be very credible as an objective news organ if a color cartoon preached a political creed from page one every day."[22]

One of his hardest struggles, partly because the advertising department claimed the same space, was installing an Op-Ed page on which to present various opinions, not a trait of the paper under McCormick. "The old McCormick hands fought vigorously against it," Freeburg said. "They didn't want anyone else to share the power to sway opinion. That was for the editorial page."[23] Nevertheless, although the sentinels warned him that it would cause the demise of the *Tribune*, Kirkpatrick did install an Op-Ed page. The blossoming of Op-Ed pages around the country should be credited to the *New York Times*, which on September 21, 1970, installed such a page, originally an innovation of the old New York *World*.

When Lawrence S. Fanning, then editor of the *Chicago Daily News*, transferred the reporter James Hoge to Washington in the sixties, he told him, "I want you to learn how to report in the TV age."[24] Fanning instructed him to write in a way that would tell the reader not just what had *happened* but what was *happening*—a critical distinction and one not easy to achieve in daily journalism. Even the Washington staff of *Time* used to dread it when their editor-in-chief, Henry R. Luce, visited the bureau and asked them what was happening in the capital. Of course, Luce would have known what had happened that week. What he was seeking was its longer-term significance.

To maintain its standing a major newspaper today must offer news as well as analysis, interpretation, background, and features. The *New York*

Times divides its New York staff between wire service–type reporters and reporters who take a broader and deeper approach. In order to accommodate both kinds of writing, papers now save space for the longer special articles by running summaries of minor news items, each limited to a paragraph or so. The old practice of almost automatically allotting five or six hundred words to any story that happened along, regardless of its importance or interest to readers, is another casualty of the television age. The corollary of this is that it takes planning to have on hand copy that is better than that which is to be discarded.

Such planning is the responsibility of editors, who now must play a more active role than many of them were accustomed to playing thirty or forty years ago. In the old days desk editors just shoved along to the composing room stories their Washington bureau, for example, had chosen to cover. No more. Hoge, who became publisher of the *New York Daily News*, said in 1987: "There is a lot more emphasis on editors' functions—on editing with the audience in mind. And, remember, editors today are people who grew up in the television age."[25]

Further problems of the new age confronted newspaper reporters after the mid-1960s when television sets began appearing in newsrooms for editors to scan. In the past reporters were, with some beery exceptions, the trusted eyes and ears of a newspaper. Although stories a reporter brought back from an assignment were always subject to check against the wire service copy, editors largely relied on the judgment of their good reporters. In the days before television, a reporter normally would return to his or her office from a White House press conference, tell the desk editor what the president had said, file a schedule of the day's stories to the paper, and then write. No longer. While a reporter is at the White House, his or her editor is glued to the television set. By the time the reporter gets back to the office, the editor has already formed an opinion and scheduled the story as he or she saw it. Murrey Marder, long a meticulous diplomatic correspondent for the *Washington Post*, explained what it's like:

They send their experts out to cover, but by the time the expert is back in the office *they* tell *him* the meaning of what happened. Now everybody's an expert on foreign policy, including the editor. By the time the reporter gets back with his judgment, space has already been allotted for his story, follow-ups for the succeeding day have been mapped out. You are no longer the first messenger when you get back to the office; you are the second or third. Your whole function is changed. . . . Instead of reporters and editors talking to each other, they talk through messages on the computer. An editor may face three TVs—one for each network—and his computer—his umbilical cord to the outside world. He doesn't need anyone else. A reporter back from the White House may point out that Reagan said this. "Yes," the editor will reply, "but he smiled when he said it. He didn't mean it." The first thing you know you are in a debate.[26]

Marder has long remembered one such disagreement. At the United Nations General Assembly session in New York in 1960 he had just covered one of the bizarre scenes of the cold war. During an uproarious debate Soviet Premier Nikita S. Khrushchev took off a shoe, brandished it at the podium, and then, for emphasis, hammered it on his desk, as it appeared to millions of viewers of the television film. As soon as the session ended, Marder and a colleague from *Time* hastened to Khrushchev's vacated seat to question all nearby eyewitnesses they could find. The upshot was that the two reporters were convinced that Khrushchev had not actually touched the desk with his shoe. Rather, he had pounded the desk with his fist, in which the shoe was held. This made sense to Marder because of his familiarity with the custom of desk-pounding in Eastern European parliaments, and he wrote the story that way. A desk editor in Washington, who had watched the scene on television, balked. It had looked to him as if Khrushchev had struck the desk with his shoe.

"People will think we are out of our minds," the editor said, as Marder has recalled. "Everyone is watching television. We are going to tell them it didn't happen when they saw it with their own eyes?" Those were the editor's last words. Marder was irritated that the television networks would be allowed, in effect, to edit the *Washington Post*. Later when he saw his story in print he was surprised to discover that his version had prevailed after all. If Marder's colleague on *Time* went through a similar office debate, he was less successful. *Time* reported that Khrushchev had pounded the desk with his shoe.[27]

Certainly, television has forced newspapers to be more honest, or at least more careful. "In the old days a politician who was on good terms with a reporter and understood that the reporter was familiar with his positions would often say to him, 'Just quote me any way you want to on that,' " recalled Clayton Kirkpatrick. "A reporter who did so today might discover that the quote he made up was different from what the politician went on television and said."[28] Nowadays, when scarcely any reporters write shorthand, the tape recorder has largely replaced the notebook and pencil. "If I misquoted one word of what Mayor Koch said before television cameras, he would call me a fool," Todd S. Purdum, city hall reporter for the *New York Times,* said in 1988.[29]

On the question of what is news, editors and reporters now take a much broader view than before. "Especially in the first half of this century we on newspapers blew some of the most important stories of the time," Eugene Roberts acknowledged.

Take migration of blacks to cities in the Thirties and Forties and the postwar migration of whites to the suburbs. We didn't cover that the way we do today. Another was the shift of the U.S. from a rural to an urban society. Papers were event-oriented. . . . Today that would not have happened. Show me a reporter who went to Europe in the years between 1910 and 1920 and got in a boat with the immigrants and came to this country.[30]

To compete with television news, Roberts and other good newspaper editors now seek exactly this kind of story. Moreover, they are finding the writers who have the talent and the eagerness to write them. Although the *Wall Street Journal* has produced its share of such articles in the past generation, the appeal of the Kilgore genre was to seasoned editors who regularly saw the *Journal.* A number of able young reporters who entered the newspaper business in the late 1960s and early 1970s were not *Wall Street Journal* readers. Their ideal, rather, was the journalism of *New York* magazine under the editorship of Clay Felker, *Rolling Stone* under Jann S. Wenner, *Harper's* under Willie Morris, and the essays of Joan Didion.

The spirit of progressive newspapers in the mid-1960s was caught by George Beebe, managing editor of the *Miami Herald,* when he told fellow editors:

Let me recommend that each of you when you return to your office take a look at your back files of three, five, and even ten years ago. You should be pleasantly surprised to discover how much more informative and attractive your product has become. If your paper looks the same as it did ten years ago, you are indeed in deep trouble.[31]

Although change overtook newspapers of all sizes, it was understandably more conspicuous on the large newspapers. Change on these newspapers, however, has a ripple effect. Their stories get into hundreds of smaller papers through such agencies as the *Los Angeles Times–Washington Post,* the *New York Times,* the *Chicago Tribune,* Gannett, and the Knight-Ridder news services. In fact, a strong reason why the AP turned to team journalism, investigations, broader news horizons, and series of articles was to try to keep pace with the newspaper wire services and supply its own similar copy to papers feeling the need to modernize in the face of television.

21

·0➤0➤0➤0➤0➤0➤0➤0➤0➤0➤0➤0➤0➤0➤0➤0➤0➤0➤0➤0➤0➤0➤0

Television's intrusion in the press box

Television never seemed more magical to Americans than when, after World War II, it began bringing baseball and football games into their homes. And nothing ever changed the sports department of a newspaper so much as television cameras in the stands behind home plate and on the fifty-yard line. Old ways of doing things went out of style fast. It was a melancholy time for many veterans whose best days had been devoted to writing about Joe DiMaggio, Sid Luckman, Jesse Owens, Gene Sarazen, and Don Budge. Largely because of television, the United States experienced an explosion in sports after 1945. By 1953 the sports committee of the Associated Press Managing Editors (APME) reported: "Television, more than any other single factor, has brought about a need for reassessment of sports writing."[1] A 1977 report by the APME captured the problem: "No reporter could describe the drama of St. Louis pitcher Al Hrabosky striking out three Cincinnati sluggers with the bases loaded, as TV did simply by showing it."[2] The "living room fans," Norman E. Isaacs, former executive editor of the Louisville *Courier-Journal,* later wrote, "have better seats than even the fat cats in the luxury boxes— and better closeups than the coach himself gets."[3]

By heightening public interest in football, baseball, and basketball, and by popularizing other sports that used to be slighted on sports pages, television forced newspapers to expand their sports sections. In the mid-1980s the appearance of *USA Today* with its remarkably complete national sports section prompted other papers, such as the *Washington Post,* to extend their sports coverage.

Sports news is vital to the prosperity of most general-circulation newspapers. It takes up about 20 percent of the news hole of these papers—

more than that of *USA Today.* "*USA Today* would not be here without sports," Thomas Curley, its president, said.[4]

A prototype of an upstate sports editor in the 1930s and 1940s was the likable Billy Kelly of the now defunct *Buffalo Courier-Express.* A hearty, fatherly man with unruly white hair and a florid complexion, Kelly sat in the city room telling stories about athletes he had never seen and games he had never covered. During the Great Depression no travel money was available, except maybe occasionally for a world's heavy-weight championship fight. In summers Kelly frequented regional race tracks, no doubt more interested in what bookies could do for him than in what he would write later. He always had a supply of passes for senior reporters on the city staff who went out and watched night baseball games instead of covering the usually idiotic night assignments an indifferent city editor had thought up for them. Every week each fall the Associated Press would poll Kelly, along with all other sports editors across the country, for a judgment on the top ten college football teams. He would invariably list Notre Dame as number one, followed by what other teams came to mind, none of which he had ever seen in action.

The *Courier-Express* subscribed to Arch Ward's popular sports col-umn in the *Chicago Tribune.* It was transmitted in the evening by Morse code. Now and then a telegraph key would click in the wire room with a message from Chicago, cautioning subscribers that Ward's column was to appear only in its entirety under his byline and that no parts of it were to be used elsewhere. When a copyboy would bring the message to Kelly, he would glance at it casually and say, "Just set it over there," pointing to a far corner of his desk. But then a deadline for his own column would loom. With Ward's piece beside his typewriter, Kelly would bang the keys so fast that in no time he would be calling, "Boy!" and his column would be whisked to the composing room through a pneumatic tube.

In November 1980 the *Bulletin* of the American Society of Newspaper Editors carried a special section on newspapers' handling of sports. One of the articles was entitled "Today's Button-Down Sports Editor." Writ-ten by Hal Bodley, sports editor of the *Wilmington News Journal,* it began:

Dressed in a neat three-piece suit, he sometimes looks like an attorney preparing a brief. He is bright, creative, a skilled manager who probably keeps up with the Dow Jones average as well as George Brett's. He—and nobody said he can't be a she—is between 30 and 40 . . . earns between $30,000 and $60,000 a year and has the ear of the person who runs the whole show. . . . Editorial executives are now hiring sports editors who could drop the word "sports" from the title and step comfortably into a key position in any other department of the paper.[5]

This last claim is debatable. Sports writers and columnists definitely have their own muse. Bill Shirley, former sports editor of the *Los Angeles Times,* said that whenever he needed to hire a reporter, what he looked for most of all was "flair." Sports writers are exuberant, and fans seem to like exuberance. Managing editors sometimes despair over the free-wheeling style of sports writing and the difficulty of getting sports writers to come to the point of a story immediately. On the other hand, the contrast between Billy Kelly and the fellow in the button-down collar does underscore the change in sports departments in the past forty years. The publication of special sections, like Sports Monday in the *New York Times* and Sports Plus in the *Boston Globe,* could not have been managed satisfactorily by most sports editors of the prewar period. The altered scene today would have bewildered Billy Kelly, if he could have returned to life to visit, say, the sports department of the *Washington Post.* In 1987, he would have found that the reporter who covered the Washington Redskins was Christine Brennan. The reporter who covered a top college football game in the country each Saturday in the fall was Sally Jenkins. Perhaps what would have surprised Kelly the most was the proliferation of women's sports demanding newspaper coverage.

Almost from the start of the televising of games and matches, sports writers were cautioned to take the needs of women readers into account. The rationale for this was that millions of women who had not regularly attended sporting events would now cultivate an interest in games their husbands watched at home. They might need more rudimentary explanations in newspapers than had been offered in old-style reporting for mostly male readers. Some sports editors reported being surprised to receive telephone calls from women with questions about boxing matches they had watched on television and were curious enough to read about in their newspapers. "To woo the new female reader," admonished one editor of the APME sports committee in 1955, "your story must be written in language she can understand."[6]

An article about the flex defense of the Dallas Cowboys might not interest a woman reader, Joe McGuff, sports editor of the *Kansas City Star,* observed, but

I believe she would read a column about what kind of man Tom Landry really is, how his wife views him and how she deals with the pressures of his job. I suspect she would read a story telling how a woman became a general manager of a minor league baseball team or how Gloria Conners raised Jimmy to be the sunny little chap he is.[7]

Wick Temple, managing editor of the Associated Press, remarked that a contemporary sports page without opinion is regarded as lifeless. Readers, he said, "want to know what their man on the scene thought of an event, and even if that is an outgrowth of television reporting, it certainly makes for livelier reading." Temple went on to describe the new style of sports writing, which is basically a feature story rather than a straight news story:

It's not the old-fashioned interview with the second baseman. It is often investigative, often gossip, sometimes muckraking. It covers a lot of what television sportsfolk are doing, because the tube is where most consumers get their sports. It may be a story of pressures on the marriages of professional athletes, drugs in sports, abuses in college recruiting and phony classroom grades. It may have to do with betting, running, the wonders of racketball. The Minneapolis Star did a takeout on the swingingest ski resorts.[8]

Some old sports editors lament that such stories on marriages, drugs, and college recruiting have robbed sports pages of humor. The new probing style of sports reporting hasn't been all fun for reporters either. They have encountered gruff resistance from some professional athletes with private lives far short of the athletic ideal. And when professional athletes became wealthy as a result of their clubs' television contracts, they felt, according to Temple, that they could "afford to clam up, tell a reporter to go to hell, or in some cases punch him out."[9] Joe Willie Namath, first of the rich quarterbacks, once said he was not going to talk to any "hundred-dollar-a-week creep."

Because of television, Bill Shirley said, "we had to start tailoring our stories to give the reader something different."[10] In quest of angles and anecdotes, reporters began to invade the players' dressing rooms after games. Some reporters were so intent on the new approach that they all but forgot to mention the score of a game or else put it so far down in their stories that readers had to search for it. Wallace Carroll, former executive editor of the *Winston-Salem Journal* and *Sentinel,* abhorred such "tricky leads."[11] But Jack Hairston, sports editor of the *Jacksonville Journal,* liked them. Deploring sports stories that still led with the score of a game, he said, "The lead heads and lead story should be something to the effect . . . 'Micky Mudrock Wins Game Despite Anxiety Over His Wife and His Girl Friend Occupying Seats in the Same Box.'"[12] Eugene C. Patterson, an outstanding editor in Atlanta, Washington, and St. Petersburg, commented: "TV has had great influence on sports pages— more than anywhere else. It led to some awful writing. Whenever you can push to excess, sports writers will do it."[13]

In general, however, sports writing today is the best it has ever been. Some of it is first-rate, as exemplified in a Thomas Boswell lead in the *Washington Post* in 1988:

Music is not the universal language. The expressions of the human face cross frontiers and make language moot with far greater ease. When the Olympic flame is extinguished, as it was at the XV Winter Games tonight, we are left not primarily with medal counts or records but with memories of faces.[14]

Before television, and certainly before radio, newspapers reported straight off which side had won a game and by what score. Such information was news to most readers. But after sports became popular on television, information of this kind did not convey anything new to newspaper readers. The change in sports writing may be seen by comparing coverage of the Detroit Tigers in their battle for the American League pennant in 1950 and in 1987.

At the close of the 1950 season, the Tigers were running stride for stride with the New York Yankees. The *Washington Post* relied for coverage on Associated Press stories. Here are samples of direct, clear, comprehensive leads:

Detroit, Sept. 21—The Detroit Tigers today brushed passed the hapless Philadelphia Athletics 8–2 to climb into a first-place tie with the idle New York Yankees.

The victory gave the Detroiters a sweep of the three-game series with the A's and left them in a good position to grab sole ownership of the No. 1 spot when they meet Cleveland tomorrow. The Yankees will be idle again tomorrow.[15]

Cleveland, Ohio, Sept. 22—Joe Gordon's home run over the left field fence to open the last half of the ninth inning gave the Cleveland Indians a dramatic 4–3 victory over Detroit tonight to knock the Tigers out of a first-place tie with the New York Yankees.

The defeat dropped the Tigers one-half game behind the idle Yankees and cut their second-place margin over the Boston Red Sox to a game and a half.[16]

The Yankees won the pennant. Thirty-seven years later, the Tigers played the Toronto Blue Jays in another exciting finale. This time the *Post* did its own coverage in the style of the television age. The leads little resembled those in 1950:

Toronto, Sept. 24—They came here hoping to sample the rock music on Yonge Street, the Chinese food on the west side and to, maybe, swing the American

League East race in their favor. When Tony Fernandez's right elbow banged off a board in the artificial turf three innings into the game, the Detroit Tigers had accomplished the last objective.[17]

Toronto, Sept. 26—The absurd mixed with the ridiculous and combined with the silly. How ridiculous? Sparky Anderson made so many moves he was forced to let rookie reliever Mike Henneman bat with two runners in scoring position in the top of the ninth inning.

How ridiculous? Toronto Manager Jimmy Williams countered by bringing in reliever Jose Nunez to pitch to Henneman, who hadn't batted in a game since high school.[18]

From Toronto the Tigers returned home for their final games.

Detroit, Sept. 30—On the last day of September, with temperatures dipping into the 40s and the pungent smell of Italian sausage drifting through Tiger Stadium, Sparky Anderson gambled on a Dan Petry comeback.[19]

Television was at a disadvantage in not being able to pick up the smell of Italian sausage. The scores of the games did appear in the headlines above these stories. (Detroit won the American League East but lost to the Minnesota Twins in the playoffs for the pennant.) The *Post*, however, usually uses straight leads on stories about games that are not shown on television in Washington.

Despite some critics, the new style of reporting major sports events has its supporters, including the novelist James Michener. In *Sports in America,* he wrote, "Don't give the scores, give the inside stories behind the scores. And deal openly with those topics which men in saloons talk about in whispers." According to Michener, *Sports Illustrated* "has become the bible of the industry, and it has done so because it appreciated from the start the facts that faced printed journalism in the age of television."[20]

The influence of television on sports writing is unmistakable. In the mid-1950s while covering a big game that was being televised, the sports editor for the *Chicago Tribune* was Wilfred Smith, a burley former football player. "Big Smith," as he was known around the office, would monitor the telecast while maintaining an open telephone line to his reporter in the press box. "When something unusual happens," Smith explained, "we give him a quick call to have him bear down on that particular incident. We've used this to advantage to keep our coverage interesting to the fan who watched the event on TV."[21]

For certain kinds of events a television set is essential for sports writers nowadays. A story might turn, for example, on reviewing an instant replay in football. For a good while, however, sports reporters worked without their own television sets, yet continually wondered how television was handling the story. At the end of an out-of-town game in those days, according to Bill Shirley, Bob Oats, Sr., who covered the Los Angeles Rams for the *Los Angeles Times,* did not write his story until he had put in a long-distance call to his son, who also wrote about football, to learn how television had viewed the game. Bill Shirley, when he was covering the University of Southern California Trojans in an out-of-town game, would call Bob Oats, Sr., in Los Angeles at the end of the first half for a similar assessment.[22]

Under no less pressure than writers are newspaper photographers, scurrying to catch action on the field that readers might not have noticed on television. At the APME meeting in 1955, F. A. Resch, the AP's general newsphoto editor, praised newspaper photographers who took shots at the World Series earlier that fall. He said they demonstrated how the still camera could hold its own in an event that also was being covered by television. "In case after case," he said, "both the single pictures and in sequences, you got detail on action which the television cameras either missed entirely or skipped by so fast that everybody wondered what really did happen. Our available camera devices enable us in many cases to catch that moment, or a succession of moments, that go by in a split second on television."[23] Since then television has perfected its own capability for isolating still shots of fleeting actions.

A generation ago it was commonplace for some newspapers to run one or two full pages of photographs on a major sporting event in their area. Television has put an end to that practice; the same scenes have already appeared on television screens.

In the past thirty years television has swept in to cover the Olympic Games with such spectacular effect as to require mobilization of newspaper sports departments. Throughout the 1950s most newspapers offered light coverage at best of the Winter Olympics. Then, in 1960, for a fee of $50,000, CBS moved its cameras and Walter Cronkite into Squaw Valley in California for the Winter Games. The whole scene was so enchanting and aroused so much enthusiasm everywhere that newspapers had to make a belated rush to expand their coverage. But in 1972 they and the news magazines were again caught by surprise, this time in the gymnastic contests at the Summer Olympics in Munich. As had been the case for years, American reporters avoided gymnastics. It had not been a popular spectator sport in the United States. "Furthermore," Bill Shirley recalled, "our reporters felt gymnastics were not macho enough. At Munich we didn't even have a ticket for gymnastic events."[24] Yet while newspapers were covering running, pole vaulting, and high diving, ABC cameras were enthralling Americans at home with the breathtaking performances of a young Soviet gymnast named Olga Korbut. She not only became the talk of the country but also the catalyst for keen and lasting popular interest in the United States in gymnastics. Newspaper reporters in Munich had a hard time catching up with the story. Actually, the AP had moved a piece on Korbut early in the games, describing "her elfin grace and her tears," but it was little used. By the time she became a true star on television, demands from editors compelled the AP to repeat the story twice. At *Newsweek* editors reportedly were dismayed that the week's file from the Munich games contained little or no mention of Olga Korbut. As a result of the embarrassment, however, the American press was fully prepared in 1984 for television's glorification of Mary Lou Retton for her whirlwind performance at the Summer Olympics in Los Angeles.

For newspapers even the Winter Olympics have become an event that requires coverage on a scale that used to be reserved for the national political conventions. At Calgary in the winter of 1988, the Knight-Ridder papers alone had a staff consisting of seven editors, two photographers, and twenty reporters and columnists. In discussing this assignment, James Batten, president of Knight-Ridder, observed, "We would not remotely cover the Olympics as we are doing if it weren't for the fascination of the public with TV."[25]

Golf and tennis were popularized by television to a degree never before experienced. "We didn't start covering Wimbledon until 1978," Shirley of the *Los Angeles Times* recalled. "Even then there were only a handful of American reporters there. Now everyone goes." The same is true of championship golf tournaments and the annual spring basketball tournament of the National Collegiate Athletic Association. Over the years television has turned NCAA games into a noisy rite. To hold the television audiences at the weekend level, the championship game is played on Monday night, squeezing morning newspaper deadlines.

In the fall of 1970, a new problem hit newspaper sports departments—Roone Arledge and his "Monday Night Football" on ABC. A television genius in sports as well as news programs, Arledge challenged the old style of football coverage. He dressed the game up as entertainment, dared the American people to live with Howard Cosell, converted Don Meredith into a crooner, and outdid the matinee idols of old with Frank Gifford. Multiplication of commercials finally kept the games going until after midnight, eastern time, to the great inconvenience of morning newspapers.

For all the changes and all the headaches televised sports have caused the press, television has made readers hungry for sports pages. Ralph McGill said in 1951 something that is true of sports editors today: "We have had people call up and say, 'You know, I never read your sports pages because I wasn't interested in sports, but now on television I have seen horse races and fights and wrestling, so I am reading your sports pages.' "[26]

Speaking broadly of the effect of television on newspapers, A. M. Rosenthal once observed:

TV is one of the best things that ever happened to the newspaper business. . . . It spreads information instantly, arousing the news appetites of tens of millions of people. TV is one vast free promotion machine for us. Day in and day out, almost all day long, TV sharpens people's interest in the very thing we're in business for.[27]

Times have changed since the day in 1921 when a newspaper editor in Green Bay, Wisconsin, received a letter from the Associated Press bureau chief in Milwaukee saying that interest in professional football was insufficient for the AP to move the scores of games on its wires.[28]

22

Two different mediums:
newspapers and television news

Newspapers and television news are alike in many ways. Both can inform, entertain, and advertise. Both enjoy the protection of the First Amendment against infringement of free speech. Both have similar aims and ideals. Both attract articulate, well-educated men and women who are curious about the world around them. But newspapers and television news are different mediums. Print on a page is naturally different from images and words transmitted through the airwaves. Despite this difference and the competition it fosters, newspapers and television news have benefited each other in fascinating ways for more than forty years.

One night during an Apollo space mission, Eugene Patterson, then the managing editor of the *Washington Post,* sat in his office with his staff watching a television screen for sight of any last-minute developments before the late-edition deadline. A young functionary, known in earlier days as a copyboy, entered, looked around—saucily, Patterson thought—and said, "I always wondered how a great American newspaper covered a space mission."

"Well, you know," Patterson observed long afterward, "that *is* how we kept up with the story." [1]

Once considered the enemy by some newspaper reporters, television news had become one of their tools by the 1960s. Thus, some years after the scene at the *Post,* Robert S. Boyd could be observed at his desk in the National Press Building as he watched C-SPAN while writing about the day in Congress. Senior writer and formerly chief of the Knight-Ridder Washington bureau, Boyd had not always been a fan of television. At the 1956 Republican National Convention he had so detested tripping over

292

television cables that he wanted, he said, "to reach down and pull them out like crab grass." Times had changed since then, he acknowledged:

Whenever there is a big event, an interview at a hijacked plane, or a sudden statement by the president, our people are sitting in front of TV with pencil and yellow pad—that is my vision of a reporter at work today. . . .

The last four political conventions I have done the lead stories, sitting at my desk with two TVs on. Wire copy was brought to me, but basically I was watching TV. . . . Background, analysis, investigation—almost our only function now.[2]

John Finney, formerly of the *New York Times* Washington bureau, recalled how reporters could cover Congress from C-SPAN. "Important debates, important votes always seemed to come at deadline in the evening, so we would turn on C-SPAN in the bureau. Furthermore, using TV you could follow the action better than from the press gallery. You could see members' expressions better and hear their voices more distinctly."[3]

For sports reporters, television also can be essential. It was on the final day of the Masters' tournament at the Augusta National Golf Club in 1986. What sports reporter would have committed himself to follow Jack Nicklaus, hole by hole? Nicklaus had long been a great champion, but his championship days seemed behind him. He was forty-six years old. A score a few points off the winning pace was what was expected of him. The most likely place to look for the winner was among the outstanding younger players like Greg Norman, Bernhard Langer, or Severiano Ballesteros. Yet if a reporter had followed one of them the last day at Augusta, he or she would have missed the story. A tremendous rally by Nicklaus on the last five holes carried him to a famous victory. Obviously, events on the course were so widely separated in distance and time that a reporter could not cover all of them. At best he or she might risk following certain players on early holes to gather useful material. But to get the whole picture of the climax of the Masters' there was only one sure place to be: the television room.

During an American League baseball game in the mid-1970s between the Texas Rangers and the Kansas City Royals, a melee erupted among the players of both teams and quickly spread all over the field. For twenty minutes, according to one report, the "action was so fast and furious, with fights being touched off like sparks, many reporters present couldn't keep up with the three-ring circus." A television crew agreed to run the tape over and over "until the reporters could single out almost every incident."[4]

Although "print" and "electronic" journalists share similar purposes, interests, and attitudes, their professional skills are differently applied. Their rewards also are very different. John Chancellor calculated that a young reporter breaking in with the City News Bureau in Chicago would have to work for ten months to earn as much money as Dan Rather of CBS made on a single day. As for fame, the respective chances for print and electronic journalists are hardly comparable.

Unless they appear on a television program, newspaper and magazine reporters, columnists, and editorial writers are faceless to the public. A television journalist, especially an anchor, has rare and continuing access to people. Walter Cronkite is a classic example. With his wholesome manner and appearance, his studied fairness, his twinkle in the midst of seriousness, Cronkite was deeply trusted by millions when he was the anchor of the "CBS Evening News." He was even mentioned as a suitable candidate for vice-president.

After Cronkite's final regular broadcast in 1980, the CBS studios in New York were bombarded with telephone calls lamenting his departure. One woman, unknown to Cronkite, was particularly distressed. She had been invoking him as an authority to enforce a regimen on her aged mother. The daughter was wont to say, "Mother, Walter says you should take your medicine now," or "Walter says it is time for you to go to bed, Mother." [5]

As a *New York Times* war correspondent in Vietnam, Eugene Roberts was going about the grim task of covering the Tet offensive in 1968 when a letter arrived from his mother. She told him she was feeling much reassured about the war because she had heard Walter Cronkite was going to Vietnam. [6]

Years later when Roberts was in Philadelphia as executive editor of the *Inquirer,* he had to cancel a speech he had agreed to make in Harrisburg. He suggested to the woman in charge of the affair that Jack Nelson, the outstanding Washington bureau chief of the *Los Angeles Times,* would make a good substitute. Never having heard of Jack Nelson of the *Los Angeles Times,* the woman was disappointed. She said she wished Roberts had suggested the Jack Nelson who was a regular panelist on the Public Broadcasting Service program "Washington Week in Review." [7] Of course, he was. The woman's mix-up underlines the higher public recognition television journalists receive compared with newspaper journalists. Time and again this gives them an important advantage.

In the 1950s and 1960s, Bernard Kilgore refused to allow *Wall Street*

Journal reporters to appear on the NBC program "Meet the Press," a rule also followed then by the *New York Times,* the *Chicago Tribune* and the Associated Press. Apprehensive about the competition of television news, Kilgore, like many other editors, believed that newspapers should not do anything to help television flourish. Henry Gemmill, Washington bureau chief of the *Wall Street Journal* in the mid-1960s, disagreed with Kilgore's rule. Gemmill finally won their running argument and became the first *Wall Street Journal* reporter to appear on "Meet the Press." Kilgore yielded to Gemmill's point that it was easier for a reporter to get his telephone calls to government officials returned if the reporter's face had become familiar in Washington through television appearances.

Because of television, largely, the number of accredited correspondents in the capital has ballooned over the years. A government official who is likely to have information on a breaking story may have a stack of calls from reporters by the end of the day. With time to return only a few, the chances are he will call those whom he knows, trusts, and considers important. This may well work in favor of a reporter who is familiar through television. Today many, though not all, editors, whose predecessors frowned on members of their staffs performing on television, welcome it. In 1988 the *Chicago Tribune* retained the services of a media consultant to help get its Washington reporters on national news shows. On the other hand, Steven Roberts, a frequent participant on "Washington Week in Review," resigned his regular job on the *New York Times* when Max Frankel, the executive editor, asked his staff to limit television appearances. Frankel frowned on having television programs build reputations on the shoulders of *Times* reporters. Roberts subsequently joined the staff of *U.S. News & World Report.* Newspaper and magazine reporters continue to fill the panels of television news discussion programs, earning their publications national mention and themselves renown and bloated speakers' fees.

To be spotted as a television newscaster by a restaurateur is to enjoy a celebrity status seldom achieved by a newspaper reporter. In the early years of the United Nations, Larry LeSueur of CBS had a daily television program, beginning at 5:00 P.M., covering the diplomats' day. He met a French woman whom he liked and one evening invited her to have champagne with him at the old El Morocco on East Fifty-fourth Street. She accepted, and they spent a pleasurable evening dancing and sipping champagne. Suddenly, LeSueur made a horrid discovery. He had no money with him. El Morocco was no place to run up a bill when one's wallet was home on the dresser.

"I explained to the waiter I was embarrassed over the fact I had no cash with me," LeSueur recalled long afterward. "He took this rather grimly and said he would have to call the manager." When the manager came over, he exclaimed happily: "You are Larry LeSueur!" A foreigner eager to learn news of world events, the manager watched LeSueur's U.N. broadcasts daily. Did LeSueur have to make a commitment to pay the bill? No. The manager was so taken by the newscaster's appearance at his restaurant that he picked up the tab.[8]

To be the after-hours guest of a maître d'hôtel is delightful, of course. A newscaster may fare even better, however, if recognized while working on a breaking story, as happened to John Tillman, who had a regular evening news show on WPIX-TV in New York. At home the morning of January 22, 1957, Tillman received an urgent call from his office. The "Mad Bomber," he was told, had just been arrested in Waterbury, Connecticut. Beginning in 1950 this mysterious terrorist had planted thirty-two homemade bombs in such places as Grand Central Terminal, Pennsylvania Station, and Radio City Music Hall. Fifteen persons had been injured, some gravely, and the fear in the city was credited with reducing attendance at theaters. Excited by word of the arrest, Tillman telephoned his camera crew to meet him in Waterbury and then sped to Connecticut himself. Several miles short of Waterbury his engine stalled. He was infuriated at the thought of missing a big story. When he finally did reach the courthouse through the courtesy of a passing motorist, at about the same time as his crew arrived, Tillman was mystified to find the place quiet, almost deserted. A lone detective came up to him and his crew and explained the reason for the quiet. Reporters and photographers were in a basement room at a press conference with New York police authorities.

Tillman long remembered that the detective's name was Ed Sullivan. Their conversation went roughly as follows:

Sullivan: "Aren't you John Tillman of 'Telepix Newsreel'?"
Tillman: "Yes."
Sullivan exuded cordiality. He was a regular viewer of the program.
Sullivan: "Would you like to see him?"
Tillman: "See who?"
Sullivan: "Would you like to see the 'Mad Bomber'?"
Tillman: "Are you kidding?"
Later he surmised that Detective Sullivan acted out of resentment against

the New York police for having stolen the show from the Waterbury cops.

Sullivan led Tillman and his crew up a back stairway to the second floor and then into an ample room with an oak desk in the center. Around it huddled several policemen.

Sullivan: "There he is."

Tillman: "Where?"

Sullivan (pointing to a fifty-four-year-old man named George Peter Metesky, who was sitting alone in a far corner): "*There*. He's a good old Waterbury boy."

Tillman: "Can I interview him?"

Sullivan: "Why not?"[9]

Tillman and his crew sprang to work, using all the film they had. After the press conference in the basement ended, the other reporters and photographers got wind of what had happened on the second floor and stormed up to talk to the bomber. They were too late. By then Sullivan had clamped Metesky in a detention cell beyond the reach of outsiders. That evening WPIX had a sensational beat. The story of the insane Metesky was that he had planted bombs out of resentment against his employer, the Consolidated Edison Company of New York. He believed that an accident he had suffered while an employee of the company had left him with tuberculosis.

Most newspapers, certainly the major ones, monitor television news. If television comes up with a significant exclusive story, newspapers react. This is not frequent, however. In the main, television reports the principal events of the day, which newspapers and wire services have covered routinely. Some papers more than others may upgrade the display they plan to give a story if television leads with it. At a 5:00 P.M. news conference at *USA Today* on December 8, 1982, Nancy Woodhull, managing editor for news, recommended front-page play for a bizarre event that day at the Washington Monument. A man in a truck backed against the monument and threatened to blow it up with explosives. Woodhull's recommendation was turned down on the grounds that the story was a local one. Then, at 7:00 P.M., Rather led the "CBS Evening News" with it. Promptly, the editors of *USA Today* yanked their story from an inside page and put it on page one. Peter Prichard wrote in his history of *USA Today*, "Editors were very aware of what people saw and heard on the television news and shaped *USA Today*'s print report to take that into account."[10] Because of the paper's national circulation, it is more sensitive than most to how television plays the news.

Coincidentally, the emergence of *USA Today* in the 1980s was a vehicle for indirect impact of television on newspapers in general. This came about because many newspapers adopted innovations in *USA Today*, which, in turn, had modeled itself on television. *USA Today* was designed to look in a sidewalk vending machine like a television screen. A number of other papers were then redesigned to look like television screens. *USA Today* sought the living colors of television screens. Many newspapers followed suit. *USA Today* went heavily into graphics and boxes. Many newspapers greatly increased their use of graphics and boxes.

Abe Rosenthal, executive editor of the *New York Times,* asserted in 1983 that he and his fellow editors "do not edit by TV or as a result of TV. . . . We are smart enough to know that the very ubiquitous quality of television makes it more important than ever that we continue to put out a newspaper that uses different judgments, different values, different techniques."[11] This was another way of saying, correctly, that newspapers and television are different mediums, each with its own functions and standards. Neither the *Times* nor any other newspaper worthy of the name allows itself to be edited by television news. And, surely, Peter Jennings would not edit "World News Tonight" according to the *Washington Post.* Yet television news and the press are part of the same continuum. Crosscurrents of influence are inevitable. The *New York Times Magazine* has killed pending articles because the subjects turned up first on Ted Koppel's "Nightline" or on an evening news program. Reporters from many papers, including the *New York Times,* have occasionally written late stories off television screens in order to make a deadline. If a skyscraper were to topple into Fifth Avenue some afternoon, *Times* editors would watch the scene on television while supervising their own coverage. In many newspaper offices and bureaus, television sets continually carry CNN for the benefit of editors and reporters. On the other hand, every morning in New York, Washington, Los Angeles, Chicago, Miami, Boston, and other cities television reporters, producers, and anchors feed on the principal newspapers. They are not likely to forget what they read. No television network ignored the story when the *New York Times* broke the Pentagon papers, secret documents about the Vietnam War, in 1971. Local television stations especially have been notorious for picking up news from local papers. In the late 1940s, for example, the morning news editor at WRC-TV, the NBC-owned station in

Washington, would begin a typical day by clipping local stories from the *Post* and the *Times-Herald* and giving them to his lone cameraman to convert into news film for the station's dinnertime program. Over the silent film the announcer would narrate the stories that had originated in the papers that morning.

Which medium exerts greater influence on the workings of the other has never been proved. The answer would probably change from day to day. After television news was established and came to deliver the news not only first but also with high visual effects, it was the printed press that over the long run had to accommodate.

The postwar period was a time of great prosperity. Papers around the country earned unprecedented profits. This was especially true of small and medium-sized papers equipped with the new technology and enjoying a monopoly or quasi monopoly. Rich newspaper chains such as Times Mirror, Knight-Ridder, Gannett Newspapers, and Newhouse Newspapers bought such papers almost wherever they could find them. Many independent papers, instead of reinvesting profits to improve their own product for the benefit of readers, used the money to buy other papers. Prices soared. For the *New Orleans Times-Picayune*, Newhouse in 1962 paid $42 million, nearly three times what the United States laid out for the Louisiana Purchase.

But large cities, particularly New York, were death wards for major newspapers in the sixties and seventies. Many folded, were merged with another paper, or disappeared through sale to another newspaper. Examples include the *New York Herald Tribune*, the *New York Mirror*, the *Boston Post*, the *Buffalo Courier-Express*, and the *St. Louis Globe-Democrat*—all morning papers. Afternoon papers fared even worse. Among the fallen were the *New York Sun*, the *New York World-Telegram*, the *New York Journal-American*, the *Brooklyn Eagle*, the *Chicago Daily News*, Chicago's *American*, *Chicago Today*, the *Washington Star*, the *Washington Daily News*, the *Philadelphia Evening Bulletin*, the *Los Angeles Mirror*, the *Minneapolis Star*, the *Indianapolis Times*, the *Baltimore News-American*, the *Newark News*, the *Detroit Times*, the *Cleveland Press*, the *Kansas City Star*, and the *Los Angeles Herald-Examiner*. All were afternoon papers.

Afternoon papers had long been dominant in the United States. In the age of television, however, the balance shifted dramatically in favor of morning papers. The reasons for it were many. Smokestack industries declined, and fewer workshifts ended in the afternoon when droves of homeward-bound laborers used to pick up afternoon newspapers at the factory gate and read them on the trolley. Now most people cannot read on the way home because they drive. Traffic has been a problem not only for commuters but also for afternoon papers. The *Washington Star,* one of the wealthiest and most influential afternoon newspapers, once had a slogan "From Press to Home Within the Hour." Worsening congestion made such a claim ludicrous. The daily rivers of vehicles made it impossible for afternoon papers in Washington and other cities to deliver editions with late news to outlying neighborhoods and suburbs.

Eugene Roberts recalled that the story of Egyptian President Anwar Sadat's assassination on October 6, 1981, broke early and ran all day in Philadelphia. "People on the way home were listening to it on their car radios. They looked forward to reading about it in the evening paper. But when they got home they found that the edition of the *Bulletin* that had been delivered did not have a line on Sadat." [12] The curse of traffic and sprawling suburbs, which staggered the *Bulletin* and other afternoon newspapers, did not affect the morning papers because they are delivered during the hours of darkness. Television news was an important element in the demise of many afternoon papers, yet it was not the sole cause. Traffic, suburban growth, and social change contributed to the problem. With more women in offices, not homes, during the afternoon, advertisers began to shift their business to morning papers. And in the many one-parent homes today the parent is likely to have little time for an afternoon newspaper. Indeed, the readers most eagerly sought by newspapers—namely, the young and the up-and-coming—do not stay home in the evening.

As Sam McKeel observed:

Life has changed, and TV is a major part of it. There has been a change in lifestyles since World War II. Affluence. Automobiles. Highways. Many people go out to dinner. They don't come home from work and read a book or sit around and talk. People travel. They have the money to pay for it. Those who come home from work turn on TV. They have dinner in front of a set and may spend the whole evening watching it.

The decline in newspaper readership reflects the disappearance of multiple newspaper readers. People used to read two or three newspapers a day. There has been a vast reduction of these readers. Not that many papers are available to them any more. [13]

Tottering afternoon papers tried almost every way to save themselves. The *Washington Star* was owned by the Noyes and Kauffmann families from 1867 to 1974. For the last seven of those years, Charles Seib was managing editor. Later he described how the paper struggled in reacting to television competition.

It had been a staid paper for years. But in the face of television news we went into new coverage, like special reports. The *Star* never did anything like that before. Haynes Johnson traveled around reporting on the mood of America, taking the temperature. We tried to do stories along the lines high-quality television was doing. . . . TV forced us into more featurish, or human, news.[14]

The event that sent the *Star* into a final tailspin, however, was not the coming of television but the sudden dominance of the *Washington Post*, resulting from its purchase of the rival *Washington Times Herald* on March 17, 1954. In 1974 the flickering *Star* was sold to the Texas multimillionaire Joe L. Allbritton, who hired James Bellows as editor. Characteristically, Bellows put all the instruments in the band to work *fortissimo*, bringing the *Star* to life in a way it never had been. Exploiting the public's interest in the capital's political and social celebrities, he spiced the *Star* with a popular gossip column "The Ear," by Diana McLellan. Bellows enticed the cartoonist Pat Oliphant from the *Denver Post* and peppered the front page with articles by Jimmy Breslin and Willie Morris. Bellows's approach to news was generally offbeat.

Despite his efforts to increase circulation, the *Star* remained squeezed for money. Bellows resigned to protest the editorial budget. In 1978 Allbritton sold the *Star* to Time, Inc. Veering away from Bellows's approach, Murray Gart, the new editor, played the hard news and used serious copy from *Time* correspondents around the world. He started special sections for suburban Virginia and Maryland and contrived to get Garry Trudeau's syndicated comic strip *Doonesbury* away from the *Post*. Gart even published an early morning edition in competition with the *Post*. But reviving the *Star* in the face of the *Post*'s momentum and the hazards for afternoon newspapers proved hopeless. Time, Inc., closed the 129-year-old newspaper in 1981.

During the late 1970s the spreading malady crippling afternoon newspapers struck the *Minneapolis Star*. The people who worked for the faltering paper, however, fought back by designing a new newspaper. This model, they hoped, not only would rescue the *Star* but also would serve as a successful guide for other afflicted afternoon papers. Stephen D. Isaacs, editor of the *Star* and son of the newspaper editor and philosopher Norman Isaacs, directed the "Minneapolis experiment," as it was called. According to Isaacs, the conferences brought together editors, photogra-

phers, reporters, editorial writers, even copy aides as well as representatives
of management. By 1978, when the experiment began, the circulation of
the *Star* had fallen seventy-five thousand copies below the 1960 level of
three hundred thousand. The planners decided that a potential reader got
home from work at five or six in the evening in time to put dinner in the
microwave oven and turn on Walter Cronkite before leaving for the theater or some other diversion. Hence, they agreed that their new model
must not be what they called *printed television*. The new goal, Isaacs
wrote,

> was to transform what was essentially a traditional, heavily spot-news oriented,
> somewhat disorganized but eminently responsible (and quite dull) editors' news-
> paper. We hoped to remake it into an exciting, indispensable, vital reporters'
> newspaper that placed its highest premium on its own staff's enterprise. We wanted
> our reportage to avoid being hemmed in by the customary editing taboos that
> prevail mostly because they always seemed to have been there.[15]

Miscellaneous small, insignificant stories were replaced by long,
thoughtful, analytical, and, if possible, definitive ones. Two facing and
typograhically attractive editorial pages featured articles by members of
an eminent board of contributors from the Minneapolis region. Pontifi-
cating editorials were ruled out, and fewer syndicated columns appeared
than formerly.

In sum, a modern, bold, streamlined state-of-the art afternoon newspaper was created. It did not work. The afternoon market of old had
shrunk. In 1982 the Cowles family, which also owned the *Minneapolis
Tribune,* a morning paper, merged the two papers. The paper is now
called the *Star Tribune,* omitting the name "Minneapolis" because the
paper circulates also in the twin city of St. Paul.

Afternoon newspapers, in their traditional role of reporting local affairs, have prospered in suburbs, towns, and small cities. In large cities,
however, the gradual disappearance of evening papers contrasts with the
almost unassailable position of the established morning newspapers. Unfortunately, a question raised by the omnipresence of television is whether
a large city any longer needs more than one metropolitan newspaper.

The quality of a newspaper has not necessarily determined whether it
survived in the postwar period. Good newspapers have disappeared, while
others that have made little pretense at editorial excellence, many of them
owned by chains, have prospered. Especially if it has a monopoly in its
market, a professionally undistinguished paper can still be a profitable
one by cutting costs, building circulation, and selling a lot of advertising.

Such papers fare all the better if they own a television station, as many do.

The plight of an independent newspaper, morning or afternoon, with the second-largest circulation in a city never has been a comfortable one, because the paper with the larger circulation gets more advertising. Long before television, many a second paper collapsed. A generation ago, however, a number of them were still able to sell enough advertising, particularly to local businesses, to survive. Still, the advertising in the second-largest paper essentially duplicated the advertising in the larger one. In recent times as retail chains have purchased local businesses and as shopping malls have proliferated, advertising has been bought by formula free of any sentiment for supporting second papers. Rather than duplicating advertising in metropolitan newspapers, advertisers pulled their money out of second papers and put it in television or in expanding suburban newspapers. As Leo Bogart of the Newspaper Advertising Bureau remarked, "Business people had a sense of need to be in the new medium, television. Their competitors were getting in, so they felt they had to." As a result, television "has eaten into the total available advertising resources in a market."[16]

Competing with television for advertising forced a change in the appearance of newspapers. Until recent years the dimensions of pages and columns varied, however minutely, from one paper to another. If a retailer wished to place a certain display advertisement in different newspapers, a common practice, he or she had to endure the time-devouring process of having the ad's layout tailored to different sizes. Walter E. Mattson, president of the New York Times Company, commented that it was much easier "to place your ad on TV where thirty seconds is always thirty seconds."[17]

Reacting to this problem, major publishers went through the long task of making width and column sizes more uniform. One display advertisement had to fit them all. Standardization reduced the width of most newspapers from eight columns to six wider columns. As a result, the papers had a less solemn, more open appearance. The change also led to new layouts throughout a newspaper. The pages, although more readable, sometimes contained a smaller volume of news.[18] "The American press," Bogart declared, "has changed rapidly under the pressures of urban depopulation and transformation, the explosion of broadcast news, and technological improvements in newspaper production methods."[19]

Television had prompted newspapers to use more and larger photographs. Surprisingly, on September 8, 1976, the once conservatively made up *New York Times* carried sixty-five photographs, ten more than New York's "picture newspaper," the *Daily News*. (Promotional head shots of syndicated columnists in the *News* were excluded from the tally.)

Television also put pressure on newspapers to use color. Advertisers helped force the issue because color drew attention to their displays. In the 1960s, when local television stations began using color in their news broadcasts, managing editors of newspapers talked as if they were victims of unfair competition. "Over and over again," said Robert Haiman of the *St. Petersburg Times* in 1969, "we heard editors grumbling at the ease with which local news departments of TV stations could use color on the daily news report and the difficulty involved in using color in local newspapers."[20] Haiman spoke as a member of the APME committee on media competition. Despite the grumbling, however, an inquiry by Haiman's committee suggested that managing editors complained more than they tried to get color photography in their papers. Such indifference ended with a jolt when *USA Today* began appearing on newsstands nationwide in the 1980s. By the early 1990s practically all metropolitan newspapers were using color.

Graphics, boxlike forms of news presentation, also were made more popular by *USA Today*. They are a composite of such elements as photographs, sketches, maps, charts, graphs, and synopses. Suitable for any subject, graphics frequently appear in different sections of newspapers. On December 30, 1987, the *Boston Globe* devoted an entire page to such a presentation, entitled "The Gulf War" (about the first Gulf War between Iran and Iraq), by Richard H. Stewart.

The most dramatic example of graphics in a newspaper to date was the one by David Miller, Dale Glasgow, and Web Bryant, to which *USA Today* devoted three-quarters of its front page on January 29, 1986, reporting on the disaster of the *Challenger* space shuttle. A fiery red with streaks of steam and smoke, the display dramatized the ill-fated liftoff of the spacecraft. At the bottom of the page were sketches of the rocket on the launch pad and of the seating arrangement of the astronauts. Along the flight path were strung several boxes showing where the craft had passed at intervals until 1 minute, 51 seconds, when it exploded. Cut into the picture was a photograph of the parents of Christa McAuliffe, the schoolteacher who died in the explosion, in the grandstand, looking aghast toward the sky. And in block letters at the top of the display, just under the *USA Today* logo, were the words "Oh, my God, no!" uttered by Nancy Reagan before a television screen in the White House.

Perhaps the most disturbing problem for newspapers in the age of television has been the loss of a generation of readers. It consists of those who were born after World War II, who have watched television since their infancy, and who, having matured, do not now regularly read the papers. The next generation is following in the same direction. By the end of 1988, according to David Shaw, who writes about journalism for the *Los Angeles Times,* most young people in the United States today—children, teenagers, and even men and women in their early twenties—did not regularly read a daily newspaper. Social conditions and modern lifestyles heighten the problem. The movement of people to outer suburbs, for example, lengthens the distances of their commuting and lessens the time they have for reading newspapers. Newspaper circulation is also affected by the trend toward later marriages. Historically, people begin to subscribe to newspapers when they have a vested interest in a community, which comes with getting married, having children, paying local taxes. In 1967, according to Shaw, 73 percent of people polled by the National Opinion Research Center at the University of Chicago said they read a newspaper every day. By March 1989, the proportion of everyday readers had fallen to 50.6 percent. In the eighteen to twenty-nine age group during the same span, the number had dropped by more than half—from 60 percent to 29 percent. Most young people are not hostile toward newspapers, just apathetic, Shaw wrote, adding, "Study after study has shown that they do not consider a daily newspaper either essential or relevant."[21]

Well aware what this attitude may mean to newspaper circulation as older readers die, editors of more than a hundred newspapers are now reaching for young readers with special coverage directed at their interests and even special sections. The latter field was pioneered in 1978 by *Newsday of New York* with "Kidsday," a four-page section with color published every Sunday and a half-page published on weekdays. Not surprisingly perhaps, *USA Today,* which was designed for the television age, goes after young readers aggressively. Its simple stories, abundance of color photographs and catchy headlines, optimism, froth, and emphasis on sports and celebrities got it off to an advantageous start.

For newspapers the first four decades of competition with television news, together with the effect of postwar changes in lifestyles, were often difficult, sometimes disastrous, always challenging, and, for the survivors, rewarding. The competition raised newspaper standards. But the strains of the marketplace were severe. In 1948 there were 1,781 daily newspapers in the United States. Mergers, sales, and closings, especially in the evening field, reduced the number as of September 30, 1990, to 1,611.[22] This was a period, incidentally, when many businesses enjoyed enormous expansion.

By no means were the changes wrought in journalism by television limited to newspapers. Since the 1960s, change among magazines has been epidemic, and television has had a great deal to do with it. In the advertising market, television has been a daunting competitor. Its programs have been no less a rival for the time and interest of magazine readers. The news magazines—*Time, Newsweek,* and *U.S. News & World Report*—have largely assumed a different function over the years. As newspapers have shifted emphasis from the straightforward news of the day, news magazines, too, have turned from summarizing news of the week to commentary, background, analysis, criticism, and thoroughgoing articles on politics, the arts, diplomacy, the environment, profiles, gossip, and twentieth-century society in general. *Newsweek* and *U.S. News,* especially, have featured articles of service to readers in fields such as personal finance and health.

Caught in the middle between newspapers and magazines are the news magazines. Their plight is epitomized by a saying at the *New York Times,* "Television ate our breakfast, and we are eating the news magazines' lunch." In other words, television beats the *Times* in delivering the news, and so the *Times,* by writing the very kinds of articles the news magazines are writing, beats them to the newsstands. And just as major newspapers have been thinking more like the news weeklies, so the news weeklies have been thinking more like the monthlies in developing articles. It is a particular burden for the news magazines that Sunday newspapers have been getting more profitable. People have more time to read on Sundays than on weekdays. Publishers have responded with thicker Sunday papers more replete with magazine-style articles. Although the circulation of dailies has remained flat, circulation of Sunday papers throughout the country increased from 49.2 million in 1970 to 62.6 million in 1990.[23]

Like newspapers, magazines have changed their appearance in the television age. Lester Bernstein, former editor of *Newsweek,* described a 1988 revision of *Time*'s format as "graphic glitz." "To snag an attention span conditioned by watching TV with a channel-switching zapper," he wrote, "there are bigger pictures and headlines, an abundance of bite-sized shorts and fragmented stories, plus more maps, charts, and boxes."[24]

The most devastating havoc created by the inroads of television in

American journalism was among mass-circulation magazines. Between 1956 and 1972 the four giants—*Collier's,* the *Saturday Evening Post, Look,* and *Life*—collapsed. At their peaks they had a combined circulation of 128.2 million. The unconquerable problem for the mass-circulation magazines was the huge loss of advertising to all departments of television. The growing popularity of color television did not abate. Returning from a trip abroad in 1962, C. D. Jackson, a top executive of Time, Inc., wrote to his boss, Henry R. Luce: "I felt an ominous shiver . . . when I read all about Telstar. . . . What I read was the warning of instant color TV all over the world."[25] In a few years the nightly television pictures of combat in Vietnam confirmed his anxieties. Television news forced magazines to compete in a losing battle. As Stanley Tretick, *Look*'s premier photographer, asked, "Why [would] anyone want to see seventeen pages of a national convention in glorious color when you had already seen the whole convention on television?"[26]

Established in 1821, the *Saturday Evening Post* became the first truly national magazine in the United States. In its heyday before the Second World War, it captivated subscribers with charming covers by Norman Rockwell. Its demise with the issue of February 8, 1969, was national news. On the last day television cameramen were shooting scenes all over the *Post*'s editorial offices in New York. Many of the staff hung around to watch themselves on television news—a perfect commentary on the competition that brought the magazine down.

23

Conclusion: Tiananmen Square, the Berlin Wall, the Persian Gulf War, and the Russian coup

The climax of roughly four decades of television news came in a succession of gripping events abroad: the students' protest in Beijing in June 1989, the toppling of the Berlin Wall and the collapse of the Communist regimes in Eastern Europe in November 1989, the war in the Persian Gulf in 1991 following Iraq's invasion of Kuwait, and the decline and fall of communism in the USSR.

Television pictures of the bloody deaths in Tiananmen Square disillusioned Americans about the once-promising government of Deng Xiaoping, chairman of the Central Military Commission of the Chinese Communist Party. Television coverage of the Berlin Wall extravaganza and the overthrow of former Soviet satellite states showed Americans one of the great revolutions of the twentieth century. Being transformed before their eyes was the postwar order in Europe. Radio and television coverage of upheaval in East Germany helped galvanize the people of Poland, Czechoslovakia, and Romania to change their own Communist governments. Only a war, waged and watched at the same time, could provide television drama as rare as that which Americans witnessed in the winter of 1991. To be sure, the spectacle as broadcast was limited by U.S. military censors. Nevertheless, the screen was a magnet for a people trembling over the fate of its sons and daughters. Stationed in the Middle East were 541,425 Americans. Early in the conflict Iraqi leader Saddam Hussein had warned that American casualties might total ten thousand in a single day. Fortunately, he was wrong. U.S. casualties were light. Television coverage of the speed of the final campaign against Hussein restored America's faith in its own role and power in the world, a faith badly shaken in Vietnam.

In Beijing on May 15, 1989, Deng welcomed Soviet leader Mikhail Gorbachev for a state visit. The television networks of the world waited in Tiananmen Square in the heart of the Chinese capital to capture everything that could be seen of the event. Chinese students and workers, who had been demonstrating in Beijing for nearly seven weeks for a more democratic form of government, quickly sensed the unparalleled opportunity at hand. Television could help them communicate their cause to peoples around the globe.

Until then Deng had enjoyed, abroad at least, a reputation for "liberalization." In the decade since the death of Mao Zedong and the end of the Cultural Revolution, he had restored order in China. Particularly relieved by his moderate course were the people of Hong Kong, due to be reclaimed by China from British rule in 1997. Deng was credited with trying to open China's economy, thereby attracting new foreign investment. But in the spring of 1989, he, and the rest of the octogenarian leadership of the country, feared anarchy. They summoned more military forces to Beijing. Anxious viewers everywhere wondered whether the government really intended to fire on the students encamped in Tiananmen Square.

Undaunted, the students erected a gleaming white, handmade replica of the Statue of Liberty. They proclaimed their cause before international television cameras. Then on June 3 the two-day crackdown began. Tanks, armored personnel carriers, and tens of thousands of troops, some of them firing AK-47 automatic rifles, blasted through the encampment. They downed flags, crushed tents, splintered the Goddess of Liberty, and killed perhaps a thousand of the demonstrators; the exact number may never be known.

The single most dramatic episode was broadcast worldwide. It centered on a lone, unarmed protester, a man perhaps in his late twenties, who was hatless and wore a white shirt and dark trousers. As tanks approached along a thoroughfare named, ironically, the Avenue of Eternal Peace, he stood in their path. On the tanks came. He refused to move. The lead tank came so close it towered above him. He did not budge. The steel monster was within several feet of crushing him to death. Then, in an unforgettable test of wills, the tank stopped. A few seconds later it started up again and tried to encircle him. The man moved into its path.

The tank took another turn. He was there, too. This time the advance halted. The man scrambled aboard the tank and pounded on the gun turret. A member of the crew emerged. The man in the white shirt cried out, according to a witness, "Why are you here? You have done nothing but create misery."[1] Then he climbed down. His colleagues hurried him away to safety.

After the voices of protest were finally silenced in Beijing, echoes still sounded around the world. Outside the Chinese consulate in New York City, pickets carried a sign, "People's Republic—What a Joke!" In his television column Walter Goodman wrote in the *New York Times*, "Television had made heroes of the youths."[2] Anchoring an ABC broadcast, Peter Jennings commented that the Chinese rulers were driving their nation "back, back, not forward."[3] "So far," the *Wall Street Journal* reported, "foreign bankers and other investors, shocked by the graphic television pictures of carnage in the Chinese capital, are concentrating on protecting their employees based in China. Most are taking a wait-and-see attitude toward current and planned investments and technology transfers, whose value totals billions of dollars."[4]

The televised scenes from Tiananmen Square spread dismay in Hong Kong. Since then, many citizens have emigrated rather than face Chinese rule in 1997. In the United States the impact of the television coverage was sufficient to bring public demands for curtailed relations with China. It was not strong enough to drive the Bush administration into grave reprisals. To the disgust of his critics, President Bush merely suspended military sales to China and suspended exchange visits of Chinese and American military delegations. "I don't want to see a total break in this relationship," Bush insisted.[5]

In the minds of some writers, the German revolution began in Tiananmen Square, wrote Tara Sonenshine in the *Washington Post*. An editorial producer for ABC's "Nightline," Sonenshine quoted a Leipzig clergyman as saying, "Although people [who watched television scenes from Beijing] were afraid, they were also filled with hope." They speculated about what events in China might mean for the burgeoning protest movement in East Germany against the oppressive regime of Erich Honecker.

Honecker acted to keep East German television from covering the Tiananmen Square spectacle, according to Professor James McAdams of Princeton University, an authority on Eastern Europe who is quoted in Sonenshine's article. But West German television, seen by East Germans, filled the gap. Sonenshine described it as a "window through which they could witness the revolutionary changes taking place around them."[6]

Dieter Buhl, a West German newspaper editor, also noted the political impact of West German television: "By becoming an ever more important pulpit for dissidents and by massively supporting the escape from East Germany, West German television (and to some degree radio) permanently increased the pressure on the East German rulers. The electronic needle again and again punctured the seemingly safe armor of the regime."[7] The capability of television news to cross boundaries and help set the pace of events was termed "terrestrial overspill" by David Webster, a former director of the British Broadcasting Corporation. When the forces of oppression began to weaken, he observed, the spread of this news hastened the process of self-government.[8]

The besieged East German government on November 9, 1989, decided to lift restrictions on travel to the West. That night jubilant East German men, women, and children poured over the Berlin Wall, prime symbol of the cold war. The scene was floodlighted for television cameras. Tom Brokaw of NBC stood by the wall, not reporting as much as celebrating the epic. His broadcast captured the joy on the faces of thousands being released from forty-four years of Communist restrictions. Seeing the East Germans on the wall dancing, hugging, shouting, drinking sparkling wine, and happily chipping away at it with hammers and chisels was a supreme lesson on the dankness of communism, Soviet style. If the memory of a television broadcast is a measure of its impact, this one will stand with the greatest. It was a broadcast that showed with utter clarity the welcome end of an era. For Americans, the scene was particularly sweet because the policies initiated by the Truman administration after World War II helped bring about the revolutionary events of 1989.

After watching television coverage of the Vietnam War in the years before his death on March 28, 1969, Eisenhower used to say it would be impossible for Americans to fight another world war because of television. They could not, he believed, stand to watch a long, bloody ordeal that would be the price of winning such a conflict. After the Persian Gulf War it is obvious that on this subject no general rule applies. Each war will have to be taken as a distinct case. When the televising of the Gulf War began, American viewers could not get enough of it. American casualties were extraordinarily light, of course, and somehow Iraqi corpses remained out of sight of television cameras. Instead of being angry and disgusted, as they were after the Vietnam War, Americans hung yellow ribbons everywhere in honor of their armed forces. People were happy, contented, proud of winning, thrilled by their military technology and the professionalism of their forces, and at least willing to listen to talk about America's becoming the "policeman of the world." Such was the irresistibility of televised news from the Gulf War that many people refrained from going out for dinner. On January 16, 1991, the first day of the fighting, almost no serious crime was reported in Washington, D.C., a crime-infested city. Evidently, criminals could not tear themselves away from television either.

That first night those in the East who were watching the 6:30 "CBS Evening News with Dan Rather" suddenly saw a quizzical look come over his face while he was talking about another topic. Reports were coming in, he said, of flashes in the sky over Baghdad. A moment later he announced that the war seemed to be starting.

CNN correspondents Peter Arnett, Bernard Shaw, and John Holliman had exclusive audio reports of the first night's fighting because in previous weeks they had badgered the Iraqis into renting them a private open phone line known as a "four-wire." This proved an enormous coup. From a room on the sixth floor of the Rashid Hotel in Baghdad, they could hear the thud of bombs and missiles and see streams of antiaircraft tracers racing into the greenish sky. Bravely they stayed on the air and told the world what was happening.

"The sky is lighting up to the south with antiaircraft and red and flashes of yellow light," Arnett reported. "There's another attack coming in. . . . It looks like the Fourth of July."

"It's like the center of hell," reported Holliman.

"We are crouched at the window, three miles from the center of the action," Arnett added. "The antiaircraft. Four bomb flashes. Planes circling for more targets, I guess."[9]

Because of transmission delays, no such unfolding drama had come live from Vietnam. But what a viewer at home saw of Baghdad that night was happening before his or her eyes. It gave television coverage a storybook effect. A writer for "The Talk of the Town" in the *New Yorker* confessed: "Sitting at my home by my TV set, I had felt not only horror at Saddam Hussein's deeds and potential deeds but (as someone brought up on Vietnam) an unfamiliar pride in our armed forces and their commanders. And the arguments against the war, which had been clear enough to me before it started, had begun to seem unreal."[10] Soon, however, he snapped out of it and was back on the side of the antiwar movement.

For most, the religion inspired by television scenes was old-fashioned patriotism. High mass was the Super Bowl in Tampa on January 27. Seventy-two thousand hand-sized flags were distributed to the arriving faithful.

"The Pentagon," remarked Walter Goodman, "won ground superiority over the press before it achieved air superiority over the Iraqis."[11] Television showed troops in preparation, convoys moving, artillery pieces firing at unseen targets, and fighter planes streaking down runways and dropping "smart" bombs on factories and bridges. Much of this action, however, had occurred hours earlier. Apart from the opening scenes in Baghdad and the later flashes of incoming Scuds and Patriot missiles rising in attack, little live action appeared on television during the hundred hours of the ground war.

Television made a folk hero of Gen. H. Norman Schwarzkopf, the able allied commander with a strapping frame and chubby face. Nicknamed "the bear" by his family, he was gruff on one side, warm on the other, and perfectly cool on television. After firing in the desert had ceased, he gave an hour-long news briefing on the winning strategy, an exposition that for fascinating narrative and clarity probably has no parallel in the history of television. Since Eisenhower and MacArthur, no other military figure has made such an impression on Americans as Schwarzkopf did. And with his plain talk and modesty, he resembled Eisenhower in manner much more than he did the haughty MacArthur. Eisenhower's genius as a leader was in instilling confidence in the public as well as in his forces. Aided by television, Schwarzkopf's impact was similar.

In different ways the shadow of Vietnam overhung the Gulf War. President Bush successfully exploited the power of television to assure the American people that he had not taken them into a futile, open-ended war like the detested conflict in Vietnam. The military, convinced that the United States lost the Vietnam War because of uncensored press and television coverage, imposed censorship with a vengeance in the Persian Gulf theater. Expertly indeed, the Pentagon almost completely controlled information about Operation Desert Storm. Reporters and photographers were not allowed to roam on their own in search of action. They were chaperoned by military public affairs officers and forced to operate in pools, which went only where the military wanted them to go. Reporters and photographers had little or no access to the fighting. Consequently, CNN and the other networks for hours lacked up-to-date action to broadcast. Even viewers who vigorously approved of military censorship were furious at the frequent reruns of old news from the Gulf. Photographers were not free to cover what viewers were impatient to see.

The Bush administration fetched up old stratagems that had paid off well in the 1988 presidential campaign. In Michael Deaver style, the White House concentrated on a message-of-the-day to keep people's minds straight about the administration's aims and concerns. As in the 1988 campaign, statements by Saddam Hussein or other criticisms were to be answered within hours. Public relations was always a high priority. "When you have, day after day . . . and hour after hour repetition of television coverage of our people out there in the Gulf," Secretary of Defense Richard B. Cheney observed, "it's just one tremendous piece of advertising for the United States military and for the people who serve in it."[12]

Lt. Gen. Thomas E. Kelly, the Pentagon's operations briefer, became an overnight celebrity. He conceded that the administration had "very much" used satellite television to send signals to Baghdad. "Every single time I mentioned the use of chemical weapons in a press briefing," he said in an interview after the cease-fire, "I would look into the camera and say, 'You must understand, any commander who uses chemical weapons is going to be held accountable for his actions.' I knew they watched CNN in Iraq, and I wanted those guys to hear that."[13]

After the first stage of the allied bombing of Baghdad, the Hussein government ordered all foreign journalists except Arnett to leave the country. Familiar with the unique worldwide audience of CNN, the Iraqis believed their purposes might be well served by keeping that network in operation in Iraq. Indeed, Saddam Hussein gave Arnett an exclusive interview. In his rounds of Baghdad, however, Arnett could cover only scenes authorized by the Iraqi government, which invariably meant broadcasting footage of damage to nonmilitary targets. Arnett and his network repeatedly explained the circumstances to audiences who would not otherwise have been able to see anything in the besieged Iraqi capital. The very purpose of a free press is to give citizens legitimate information. In such an emotional time, however, some Americans overlooked the matter of freedom of the press and practically accused Arnett, one of the best reporters of his time, of being a traitor. From Schwarzkopf down, the military resented his reports of damage to civilian property while American briefers were reporting damage inflicted almost entirely on military targets. In fact, Arnett caught barely a speck of the total damage the United States wreaked on Iraq. For instance, bombing by the United States and its allies reduced Iraq's electrical generating capacity to the level of 1920.[14] In less emotional times, Arnett's audience would have had the good sense to realize that filling the air with bombers and missiles would lead to death and destruction below. But a great many overwrought people at home did not want any reporting at all except unquestioning coverage of encouraging statements by military briefers. Arnett had a right to broadcast news from Baghdad. When the fighting ended, the worst of the controversy about him subsided.

A middle ground existed in these disputes. It was that in Baghdad CNN leaned too far beyond legitimate news by also making its facilities available for Iraqi propaganda. Those who held this view did not suppose such propaganda would sway opinion and public policy in the United States. Their main concern was its effect elsewhere in the Middle East and other parts of the world serviced by CNN. The war ended too quickly for any satisfactory judgment to be formed on this position. Nothing CNN ever broadcast weakened the anti-Iraq coalition. Hostilities lasted long enough to demonstrate a classic case of news management by the White House and the Pentagon.

Although curtailed by censorship, television news was powerful enough to arouse passionate support in America for the nation's war aims. Following the cease-fire, television news again proved its power: it placed heavy pressure on the high-riding Bush administration to do an about-face on its policy regarding Kurdish refugees on the northern Iraqi borders. At first the president's policy had been to bring American forces home from the desert as quickly as possible and to keep Americans out of the internal affairs of devastated Iraq. But then Saddam Hussein, still in power, turned his guns on hundreds of thousands of rebelling Kurds inhabiting Iraq and sent them fleeing for safety. Day after day television news flooded American homes with intimate scenes of refugees, many of them babies and small children, freezing, starving, and dying. Viewers found the tragedy intolerable.

Bush had publicly called on the Kurds and others in Iraq to rise up and drive Hussein from power. But when the Kurds tried to do so, Bush made no attempt to save them from Hussein's armed forces. Later the president modified his policy. Reacting to the public mood and to pressures from the British, French, and Turks, he sent American troops into Iraq to protect, feed, and shelter the refugees.

The government's reliance on television, especially CNN, in critical situations, has become a familiar story. As Michael Deaver, President Ronald Reagan's television adviser, recalled,

Any time there was a world crisis, where would we be? The president and all of us—we'd be back there in his little alcove with the television on. The National Security Council and the situation room would bring us bulletins, but we knew things from watching television ten minutes before the NSC and the Situation Room.[15]

Again, beginning August 19, 1991, satellite television images held the world in thrall. A Soviet hardliners' coup against Soviet President Mikhail Gorbachev collapsed on live television. For three days television pulsated with the kind of electronic pictures that producers dream about—tanks on the move in Moscow streets; Russian leader Boris Yeltsin atop a tank, calling for defiance; the towering statue of Feliks Dzershinsky, godfather of the Soviet secret police, toppled from its pedestal; defiant Muscovites bestowing garlands on soldiers; Gorbachev at the air terminal, smiling wanly as he returns from his brief captivity—the world saw it all.

Another little TV drama was the appearance of the conspirators. Grim and gray, they used television to plead their case to their own people and the world beyond. This proved a mistake. Robert Abernethy, the NBC Moscow correspondent, reported, "Many Russians told me that they watched that press conference and saw the confusion, ineptness and fumbling of those people and realized they were not competent to run the country. So they went to the barricades."[16]

In the eyes of American televiewers the cold war was finally ending. A woman in Houston who watched the panoply of pictures from Moscow told the *New York Times*, "I realized that they lived, they love, they bleed, they die the same as anyone else even though for years we have been taught different."[17] More than at any time since World War II, Americans found the people of Russia kindred souls who shared a love of freedom. Jonathan Yardley wrote in the *Washington Post* that the event was a "genuinely new world order in which boundaries between cultures have been lowered if not indeed obliterated by television."[18]

George F. Kennan, the father of Soviet containment and leading diplomatic authority on the USSR, who found it difficult "to find any other turning point in history that is so significant as this one," attributed the resolve of the Russian people in resisting the coup "to the modern communications revolution."[19]

Because of the electric eye, the bumbling moves of the "gang of eight" could not be hidden. It was widely expected that they would pull the plug on television news transmissions to the outside world; but they could not, and this proved a major setback. The plotters several times ordered that CNN be shut down, and the head of Soviet TV, Leonid Kravchenko, gave orders to his staff to turn it off, "but they silently sabotaged his orders," according to Eason Jordan, CNN vice-president for international news gathering.[20]

CNN again became an agent of history. When Yeltsin stood on a tank to rally the people, he knew that although the event might not appear on Soviet TV, it would be picked up by CNN and the other Western networks and beamed back to the Russian people. One administration official told the *Washington Post* that the first consideration on hearing about the coup was not how to cable instructions to American diplomats but how to get a statement on CNN that could shape the response of all the allies. "Diplomatic communications just can't keep up with CNN," the official said.[21] When President Bush spoke out at news conferences in support of the democratic forces in Moscow, his words would travel much swifter by global TV than by any diplomatic channel. These facts, in addition to the pictures of resistance inside and outside the Russian parliament building, energized the resisters.

During Gorbachev's time of greatest peril on the second day of the coup, while he was being held captive in the Crimea, he turned to television as a possible means of escape. At 2 A.M. he turned off all the lights at his vacation home, closed the windows and doors, and went to an upstairs bedroom with his son-in-law to videotape a message to the Soviet people that he was not ill, as the plotters had asserted, and that he was resisting their attempt to put him down. As his daughter's husband operated a home videocamera Gorbachev taped his message in the hope of smuggling it out, thus alerting the Soviet people to the true circumstances surrounding the coup attempt. As it turned out, he was rescued the next day, and the clandestine tape was broadcast later as part of the historical record.

Still another sign of television's central role in the second Russian revolution was noted by, among others, Tom Fenton of CBS News. Fenton was watching the Soviet TV news program "Vestnik." A gray-suited TV announcer caught himself in mid-sentence, "stared confusedly at the sheet of paper he had been handed, and in one breath, switched from the coup leaders' line to the reformers'."[22]

The television eye remained in close-up as the weeks tumbled on and sweeping change engulfed the Soviet Union. No one could say how it would all sort out. If there was a lesson in the remarkable events, it was again that in the age of the satellite no country can any longer seal its borders.

In the four decades beginning with 1948, television news has become a prime medium of domestic as well as international communication. Tiananmen Square, the Berlin Wall, the Persian Gulf War, and the retreat from Soviet communism are but recent chapters in a communications revolution that will continue to affect and shape the world for years to come.

Of all the wonders brought by the television revolution, none has the prospect of contributing more to world peace and understanding than broadcasting live via satellite, the miracle of electronics that enables mankind to be everywhere instantly. Inventors toiled with remarkable speed to perfect the technology needed to send pictures and messages across national boundaries. The question is whether politicians and diplomats, as well as journalists, can summon comparable ingenuity to put to best use the new democratizing power of global television.

Notes

Preface

1 Agnew text, *New York Times,* November 14, 1969, p. 24.
2 Interview with James K. Batten.
3 Reuven Frank, commentary on "Television: The Power of Pictures," documentary on Public Broadcasting Service, September 21, 1987.
4 *Associated Press Managing Editors Redbook,* 1967 (a transcript of APME annual meetings), pp. 99, 100.

1. Police dogs, firehoses, and television cameras

1 Juan Williams, *Eyes on the Prize: America's Civil Rights Years, 1954–1965* (New York: Viking, 1987), pp. 101, 102.
2 *Covering the South: A National Symposium on the Media and the Civil Rights Movement* (hereafter, Symposium), April 3–5, 1987, University of Mississippi, comments by Robert Schakne, Panel 1, pp. 34, 35.
3 Ibid., p. 34.
4 Peter J. Boyer, *Who Killed CBS?* (New York: Random House, 1988), p. 229.
5 Letter, 1987, John Chancellor to the authors.
6 John Chancellor, "Radio and Television Had Their Own Problems in Little Rock Coverage," *The Quill,* December 1957, pp. 9, 10.
7 Symposium, Karl Fleming, oral history transcript, p. 14.
8 Symposium, John Chancellor, Panel 1, p. 42.
9 Wallace Westfeldt, quoted in Gwenda Blair, *Almost Golden: Jessica Savitch and the Selling of Television News* (New York: Simon & Schuster, 1988), pp. 71, 72.
10 Symposium, Jack Nelson, oral history transcript, pp. 33, 34.
11 Symposium, Eugene Roberts, oral history transcript, pp. 17, 18.
12 Symposium, Hodding Carter III, Panel 5, p. 3.
13 Symposium, John Seigenthaler, Panel 3, p. 41.
14 Symposium, John O. Emmerich, Jr., Panel 2, pp. 7, 8.
15 Symposium, Arlie W. Schardt, oral history transcript, p. 10.
16 Symposium, John Herbers, oral history transcript, p. 4.
17 Symposium, Richard R. Sanders, oral history transcript, p. 22.

18 Symposium, Cliff Sessions, oral history transcript, p. 4.
19 "The Negro on TV," editorial in the *Nation,* November 22, 1965, p. 374.
20 Fred W. Friendly, *The Good Guys, the Bad Guys and the First Amendment: Free Speech Versus Fairness in Broadcasting* (New York: Random House, 1975), p. 91.
21 Dan Rather, with Mickey Herskowitz, *The Camera Never Blinks: Adventures of a TV Journalist* (New York: William Morrow, 1977), pp. 76, 77.
22 Symposium, Claude F. Sitton, oral history transcript.
23 Rather, *The Camera Never Blinks,* p. 71.
24 Symposium, Karl Fleming.
25 Peter Jennings, "There's More I Want to Know," *Parade,* October 15, 1989, p. 4.
26 Rather, *The Camera Never Blinks,* pp. 79–82.
27 Ibid., pp. 79–82.
28 Interview with Richard Valeriani, 1987.
29 Symposium, Charles Quinn, Panel 2, p. 24.
30 David J. Garrow, *Bearing the Cross: Martin Luther King, Jr. and the Southern Christian Leadership Conference* (New York: Vintage Books, 1988), p. 66.
31 Ibid., p. 97.
32 Symposium, Herbert Kaplow, oral history transcript, pp. 22, 23.
33 Symposium, Charles Quinn, Panel 2, pp. 24, 25.
34 Garrow, *Bearing the Cross,* p. 239.
35 Symposium, Hodding Carter III, Panel 5, p. 4.
36 Interview with Joseph L. Rauh, Jr., 1987.
37 Robert Kennedy, Jr., *In His Own Words: The Unpublished Recollections of the Kennedy Years* (New York: Bantam, 1988), pp. 171, 172.
38 Howard Schuman, Charlotte Steeh, and Lawrence Bobo, *Racial Attitudes in America* (Cambridge, Mass.: Harvard University Press, 1985), pp. 25, 26.
39 *Presidential Papers of the Presidents: John F. Kennedy, 1963* (Washington, D.C.: U.S. Government Printing Office, 1964), p. 469.
40 Robert E. Kintner, *Broadcasting and the News,* reprint from *Harper's Magazine* by special permission (New York: Harper & Row, 1965), p. 95.
41 Williams, *Eyes on the Prize,* p. 252.
42 Garrow, *Bearing the Cross,* p. 381.
43 Symposium, Jack Bass, oral history transcript, p. 27.
44 Symposium, Richard Valeriani, oral history transcript, p. 18.
45 Lyndon Baines Johnson, *The Vantage Point: Perspectives of the Presidency, 1963–1969* (London: Weidenfeld & Nicolson, 1971), p. 162.
46 Ibid., p. 165.
47 Ibid.
48 Interview with Burke Marshall, 1987.
49 Stephen F. Lawson, *In Pursuit of Power: Southern Blacks and Electoral Politics, 1965–1982* (New York: Columbia University Press, 1985), p. 14.
50 Quoted in Johnson, *The Vantage Point,* p. 159.

51 Eugene Patterson, "A Flower for the Grave," *Atlanta Constitution*, September 16, 1963, p. 4.

52 Interview with Eugene Patterson, 1987.

53 Frank Mankiewicz and Joel Swerdlow, *Remote Control: Television and the Manipulation of American Life* (New York: Times Books, 1978), p. 104.

2. Exit Joe McCarthy

1 Robert Griffith, *The Politics of Fear: Joseph R. McCarthy and the Senate*, 2d ed. (Amherst: University of Massachusetts Press, 1987), p. 320.

2 Stephen E. Ambrose, *Eisenhower*, Vol. II: *The President* (New York: Simon & Schuster, 1984), pp. 161, 162.

3 Griffith, *Politics of Fear*, pp. 244, 260.

4 A. M. Sperber, *Murrow: His Life and Times* (New York: Bantam, 1986), p. 428.

5 Ibid., p. 434.

6 Barbara Matusow, *The Evening Stars: The Making of the Network News Anchor* (Boston: Houghton Mifflin, 1983), pp. 67, 68.

7 The foregoing passage draws on Alexander Kendrick, *Prime Time: The Life of Edward R. Murrow* (Boston: Little, Brown, 1969), p. 52; and Sperber, *Murrow*, pp. 436, 437.

8 Sperber, *Murrow*, pp. 438, 439.

9 Ibid., p. 440.

10 *Public Papers of the President of the United States: Dwight D. Eisenhower, 1954* (Washington, D.C.: U.S. Government Printing Office, 1960), p. 382.

11 John Charles Daly, transcript, "A Free Press: Endangered or Dangerous?" Smithsonian Institution Symposium, November 26, 1986.

12 Max Wilk, *The Golden Age of Television* (New York: Delacorte Press, 1976), pp. 257, 258.

13 Daly transcript.

14 *Newsweek*, May 24, 1954, p. 84.

15 Wilk, *Golden Age*, p. 257.

16 *Congress and the Nation, 1945–1964: A Review of Government and Politics in the Postwar Years* (Washington, D.C.: Congressional Quarterly, 1965), pp. 1721, 1725.

17 *Congress and the Nation*, p. 1721.

18 Griffith, *Politics of Fear*, pp. 260, 261.

19 U.S. Senate, *Hearings Before the Special Subcommittee on Investigations of the Committee on Government Operations, 83d Cong., 2d sess., Pt. 59*, pp. 24, 26–30.

20 Ibid., pp. 26–30.

21 Sperber, *Murrow*, p. 369.

22 Roy Cohn, *McCarthy* (New York: New American Library, 1968), p. 204.

23 Edwin R. Bayley, *Joe McCarthy and the Press* (Madison: The University of Wisconsin Press, 1981), pp. 208, 209.

24   Kendrick, *Prime Time*, pp. 53, 54.
25   Griffith, *Politics of Fear*, p. 270.
26   Sperber, *Murrow*, p. 471.
27   Griffith, *Politics of Fear*, p. 264.
28   Gladys Engel Lang and Kurt Lang, *The President, the Press and the Polls During Watergate* (New York: Columbia University Press, 1983), p. 67.
29   Marya Mannes, *The Reporter*, June 8, 1954, pp. 40–42.

3. Television news and the ups and downs of Richard Nixon

 1   Richard M. Nixon, "Memo to President Bush: How to Use TV—and Keep from Being Abused by It," *TV Guide*, January 14, 1989, pp. 26ff.
 2   Newton Minow, John Bartlow Martin, Lee M. Mitchell, *Presidential Television: A Twentieth Century Fund Report* (New York: Basic Books, 1973), pp. 55, 56.
 3   Thomas Whiteside, "Annals of Television: Shaking the Tree," *New Yorker*, March 17, 1975, pp. 41, 42, 46.
 4   Memo for Haldeman from the President, April 30, 1972, Folder: HRH 1972 memoranda from the President, Box 162, Nixon Presidential Materials, National Archives, Alexandria, Va. (hereafter NPM).
 5   Whiteside, "Annals of Television," p. 45.
 6   Haldeman Memo to the President, October 14, 1971, Folder: Haldeman Action Memos, Box 179, NPM.
 7   RN Memo to Haldeman, April 30, 1972, Box 162, Folder: HRH Memoranda from the President, NPM.
 8   Haldeman Files, Box 112, Folder: Haldeman Action Memos, November 10, 1972, NPM.
 9   William Safire, *Before the Fall: An Inside View of the Pre-Watergate White House* (Garden City, N.Y.: Doubleday, 1975), pp. 352, 353.
10   Nixon, "Memo."
11   Richard M. Nixon, *RN: The Memoirs of Richard Nixon* (New York: Grosset & Dunlap, 1978), p. 92.
12   Richard M. Nixon, *Six Crises* (Garden City, N.Y.: Doubleday, 1962), p. 115.
13   Ibid.
14   Ibid., p. 117.
15   Nixon, *Memoirs*, p. 105.
16   Theodore H. White, *Breach of Faith: The Fall of Richard Nixon* (New York: Atheneum, 1975), p. 40.
17   Garry Wills, *Nixon Agonistes: The Crisis of the Self-Made Man* (Boston: Houghton Mifflin, 1970), p. 92.
18   Nixon, *Memoirs*, p. 208.
19   Safire, *Before the Fall*, p. 6.
20   Nixon, *Memoirs*, p. 208.
21   Safire, *Before the Fall*, pp. 5, 6.

22   Theodore H. White, *The Making of the President, 1960* (New York: Atheneum, 1961), p. 178.
23   Stephen E. Ambrose, *Eisenhower, Volume Two, The President* (New York: Simon & Schuster, 1984), p. 601.
24   Lawrence F. O'Brien, *No Final Victories: A Life in Politics from John F. Kennedy to Watergate* (Garden City, N.Y.: Doubleday, 1974), p. 94.
25   Nixon, *Memoirs*, p. 217.
26   Erik Barnouw, *Tube of Plenty: The Evaluation of American Television* (New York: Oxford University Press, 1975), p. 274.
27   Nixon, *Six Crises*, p. 337.
28   O'Brien, *No Final Victories*, p. 94.
29   Text of Bill Moyers Special (PBS), *Campaign: The Prime Time President,* October 3, 1988, pp. 7, 8.
30   Ibid.
31   White, *Making of the President, 1960*, pp. 287, 288.
32   Philip Deane in *The London Observer*. Quoted in Joe McGinniss, *The Selling of the President 1968* (New York: Trident Press, 1969), pp. 185, 186.

4. *Television's march on Cape Canaveral*

1   Figure supplied by Professor John M. Logsdon of George Washington University.
2   Interview with Robert Asman, 1987.
3   Interview with Herbert Kaplow, 1987.
4   Ibid.
5   John M. Logsdon, *The Decision to Go to the Moon* (Chicago: University of Chicago Press, 1970), p. 20.
6   "Statement by the President on the flight of Astronaut Alan B. Shepard," *Public Papers of the Presidents, John F. Kennedy, 1961*, p. 353.
7   Memorandum, Abraham Silverstein to James E. Webb, September 6, 1961, NASA Historical Archives, Washington, D.C.
8   Interview with Robert J. Shafer, director of Television Development for NASA, 1987.
9   Interview with James Kitchell, 1987.
10   Interview with Julian Scheer, 1987.
11   Ibid.
12   Interview with Brian Duff, 1987.
13   Interview with John Finney, 1987.
14   Interview with Howard Simon, 1987.
15   Edwin Diamond, "Perfect Match: TV and Space," *Columbia Journalism Review* (Summer 1965): 20.
16   Barbara Matusow, *The Evening Stars: The Making of the Network News Anchor* (Boston: Houghton Mifflin, 1983), p. 127.
17   *Broadcasting*, February 26, 1962, p. 50.
18   *New York Times*, February 2, 1962, p. 91.

19   Letter, John Glenn to Joseph Angotti, April 25, 1964, supplied by Angotti.
20   Interview with Brian Duff, 1987.
21   Ibid.
22   Interview with Julian Scheer, 1987.
23   "Visions of the Lunar Voyage," *Life,* May 30, 1969, p. 51.
24   Crosby Noyes, *Washington Star,* August 6, 1971, p. 13.
25   Letter, Chet Hagan to Angotti, November 11, 1963, supplied by Angotti.
26   *New York Times,* January 29, 1986, p. C21.

5. Television's supreme hour

1   Robert MacNeil, *The Right Place at the Right Time* (Boston: Little, Brown, 1982), pp. 212, 213. Also William Manchester, *The Death of a President: November 20–November 25, 1963* (New York: Harper & Row, 1967), p. 279.
2   Barbara Matusow, *The Evening Stars: The Making of the Network News Anchor* (Boston: Houghton Mifflin, 1983), p. 104.
3   The foregoing passage is based on Albert R. Kroeger, "The Four Days," *Television,* January 1964, pp. 31, 32; Elmer W. Lower, "A Television Network Gathers the News," in *The Kennedy Assassination and the American Public,* ed. Bradley S. Greenberg and Edwin B. Parker (Stanford, Calif.: Stanford University Press, 1965), p. 69.
4   Interview with Julian Goodman, 1988.
5   Matusow, *Evening Stars,* p. 5.
6   Interview with William B. Monroe, 1988.
7   Special Report, "A World Listened and Watched," *Broadcasting,* December 2, 1963, p. 36.
8   Thomas J. Schoenbaum, *Waging Peace and War: Dean Rusk in the Truman, Kennedy, and Johnson Years* (New York: Simon & Schuster, 1986), p. 402.
9   Interview with Julian Goodman, 1988.
10 Lower, "A Television Network," p. 70.
11 Tom Pettit, "The Television Story in Dallas," in *The Kennedy Assassination and the American Public,* p. 65.
12 National Broadcasting Company, News Division, *Seventy Hours and Thirty Minutes as Broadcast on the NBC Television Network by NBC News* (New York: Random House, 1966), p. 92.
13 Kroeger, "The Four Days," p. 58.
14 Manchester, *Death of a President,* p. 452.
15 Ibid., p. 590.
16 William A. Mindak and Gerald D. Hursh, "Television's Function on the Assassination Weekend," in *The Kennedy Assassination and the American Public,* p. 137.
17 Ibid., p. 140.
18 Ibid., p. 141.
19 Report, A. C. Nielsen Co., "TV Responses to the Death of a President," New York, 1964.

6. In the eye of the storm

1   Juan Williams, *Eyes on the Prize, America's Civil Rights Years, 1954–1965* (New York: Viking Penguin, 1987), p. 287.
2   McCone Commission Report, quoted in Jerry Cohen and William S. Murphy, *Burn, Baby, Burn* (New York: E. P. Dutton, 1986), p. 317.
3   Ibid., p. 98.
4   Ibid., pp. 98–100.
5   Frank Haven, *Associated Press Managing Editors* (APME) *Red Book,* 1965, pp. 106–8.
6   Hal Humphrey, "TV Riot Coverage Too Sensitive," *Los Angeles Times,* August 17, 1965, pt. 4, p. 14.
7   "How Do You Cover Hell?" *Newsweek,* August 30, 1965, p. 50.
8   Elmer Lower, speech before Sigma Delta Chi, Buffalo, N.Y., September 21, 1967, quoted in *Congressional Record,* October 11, 1967, p. S14655.
9   Neil Hickey, "Do TV Cameras Add Fuel to Riot Flames?" *TV Guide,* September 16, 1967, p. 11.
10 Lower, Buffalo speech, quoted in *Congressional Record,* p. S14654.
11 Interview with Robert Shafer, 1988.
12 Interview with Fred Rheinstein, 1988.
13 Lower, Buffalo speech, quoted in *Congressional Record,* p. S14653.
14 Report of the National Advisory Commission on Civil Disorders, March 3, 1968, pt. III, Chap. 15, p. 11.
15 Ibid., pp. 19, 20.
16 Ibid., pp. 30, 31.
17 Ibid., pp. 10, 11.
18 Ibid., pp. 3, 27, 48.

7. Vietnam, 1965–1967

1   Morley Safer, *Flashbacks: On Returning to Vietnam* (New York: Random House, 1990), pp. 89, 90.
2   Quoted in William M. Hammond, *The U.S. Army in Vietnam: Public Affairs, the Military and the Media, 1962–1968* (Washington, D.C.: Center for Military History, 1988), p. 187.
3   Ibid., p. 188.
4   Ibid., p. 189.
5   Ibid., p. 189.
6   Ibid., p. 190.
7   Ibid., p. 191.
8   Interview with Barry Zorthian, 1988.
9   Barry Zorthian, oral history transcript, pt. 2, pp. 17–19, Lyndon Baines Johnson Library, Austin, Texas.
10 Lawrence W. Lichty and Edward Fouhy, "Television Reporting of the Vietnam War," *The World and I,* April 1987, p. 581.
11 Hammond, *U.S. Army in Vietnam,* p. 188.

12 "CBS Evening News with Walter Cronkite," August 5, 1965, quoted in Lichty and Fouhy, "Television Reporting," p. 581.
13 William M. Hammond, "The Press in Vietnam as Agent of Defeat: A Critical Examination," in *Reviews in American History,* ed. by Stanley Kutler (Baltimore: Johns Hopkins University Press, 1989), p. 11.
14 Lichty and Fouhy, "Television Reporting," p. 582.
15 Richard Nixon, *RN: The Memoirs of Richard Nixon* (New York: Grosset & Dunlap, 1978), p. 350.
16 William Westmoreland, *A Soldier Reports* (Garden City, N.Y.: Doubleday, 1976), p. 420.
17 Robert Elegant, "How to Lose a War: Reflections of a Foreign Correspondent," in *Vietnam Reconsidered: Lessons from a War,* ed. Harrison Salisbury (New York: Harper & Row, 1984), pp. 145, 146.
18 Quoted in "Vietnam and Electronic Journalism," *Broadcasting,* May 19, 1975, p. 26.
19 John Mueller, *War, Presidents and Public Opinion* (Lanham, Md.: University Press of America, 1985), p. 53.
20 Hammond, *U.S. Army in Vietnam,* p. 181.
21 Ibid., p. 182.
22 Edward J. Epstein, "Changing Focus," *TV Guide,* October 13, 1973, p. 49.
23 George Bailey, "Interpretive Reporting of the Vietnam War by Anchormen," *Journalism Quarterly* (Summer 1976): 319–24.
24 Daniel Hallin, *The Uncensored War: The Media and Vietnam* (New York: Oxford University Press, 1986), p. 133.
25 Ibid., p. 110.
26 Raymond L. Carroll and Lawrence W. Lichty, "National Network Television Programs About the Vietnam War, 1957–1971," paper presented at the Speech Communications Association, Chicago, December 28, 1972.
27 Hammond, *U.S. Army in Vietnam,* p. 387.
28 Ibid.
29 Ibid.
30 Westmoreland, *A Soldier Reports,* p. 420.
31 "The Air: The Falklands, Vietnam and Our Collective Memory," *New Yorker,* August 16, 1982, p. 71.
32 Lichty and Fouhy, "Television Reporting," p. 584.
33 Hammond, "The Press in Vietnam," p. 316.
34 Edward J. Epstein, "What Happened vs. What We Saw," *TV Guide,* September 29, 1973, p. 10.
35 Lichty and Fouhy, "Television Reporting," pp. 583, 584.
36 Neil Hickey, *TV Guide,* October 1, 1966, pp. 12, 13.
37 Ibid., p. 8.
38 Figures supplied by the Center of Military History, U.S. Army, Washington, D.C.
39 Hammond, *U.S. Army in Vietnam,* pp. 387, 388.
40 Ibid., pp. 153, 155.
41 Hallin, *Uncensored War,* pp. 140–41.

42 Ibid., p. 146.
43 Michael Arlen, "The Road from Highway 1," *New Yorker,* May 5, 1975, p. 122.

8. Vietnam, 1968–1975

1 Godfrey Sperling, Jr., "A Memorable Breakfast with RFK," *Christian Science Monitor,* June 14, 1988, p. 3.
2 Ibid.
3 Don Oberdorfer, *TET!* (Garden City, N.Y.: Doubleday, 1971), p. 18.
4 President's Daily Diary, January 30, 1968, Lyndon Baines Johnson Library, Austin, Texas.
5 Memos for the President. National Security File, NSC History, March 31 speech, Box 47, vol. 2, nos. 6–10, LBJ Library.
6 Peter Braestrup, *Big Story: How the American Press and Television Reported and Interpreted the Crisis of Tet 1968 in Vietnam and Washington,* abridged ed. (New Haven: Yale University Press, 1977), p. 117.
7 Ibid., p. 116.
8 Daniel Hallin, *The Uncensored War: The Media and Vietnam* (New York: Oxford University Press, 1986), p. 169.
9 Braestrup, *Big Story,* pp. 508ff.
10 Ibid., p. 132.
11 Ibid., p. 133.
12 Hallin, *Uncensored War,* p. 345.
13 William C. Berman, *William Fulbright and the Vietnam War* (Kent, Ohio: Kent State University Press, 1988), pp. 55, 56.
14 David J. Garrow, *Bearing the Cross: Martin Luther King, Jr., and the Southern Christian Leadership Conference* (New York: Vintage Books, 1988), p. 454.
15 William M. Hammond, *United States Army in Vietnam: Public Affairs, the Military and the Media, 1962–1968* (Washington, D.C.: Center for Military History, United States Army, 1988), pp. 288, 289.
16 Curtis Prendergast, with Geoffrey Colvin, *The World of Time, Inc.: The Intimate History of a Changing Enterprise,* vol. 3: *1960–1980* (New York: Atheneum, 1986), pp. 241, 242.
17 Ibid., pp. 250, 251.
18 George A. Bailey and Lawrence W. Lichty, "Rough Justice on a Saigon Street: A Gatekeeper Study of NBC's Tet Execution Film," *Journalism Quarterly* (Summer 1972): 221–29, 238.
19 Ibid., p. 223.
20 Ibid., p. 226.
21 Ibid., p. 238.
22 David Culbert, "Television's Vietnam and Historical Revisionism in the United States," *Historical Journal of Film, Radio and Television,* November 3, 1988, p. 261.
23 Hallin, *Uncensored War,* p. 168.

24   Peter Grose, "Rusk Says Enemy Rules Out Talks," *New York Times,* February 5, 1968, pp. 1, 14.
25   Braestrup, *Big Story,* p. 468.
26   Hammond, *U.S. Army in Vietnam,* p. 369.
27   Interview with George Christian, 1988.
28   Hallin, *Uncensored War,* p. 168.
29   John E. Mueller, "Reflections on the Vietnam Antiwar Movement and on the Curious Calm at the War's End," in *Vietnam as History Ten Years After the Paris Accords,* ed. Peter Braestrup (Lanham, Md.: University Press of America, 1984), p. 106.
30   "Westmoreland Requests 206,000 More Men," *New York Times,* March 10, 1968, p. 1.
31   "U.S. Is Losing War in Vietnam," *New York Times,* March 11, 1968, p. 82.
32   Braestrup, *Big Story,* p. 470.
33   Neil Sheehan, *A Bright Shining Lie: John Paul Vann and America in Vietnam* (New York: Random House, 1988), p. 702.
34   Newton N. Minow, John Bartlow Martin and Lee M. Mitchell, *Presidential Television, A Twentieth Century Fund Report* (New York: Basic Books, 1973), p. 59.
35   Ibid., p. 62.
36   Lawrence W. Lichty and Edward Fouhy, "Television Reporting of the Vietnam War," *The World and I,* April 1987, p. 577.
37   Ibid., p. 579.
38   Mueller, "Reflections," pp. 51ff.
39   Michael Arlen, "The Road from Highway 1," *New Yorker,* May 5, 1975, pp. 122ff.
40   Hammond, *U.S. Army in Vietnam,* p. 388.

9. Nixon's presidency, a difficult time

1   Richard M. Nixon, *RN: The Memoirs of Richard Nixon* (New York: Grosset & Dunlap, 1978), pp. 244, 245.
2   Text of Nixon press conference, *New York Times,* November 8, 1962, p. 20.
3   Jules Witcover, *The Resurrection of Richard Nixon* (New York: G. P. Putnam's Sons, 1970), p. 14.
4   Nixon, *Memoirs,* p. 246.
5   "Many Chicagoans Assail Hiss Appearance on TV," *Chicago Tribune,* November 12, 1962, p. 1.
6   Nixon, *Memoirs,* p. 246.
7   *Public Papers of the Presidents of the United States, Richard Nixon, 1969* (Washington, D.C.: U.S. Government Printing Office, 1971), p. 246.
8   Haldeman Files, Box 30, March 1969 folder, Nixon Presidential Materials, National Archives, Alexandria, Va. (hereafter NPM).
9   J. Anthony Lukas, *Nightmare: The Underside of the Nixon Years* (New York: Viking Press, 1976), p. 270.

10 Haldeman Files, Box 30, September 1969 folder, NPM.
11 Memo for the President from Buchanan, September 28, 1969, Haldeman File, Folder: President's Office Files: Annotated News Summaries, September 1969, Box 30, NPM.
12 Stephen E. Ambrose, *Nixon, The Triumph of a Politician 1962–1972,* vol. 2 (New York: Simon & Schuster, 1989), pp. 248, 249.
13 William Safire, *Before the Fall* (Garden City, N.Y.: Doubleday, 1975), p. 343.
14 Nixon, *Memoirs,* p. 245.
15 Memo for Haldeman from J. S. Magruder, October 17, 1969, Box 141, HRH Public Relations file, NPM.
16 Haldeman File, December 8, 1969, Box 152, Folder: Talking Papers, NPM.
17 *Public Papers of the Presidents, Nixon, November 3, 1969,* pp. 901–9; letters 910, 911.
18 Interview with Marvin Kalb, 1988.
19 Text supplied from CBS files.
20 Safire, *Before the Fall,* pp. 346, 352.
21 Thomas Whiteside, "Annals of Television: Shaking the Tree," *New Yorker,* March 17, 1975, pp. 42, 43.
22 *New York Times,* November 14, 1969, p. 24.
23 Ibid.
24 Nixon, *Memoirs,* pp. 411, 412.
25 Sig Mickelson, *The Electric Mirror: Politics in the Age of Television* (New York: Dodd, Mead, 1972), p. 165.
26 Daniel Schorr, "The Establishment Press," *The Center,* July–August 1979, pp. 2ff.
27 Interview with Marvin Kalb, 1988.
28 Marilyn A. Lashner, *The Chilling Effect in TV News* (New York: Praeger Publishers, 1984), p. 5.
29 Memorandum for Frank Haven from Nick B. Williams, August 16, 1968, *Los Angeles Times,* History Center.
30 Memo for the President from Buchanan, March 30, 1970, Haldeman Files, Folder: Memos for President, March 1970, Box 139, NPM.
31 *New York Times,* April 10, 1970, pp. 1, 14.
32 Memo for Herbert Klein and Ronald Ziegler from the President, April 21, 1970, Haldeman Files, Folder: Memos from the President, April 1970, NPM.
33 Memo for Haldeman from Charles Colson, September 25, 1970, Haldeman Files, Folder: Press and Media, Part 1, Box 141, NPM.
34 Memo for Alexander Butterfield from Haldeman, October 7, 1969, Haldeman Files, Folder: Memoranda for the President's File, November 1969, Box 138, NPM.
35 Memo for the President from Butterfield, October 7, 1969, Haldeman Files, Folder: Memoranda for the President's File, November 1969, Box 138, NPM.
36 Ibid.
37 Memo for Haldeman from the President, Haldeman Files, Folder: HRH Memoranda from the President, November 1970, Box 138, NPM.

38 Memo for Haldeman from Herbert Klein, December 18, 1970, Chapin Files, Box 18, NPM.
39 Thomas Thompson, "Chet Heads for the Hills," *Life,* July 17, 1970, p. 36.
40 Whiteside, "Annals of Television," p. 45.
41 Draft memo dealing with the media, November 23, 1970, Haldeman Files, Folder: HRH Memoranda for the President, Box 139, NPM.
42 Memo for Haldeman from the President, January 5, 1971, Haldeman folder, 1971, Box 140, NPM.
43 National Archives oral history interview with Charles Colson, June 15, 1988, p. 38, NPM.
44 Magruder folder, January 1971, Haldeman Files, Box 72, NPM.
45 Memos from Haldeman folder, January/February 1971, Chapin Files, Box 18, NPM.
46 Joseph C. Spear, *Presidents and the Press: The Nixon Legacy* (Cambridge: MIT Press, 1984), p. 89.
47 Memo to Haldeman from Roger Ailes, December 16, 1970, Haldeman Files, Box 139, NPM.
48 Memo from the President to Haldeman, January 14, 1971, Haldeman Files, Box 140, NPM.
49 Ibid.
50 Memo from the President to Haldeman, March 8, 1971, Haldeman Files, Box 140, NPM.
51 Memo from the President to Haldeman, June 2, 1971, Haldeman Files, Box 140, NPM.
52 Memo from the President to Haldeman, May 9, 1971, Haldeman Files, Box 141, NPM.
53 H. R. Haldeman, with Joseph Di Mona, *The Ends of Power* (New York: New York Times Books, 1978), p. 184.
54 Ibid., p. 185.
55 *The Washingtonian,* January 1989, p. 193. For the full quotation see *The President: Richard Nixon's Secret Files,* ed. Bruce Oudes (New York: Harper & Row, 1989).

10. Nixon in China and Watergate

1 Advertisement by Communications Satellite Corporation, *New York Times,* February 22, 1972, p. 13.
2 John J. O'Connor, "TV: Camera in Peking Shows Affairs of State," *New York Times,* February 22, 1972, p. 74.
3 Max Frankel, "Reporter's Notebook: But a Wall Survives," *New York Times,* February 25, 1972, p. 1.
4 Ibid.
5 Ibid.
6 *Washington Post,* February 28, 1972, p. A20.
7 "753 Dailies for Nixon; 56 Support McGovern," *Editor & Publisher,* November 4, 1972.

8 Memo for Buchanan from President, Haldeman Files, Box 162, Folder: HRH 1972 memos from President, Nixon Presidential Materials, National Archives, Alexandria, Va. (hereafter NPM).

9 Memo for the President from Buchanan, November 10, 1972, Haldeman Files, Box 162, Folder: Goal Memos, NPM.

10 Gladys Lang and Kurt Lang, *The President, the Press, and the Polls During Watergate* (New York: Columbia University Press, 1983), p. 40.

11 Theodore White, *Breach of Faith: The Fall of Richard Nixon* (New York: Atheneum, 1975), p. 177.

12 Richard M. Nixon, *RN: The Memoirs of Richard Nixon* (New York: Grosset & Dunlap, 1978), p. 978.

13 Ibid.

14 J. Anthony Lukas, *Nightmare: The Underside of the Nixon Years* (New York: Viking Press, 1976), p. 338.

15 Nixon, *Memoirs*, p. 850.

16 Ibid.

17 *New York Times*, November 18, 1973, p. 62.

18 *New York Times*, April 30, 1974, p. 32.

19 Lukas, *Nightmare*, p. 487.

20 Ibid., pp. 490, 491.

21 "A Triumphant Middle East Hegira," *Time*, June 24, 1974, p. 13.

22 Nixon, *Memoirs*, p. 1017.

23 Howard Fields, *High Crimes and Misdemeanors: "Wherefore Richard M. Nixon ... Warrants Impeachment." The Dramatic Story of the Rodino Committee* (New York: W. W. Norton, 1978), p. 274.

24 Ibid., pp. 229, 239.

25 Ibid., p. 241.

26 White, *Breach of Faith*, p. 316.

27 "Two Decades of Crisis Between Nixon and the Media," *Broadcasting*, August 19, 1974, p. 23.

28 Richard Nixon, "Memo to President Bush: How to Use TV—And Keep from Being Abused by It," *TV Guide*, January 14, 1989.

29 Ibid.

30 Ibid.

31 Ibid.

11. Infuriating pictures from Iran

1 Walter Goodman, "Day 3,650: Looking Back at the Hostage Crisis," *New York Times*, November 7, 1989, p. C22.

2 Howard Husock and Pamela Varley, "Siege Mentality: ABC, the White House, and the Iran Hostage Crisis," Kennedy School of Government Case Program, Harvard University, 1988, p. 3.

3 Ibid., p. 1.

4 Edward W. Said, "Iran," *Columbia Journalism Review* (March–April 1980): 25–27.

5   Ibid., p. 29.
6   William Safire, *Before the Fall: An Inside View of the Pre-Watergate White House* (Garden City, N.Y.: Doubleday, 1975), p. 458.
7   William A. Dorman and Mansaur Farhang, *The Press and Iran: Foreign Power and the Journalism of Deference* (Berkeley: University of California Press, 1987), pp. 139, 145, 147, 229.
8   James A. Bill, *The Eagle and the Lion: The Tragedy of American-Iranian Relations* (New Haven: Yale University Press, 1988), pp. 328–49.
9   Hedley Donovan, *Roosevelt to Reagan: A Reporter's Encounters with Nine Presidents* (New York: Harper & Row, 1985), p. 173.
10 Michael O'Neill, *Terrorist Spectaculars: Should TV Coverage Be Curbed?* A 20th Century Fund Paper (New York: Priority Press Publications, 1986), p. 43.
11 Husock and Varley, "Siege Mentality," p. 7.
12 Donovan, *Roosevelt to Reagan,* p. 181.
13 Robert Pierpoint interview with Jimmy Carter for "CBS Sunday Morning," aired October 15, 1989.
14 Tom Mathews, "America Closes Ranks," *Newsweek,* December 17, 1979, p. 42.
15 David Hoffman, "A Week of Crises Management," *Washington Post,* August 6, 1989, pp. 1, 14.
16 Hamilton Jordan, *Crises: The Last Year of the Carter Presidency* (New York: G. P. Putnam's Sons, 1982), p. 56.
17 Warren Christopher, "Introduction," in *American Hostages in Iran: The Conduct of a Crisis,* ed. Paul H. Kreisberg (New Haven: Yale University Press, 1985), pp. 25, 26.
18 Interview with Walter Mondale, 1987.
19 Interview with Walter Cronkite, 1988.
20 Edwin Diamond, *Sign Off: The Last Days of Television* (Cambridge, Mass.: MIT Press, 1983), 1st MIT Paperbacks ed., p. 110.
21 Interview with Walter Cronkite, 1988.
22 Ibid.
23 Arlie Schardt, "Dateline Teheran," *Newsweek,* December 3, 1979, p. 87.
24 Husock and Varley, "Siege Mentality," p. 13.
25 Michael Mossettig, "Diplomat Without Portfolio," *Channels* (June–July 1981): 48.
26 Mike Wallace and Mary Paul Yates, *Close Encounters* (New York: William Morrow, 1984), p. 327.
27 Ibid.
28 Interview with Walter Mondale, 1987.
29 Interview with Bill Leonard, 1989.
30 *New York Times,* April 2, 1980, p. A8.
31 *Washington Post,* April 2, 1980, p. 1.
32 *New York Times,* April 2, 1980, p. A1.
33 Interview with Walter Mondale, 1987.
34 Interview with Ray Jenkins, 1989.

35 ABC News "Nightline," November 3, 1989.
36 Ibid.

12. The call

1 Transcript of a talk by Joseph Angotti before the Ethiopian Famine Coverage Seminar on Philanthropy at Columbia College in New York, March 10, 1986.
2 Ibid.
3 Peter J. Boyer, "Famine in Ethiopia: The TV Accident That Exploded," *Washington Journalism Review* (January 1985): 21.
4 "Finally Relief," *Time,* November 12, 1964, pp. 65, 66.
5 Angotti transcript.
6 Boyer, "Famine in Ethiopia."
7 Joseph Berger, "Offers of Aid for Stricken Ethiopia Are Pouring into Relief Agencies," *New York Times,* October 28, 1984, p. 1.
8 Boyer, "Famine in Ethiopia," p. 19.
9 Joanne Omang, "TV Film of Emaciated Children Ended Apathy on Ethiopian Famine," *Washington Post,* November 21, 1984, p. A10.
10 "A Flood of Generosity," *Newsweek,* November 26, 1984, p. 56.
11 Interview with Peter Davies, 1988.
12 *Washington Post,* July 15, 1985, p. A19.
13 Keith Richburg, "Relief Office Battles World Disasters," *Washington Post,* October 24, 1985, p. A19.
14 Figures provided by the Ethiopian desk, Agency for International Development, Washington, D.C.
15 Robert J. McCloskey, "Opinion Shapes Policy on Famine Relief," *Los Angeles Times,* January 29, 1985, pt. II, p. 5.
16 "Millions Starve in Ethiopia as Drought Intensifies," *Facts on File,* November 30, 1984, p. 889.
17 Boyer, "Famine in Ethiopia," pp. 19, 20.

13. The White House in the television age

1 Gerald Rafshoon, "President McLuhan," *Nation,* February 11, 1978, p. 132.
2 Lloyd Cutler, "Foreign Policy on Deadline," *Foreign Policy* (Fall 1984): 1, 21.
3 *Public Papers of the Presidents of the United States: 1955: Dwight D. Eisenhower* (Washington, D.C.: U.S. Government Printing Office, 1959), p. 185.
4 *Public Papers of the Presidents of the United States: 1957* (Washington, D.C.: U.S. Government Printing Office, 1958), pp. 214, 215.
5 Sig Mickelson, *From Whistle Stop to Sound Bite* (New York: Praeger Publications, 1989), pp. 110, 111.
6 *Interview with Ray Scherer, April 11, 1961,* NBC files, *J.F.K. Report No. 2.*
7 *Time,* March 1, 1964, p. 10.

8   Hugh Sidey, *A Very Personal Presidency: LBJ in the White House* (New York: Atheneum, 1968), pp. 74–77.

9   Juan Williams, *Eyes on the Prize: America's Civil Rights Years, 1954–65* (New York: Viking Penguin, 1987), p. 242.

10 *Public Papers of the Presidents of the United States, Lyndon Baines Johnson, 1967* (Washington, D.C.: U.S. Government Printing Office, 1968), pp. 1045–48.

11 *Chicago Daily News,* November 18, 1967, p. 2.

12 *Public Papers of the Presidents of the United States, Richard M. Nixon, 1972* (Washington, D.C.: U.S. Government Printing Office, 1974), p. 705.

13 Helen Thomas, "Introduction," *The Nixon Presidential Press Conferences* (New York: Earl M. Coleman Enterprises, 1978), p. vi.

14. The television president

1   Interview with Benjamin C. Bradlee, 1988.

2   Interview with Michael Deaver, 1990.

3   Robert H. Kupperman and Jeff Kamen, "When Terrorists Strike: The Lessons TV Must Learn," *TV Guide,* September 23, 1989, p. 20. The article was adapted from their book, *Final Warning: Averting Disaster in the New Age of Terrorism* (Garden City, N.Y.: Doubleday, 1989).

4   Text supplied by Mike Jensen.

5   CBS transcript of "Sunday Morning," November 21, 1982, pp. 9–14.

6   CBS transcript, "CBS Evening News with Dan Rather," November 23, 1982.

7   Michael K. Deaver with Mickey Herskowitz, *Behind the Scenes: In which the Author Talks about Ronald and Nancy Reagan and Himself* (New York: William Morrow, 1987), pp. 165, 166.

8   Ze'ev Schiff and Ehud Ya'ari, ed. and trans. by Ina Friedman, *Israel's Lebanon War* (New York: Simon and Schuster, 1984), pp. 225, 226.

9   Quoted in Roderick Townley, "Casper Weinberger Says: Some TV Reporters Are Biased," *TV Guide,* October 15, 1988, p. 3.

10 Howell Raines, "Reagan Wounded in Chest by Gunman," *New York Times,* March 31, 1981, p. A3.

11 Ibid.

12 B. Drummond Ayers, Jr., "Amid the Darkest Moment, A Leaven of Presidential Wit," *New York Times,* April 1, 1981, p. A18.

13 *Papers of the President of the United States, Ronald Reagan, 1981* (Washington, D.C.: U.S. Government Printing Office, 1982), p. 391.

14 C. T. Hanson, "Gunsmoke and Sleeping Dogs: The Prez's Press at Midterm," *Columbia Journalism Review* (May–June 1983): 31.

15 Alexander M. Haig, Jr., *Caveat: Realism, Reagan, and Foreign Policy* (New York: The Macmillan Company, 1984), p. 160.

16 David S. Broder, "Catching up with the '80s," *Washington Post,* December 13, 1989, p. A25.

17 Lou Cannon, *Reagan* (New York: G. P. Putnam's Sons, 1982), p. 13.

18   Elizabeth Drew, "Letter from Washington," *New Yorker,* July 31, 1989, p. 76.

19   James David Barber, "Reagan's Sheer Personal Likability Faces Its Sternest Test," *Washington Post,* January 20, 1981, "Inauguration '81," supplement, p. 8.

20   Hedrick Smith, *The Power Game: How Washington Works* (New York: Random House, 1988), p. 423.

21   Mark Hertsgaard, *On Bended Knee: The Press and the Reagan Presidency* (New York: Farrar Straus Giroux, 1988), p. 16.

22   Interview with Michael Deaver, 1989.

23   Hertsgaard, *On Bended Knee,* pp. 37, 38.

24   Stephen E. Ambrose, "Mr. President! Mr. President!," *New York Times Book Review,* November 20, 1988, p. 34.

25   David Gergen, quoted in Hertsgaard, *On Bended Knee,* p. 25.

26   Deaver, *Behind the Scenes,* pp. 175, 176.

27   *The Tower Commission Report: The Full Text of the President's Special Review Board,* introduction by R.W. Apple, Jr. (New York: Bantam Books, The New York Times, 1987), pp. 79, xiii.

28   Interview with Michael Deaver, 1989.

29   Larry Speakes with Robert Pack, *Speaking Out: The Reagan Presidency from Inside the White House* (New York: Charles Scribner's Sons, 1988), p. 237.

30   Ibid., p. 239.

31   Interview with Michael Deaver, 1989.

32   Thomas P. O'Neill, Jr., with William Novak, *Man of the House: The Life and Political Memoirs of Speaker Tip O'Neill* (New York: St. Martin's Press, 1987), p. 413.

33   Denis Steven Rutkus, *President Reagan, The Opposition and Access to Network Airtime* (Washington, D.C.: Congressional Research Service, The Library of Congress, 1984), p. 8.

34   Ibid., p. 7.

35   Ibid., p. 9.

36   Ibid., pp. 11, 12.

37   Ibid., pp. 32, 33.

15. The television occupation of Capitol Hill

1   Ronald Garay, *Congressional Television: A Legislative History* (Westport, Conn.: Greenwood Press, 1984), pp. 25, 26.

2   Patricia Henry Yeomans, ed., *Behind the Headlines with Bill Henry* (Los Angeles: Ward Ritchie Press, 1972), p. 169.

3   Interview with Robert Clark, ABC Senate Correspondent, 1989.

4   Thomas P. O'Neill, Jr., with William Novak, *Man of the House: The Life and Political Memoirs of Speaker Tip O'Neill* (New York: St. Martin's Press, 1987), paperback ed., p. 346.

5   Ibid.
6   Garay, *Congressional Television*, p. 103.
7   Interview with Daniel Glickman, 1989.
8   Hedrick Smith, *The Power Game: How Washington Works* (New York: Random House, 1988), p. 129.
9   Garay, *Congressional Television*, p. 20.
10 Robert Michel, speech at the National Press Club, December 6, 1989.
11 Interview with Patrick Moynihan, 1989.
12 Ibid.
13 Interview with Daniel Glickman, 1989.
14 Interview with Jerry Ray, 1989.

16. From Dulles to Gorbachev

1   Sandra Burton, *Impossible Dream: The Marcoses and the Aquinos and the Unfinished Revolution* (New York: Warner, 1989), pp. 290–91.
2   *Public Papers of the Presidents of the United States, Dwight D. Eisenhower, 1957* (Washington, D.C.: U.S. Government Printing Office, 1958), pp. 431, 433, 438, 440.
3   Robert E. Kintner, *Broadcasting and the News*, reprint from *Harper's Magazine* by special permission (New York: Harper & Row), 1965, pp. 35, 36.
4   Erik Barnouw, *Tube of Plenty: The Evaluation of American Television* (New York: Oxford University Press, 1975), pp. 320, 321.
5   Kintner, *Broadcasting and the News*, pp. 35–37.
6   Barnouw, *Tube of Plenty*, pp. 321, 322.
7   Kintner, *Broadcasting and the News*, p. 38.
8   Barnouw, *Tube of Plenty*, p. 322.
9   Michael J. O'Neill, *Terrorist Spectaculars: Should TV Coverage Be Curbed? A 20th Century Fund Paper* (New York: Priority Press, 1986), p. 2.
10 Ibid., pp. 3, 4.
11 Joseph Berger, "Gunmen Seize Jet in Mideast Flight, Passenger Killed," *New York Times*, June 15, 1985, p. 1.
12 O'Neill, *Terrorist Spectaculars*, pp. 3, 4.
13 *New York Times*, June 21, 1985, p. A6.
14 Michael J. O'Neill, "Terrorism and the News," speech delivered to the Associated Press Managing Editors, *APME Red Book*, 1985, p. 28.
15 Robert Kupperman and Jeff Kamin, "When Terrorists Strike: The Lessons TV Must Learn," *TV Guide*, September 23, 1989, p. 19.
16 William C. Adams, "The Beirut Hostages: ABC and CBS Seize an Opportunity," *Public Opinion* (August–September 1985): 45.
17 O'Neill, *Terrorist Spectaculars*, p. 26.
18 Ibid., p. 27.
19 Interview with Paul Bremer III, 1989.
20 O'Neill, *Terrorist Spectaculars*, p. 7. Quoted from Henry Kissinger, "The Impact on Negotiations—What the Experts Say," *TV Guide*, September 21, 1985; ABC "Nightline," July 25, 1985.

21 Katharine Graham, "Terrorism and the Media," speech at the English-Speaking Union, London, December 6, 1985.

22 O'Neill, *Terrorist Spectaculars,* p. 51.

23 Maureen Dowd, "White House," *New York Times,* August 11, 1989, p. A12.

24 Stanley Karnow, *In Our Image: America's Empire in the Philippines* (New York: Random House, 1989), pp. 412–13.

25 Richard G. Lugar, *Letters to the Next President* (New York: Simon & Schuster, 1988), p. 98.

26 O'Neill, *Terrorist Spectaculars,* p. 15.

27 Interview with Mark Helmke, 1989.

28 Lugar, *Letters to the Next President,* p. 146.

29 Ibid.

30 Ibid., p. 151.

31 Ibid., pp. 162, 163.

32 David K. Shipler, "Gorbachev Mix on TV Is Tough but Cooperative," *New York Times,* December 1, 1987, pp. A1, A12.

33 Tom Shales, "On the Air: The Pageant on a Day of Grace," *Washington Post,* December 9, 1987, p. B1.

34 Maureen Dowd, "As 'Gorby' Works the Crowd, Backward Reels the K.G.B.," *New York Times,* December 11, 1987, p. 1.

35 Gary Lee, "Gorbachev Displays Verve," *Washington Post,* December 11, 1987, p. A29.

36 Walter Goodman, "Summit Coverage: Is Camera Turning Cruel?" *New York Times,* June 2, 1988, A18.

37 From "Americans Talk Quietly," twelve national surveys on national security issues conducted by Marttila and Kiley, Inc., of Boston. Copies made available to the authors by the State Department.

17. Television and the transformation of American politics, 1952–1984

1 William Manchester, *The Glory and the Dream: A Narrative History of America, 1932–1972* (Boston: Little, Brown, 1973), p. 617.

2 A. M. Sperber, *Murrow: His Life and Times* (New York: Bantam, 1986), p. 385. This chapter draws extensively on this excellent book.

3 Herbert S. Parmet, *Eisenhower and the American Crusades* (New York: Macmillan, 1972), pp. 78, 79.

4 Charles McDowell, "Television Politics: The Medium in the Revolution," in *Beyond Reagan: The Politics of Upheaval,* ed. Paul Duke (New York: Warner Books, 1986), pp. 237–39.

5 Ibid.

6 *New York Herald Tribune,* July 7, 1952, p. 7.

7 Edwin Diamond and Stephen Bates, *The Spot: The Rise of Political Advertising on Television,* rev. ed. (Cambridge, Mass.: MIT Press, 1988), p. 60.

8 John Bartlow Martin, *Adlai Stevenson of Illinois* (Garden City, N.Y.: Doubleday, 1976), p. 614.

9   Diamond and Bates, *The Spot*, p. 54.

10 Ibid., p. 57.

11 Ibid., pp. 58, 60.

12 Ibid., p. 65.

13 *Public Papers of the Presidents of the United States, Harry Truman, 1952–53* (Washington, D.C.: U.S. Government Printing Office, 1966), p. 132.

14 Figure supplied by the Television Bureau of Advertising.

15 Richard L. Berke, "For Political Incumbents, Loopholes That Pay Off," *New York Times*, March 20, 1990, p. 1.

16 Norman Ornstein, Thomas Mann, and Michael Maldin, *Vital Statistics on Congress* (Washington, D.C.: American Enterprise Institute, 1987), p. 56, table 2-7.

17 Figure supplied by the office of the historian of the House of Representatives.

18 Sig Mickelson, *From Whistle Stop to Sound Bite: Four Decades of Politics and Television* (New York: Praeger Publications, 1989), p. 59.

19 Tom Wicker, *On Press* (New York: Berkeley, 1979), pp. 1–3.

20 Theodore H. White, *The Making of the President, 1964* (New York: Signet Books, 1964), p. 261.

21 Jack W. Germond and Jules Witcover, *Whose Broad Stripes and Bright Stars? The Trivial Pursuit of the Presidency 1988* (New York: Warner, 1989), p. 54.

22 Diamond and Bates, *The Spot*, p. 129.

23 Richard N. Goodwin, *Remembering America: A Voice from the Sixties* (New York: Harper & Row, 1988), pp. 305, 306.

24 Nixon, *Six Crises*, p. 340.

25 Germond and Witcover, *Whose Broad Stripes?* p. 55.

26 Joe McGinniss, *The Selling of the President, 1968* (New York: Trident Press, 1969), p. 28.

27 Ibid., pp. 193–95.

28 Ibid., p. 181.

29 Ibid., pp. 199, 200.

30 Reprinted in David S. Broder, *Behind the Front Page: A Candid Look at How the News Is Made* (New York: Simon & Schuster, 1987), p. 91.

31 Ibid., p. 92.

32 Jules Witcover, *Marathon: The Pursuit of the Presidency, 1972–1976* (New York: Viking Press, 1977), p. 135.

33 Ibid., pp. 201, 202.

34 Jeff Greenfield, *The Real Campaign: How the Media Missed the Story of the 1980 Campaign* (New York: Summit, 1982), pp. 18, 19.

35 Witcover, *Marathon*, p. 598.

36 Gerald R. Ford, " 'Poland. I Told You So,' " *Washington Post*, October 11, 1989, p. A29.

37 James H. McCartney, "The Triumph of Junk News," *Columbia Journalism Review* (January–February 1977): 17ff.

38 Ibid.

39 Greenfield, *The Real Campaign*, p. 63.
40 Ibid., p. 64.
41 Mary McGrory, *Boston Globe*, November 5, 1977, p. 11.
42 Greenfield, *The Real Campaign*, p. 160.
43 Ibid., pp. 163, 164.
44 Broder, *Behind the Front Page*, p. 289.
45 Greenfield, *The Real Campaign*, p. 167.
46 Ibid., p. 169.
47 Martin Schram, *The Great American Video Game: Presidential Politics in the TV Age* (New York: William Morrow, 1987), p. 27.
48 Interview with Joseph Angotti, 1988.
49 Jack W. Germond and Jules Witcover, *Wake Us When It's Over: Presidential Politics of 1984* (New York: Macmillan, 1985), p. 510.
50 Interview with Walter Mondale, 1987.
51 Greenfield, *The Real Campaign*, p. 14.
52 *New York Times*, November 11, 1948, p. 7.
53 Theodore H. White, *The Making of the President, 1960* (New York: Atheneum, 1961), p. 294.

18. 1988

1 Mark Shields, "Don't Blame the Political Consultants," *Washington Post*, March 31, 1990, p. A27.
2 Bob Schieffer and Garry Paul Gates, *The Acting President: Ronald Reagan and the Men Who Helped Him Create the Illusion That Held America Spellbound* (New York: E. P. Dutton, 1989), p. 348.
3 Jack W. Germond and Jules Witcover, *Whose Broad Stripes and Bright Stars?: The Trivial Pursuit of the Presidency, 1988* (New York: Warner, 1989), p. 120.
4 Ibid., p. 122. Excerpts from the transcripts are from pp. 122, 123.
5 Schieffer and Gates, *The Acting President*, p. 10.
6 Germond and Witcover, *Whose Broad Stripes?* p. 124.
7 *Washington Post*, January 28, 1988, p. A2.
8 Germond and Witcover, *Whose Broad Stripes?* p. 141.
9 Ibid., p. 145.
10 Speech by Robert J. Dole at a meeting of the Electronic Industries Association, Washington, D.C., March 27, 1990.
11 Germond and Witcover, *Whose Broad Stripes?* p. 357.
12 Paul Taylor and David S. Broder, *Washington Post*, October 28, 1988, p. A1.
13 *Time*, November 21, 1988, p. 49.
14 Germond and Witcover, *Whose Broad Stripes?* pp. 10–12.
15 Ibid., p. 11.
16 Ibid., pp. 162, 163.
17 Kathleen Hall Jamieson, *Washington Post*, October 30, 1988, p. C1.
18 *New York Times*, November 3, 1988, p. 1.

19   Sidney Blumenthal, *Washington Post,* October 28, 1988, p. D1.
20   Russell Baker, "Not a Vintage Year," *New York Times,* December 31, 1988, p. 23.
21   Peter Goldman, Tom Matthews, and the *Newsweek* Election Team, *The Quest for the Presidency, 1988* (New York: Simon & Schuster, 1989), p. 133.
22   For an account of these incidents, see William Boot, "Campaign '88: TV Overdoses on the Inside Dope," *Columbia Journalism Review* (January–February 1989): 25, 26.
23   Walter Goodman, "Toward a Campaign of Substance in '92," *New York Times,* March 26, 1990, p. C16.
24   Germond and Witcover, *Whose Broad Stripes?* p. 386.
25   Ibid., p. 388.
26   Transcripts of the polls were supplied by the Roper Center for Public Opinion Research, University of Connecticut.
27   Excerpts taken from Germond and Witcover, *Whose Broad Stripes?* p. 440.
28   Roone Arledge, transcript, Du Pont Award Symposium, Columbia University, 1988.
29   "Sound Bite Democracy: Network Evening News Presidential Campaign Coverage 1968 and 1988," Research Paper B-2, Joan Shorenstein Barone Center, Harvard University, June 1990.
30   Kathleen Hall Jamieson, "Pictures Speak Louder (and Less Truthfully) Than Words," *The Woodrow Wilson Center Report,* October 1989, p. 6.

19. Profound change in print journalism

1   Norman Chandler, "The Television Station of Today and Tomorrow." Text of speech apparently delivered in May 1954. See Norman Chandler Collection III 1/2, *Los Angeles Times* History Center, Los Angeles.
2   John Seigenthaler, "Is It a Question of Being Nice to the Competition?" *Bulletin of the American Society of Newspaper Editors* (hereafter *ASNE Bulletin*), October 1964, p. 16.
3   Interview with John W. Finney, 1987.
4   *ASNE Bulletin,* August 1952, p. 1.
5   Interview with Martin Hayden, 1987.
6   Interview with Ben Bagdikian, 1988.
7   *Proceedings of the American Society of Newspaper Editors* (hereafter *ASNE Proceedings*), 1951, pp. 146ff.
8   Ibid., pp. 146, 147.
9   Ibid., pp. 152, 153.
10   Ibid., pp. 158, 159.
11   Ibid., p. 144.
12   *New York Times,* March 18, 1951, p. 3, section 2.
13   *ASNE Proceedings,* 1951, p. 95.
14   Ibid., p. 147.
15   Ibid., pp. 159, 162.

16 Ibid., p. 149.
17 *Associated Press Managing Editors Red Book* (hereafter *APME Red Book*), 1955, p. 124.
18 Rebecca F. Gross, "More Features or Improved News Coverage?" *ASNE Bulletin,* October 1, 1952, p. 10.
19 *APME Red Book,* 1955, pp. 122, 123. Italics added.
20 "Sitting in at the Summit," *Detroit Free Press,* July 18, 1955, p. 1.
21 Ibid., July 19, 1955, p. 1.
22 Ibid., July 20, 1955, p. 1.
23 *APME Red Book,* 1955, p. 149.
24 *APME Red Book,* 1980, pp. 61, 62.
25 Sig Mickelson, *From Whistle Stop to Sound Bite: Four Decades of Politics and Television* (New York: Praeger Publishers, 1989), p. 52.
26 Ibid.
27 *New York Times,* June 15, 1952, p. 9, section 2.
28 *ASNE Bulletin,* August 1, 1952, p. 3.
29 Interview with Clifton Daniel, 1988.
30 Ibid.
31 Gay Talese, *The Kingdom and the Power* (New York: World Publishing, 1966), p. 208.
32 Bruce Porter, "The 'Max' Factor at the New York Times," *Columbia Journalism Review* (November–December 1988): 29–35.
33 Thomas B. Rosenstiel, "News Giant Makes Big Changes," *Los Angeles Times,* June 11, 1991, p. 1.
34 Interview with William D. Rinehart, 1987.
35 Chalmers M. Roberts, *The Washington Post: The First 100 Years* (New York: Houghton Mifflin, 1977), p. 262.
36 Gene Gilmore, "How Chicago Lost Another Paper," *Columbia Journalism Review* (May–June 1978): 57.
37 *Editor and Publisher Year Book, 1988.*
38 *Covering the South: A National Symposium on the Media and the Civil Rights Movement,* April 3–5, 1987, University of Mississippi, William R. Shipp, oral history transcript, pp. 23, 24.

20. Newspapers in the age of television

1 Interview with Sam S. McKeel, 1987.
2 Interview with Richard Harwood, 1988.
3 *Associated Press Managing Editors Red Book* (hereafter *APME Red Book*), 1965, p. 9.
4 George A. Cornish, letter to the authors, 1988.
5 Interview with Mel Elfin, 1987.
6 Interview with Clayton Kirkpatrick, 1988.
7 *Proceedings of the American Society of Newspaper Editors,* 1970, pp. 180, 181.
8 Interview with Benjamin C. Bradlee, 1988.

9   *APME Red Book,* 1957, pp. 116, 117.
10 *APME Red Book,* 1955, p. 125.
11 Interview with Reg Murphy, 1987.
12 Interview with Nick B. Williams, 1990.
13 Nick B. Williams, letter to authors, 1988.
14 Marshall Burges, *The Life and Times of Los Angeles: A Newspaper, a Family and a City* (New York: Atheneum, 1984), pp. 115, 116.
15 Memorandum, Nick B. Williams to Frank Haven, August 16, 1968, *Los Angeles Times* History Center.
16 Ibid.
17 Interview with Robert Gibson, 1988.
18 Nick B. Williams, letter to Victor M. Carter, March 10, 1970, Williams Papers, Box I, 1963–1973, *Los Angeles Times* History Center.
19 Interview with Clayton Kirkpatrick, 1989.
20 Ibid.
21 Interview with Russell W. Freeburg, 1987.
22 Interview with Clayton Kirkpatrick, 1990.
23 Interview with Russell W. Freeburg, 1987.
24 Interview with James Hoge, 1988.
25 Ibid.
26 Interview with Murrey Marder, 1988.
27 Ibid.
28 Interview with Clayton Kirkpatrick, 1990.
29 Interview with Todd S. Purdum, 1990.
30 Interview with Eugene Roberts, 1987.
31 *APME Red Book,* 1965, p. 10.

21. Television's intrusion in the press box

1   *Associated Press Managing Editors Red Book* (hereafter *APME Red Book*), 1953, p. 204.
2   *APME Red Book,* 1977, p. 173.
3   Norman E. Isaacs, "Circuit Preacher on Journalism's Sins," *Bulletin of the American Society of Newspaper Editors* (hereafter *ASNE Bulletin*), March 1984, p. 23.
4   Thomas Curley, speech to Conference on Media Economics and Sports Coverage, The Gannett Center for Media Studies, Columbia University, November 3, 1987.
5   Hal Bodley, "Today's Button-Down Sports Editor," *ASNE Bulletin,* November 1980, p. 15.
6   Report of the Sports Committee, *APME Red Book,* 1955, p. 205.
7   Joe McGuff, article in *APME Red Book,* 1978, pp. 101, 102.
8   Wick Temple, article in *ASNE Bulletin,* November 1980, pp. 12ff.
9   Ibid.
10 Interview with Bill Shirley, 1990.
11 Interview with Wallace Carroll, 1987.
12 *APME Red Book,* 1963, p. 27.

13 Interview with Eugene Patterson, 1988.
14 *Washington Post,* February 29, 1988, p. 1.
15 *Washington Post,* September 22, 1950, p. 21.
16 *Washington Post,* September 23, 1950, p. 12.
17 *Washington Post,* September 25, 1987, p. D1.
18 *Washington Post,* September 27, 1987, p. C1.
19 *Washington Post,* October 1, 1987, p. E1.
20 James A. Michener, *Sports in America* (New York: Random House, 1976), p. 322.
21 *APME Red Book,* 1957, p. 58.
22 Interview with Bill Shirley, 1990.
23 *APME Red Book,* 1955, p. 89.
24 Interview with Bill Shirley, 1990.
25 Interview with James Batten, 1989.
26 *ASNE Proceedings,* 1951, pp. 146ff.
27 A. M. Rosenthal, "Television and Us," excerpts from a talk at an ASNE panel, *ASNE Bulletin,* October 1983, p. 34.
28 *ASNE Bulletin,* November 1980, p. 14.

22. Two different mediums

1 Interview with Eugene Patterson, 1987.
2 Interview with Robert S. Boyd, 1987.
3 Interview with John Finney, 1988.
4 *Associated Press Managing Editors Red Book* (hereafter *APME Red Book*), 1977, p. 173.
5 Interview with Barbara Matusow, 1988.
6 Interview with Eugene Roberts, 1987.
7 Ibid.
8 Interview with Larry LeSueur, 1987.
9 Interview with John Tillman, 1987.
10 Peter Prichard, *The Making of McPaper: The Inside Story of USA Today* (Kansas City: Andrews, McMeel & Parker, 1987), p. 177.
11 A. M. Rosenthal, "Television and Us," *Bulletin of the American Society of Newspaper Editors* (hereafter *ASNE Bulletin*), October 1983, p. 34.
12 Interview with Eugene Roberts, 1987.
13 Interview with Sam McKeel, 1987.
14 Interview with Charles Seib, 1987.
15 Stephen D. Isaacs, "Solving the P.M. Dilemma: Will Soft News Succeed?" *ASNE Bulletin,* September 1980, p. 3.
16 Interview with Leo Bogart, 1987.
17 *APME Red Book,* 1983, p. 109.
18 Fred Shapiro, "Shrinking the News," *Columbia Journalism Review* (November–December, 1976): 26.
19 Leo Bogart, "How U.S. Newspaper Content is Changing," *Journal of Communications,* September 1985, p. 82.
20 Robert Haiman, *APME Red Book,* 1969, p. 78.

21 David Shaw, "For Papers a Generation is Missing," *Los Angeles Times,* March 15, 1989, Part 1, p. 14.
22 *Editor & Publisher International Year Book* (New York: Editor & Publisher, 1991).
23 Figures supplied by the Newspaper Advertising Bureau.
24 Lester Bernstein, "Time, Inc., Means Business," *The New York Times Magazine,* February 26, 1989, p. 22.
25 Curtis Prendergast, with Geoffrey Colvin, *The World of Time, Inc.: The Intimate History of a Changing Enterprise,* Vol. 3: *1960–1980* (New York: Atheneum, 1986), pp. 54, 55.
26 Interview with Stanley Tretick, 1988.

23. Conclusion

1   James P. Sturba, "For a Moment This Man's Lonely Act of Defense Held the Chinese Army at Bay," *Wall Street Journal,* June 6, 1989, p. A25.
2   *New York Times,* June 5, 1989, p. A11.
3   Quoted in ibid.
4   "Foreign Investors Shudder over China," *Wall Street Journal,* June 6, 1989, p. A25.
5   *New York Times,* June 6, 1989, p. 1.
6   Tara Sonenshine, "Revolution Has Been Televised," *Washington Post,* October 2, 1990, p. A19.
7   Dieter Buhl, "Window to the West: How Television from the Federal Republic Influenced Events in East Germany," Discussion Paper D-5, The Joan Shorenstein Barone Center, John F. Kennedy School of Government, Harvard University.
8   David Webster, "Television's Ricochet," *Washington Post,* December 12, 1989, p. A19.
9   Eric Malnic and Thomas B. Rosenstiel, "World Hears War Begin Live from Baghdad," *Los Angeles Times,* January 17, 1991, p. 1.
10 "The Talk of the Town," *New Yorker,* February 11, 1991, p. 25.
11 Quoted in interview with Richard Valeriani in the *Columbia Journalism Review* (March–April 1991): 24.
12 David Broder in *Washington Post,* February 27, 1991, p. A25.
13 Interview with Garrick Utley, "Sunday Today," March 31, 1991.
14 Pentagon experts made this claim. See Barton Gellman, "Allied Air War Struck Broadly in Iraq," *Washington Post,* June 23, 1991, p. 1.
15 Interview with Michael Deaver, 1990.
16 Neil Hickey, "TV's Biggest Coup: Covering the Week that Shook the World," *TV Guide,* September 21–27, 1991, p. 20.
17 Robert Suro, "Watching the Distant Storm, Americans Feel for Russians," *New York Times,* August 23, 1991, p. A1.
18 Jonathan Yardley, "In the Soviet Union, the Tube Test," *Washington Post,* August 26, 1991, p. C2.
19 George F. Kennan, "MacNeil/Lehrer NewsHour," August 22, 1991.

20 John Carmody, "The TV Column," *Washington Post,* September 3, 1991, p. D6.
21 David Hoffman, "Global Communications Network Was Pivotal in Defeat of Junta," *Washington Post,* August 23, 1991, p. A27.
22 Robert Goldberg, "Five Days in August," *Wall Street Journal,* August 26, 1991, p. A8.

Index

Index